Data Mining in E-Learning

WITPRESS

WIT Press publishes leading books in Science and Technology.
Visit our website for the current list of titles.
www.witpress.com

WITeLibrary

Home of the Transactions of the Wessex Institute, the WIT electronic-library provides the
international scientific community with immediate and permanent access to individual
papers presented at WIT conferences. Visit the WIT eLibrary at
http://library.witpress.com

Objectives of the Series

Advances in Management Information Series

Information and Communications Technologies have experienced considerable advances in the last few years. The task of managing and analysing ever-increasing amounts of data requires the development of more efficient tools to keep pace with this growth.

This series presents advances in the theory and applications of Management Information. It covers an interdisciplinary field, bringing together techniques from applied mathematics, machine learning, pattern recognition, data mining and data warehousing, as well as their applications to intelligence, knowledge management, marketing and social analysis. The majority of these applications are aimed at achieving a better understanding of the behaviour of people and organisations in order to enable decisions to be made in an informed manner. Each volume in the series covers a particular topic in detail.

The volumes cover the following fields:

Information
Information Retrieval
Intelligent Agents
Data Mining
Data Warehouse
Text Mining

Competitive Intelligence
Customer Relationship Management
Information Management
Knowledge Management

J. Rao
Case Western Reserve University
USA

D. Riaño
Universitat Rovira I Virgili
Spain

J. Roddick
Flinders University
Australia

F. Rodrigues
Poly Institute of Porto
Portugal

F. Rossi
DATAMAT
Germany

D. Sitnikov
Kharkov Academy of Culture
Ukraine

R. Turra
CINECA Interuniversity Computing
Centre
Italy

D. Van den Poel
Ghent University
Belgium

J. Yoon
Old Dominion University
USA

N. Zhong
Maebashi Institute of Technology
Japan

H.G. Zimmermann
Siemens AG
Germany

Data Mining in E-Learning

Editors

C. Romero
University of Cordoba, Spain

S. Ventura
University of Cordoba, Spain

C. Romero
University of Cordoba

S. Ventura
University of Cordoba

Published by

WIT Press

Ashurst Lodge, Ashurst, Southampton, SO40 7AA, UK
Tel: 44 (0) 238 029 3223; Fax: 44 (0) 238 029 2853
E-Mail: witpress@witpress.com
http://www.witpress.com

For USA, Canada and Mexico

WIT Press

25 Bridge Street, Billerica, MA 01821, USA
Tel: 978 667 5841; Fax: 978 667 7582
E-Mail: infousa@witpress.com
http://www.witpress.com

British Library Cataloguing-in-Publication Data

A Catalogue record for this book is available
from the British Library

ISBN: 1-84564-152-3
ISSN: 1742-0172

Library of Congress Catalog Card Number: 2006920597

Contents

Chapter 3
Data mining for the analysis of content interaction in web-based
learning and training systems... 41
C. Pahl

Chapter 4
On using data mining for browsing log analysis in learning environments..... 57
F. Wang

Chapter 8
B. Minaei-Bidgoli, P. Tan, G. Kortemeyer &, W.F. Punch

Chapter 9
W. Hämäläinen, T.H. Laine & E. Sutinen

Chapter 13
E. Mor, J. Minguillón & J.M. Carbó

Chapter 14
J. Chen & Q. Li

Preface

The design and implementation of web-based education systems have grown exponentially in the last years, spurred by the fact that neither students nor teachers are bound to a specific location and that this form of computer-based education is virtually independent of any specific hardware platforms. These systems accumulate a vast amount of information which is very valuable in analyzing students' behavior and to assist authors in detecting possible errors, shortcomings and improvements. However, due to the vast quantities of data these systems can generate daily, it is very difficult to manage manually, and authors demand tools which assist them in this task, preferably on a continuous basis. A very promising area to attain this objective is the use of data mining.

In the last years, researchers have begun to investigate various data mining methods to help teachers improve e-learning systems. These methods allow them to discover new knowledge based on students' usage data. The same idea has already been successfully applied in e-commerce systems and is now very popular. Comparatively little work in this direction has yet been released in e-learning systems. However, the number of contributions in this area have grown, both in international conferences (International Conference on Computers in Education, International Conference on Web-based Learning, World Conference on Open Learning and Distance Education, International Conference on Adaptive Hypermedia and Adaptive Web-based Systems, International Conference on User Modeling, International Conference on Intelligent Tutoring Systems, Pacific-Asia Conference on Knowledge Discovery and Data Mining, Genetic and Evolutionary Computation Conference, etc.) and in scientific journals (International Journal on E-Learning, IEEE Education, Computers & Education, Journal of Educational Technology Systems, Journal of Interactive Learning Research, User Modeling and User-Adapted Interaction, etc.). The main purpose of this book is to show the current state of this research area.

This book consists of openly solicited and invited chapters, written by international researchers and leading experts on the application of data mining techniques in e-learning systems. The book consists of 16 chapters organized in two parts. In the first part of the book (Chapters 1–4) we present an introduction to e-learning systems, data mining and the interaction between the two areas. In the second part of the book (Chapters 5–16) we present several case studies and experiences of applying data mining techniques in e-learning systems. In particular, the chapters cover the following:

Chapter 1 describes recent and ongoing research in web-based education systems, in particular adaptive web-based educational hypermedia.

Chapter 2 describes specific examples of self-directed e-learning and how their functionality and utility can be improved through the use of web mining technology.

Chapter 3 proposes the use of web usage mining for the analysis and evaluation of learner interactions with contents in web-based learning and training systems.

Chapter 4 describes some models and methods of analyzing browsing log data to construct a browsing behavioral model which is helpful in supporting e-learning applications.

Chapter 5 suggests the use of web mining techniques as non-intrusive method to build an agent that could recommend actions, resources or simply links to follow, in a e-learning environment.

Chapter 6 proposes an e-learning system that recommends research papers to students wishing to study an area of research.

Chapter 7 describes a case study and an extensible and customizable pre-processing and pattern analysis tools for supporting the web usage mining process.

Chapter 8 introduces an approach for predicting student performance by the discovery of interesting contrast rules within a web-based educational system.

Chapter 9 introduces general paradigms for tackling intelligent tutoring systems and applies various data mining schemes to describe and predict student performance.

Chapter 10 proposes the use of evolutionary algorithms as an association rule mining method for discovering interesting relationships in student's usage data.

Chapter 11 proposes a neural network model for identification of gifted students and a web mining framework for distance education to provide their learning path.

Chapter 12 reviews some experiences using data mining to analyze data obtained from e-learning courses based on virtual communities.

Chapter 13 describes a framework for studying the navigational behavior of the users in an e-learning environment integrated in a virtual campus to include the concept of recommended itinerary.

Chapter 14 proposes the construction of an e-textbook automatically using data mining methodologies for a user-specified topic hierarchy and examines how web content mining can be applied to aid e-learning experiences.

Chapter 15 proposes a method of online outlier detection of learners' irregular learning processes using their response time to e-learning content.

Finally, Chapter 16 proposes the use of data mining in enrollment management.

In conclusion, we hope the reader will find this book a truly helpful guide and a valuable source of information about the application of data mining techniques in e-learning systems.

Cristóbal Romero & Sebastián Ventura
Córdoba, July 2005

Biography

 Dr. Cristóbal Romero is an Assistant Professor in the Computer Science Department of the University of Córdoba, Spain. He received his Ph.D. in Computer Science from the University of Granada in 2003. His research interests lie in artificial intelligence and data mining in education.

 Dr. Sebastián Ventura is an Associate Professor in the Computer Science Department of the University of Córdoba, Spain. He received his Ph.D. in Sciences from the University of Córdoba in 1996. His research interests lie in soft-computing and its applications.

PART 1

An introduction to e-learning systems, data mining and their interactions

CHAPTER 1

Web-based educational hypermedia

P. De Bra
Department of Computer Science, Eindhoven University of Technology, The Netherlands.

Abstract

The Web has revolutionized the way information is delivered to people throughout the world. It did not take long for learning material to be delivered through the Web, using electronic textbooks. The use of hypertext links gives the learner a lot of freedom to decide on the order in which to study the material. This leads to problems in understanding electronic textbooks, which can be solved using *adaptive hypermedia* methods and techniques. In this chapter we describe how the field of educational hypermedia benefits from *user modeling* and *adaptation*. We also show that the information gathered about the learners and their learning process can be used to improve the quality of electronic textbooks.

1 Introduction

For a long time the use of *hypermedia* in education was limited because of the need for specialized hardware/software platforms for bringing hypermedia to the end user. Some readers may remember the Plato system [1], featuring personal and group notes, threaded discussions, hyperlinks, interactive elements and games, etc. Its use was restricted to institutes equipped with special terminals, connected to large mainframe computers running the Plato environment. A more affordable but also unsuccessful attempt at bringing hypermedia and interactivity to the public was the introduction of CD-Interactive by Philips and Sony (in 1986). Many other (hypermedia) environments suitable for delivering interactive learning material have been developed but never became popular. Then, in 1989, Tim Berners Lee started developing the ideas and software for the World Wide Web. The first implementations of web servers (from CERN and NCSA, much later evolved into the most popular Apache server) and browsers (NCSA Mosaic for X-Windows being the first popular one, which later evolved into Netscape and now Mozilla Firefox) initially only allowed for a fairly primitive form of hypermedia: pages with (untyped) links and possibly some embedded images. Soon a primitive form of servers-side dynamic content generation was added through Common Gateway Interface scripts. No matter how primitive, the World Wide Web immediately offered an irresistible package: a simple server running on inexpensive Unix workstations, enabling everyone to set up their own server, a simple completely text-based page format (HTML) that everyone could master very easily, and a simple browser running on everyone's workstation. This, combined with computers being connected through the Internet and a universal way to address pages on any machine anywhere on the Web, turned everyone into a potential publisher and gave everyone access to all the information published on the Web.

Around 1993 people started publishing course material on the Web rather than in paper documents (or on proprietary systems in proprietary document formats). At the Eindhoven University of Technology we started the first online course on the subject of hypermedia, using the Web as the hypermedia platform for delivering the course. (This course is currently available, in an updated form, at http://wwwis.win.tue.nl/2L690/.) Our early experience with this course [2] made us aware of a number of difficulties learners experience when using a course text that is delivered in hypermedia form:

- The first problem we encountered was *orientation*. A course text delivered through hypermedia need not have a strictly hierarchical structure of chapters, sections, subsections and paragraphs. In our hypermedia course there is a list of major topics, but quite a number of pages can be categorized as belonging to different topics and are also reachable through the introductory pages of different topics. As a result, a typical hierarchical table-of-content-like navigation aid indicating the position of the current page in the structure, as found on many web sites, would not be appropriate. (The current page often belongs in different places in the structure at once.) Not only was it difficult for learners to know 'where' in the course text they were, it was also difficult for them to know how much they had already studied and how much more there was still to be read, and where that additional material could be found.
- The second problem was *comprehension*. Giving learners access to all the material at once, through a (clickable) list of topics, meant that the learners could just pick any topic and start studying it. The unnumbered list of topics apparently did not convey a message of desired reading order, in the way the sequential order of chapters and pages in a book does. It is hard, if not impossible, to write a course text in such a way that every page, or at least every chapter, can be read without having first studied some other part of the course.
- The third problem was *assessment* of the learner's performance. We added a multiple-choice test to our hypermedia course, to assess the learner's knowledge after studying all the material. Since the reading (study) order was completely free, there was no clear place in the hypermedia structure to place tests about

partial knowledge, like at the end of each chapter (in a textbook). Students who considered themselves ready to take the final test and failed had no clear way of knowing how to remedy the problem. Intermediate tests would have revealed much earlier on whether they were studying the material in sufficient detail or not.

There are essentially only two ways to solve the above-mentioned problems: create and present a clearly hierarchical structure with chapter and section numbers to indicate a preferred reading order, or provide some form of 'automated guidance' for users who wish to follow unforeseen paths through the learning material. In the past the emphasis has often been on fairly strong guidance, in 'intelligent tutoring systems' like ELM-ART [3, 4] and SQL-Tutor [5, 6] (among many others). In this chapter we will describe how *adaptive hypermedia* methods and tools can be used to combine the desire for as much navigational freedom as possible with the need to study certain concepts before building other knowledge upon them. In Section 2 we will take a look at the different methods and techniques that are used in adaptive hypermedia in general, and adaptive learning environments in particular, and indicate their purpose. In Section 3 we will sketch the overall architecture of adaptive systems using a reference model. In Section 4 we discuss the adaptive hypermedia architecture (AHA!) system developed at the Eindhoven University of Technology and show different ways in which online course texts can be created with or for AHA!. We devote Section 5 to the issue of evaluating the learner's knowledge and using it as input for further adaptation. In Section 6 we discuss the use of adaptation to serve learners with different cognitive styles. We conclude with some advice and outlook into the future of online adaptive educational hypermedia.

2 Adaptive (educational) hypermedia

In [7, 8] Peter Brusilovsky has presented an overview of the field of adaptive hypermedia. Rather than summarizing these overviews we concentrate on the use of adaptation in an educational environment. There are two main reasons for using adaptation: to avoid problems that occur when reading material out of the intended order and to better serve the individual differences between users. The latter issue is discussed in Section 6. In the current section we concentrate on using adaptation to facilitate studying a course that offers a lot of navigational freedom (to pick topics to study at will).

In every course text there are a lot of cross-references between different chapters/ sections. In a normal paper textbook the author knows whether such a reference is a forward or a backward reference, and thus whether the reference is to a concept not yet known or already known. In an online course with navigational freedom the author cannot know whether a reference is a forward or backward reference. However, it is not difficult to track a user's path through the course text, and thus for the system to know whether for this user at this time a reference is a forward or backward reference. So if an author creates two versions of the reference the system can choose and present the appropriate one. This leads to the first important form of adaptation: *content adaptation* or, as Brusilovsky [7] defines it, *adaptive presentation*.

There are essentially three cases where content adaptation because of a reference to another concept is useful [7].

- When a reference is made to a concept the learner does not yet know, and of which at least some understanding is needed, a short *prerequisite explanation* can be inserted. This lets the learner continue with the chosen subject, rather than requiring a jump to the prerequisite concept to study that in detail first.
- Sometimes the current concept can be elaborated upon further in case the related concept is already known, or when the knowledge level of the learner is already high. For these 'expert' users an *additional explanation* can be given that is beyond the level of the average learner (at the time of visiting the current page).
- Sometimes an interesting comparison is possible with another concept, but only if that other concept is already known. Such a *comparative explanation* between the concepts can automatically be shown on the page of the second of the two concepts studied by the learner, whichever of the two is second in the chosen reading order.

When used with care the learner may not be aware that content adaptation is being performed. If content adaptation happens frequently and obviously the learners may become uneasy, thinking that they are 'missing out' on some of the information in the course.

The differences in knowledge, caused by choosing different paths through the course text can be compensated for to some extent, but sometimes it is necessary to guide users in a certain direction or to keep users away from some learning material they are really not ready for (meaning that a short prerequisite explanation is not sufficient to prepare the learner for the rest of the description of the topic). The reading order can be influenced by manipulating the hypertext links. This brings us to the second form of adaptation: *link adaptation*. Brusilovsky [7] defines it as: *adaptive navigation support*.

Link adaptation can be done in several ways, because links have a *position* on the page, a *presentation* through a link anchor and a *destination*.

- That the *position* of links has an influence on the user's behavior is best seen in the presentation of results by search engines. People are used to lists having an order of ranking from best to worst. This perceived meaning can be used to sort lists of links so that the most appropriate links for the current learner, in his current state of mind, are placed at the top. Brusilovsky [7, 8] calls this *adaptive link sorting*. Besides link sorting, links can also be made 'available' through a system of menus and submenus. A commonly used technique is to show a list of chapters, and the list of sections of the 'current' chapter. By having only the sections of one chapter listed at any one time, it is suggested to the user to only select sections from that one chapter and not jump around between sections in different chapters. Conditionally presenting (or hiding) links is also called adaptive *link removal*.

- Links are presented through a *link anchor*. This is a word or phrase or perhaps an icon, displayed in a way that hints at it being a link. On the Web links are typically represented by anchors that appear in blue and that are underlined, and images or icons that are link anchors typically have a blue border. In modern browsers the shape of the cursor changes when it is moved over a link anchor. (It usually becomes a 'hand'.) There are different ways in which the user can be guided towards or away from certain links by changing the presentation of the link anchor. Virtually all web browsers change the color of the link anchor after the link is visited. (The standard color scheme is that blue link anchors become purple.) However, using style sheets it is possible to change the appearance of link anchors in other ways, and it is also possible to add icons to indicate a special meaning of a link. The AHA! system [9] has a default link adaptation technique of *link hiding*. Link anchors can be blue, purple or black, and link anchors are not underlined in AHA!, so the black links are effectively hidden. They look just like normal text. It is also possible to change this color scheme and use three visible colors, resulting in a technique of *link annotation*. Other systems, like ELM-ART [10] and Interbook [11] for instance, use icons to recommend for or against certain links (green and red balls).

- In almost all hypermedia literature there is a close connection between *links* and *link anchors*. Users expect a link anchor to always correspond to the same link, and hence to lead to the same link destination. However, when pages are generated dynamically (e.g. by an adaptive system) there is no technical reason why the same anchor cannot lead to a different destination, depending on the circumstances. A link can for instance lead to a simplified description of a topic or a detailed description depending on the learner's progress. People are beginning to get used to (and accept) such unstable link anchors, because of 'top stories', 'joke of the day' and other links that routinely lead to information that changes frequently. In a learning context, in [12–14], the use of an adaptive course (with adaptive tests) is described in which the outcome of a test would automatically lead to the start of a chapter at a beginner's, intermediate or advanced level. It is almost like the automatic progression to higher levels in shootout or adventure games.

We conclude this section with a small example from the hypermedia course. Figure 1 shows three ways in which a short paragraph about the Xanadu system appears in a page about URLs (see http://www.xanadu.net/XUarchive/ for an archive of notes about Xanadu).

In the first version a brief comparison is made between URLs and the addressing mechanism of Xanadu. Because the learner has not yet studied Xanadu a short note on Xanadu is added between parentheses. And although there is a whole page on Xanadu, the link to that page is hidden because the user has not yet started studying the whole chapter on the history of hypertext systems. The second version also shows the short note on Xanadu, but this time the user has already started the

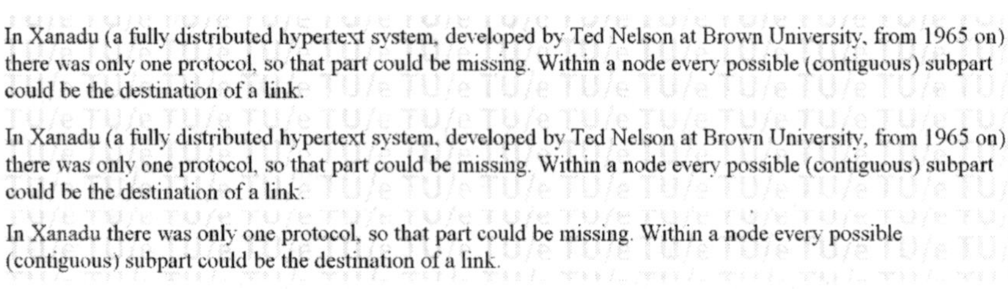

In Xanadu (a fully distributed hypertext system, developed by Ted Nelson at Brown University, from 1965 on) there was only one protocol, so that part could be missing. Within a node every possible (contiguous) subpart could be the destination of a link.

In Xanadu (a fully distributed hypertext system, developed by Ted Nelson at Brown University, from 1965 on) there was only one protocol, so that part could be missing. Within a node every possible (contiguous) subpart could be the destination of a link.

In Xanadu there was only one protocol, so that part could be missing. Within a node every possible (contiguous) subpart could be the destination of a link.

Figure 1: Content adaptation in the hypermedia course.

chapter on the history and hence the link to the page on Xanadu is recommended (shown in blue). In the third version the learner is reading this page after learning about Xanadu. The link is shown as visited (purple), meaning the learner can go to the Xanadu page but this is no longer recommended as the learner was there before. The short note about Xanadu is no longer shown, so as to not interrupt the sentence with that note. The learner already knows everything about Xanadu, so the note is no longer needed. This simple and small example shows how content adaptation and link adaptation can be combined to provide the 'appropriate' description to every learner. What the example doesn't show is that the decision which adaptation *is* 'appropriate' is often non-trivial. In most current adaptive systems an author has to decide under which circumstances which adaptation is made. This is laborious and error-prone. There is a potential benefit for some form of automated reasoning, based on data mining, machine learning or neural networks to relieve the author from this difficult task.

3 The AHAM reference architecture

In the period 1965–1990 a large number of hypertext systems were designed, built, and used, sometimes for many applications but often only for one or a few. Despite all the differences, researchers got together for a workshop (at the Dexter Inn) and this resulted in the Dexter model [15, 16], a formal model that captured the architecture of the existing (and some future) systems. The model consists of five layers covering different functional parts of a hypertext system. The most important part is the *storage layer* which describes the structure of nodes (pages) and links. This layer touches upon the anchoring and presentation-specifications layers. This model suits our purposes well because it separates the 'hypermedia' part from the user-interface or browser part and also from the database or file system part (of how data are represented inside the components). In [17] we extended the Dexter model to describe the architecture of adaptive hypermedia systems. This resulted in the adaptive hypermedia application model (AHAM), as shown in Fig. 2.

The storage layer is extended to consist of three parts: the *domain model* which roughly corresponds to the 'old' storage layer, representing the structure of the information, the *user model* which represents how the user relates to the information (e.g. in terms of knowledge), and the *teaching model*, later renamed to *adaptation*

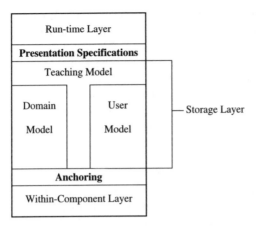

Figure 2: The adaptive hypermedia application model.

model, which represents the methods that are used to guide the learner through the information structure.

Without going into the details of the AHAM, we will describe the main elements that show clearly why adaptive educational hypermedia systems fit so easily in this model.

- When designing a course it is important to first list the concepts or topics the course should cover. A hierarchy of topics and subtopics is a good start, because it can be translated into a structure of chapters, sections and paragraphs.
- The next thing to do is to determine dependencies between the concepts. In some subject areas such dependencies are pretty clear and rigid, like an argumentation line of lemmas and theorems in mathematics (where the proofs of one theorem depend on other theorems and lemmas), but in other areas it is also sometimes advisable to study certain concepts before certain other concepts. This leads to a structure of *prerequisite relationships*. Many other types of relationships can be thought of, but prerequisites are most common in educational material.
- The different techniques (like the *link annotation* and the *conditional inclusion of fragments*) mentioned in Section 2 can be used to translate the concept relationships into adaptive behavior. For each type of relationship (e.g. prerequisites) some *generic adaptation rules* can be defined. Likewise, the translation of the action of reading pages into knowledge increments for certain concepts (small page concepts and higher-level section and chapter concepts) is also defined through such adaptation rules. The rules together form what we call the 'teaching model' or 'adaptation model' in AHAM.

A key point in AHAM is that the adaptation rules are used to translate user actions into user model updates (as well as the presentation and adaptation of content). Also, the rules use user model information together with the action information in order to determine the required user model updates. A typical example of such an adaptation rule would be (expressed in plain English): *on access of page P, if P is recommended then set the knowledge value for P to 100.* Expressed in this way the rules are so called *event–condition–action* rules, where *access of page P* is the event, *if P is recommended* is the condition checking the recommendation status of *P* in the user model, and *set the knowledge value for P to 100* is the action. A page access is just one type of event triggering such a rule. The evaluation of a test (e.g. a multiple-choice test) would be another triggering event, but user model updates are also triggers. When the knowledge of *P* is changed and *P* belongs to a section *S* which belongs to chapter *C* then the knowledge update to *P* may trigger a rule that has an action to create a (smaller) knowledge update to *S* and that update may be the trigger for an (even smaller) knowledge update to *C*. Authors of learning material need not be familiar with these adaptation rules. They can expect their authoring environment to translate concept relationships into these adaptation rules automatically. The existence of a rule system in AHAM is important because the approach of events that conditionally trigger actions suggests a system architecture that is very suitable for creating logging information that can be mined in order to find interesting access, test and user model update patterns.

Many seemingly very different authoring and delivery platforms for adaptive electronic textbooks exist (e.g. KBS-HyperBook [18, 19], Interbook [11], TANGOW [20], MOT [21] and AHA! [9]). However different, all systems consider concepts and concept relationships and have some type of intelligence to perform adaptation based on the concept relationships. In this sense all systems follow the general architecture of the AHAM reference model (but possibly with a different kind of rule or reasoning language and engine). In the next section we are going to look at AHA!, a system that corresponds closely to AHAM, including the structure of the adaptation rule language.

4 A general-purpose adaptive web-based platform

AHA! is an open source web server extension to add adaptation to applications such as online courses. In this section we concentrate on how AHA! can adapt a course to the individual learner. However, in order to perform that adaptation AHA! stores and updates a lot of information in the *user model* and optionally also maintains a complete *log* of all the user's actions, thus providing ample opportunity for data mining applications to analyze the users' behavior and detect potential issues or problems that are experienced by a significant number of learners [12, 13].

4.1 Overall architecture of AHA!

Figure 3 shows the overall architecture of AHA!. The core is formed by the AHA! engine which is implemented using Java Servlets running on (and communicating with) the web server. The information on the server consists of three parts we describe in detail below: a combined *domain and adaptation model* (DM/AM), corresponding to these models in AHAM, a *user model* (UM) which keeps track of the user's knowledge about the domain concepts, and the *local pages* which

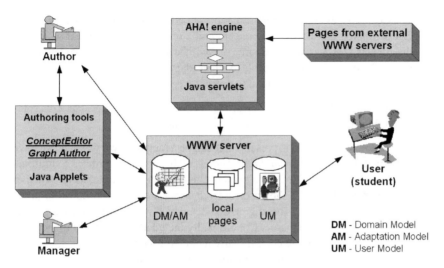

Figure 3: Overall architecture of AHA!.

contain the content of the application or course. It is possible to include external pages (retrieved from other web servers) and they are (potentially) adapted in the same way as local pages. AHA! also contains authoring and management tools, explained in a later section.

- The basis for the adaptation is the information stored in the user model (UM). Apart from some information that is specific for the user and independent of the application or course the UM is an *overlay model*. For each concept covered by the course UM contains a number of attribute values. In AHA! each concept can have arbitrarily many (named) attributes, but typically there is at least a *knowledge* value and a *suitability*. The knowledge attributes of all concepts together give a detailed impression of the knowledge the learner has of the whole course. The suitability value represents whether the concept is recommended. In AHA! attributes can be persistent or volatile. When the suitability is volatile it means that whenever a link to a concept is shown the system must decide whether the prerequisites are satisfied (in order to adapt the link). When it is persistent the suitability is calculated when it changes and simply used when needed.

- The *conceptual structure* of an AHA! application consists of *concepts* that are optionally associated with (one or more *resources*). With each concept a number of attributes are associated, each with a number of adaptation rules. When a new user logs on the concept/attribute structure is copied into the UM. For each concept there is an attribute *access* with adaptation rules that are executed when the concept is accessed (because the user clicks on a link to that concept). The adaptation rules work exactly as described in the AHAM in Section 3, including the propagation of rule execution and thus of knowledge updates from pages to sections to chapters.

- The (local) pages and fragments are represented in DM/AM as *resources*. There can be a fixed link between a concept and a resource, meaning that whenever the concept is accessed the resource that will be shown (possibly adapted) to the user is fixed. But it is also possible to let an adaptation rule (tied to a *show-ability* attribute) decide which resource to present (see below).

Figure 4 shows the adaptation performed by AHA! based on the adaptation rules and the UM. The figure is actually a slight simplification.

- When a page (resource) is presented, it can be adapted in two ways: it can have *conditional fragments* or *conditional objects*. The difference is that a conditional fragment is embedded in the page (and so is the requirement to decide whether the fragment should be shown or not), and that a conditional object is just a reference to a concept. The engine decides which resource to include, so it is more than just a yes/no issue. Conditionally included fragments or objects can themselves contain more conditionally included fragments or objects.
- When a page contains a link the engine looks at the suitability to decide whether the destination of the link (a concept or the page the concept leads to) is recommended or 'desired'. The link is then presented accordingly. The standard default scheme in AHA! is to use a *blue* link for recommended and not previously visited link destinations, *purple* for recommended but already visited destinations, and *black* for non-recommended destinations. Optionally it is also possible to add icons to the link (and presented in front of or behind the link anchor). Also, the blue/purple/black color scheme can be changed (but the number of colors is fixed at three).

In AHA! the presentation of a course can be influenced in many more ways that are beyond the scope of this chapter. AHA! uses a *layout model* to define how

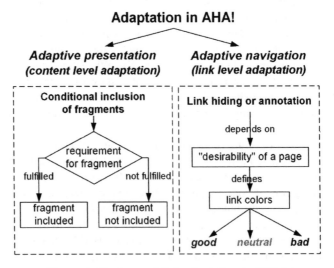

Figure 4: Content and link adaptation in AHA!.

concepts (of different types) are presented. A layout is an html frames structure, and apart from a frame that shows a page there can be frames that show part of a table of contents, concepts of which the knowledge is increased by reading the current page, prerequisite concepts (and their knowledge level), etc. Through the powerful layout model AHA! applications can be made to look very similar to applications in other adaptive educational hypermedia platforms. In [22] we made a first high-fidelity translation from Interbook [11] to AHA!, and we have since redesigned that translation to use high-level structures as described in the next section instead of the low-level adaptation rules described above.

4.2 The AHA! authoring tools

AHA! comes with two main authoring tools (and a multiple-choice test editor [14]). For fas˙ ˀnd easy authoring of the conceptual structure there is the *Graph Author*, in which ᴜ. author can use high-level concept relationships such as prerequisites. The tool generates the adaptation rules for DM/AM automatically. For specialists or for fine-tuning the generated rules AHA! offers the *Concept Editor* (sometimes called *Generatelist Editor*). Figure 5 shows a screenshot of the Graph Author. This figure shows the concept structure of an (old) AHA! tutorial. On the left the

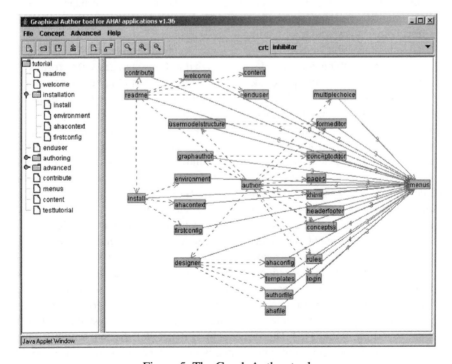

Figure 5: The Graph Author tool.

concept hierarchy is shown. This hierarchy is used to generate adaptation rules for propagating knowledge from pages to sections to chapters. On the right we see a graph of concept relationships. Each color and arrow style represents a different type of relationship. AHA! uses templates to translate the high-level relationships to the low-level adaptation rules. By using high-level relationships it is much easier for an author to understand the structure that form the basis for the adaptation than by authoring adaptation rules directly. However, the AHA! engine only works with adaptation rules. If (through data mining for instance) one discovers that a certain adaptation rule does not produce an optimal adaptation effect it is not immediately clear which high-level relationship has to be changed.

5 Questions, quizzes and tasks

Adaptive educational hypermedia systems focus on optimizing the process of reading course material. The basic idea is that adaptation is based on the system's idea of the *knowledge* of the learner. However, the system does not have very reliable information to base that estimate of the user's knowledge on. Especially in a web-based system the server-side adaptation engine (like AHA!) only receives events when the user clicks on a link. Other user actions like scrolling (to the bottom of a page) and actual reading (that could be followed by tracking eye-movement) do not result in messages being sent to the server. Also, the time between page accesses is not a reliable measure for the actual reading time as users may be distracted and perform other tasks instead of reading.

It is clear that the system can get a more accurate impression of the user's knowledge by 'probing' that knowledge through questions, quizzes, or the results of more elaborate tasks. Multiple-choice tests are the most popular, because they are easy to grade automatically. A slight variation, found in Interbook [11] for instance is a textfield in which a number, word or phrase must be entered (literally).

An interesting use of tests in an adaptive learning environment is in providing remedial content. After a test, the learner can be guided towards pages that need to be revisited because they seem not to be understood quite as well as the user model (based on reading alone) had indicated. But alternatively, tests can also be used to probe a user's knowledge before she starts reading, in order to decide which subjects can be skipped or need to be reviewed only briefly.

Another interesting part about adding tests or quizzes to an adaptive educational hypermedia environment is that the tests allow us to verify whether the knowledge level estimated through recording page accesses and the knowledge level measured through tests correspond. Monitoring this just in a single user is not meaningful because the learner may accidentally have missed something while reading, or misread something or forgotten a detail. When monitoring large numbers of users a pattern may emerge that indicates that learners systematically get certain questions wrong [13]. This does not immediately tell the course author what is wrong but it does point out which topic is not understood as well as it should have been.

6 Adapting to learning styles

In the previous sections we have only considered adaptation to the *knowledge level* of the learner. This level is mostly used in combination with *prerequisite relationships* in order to decide which content to show and how to annotate links. These adaptation methods and techniques treat every learner in exactly the same way. By considering individual differences in the way people prefer to learn the adaptation can be further improved. Some of this was tried in [23] and [24] for instance. An overview of possibilities and problems in using learning styles in adaptive hypermedia can be found in [25].

Roughly speaking there are two ways in which adaptation to learning styles is done: there are learning styles that indicate a preference for some *media type(s)* over others, and there are learning styles that influence the *order* in which learning material is studied.

Adaptation to media preferences can be easily implemented through the conditional inclusion of fragments or objects. When logging in for the first time the system can ask the learner whether she prefers presentations through text, images, video, audio or whichever media types are available. Alternatively the system can offer access to the different types of content and deduce the media preference from the choice the learner makes. ARTHUR [23] is an example of a system that uses media preferences. It distinguishes between the *visual-interactive*, *auditory-lecture* and *text* styles.

Adaptation of the *learning order* is more difficult and also more controversial. There are several classifications of learning styles, including Dunn and Dunn [26], Felder and Silverman [27], Kolb [28] and Honey and Mumford [29]. We show just two examples of how adaptation is possible to some of these categories of learning styles.

Kolb [28] distinguishes between *example-oriented* learners, or 'Reflectors' and *activity-oriented* learners, or 'Activists'. According to Kolb's learning model, 'Reflectors' are people who tend to collect and analyze data before taking an action. 'Activists' are more motivated by experimentation and attracted by challenge. In order to adapt to these individual differences one can add an attribute to concepts to indicate whether they represent an example or an activity. On a page or menu that provides links to the pages that are available on a certain topic the example can be presented and recommended first to the reflectors and the activity can be presented and recommended first to the activists. This type of adaptation can be taken one step further because often there is not just examples and activities but for instance also theory or a definition or explanation. Some learners want to see examples first, then the theory, then do an activity, whereas others may want to see the theory first, then examples, then activity, and others…Adaptation to these types of learning styles only involves *sorting, conditional inclusion of fragments* and *link annotation*.

Learners will generally not know terms like 'Reflector' and 'Activist' (in their Kolb learning style meaning). The learning style can be probed by offering the learner the free choice between example, activity or explanation at first, and by observing a pattern in the choices she makes.

A pair of more complex types of learning style to adapt to are the *field-dependent* (FD) and *field-independent* (FI) styles [30]. FI users follow an analytical approach. They pick a topic and study it in detail. FD users need to first see the global picture and ignore the details (until later). Also, FD learners are more likely to require externally defined goals and reinforcements, whereas FI ones tend to develop self-defined goals. Assuming that the 'global' picture can be gathered by reading the top-level or introductory pages of each chapter of a course, we can start by considering the lower-level pages as non-recommended for FD learners. Optionally we may even wish to write special introductory pages for each topic, pages that assume the learner wishes to get the general picture and not yet start studying the details. In other words, for FD learners the system should (at least for the top levels) suggest (or maybe even enforce) a breadth-first navigation through the concept hierarchy.

FI learners can pick a chapter and start studying it right away without visiting the introductions of other chapters. So this learning style does not require adaptation. (FI users need not be forced to stay within a chapter they start for instance.)

Detecting FD versus FI is not trivial because the beginning of a breadth-first navigation pattern is not yet a clear sign of an FD learner and by the time the system would know for sure the learner is FD the breadth-first part of the navigation may well be over. An alternative is to use a questionnaire, but reliable questionnaires for determining learning styles are long and cumbersome.

If the cognitive style of users is known beforehand it is interesting to see whether using the adaptation suggested above actually improves the learning process and outcome, and/or whether users (always) follow the advice that corresponds to their learning style. We have not performed any user studies to confirm or deny the potential positive effect of performing adaptation to learning styles in the way we suggested above.

7 Conclusions

In this chapter we have briefly reviewed the area of web-based educational hyper-media, and in particular the use of adaptive hypermedia technology in this area. We have shown a reference architecture (AHAM) for adaptive hypermedia and given some details of the AHA! system that resembles this reference architecture most closely. We have shown that high-level authoring tools can shield course authors from the low-level adaptation rules that drive the adaptation engine. The adaptation is, first and foremost, driven by the conceptual structure of the learning material. We have also looked into the use of learning styles to improve the learning process further by taking individual differences between users (independent of the topic of the learning material) into account.

Because web-based systems record access events, the updating of the user model that keeps track of the user's knowledge and also the logging of the access events provide interesting data that can be used to analyze whether course material and tests are properly matched to each other and whether the adaptation helps to provide the appropriate learning material to the learner.

We have not covered all possible uses of adaptation in e-learning. Some researchers have concentrated on providing adaptation based on information about the user's task [31] or other contextual aspects. We have also not covered the issue of *search* in adaptive educational hypermedia, which is a difficult topic because the adaptation makes it difficult to predict what exactly the content will be of search 'hit' (a link to a concept), or more precisely, of the page that will appear when the learner clicks on that link.

References

[1]   Wooley, D.R., Plato: The emergence of online community. *Matrix News* (online version at www.thinkofitcom/plato/dwplatohtm), 1994.

[2]   de Bra, P., Teaching hypertext and hypermedia through the web. *Journal of Universal Computer Science*, **2(12)**, pp. 797–804, 1996.

[3]   Weber, G. & Specht, M., User modeling and adaptive navigation support in www-based tutoring systems. *Int. Conf. on User Modeling*, pp. 289–300, 1997.

[4]   Weber, G. & Brusilovsky, P., ELM-ART: an adaptive versatile system for web-based instruction. *International Journal of Artificial Intelligence in Education*, **12**, pp. 351–384, 2001.

[5]   Mitrovic, A., Experiences in implementing constraint-based modeling in SQL-Tutor. *Int. Conf. on Intelligent Tutoring Systems*, pp. 414–423, 1998.

[6]   Mitrovic, A., Using evaluation to shape its design: results and experiences with SQL-Tutor. *User Modeling and User-Adapted Interaction*, **12(2–3)**, pp. 243–279, 2002.

[7]   Brusilovsky, P., Methods and techniques of adaptive hypermedia. *User Modeling and User Adapted Interaction*, **6(2–3)**, pp. 87–129, 1996.

[8]   Brusilovsky, P., Adaptive hypermedia. *User Modeling and User Adapted Interaction*, **11(1)**, pp. 87–110, 2001.

[9]   de Bra, P., Aerts, A., Berden, B., de Lange, B., Rousseau, B., Santic, T., Smits, D. & Stash, N., AHA! the adaptive hypermedia architecture. *ACM Conference on Hypertext and Hypermedia*, Nottingham, UK, pp. 81–84, 2003.

[10] Brusilovsky, P., Schwarz, E. & Weber, G., ELM-ART: an intelligent tutoring system on world wide web. *Int. Conf. on Intelligent Tutoring Systems*, pp. 261–269, 1996.

[11] Brusilovsky, P., Eklund, J. & Schwarz, E., Web-based education for all: a tool for developing adaptive courseware. *Computer Networks and ISDN Systems (WWW'98 Conference)*, **30(1–7)**, pp. 291–300, 1998.

[12] Romero, C., Ventura, S. & de Bra, P., Knowledge discovery with genetic programming for providing feedback to courseware author. *User Modeling and User-Adapted Interaction: The Journal of Personalization Research*, **14(5)**, pp. 425–464, 2004.

[13]   Romero, C., Ventura, S., de Castro, C. & de Bra, P., Discovering prediction rules in AHA! courses. *Lecture Notes in Artificial Intelligence*, **2702**, pp. 25–34, 2003.

[14]   Romero, C., Martin-Palomo, S., de Bra, P. & Ventura, S., An authoring tool for web-based adaptive and classic tests. *AACE ELEARN'2003 Conference*, Phoenix, AZ, pp. 174–177, 2003.

[15]   Halasz, F. & Schwartz, M., The Dexter reference model. *NIST Hypertext Standardization Workshop*, pp. 95–133, 1990.

[16]   Halasz, F. & Schwartz, M., The Dexter hypertext reference model. *Communications of the ACM*, **37(2)**, pp. 30–39, 1994.

[17]   de Bra, P., Houben, G.J. & Wu, H., AHAM: A Dexter-based reference model for adaptive hypermedia. *ACM Conf. on Hypertext and Hypermedia*, Darmstadt, Germany, pp. 147–156, 1999.

[18]   Nejdl, W. & Wolpers, M., Kbs hyperbook – a data-driven information system on the web. *Int. WWW8 Conference*, Toronto, 1999.

[19]   Henze, N. & Nejdl, W., Adaptivity in the kbs hyperbook system. *Second Workshop on Adaptive Systems and User Modeling on the WWW*, Toronto, 1999.

[20]   Carro, R.M., Pulido, E. & Rodriguez, P., TANGOW: a model for internet-based learning. *International Journal of Continuing Engineering Education and Lifelong Learning*, **11(1–2)**, pp. 25–34, 2001.

[21]   Cristea, A. & de Mooij, A., Adaptive course authoring: Mot, my online teacher. *ICT-2003, IEEE LTTF Int. Conf. on Telecommunications, Telecommunications + Education Workshop*, 2003.

[22]   de Bra, P., Santic, T. & Brusilovsky, P., AHA! meets Interbook, and more.... *AACE ELearn'2003 Conference*, Phoenix, AZ, pp. 57–64, 2003.

[23]   Gilbert, J. & Han, C., Adapting instruction in search of 'a significant difference'. *Journal of Network and Computer Applications*, **22**, pp. 149–160, 1999.

[24]   Triantafillou, E., Pomportsis, A. & Georgiadou, E., AES-CS: adaptive educational system based on cognitive styles. *Proc. of the AH2002 Workshop*, Malaga, Spain, pp. 10–20, 2002.

[25]   Stash, N., Cristea, A. & de Bra, P., Authoring of learning styles in adaptive hypermedia: Problems and solutions. *Proc. of the WWW2004 Conference*, New York, NY, pp. 114–123, 2004.

[26]   Dunn, R. & Dunn, K., *Teaching Students Through Their Individual Learning Styles: A Practical Approach*, Reston Publishing: Reston, VA, 1978.

[27]   Felder, R. & Silverman, L., Learning and teaching styles in engineering education. *Journal of Engineering Education*, **78(7)**, pp. 674–681, 1988.

[28]   Kolb, D., *Experiential Learning Experience as the Source of Learning and Development*, Prentice Hall, Englewood Cliffs, NJ, 1984.

[29]   Honey, P. & Mumford, A., *The Manual of Learning Styles*, Peter Honey: Maidenhead, 1992.

[30] Witkin, H., Moore, C., Goodenough, D. & Cox, P., Field-dependent and field-independent cognitive styles and their educational implications. *Review of Educational Research*, **47(1)**, pp. 1–64, 1977.

[31] Aroyo, L. & Dicheva, D., Aims: Learning and teaching support for www-based education. *International Journal for Continuing Engineering Education and Life-long Learning*, **11(1/2)**, pp. 152–164, 2001.

CHAPTER 2

Web mining for self-directed e-learning

P. Desikan, C. DeLong, K. Beemanapalli, A. Bose & J. Srivastava
Department of Computer Science & Engineering,
University of Minnesota, USA.

Abstract

Self-directed e-learning focuses on the independent learner, one who engages in education at his own pace, free from curricular obligation. A number of tools, some purposefully and others serendipitously, have become key enablers of this learning paradigm. For example, tools such as Google Scholar, CiteSeer Research Index, make it possible to perform literature search without stepping out of one's room. Due to the same technologies that helped make self-directed e-learning possible in the first place, these tools are in danger of delivering diminishing returns as micro-learning, lifelong education, and continuous education become the norm in our information age. Web mining, however, may potentially offer a solution to this issue. In this chapter, we investigate specific examples of self-directed e-learning and how their functionality and utility can be improved through the use of web mining technology, techniques, and practices. Our work demonstrates the usefulness of web mining as it applies to self-directed e-learning and the need to map implicit relationships in learner behavior, usage, and context.

1 Introduction

The introduction of the World Wide Web has had a profound impact on education, reducing the necessity of a learner and teacher to share the same physical space, and creating an entirely new form of knowledge delivery. With an ever-increasing number of Internet users and web sites, online learning, training, and online educational multimedia – all generally referred to as 'e-learning' – are becoming increasingly prevalent [1]. Additionally, while some educational outlets have used e-learning to supplement existing brick-and-mortar instruction (using software such as Web-CT [2]), others have replaced traditional instruction all together and replaced it with e-learning, creating a Virtual University [3]. The reasons for the increase in e-learning, and their sociological implications are almost as numerous as the systems available to enable e-learning [4].

There is, however, a common thread linking most of these systems, i.e. the user is given the ability to access expert information with some level of interaction. It is this level of interaction that is a key distinguishing feature when comparing different kinds of e-learning systems. For instance, the advantages of a web-enabled video feed may have only marginal utility over attending the lecture being taped; and may, in fact, be worse since face-to-face real time interaction is lost. Thus, e-learning must keep in mind the people it is designed for in order to be effective. Further, since individual needs differ, there is no reason why a single learning or teaching technique will work equally well for everyone.

Significant differences exist between students, such as their learning rate, personal interests, and a priori domain knowledge. If e-learning delivery can be brought into alignment with these individual traits, the learners' experience can be vastly improved over current models. As a specific example, material could be adapted to each student, or to a group of them (i.e. a class), who share some characteristics pertaining to the desired (target) knowledge or context [5].

However, designing systems that predetermine all possible usage scenarios is not feasible. Additionally, it may not be practical or efficient in many situations because of the diverse and rapidly changing requirements of learners. What is necessary is an informed e-learning system that continually 'educates' itself about the requirements of its learners, while delivering material that is most appropriate for individual learners.

Towards this, web mining techniques have been used to help identify usage behavior characteristics not obvious by other methods. There has been an extensive amount of work on web usage-based mining [6], including various aspects such as proper data preparation and pre-processing [7], web usage-based recommendations for e-learning [8–10], and models to assist online e-learning assessment [11].

Web mining can also be used to aid a user by integrating the implicit information from multiple sources of web data. At the simplest level, it can be a keyword-oriented search. However, learning is often aided by the inclusion of other kinds of data, such as a concept hierarchy and usage data. Often meta-information, such as authors, citations, and other expert-defined data, also help improve the learning process.

Given that web mining techniques can extract knowledge from the behavior of past users to help future ones, these techniques have much to offer existing e-learning systems.

In this chapter, we examine how e-learning systems can be improved using various web mining techniques and provide example applications that help illustrate our claims. Given the broad scope of e-learning, we will focus on *self-directed e-learning*, a facet of e-learning in which the learner is able to access a vast amount of expert-defined information, but is not necessarily subject to curricular constraints (i.e. semesters, grades, etc.). Thus, the focus here is on improving the user experience in self-directed e-learning systems through the use of web mining techniques.

This chapter is organized as follows. In Section 2 we provide the motivation for self-directed e-learning and present scenarios that describe its nature and significance. Section 3 presents some prominent self-directed e-learning applications that exist today in different domains, with a brief discussion on what they have to offer. In Section 4 we discuss the gaps in existing technologies by presenting issues that have not yet been addressed for an efficient self-directed e-learning. An introduction to web mining, the state-of-the art research in the area and how it can be applied to overcome the existing gaps in technologies is discussed in Section 5. We identify possible research directions to enable efficient self-directed e-learning in Section 6. Finally, in the last section we summarize the ideas discussed herein and provide conclusions.

2 Why self-directed e-learning?

W. Edwards Deming once said, 'Learning is not compulsory, but neither is survival'. In our current context – a world increasingly driven by knowledge – this is a specially salient observation. In many ways, a successful life depends on what we have learned and our understanding of the constantly evolving world around us; and thus one must engage in continuous learning to remain relevant. However, the learning that we are talking about is not restricted to traditional notions of learning bound to a specific physical location, such as high schools, colleges, and universities. Rather it is an *ongoing process* whereby its extent and nature may vary from person to person. Some may do it for pleasure, some for the love of learning, and some out of plain necessity. Some may invest more time in order to gain a deep understanding while others make merely be looking for a cursory overview. As such, self-directed e-learning is well-suited to reconcile these differing learner preferences. Such a system enjoys the benefits of access to a wealth of information via the Internet, as well as knowledge of individual learning habits, so that the specific needs of each individual learner can be catered to.

- Consider, for example, the situation of a *stay-at-home mother*. The task of raising a child can require knowledge of many kinds. Right from monitoring the hourly activities of a newborn to disciplining a young school-going child, there are numerous issues involved that need to be handled with care. While consulting a doctor for regular checkups is necessary, often mothers are faced with situations that need expert advice in monitoring the growth and daily activities of their children. Typical problems faced by such a mother are two-fold: availability of information and flexibility in time to access such information. With the advent of the Internet and e-learning systems, these problems are no more a technical issue. Mothers can access information from web sites that offer expert advice or information on child-related issues or they can participate in forums where parents can exchange their ideas and experiences. This enables them to learn from the experts, as well as experiences of other parents, on the best way to approach the issues involved with their children. The infrastructure helps provide mothers with multiple sources of information that can be accessed at their leisure or time of necessity, providing them a perfect platform to learn about the variety of aspects involved in child upbringing.

- Another common example is of a *graduate student* searching for interesting topics of research in her field. She starts out with a survey of literature pertaining to her interests and continues on to newsgroups, discussion forums, Internet search engines (like Google) and digital libraries (such as those provided by the IEEE). At the outset, she may have only a vague idea of what she is actually looking for. What she requires is a facilitator that recognizes her interests and introduces online material that can spark further research. A self-directed e-learning system can be such a facilitator: nominal input from the individual can produce a rich set of information while bringing her understanding into balance with the depth of the material being researched.

The examples above highlight some important points about learning today. It is a continuous process and the knowledge sought can vary from individual to individual in form, content, depth, and purpose. Learning for the most part is a highly focused endeavor, but flexible in its method, and directed by the individual's preferences. *Micro-learning* would be a more appropriate term for this. On the other hand material required for learning is readily available, thanks to the ubiquitous Internet. A seemingly limitless amount of information of all kinds is available through millions of web sites and web pages. We are also equipped with tools and technologies that allow us to access this data anywhere, anytime, with a few clicks of the mouse.

Even so, leveraging this enormous body of information to learn effectively and efficiently remains a challenging task. *Individualization* is a key requirement for this, and we can improve the knowledge-acquiring experience by learning from previous instances. In this way, mining data from past learning experiences can provide useful insights into human learning methodology, which in turn will go a long way in providing that personal touch to the learning experience. Data mining – and web mining in particular – can provide immense opportunities to realize the true potential of self-directed e-learning.

3 Web-based self-directed e-learning applications

A number of examples of self-directed e-learning exist. We focus on some of the most notable ones and give a short overview of what each has to offer.

3.1 Google Scholar

Google Scholar [12] is essentially a search engine for academic publications that are available online; each publication is linked to others by way of citations (Fig. 1). Both natural language and Boolean searches are possible. The searches themselves can be customized to query certain authors, publications, or within a year range

Search terms

Search preferences

Search results

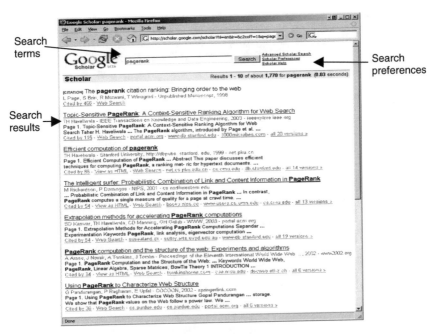

Figure 1: Google Scholar.

(e.g. 1999–2003). The search results are similar to Google's regular search and are generally in order of descending citation count (because Google's result-ranking algorithm, PageRank, relies on 'backlinks' – citations, in this case – to influence result authority).

3.2 Westlaw

Westlaw [13] is a sophisticated search and retrieval system for legal documents and other ancillary material available in Thompson West's proprietary database (Fig. 2). Similar to Google Scholar, Westlaw offers a natural language search as well as Boolean search options, called 'Terms and Connectors'. Searches are extremely customizable: by date range, document database (e.g. state, federal, circuit court), and type of document (e.g. cases and statutes). The results look similar to those found in other search engines – albeit more legal text-heavy – and also include a sidebar called 'ResultsPlus'. ResultsPlus does background searches for relevant documents using the current set of search keywords as well as metadata contained within the set of returned results. The ResultsPlus list can be customized to search specific document archives, helping pare down the results to those of interest to the user.

3.3 CiteSeer

CiteSeer [15] is one of the most popular online bibliographic indices related to computer science (Fig. 3). The key contribution of the CiteSeer repository is the

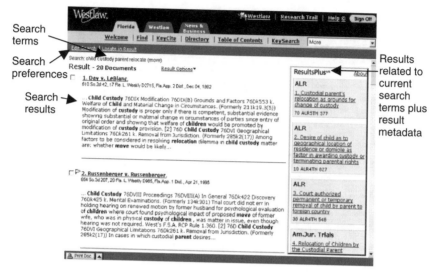

Figure 2: Westlaw: search system for law documents.

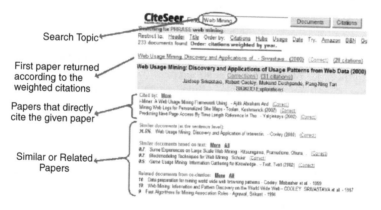

Figure 3: CiteSeer.

'autonomous citation indexing' [16]. Citation indexing makes it possible to extract information about related articles. Automating such a process eliminates significant human effort and makes the search more effective and efficient. The key concepts are depicted in Fig. 4.

Information about citations and their context is stored for each of these documents. The full text of the document is stored in several different formats. Information about documents that are similar at a sentence level (percentage of sentences that match between the documents), at a text level, or related due to co-citation is also given. Citation statistics for documents are computed that enable the user to look at the most cited or popular documents in the related field. They also maintain

Search terms

Search preferences

Display options for results

Search results

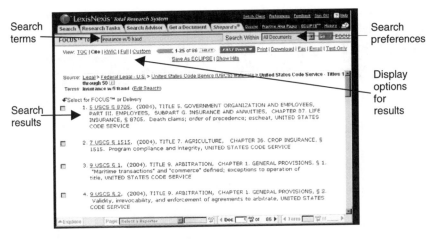

Figure 4: LexisNexis.

a directory for computer science-related papers, to make search based on categories easier. These documents are ordered by the number of citations. For a learner interested in documents related to computer science, this provides a very good repository and meta-level information for self-directed learning.

3.4 LexisNexis

LexisNexis [14] is a collection of information search and retrieval tools coupled with a vast library of available documents, including those related to law, academic, law enforcement, news, market intelligence, government, and insurance. As is the case with Westlaw, LexisNexis searches offer a wide array of search options, including natural language and Boolean searches, results customizable by document archive, similar result documents, and selected text.

LexisNexis offers additional capabilities in its display of results, of which there are five options, namely Cite (title/headline, author, source, and date), Show Hits (displays keyword matches in results), KWIC (displays 'Key Words In Context', similar to Show Hits), Full (displays full text of documents in results), and Custom (displays selected portions of documents).

3.5 Knowledge management systems

Knowledge management is defined as preserving actively and systematically the knowledge that is available in an organization. The interest in knowledge management in organizations has seen a recent surge. Companies emphasize the importance of relationship between knowledge and learning. Choenni *et al.* [17], discuss the significance of an e-learning environment in knowledge management and the challenges in its implementation. The e-learning is self-directed as the people in an organization search the knowledge base to find the required information.

Figure 5: Projistics knowledge management system.

In the industry many knowledge management solutions or software are available. Here we will discuss one of them to highlight the present trend and the types of features they provide. Figure 5 shows the snapshot of a knowledge management and document management software called Projistics [18].

The main features this knowledge management system provides are document management, knowledge bases, persistent discussion threads, check-in/check-out functionality, extensive audit trail and change history maintenance, approval routing, and configurable workflows. Though the software suite is an excellent e-learning based environment, it does not serve personalized content to its users.

3.6 Dr. Spock's child care

Figure 6 shows the web interface provided by 'The Dr. Spock Company' [19]. It is a leading parenting media and merchandising company that provides parents with latest expert advice, information, and inspiration on raising children. The company embodies the strength and identity of world-renowned pediatrician Dr. Benjamin Spock, providing parents with the latest expert content from today's leading authorities in parenting and children's health.

The search feature is a useful tool that enables parents to find information they are looking for. It also has discussion forums where parents can post questions that

Figure 6: Dr. Spock's child care.

will be answered either by experts in the field or by other parents. The information on the web site is methodically classified for easy retrieval.

4 Gaps in existing technology

The aforementioned example applications, while maintaining high levels of quality in provided content and demonstrated utility through their widespread use, have issues that remain unsolved. E-learning systems today focus on the technology aspect with apparently lesser efforts spent on developing a system that can be tailored and adapted to individual learners. A brief discussion on shortcomings in current systems follows.

4.1 Lack of community collaboration

Consider the following scenario: there is a stack of documents on a table that many people are seated at. Occasionally, someone will grab one or two documents, perhaps more, and then leave the table. Other people arrive, sit at the table, and do the same. At no time does anyone converse with each other, even if two people have looked at the same document. They do not discuss what one may have located that the other did not, despite the potential of identifying additional relevant information.

All of the previous examples share this approach. Each user of the respective services poses queries, browses results, and learns in isolation from other users.

In essence, there is no community aspect to self-directed e-learning, where like-minded users can contribute to each other's research, as is the case in a real classroom.

Despite the fact that each person's learning requirements may be different from others, there are often wide areas of overlap between individuals that can be mutually beneficial. Similarity in learning needs define *functional communities* of learners. These are virtual communities with fairly vague and overlapping definitions. Moreover, such communities are dynamic in the sense that needs of learners may change over time. Satisfying such communities is a difficult task, and yet it is conceivable to develop systems that learn from some in order to help the others. Most systems of today do barely little to tap into the colossal amounts of usage information already available.

4.2 Time management

For many users, time is a precious commodity, pressing them to accomplish as much as possible as quickly as possible. Current self-directed e-learning systems impose several requirements on their users, assuming a relatively equal distribution of a priori knowledge about the subject matter and the capability of always being able to properly formulate the 'right question'. All of us have, at some point or other, struggled to find what we were looking for on the web, essentially because we couldn't examine the right sources or pose the right queries. This imposition detracts from the experiences of users, especially the newer ones, who may spend inordinate amounts of time looking for documents that have very specific wordings. Compound this with the ever-increasing size of document repositories and querying can become difficult even for those who are well versed in the domain's knowledge.

4.3 Not self-improving

Perhaps this statement is too obvious, but it deserves mentioning anyway: the vast majority of search result lists are not 100% precise. Were they so, any query for documents would return a perfect list of relevant results. Current self-directed e-learning systems, while providing powerful sets of tools for querying, still operate from a self-contained idea of document relevancy, whereby the outcomes the results are meant to produce are not mapped back to their model of what makes a document relevant in the first place. Logs of usage of online documents, for example, constitute an implicit feedback from users about the relevance of these documents in different contexts. The challenge lies in extracting and deciphering user feedback from these massive repositories of data.

4.4 Implicit relationships not mapped

Another opportunity for improvement is in the area of inter-document relationships. Certainly, one document is related to another if it is explicitly defined through a citation, which can be considered a 'link'. However, it is also the case that one document can be related to another implicitly, even if they are not linked by citation. Search results try to map this through textual similarity, where documents are related if they share some of the same words or phrases. In general, this works fairly well, but is prone to failure when such words or phrases can be mapped to multiple contexts. It is in this, the identification of user context, where results can be distilled to match those of the user's intent. In self-directed e-learning systems – and search engines more broadly – this is a problem yet unsolved.

Deducing inter-document relationships is also a severe issue with present knowledge management systems. Knowledge management systems of today hardly mine data for new knowledge in the form of hitherto undiscovered relationships or trends connecting employees, management, or other stakeholders, their activities, and leveraging this information effectively throughout an organization.

5 Web mining

Web mining is the application of data mining techniques to extract knowledge from web data, including web documents, hyperlinks between documents, usage logs of web sites, etc. A panel organized at ICTAI 1997 [20] asked the question 'Is there anything distinct about web mining (compared to data mining in general)?' While no definitive conclusions were reached then, the tremendous attention on web mining in the past 5 years and the number of significant ideas that have been developed have answered this question in the affirmative in a big way. In addition, a fairly stable community of researchers interested in the area has been formed, largely through the successful series of WebKDD workshops, which have been held annually in conjunction with the ACM SIGKDD Conference since 1999 and the Web Analytics workshops, which have been held in conjunction with the SIAM data mining conference. Kosala and Blockeel [21] provide a good survey of the research in the field till the end of 1999.

Two different approaches were taken in initially defining web mining. First was a 'process-centric view', which defined web mining as a sequence of tasks [22]. Second was a 'data-centric view', which defined web mining in terms of the types of web data that was being used in the mining process [23]. The second definition has become more acceptable, as is evident from the approach adopted in most recent papers that have addressed the issue. In this chapter we define the data-centric view of web mining, which is described as 'the application of data mining techniques to extract knowledge from web data, i.e. web content, web structure and web usage data.'

The attention paid to web mining, in research, software industry, and web-based organizations, has led to the accumulation of a number of experiences. And its application in e-learning has also found its utility. In the following subsections, we will describe the taxonomy of web mining research and the applicability of web mining to e-learning.

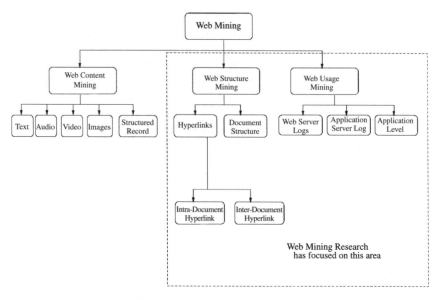

Figure 7: Web mining taxonomy.

5.1 Web mining taxonomy

Web mining can be broadly divided into three distinct categories, according to the kinds of data to be mined. We provide a brief overview of the three categories and a figure depicting the taxonomy is shown in Fig. 7.

5.1.1 Web content mining

Web content mining is the process of extracting useful information from the contents of web documents. Content data corresponds to the collection of facts a web page was designed to convey to the users. It may consist of text, images, audio, video, or structured records such as lists and tables. Application of text mining to web content has been the most widely researched. Issues addressed in text mining are: topic discovery, extracting association patterns, clustering of web documents and classification of web pages. Research activities on this topic have drawn heavily on techniques developed in other disciplines such as information retrieval and natural language processing. While there exists a significant body of work in extracting knowledge from images, in the fields of image processing and computer vision, the application of these techniques to web content mining has been limited.

5.1.2 Web structure mining

The structure of a typical web graph consists of web pages as nodes and hyperlinks as edges connecting related pages. Web structure mining is the process of discovering structure information from the Web. This can be further divided into two kinds based on the kind of structure information used.

- *Hyperlinks*: A hyperlink is a structural unit that connects a location in a web page to different location, either within the same web page or on a different web page. A hyperlink that connects to a different part of the same page is called an *intra-document hyperlink* and a hyperlink that connects two different pages is called an *inter-document hyperlink*. There has been a significant body of work on hyperlink analysis, of which [24] provides an up-to-date survey.
- *Document structure*: In addition, the content within a web page can also be organized in a tree-structured format, based on the various HTML and XML tags within the page. Mining efforts here have focused on automatically extracting document object model (DOM) structures out of documents.

5.1.3 Web usage mining

Web usage mining is the application of data mining techniques to discover interesting usage patterns from web data, in order to understand and better serve the needs of web-based applications. Usage data captures the identity or origin of web users along with their browsing behavior at a web site. Web usage mining itself can be classified further depending on the kind of usage data considered:

- *Web server data*: The user logs are collected by web servers. Typical data includes IP address, page reference and access time.
- *Application server data*: Commercial application servers, e.g. Weblogic, have significant features in the framework to enable e-commerce applications to be built on top of them with little effort. A key feature is the ability to track various kinds of business events and log them in application server logs.
- *Application level data*: Finally, new kinds of events can always be defined in an application and logging can be turned on for them, generating histories of these specially defined events.

5.2 Web mining research: state of the art

The interest of the research community and the rapid growth of the work in this area have resulted in good surveys over the past years that presents updated work and points to directions of further work [21, 23, 25]. Research on web content mining has focused on issues such as extracting information from structured and unstructured data and integration of information from the various sources of content. Earlier work on web content mining can be found in Kosala's work [21]. Web content mining together with other kinds of web data can be used for applications such as web page categorization and topic distillation. Liu and Chang [26], in their work, have presented some of the key issues in web content mining that has captured the attention of research community. Research in web structure mining has focused primarily on hyperlink analysis and has found its utility in a variety of applications. A survey on hyperlink analysis techniques and a methodology to pursue research has been proposed by Desikan *et al.* [24]. Among these techniques, PageRank [27], developed by Google founders, is the most popular metric for ranking hypertext documents according to their importance. The key idea is that a page has high rank if many highly ranked pages point it to. So the rank of a page depends upon the ranks of the pages pointing to it. This process is done iteratively till the rank of all the pages is determined. Oztekin *et al.* [28], proposed Usage Aware PageRank incorporating usage statistics into framework of PageRank model. The other popular metric is *hub* and *authority* scores. From a graph theoretic point of view, *hubs* and *authorities* can be interpreted as 'fans' and 'centers' in a bipartite core of a web graph. The hub and authority scores for a page are not based on a formula for a single page, but are computed for a set of pages related to a topic using an iterative procedure called HITS algorithm [29].

Web usage data has captured attention due to its nature of bringing user's perspective of the Web as opposed to creator's perspective. Understanding user profiles and user navigation patterns for better adaptive web sites and predicting user access patterns has evoked interest to the research and the business community. Methods for pre-processing the user log data and to separate web page references into those made for navigational purposes and those made for content purposes have been developed [7]. Perkowitz and Etzioni introduced the concept of adaptive web in their work [30]. Since then, Markov models have been used extensively to predict user behavior [31, 32, 33]. An extensive updated survey on web usage mining can be found in [34].

5.3 Web mining applicable to e-learning

We have described in the previous subsections how information can be extracted from different kinds of web data. From a direct perspective, information extraction can be viewed as a form of learning. Web mining techniques has been effectively used in search engine technologies to retrieve the most relevant and significant pages. However, the contribution of web mining has not been restricted to such explicitly available information such as page content. It must be noted that learning is often aided with inclusion of other kinds of data such as concept hierarchy on which a web structure is based or usage information. These kinds of data do not directly reflect the information in the page but help in building the context and circumstances in which such information is sought.

Web usage mining techniques as discussed earlier can be used to discover user navigation patterns. The user in our case is the self-directed learner. The creator of the web pages would represent the expert who has designed the web site to represent a series of notes. However, it is the usage information that actually reflects how a user is navigating or learning from the web site. Such usage information can not only serve as a useful feedback to the experts about the learners approach, but can also suggest to learners from the 'navigation experience' of other user's on what they found useful. Initial work on analyzing web logs to discover patterns and associations between web pages visited provided the right direction for such kind of analysis, but did not especially address the issue of e-learning. These kinds of analysis can be done either offline or online, or integrating both. A natural extension to such analysis was to develop recommender systems based on offline analysis [9] as well as an integrated approach.

Web mining techniques coupled with integrated meta-information such as author info, download info, and other additional information explicitly defined by a domain expert helps to improve the learning process. Given a large, knowledge-dense web site and a non-expert user seeking information, recommending relevant content becomes a significant challenge. Web mining has also been shown as a useful tool for providing expert-driven recommendations to non-experts, helping them understand what they *need* to know, as opposed to what is popular among other users. Another different dimension of web mining has focused on modeling user navigation behavior. The popular techniques are based on the first order Markov model where the user is modeled as a random surfer. Other models include a Markov chain model and reducing the 'randomness' factor by introducing a *bias* either based on the past usage patterns [28] or due to natural clustering of documents [35].

6 Future directions of research

Looking ahead, much can be done through the use of web mining to improve self-directed e-learning applications such that their function is in closer alignment with the expectations of their users. In particular, web mining is capable of realizing relationships that more accurately map what is known in a target domain, enabling web mining-enhanced self-directed e-learning systems to be brought into epistemological balance with other more traditional methods of learning, as in classroom education.

Several methods can be brought to bear in the realm of self-directed e-learning systems that could significantly enhance the overall user experience:

6.1 Usage rules

One of the key components of most recommender systems, such as the one used by Amazon.com, is the mining of usage patterns from server logs [36, 37]. As an indicator of how a web site is used, usage data can also be used to identify relevant documents based on the browsing and querying experiences of other users. These documents can then be presented to the user as they browse results in the form of a sidebar of recommendations.

In essence, this is akin to having the users, who are all sitting at the same table with the same set of documents, converse with each other. Not only do usage-based recommendations connect users to other documents of interest, they can also help maximize research time by reducing the number of 'guess-work' queries.

6.2 Keyword clustering: the conceptual thesaurus

Searching can be tedious work if one is unsure of how to formulate the 'question', or in this case, the query. Wouldn't it be better if the e-learning system could figure out what one might be searching for automatically? Often one has to search for something multiple times using different keywords/phrases till you found the right combination.

By clustering query keywords together into conceptually similar groups, we can suggest similar search terms/phrases or return results from closely related keyword clusters [38]. This could easily be combined with usage rules to display a sidebar of results from related searches, as well as some suggestions for related 'next' searches that are connected to the current set of keywords implicitly.

6.3 Recommendation mining

The mining of recommendations themselves – either in the search results or sidebar results – could be used to help pare down or expand sidebar results and/or search keyword recommendations by building a model of result relevancy given a user context. For instance, if one searches for 'link analysis' and the sidebar has a result no one ever clicks on, this may help identify a low confidence recommendation, which one may not want to include in the future.

6.4 Smart results: model of relevance

The most popular model of user navigation that has been used to rank Web documents of a search query has been a random surfer model. This is based on the assumption that each user who issues the query is at the same level of knowledge and wants to explore the topic to the same depth of knowledge. However, in a real world scenario that is not entirely true. Not all users have in depth knowledge about all topics. The goal of a novice browsing a topic is more likely to get an overview of the field as opposed to an expert, who is aware of what the field is about and would like to explore in depth. Existing systems do not incorporate this kind of model. Though there are systems that take into account user profile to a certain extent and current navigation sessions, the relevance of web pages to each user is not taken into account.

6.5 Intelligent knowledge management systems

Web logs are the clear indicators of users' browsing behavior. Web mining can be applied to these logs to extract valuable information regarding the user interest, his generic profile, etc. Based on this extracted knowledge, when the user accesses the system in the future, personalized recommendations can be made. Tang and McCalla [39] explain how this task can be achieved. We present an example scenario with recommendations to illustrate the type of recommendations possible in an e-learning knowledge management system.

Example scenario: A user submits the query 'Inventory Management' to the system. When the user re-visits the system, the following recommendations can be made:

- Last week you searched for 'Inventory Management'. A new paper has been published in a journal related to this topic. Would you like to look at it?
- Based on your previous visits we have discovered that you might be interested in the following topics:

- demand forecasting,
- supply-chain management,
- warehouse resources.

- Users have answered a question posted by you in the forum. Here is a link to the answer. Would you also like to look at the answers given by these users to other questions?

Such recommendations will enable the user of a knowledge management system, to find a broader range of relevant information.

7 Conclusion

Current trends are clear indicators that online learning is gaining in importance. Self-directed e-learning provides the right mix of technology and individualization that can enhance the learning experience. We have illustrated numerous examples of self-directed e-learning systems, yet there exist wide gaps in current technology that hinder the potential of e-learning. Some of these shortcomings were discussed. Web mining techniques have been immensely successful in a variety of application domains, and this leads us to believe that web mining techniques will enable us to overcome the limitations in current e-learning systems. Towards this end, we have provided a glimpse of what web mining is today, and outlined research areas in the field that have the potential to improve the efficacy of self-directed e-learning.

Acknowledgments

We would like to thank the Data Analysis and Management Research Group at the Department of Computer Science for providing valuable suggestions. This work was supported by AHPCRC contract number DAAD19-01-2-0014. The content of the work does not necessarily reflect the position or policy of the government and no official endorsement should be inferred.

References

[1]   Derek Stockely, E-learning, http://derekstockley.com.au/eindex2b.html
[2]   WebCT, http://www.webct.com
[3]   Groeneboer, T.C.C. & Stockley, D., Virtual-U: a collaborative model for online learning environments. *Second Int. Conf. on Computer Support for Collaborative Learning*, Toronto, Canada, December 1997.
[4]   Naber, L. & Köhle, M., If e-learning is the answer, what was the problem? *Proc. of AusWeb*, 2002.
[5]   Carchiolo, V., Longheu, A. & Malgeri, M., Adaptive Formative Paths in a Web-based Learning Environment. *Educational Technology & Society*, **5(4)**, pp. 64–75, 2002.

[6]   Srivastava, J., Cooley, R., Deshpande, M. & Tan, P., Web usage mining: Discovery and applications of usage patterns form web data. *SIGKDD Explorations*, **1(2)**, pp. 12–23, January 2000.

[7]   Cooley, R., Mobasher, B. & Srivastava, J., Data preparation for mining World Wide Web browsing patterns. *Knowledge and Information Systems*, **1(1)**, pp. 5–32, 1999.

[8]   Zaïane, O.R., Web usage mining for a better web-based learning environment. *Proc. of Conf. on Advanced Technology for Education*, Banff, Alberta, pp. 60–64, June 27–28, 2001.

[9]   Zaïane, O.R., Building a recommender agent for e-learning systems. *Proc. of the 7th Int. Conf. on Computers in Education (ICCE)*. Auckland, New Zealand, pp. 55–59, December 3–6, 2002.

[10] Cooley, R., Tan, P.N. & Srivastava, J., Websift: the web site information filter system. *Proc. of the Web KDD*, 1999.

[11] Guo, L., Xiang, X. & Shi, Y., Use web usage mining to assist background online e-learning assessment. *4th IEEE ICALT*, 2004.

[12] Google Scholar, http://scholar.google.com

[13] Westlaw, http://training.west.thomson.com/index.asp

[14] LexisNexis, http://www.lexisnexis.com/elearning/lexis/researchtool/search-tool.asp

[15] CiteSeer, http://citeseer.ist.psu.edu/cs

[16] Lawrence, S., Giles, C.L. & Bollacker, K., Digital libraries and autonomous citation indexing. *IEEE Computer*, **32(6)**, pp. 67–71, 1999.

[17] Choenni, S., Walker, R., Bakker, R. & Baets, W., E-learning as a vehicle for knowledge management. *Proc. of the 14th Conf. on Applications of Prolog, INAP*, 2001.

[18] Projistics, http://www.projistics.com/

[19] Dr. Spock Company, http://www.drspock.com/

[20] Srivastava, J. & Mobasher, B., Panel discussion on 'Web Mining: Hype or Reality?' *ICTAI*, 1997.

[21] Kosala, R. & Blockeel, H., Web mining research: A survey. *SIGKDD Explorations*, **2(1)**, pp. 1–15, 2000.

[22] Etzioni, O., The World Wide Web: Quagmire or Gold Mine? *Communications of the ACM*, **39(11)**, pp. 65–68, November 1996.

[23] Cooley, R., Mobasher, B. & Srivastava, J., Web mining: information and pattern discovery on the world wide web. *9th IEEE ICTAI*. 1997.

[24] Desikan, P., Srivastava, J., Kumar, V. & Tan, P.N., *Hyperlink Analysis: Techniques and Applications*, Technical Report 2002-0152, Army High Performance Computing and Research Center, 2002.

[25] Srivastava, J., Desikan, P. & Kumar, V., Web mining – concepts, applications and research directions (Chapter 21). *Data Mining: Next Generation Challenges and Future Directions*, MIT/AAAI Press: Cambridge, MA, 2004.

[26] Liu, B. & Chang, K.C.C., Editorial: Special Issue on Web Content Mining. *SIGKDD Explorations*, December, 2004.

[27] Page, L., Brin, S., Motwani, R. & Winograd, T., The PageRank citation ranking: bringing order to the web. *Stanford Digital Library Technologies*, January 1998.

[28] Oztekin, B.U., Ertoz, L. & Kumar, V., usage aware PageRank. *World Wide Web Conf.*, 2003.

[29] Kleinberg, J.M., Authoritative sources in hyperlinked environment. *9th Annual ACM-SIAM Symp. on Discrete Algorithms*, pp. 668–677, 1998.

[30] Perkowitz, M. & Etzioni, O., Adaptive web sites: an AI challenge. *IJCAI97*, 1970.

[31] Pirolli, P. & Pitkow, J.E., Distribution of surfer's path through the World Wide Web: empirical characterization. *World Wide Web*, 1, pp. 1–17, 1999.

[32] Sarukkai, R.R., Link prediction and path analysis using Markov chains. *Proc. of the 9th World Wide Web Conf.*, 1999.

[33] Zhu, J., Hong, J. & Hughes, J.G., Using Markov chains for link prediction in adaptive web sites. *Proc. of ACM SIGWEB Hypertext*, 2002.

[34] Mobasher, B., Web usage mining and personalization (Chapter 15). *Practical Handbook of Internet Computing*, ed. M.P. Singh, CRC Press: Boca Raton, FL, 2005.

[35] Padmanabhan, D., Desikan, P., Srivastava, J. & Riaz, K., WICER: a weighted inter-cluster edge ranking for clustered graphs. *Proc. of the 2005 IEEE/WIC/ACM Int. Conf. on Web Intelligence*, 2005.

[36] Mobasher, B., Cooley, R. & Srivastava, J., Automatic personalization based on web usage mining. *Communications of the ACM*, **43(8)**, pp. 142–151, 2000.

[37] Berendt, B., Hotho, A. & Stumme, G., Towards semantic web mining. *Proc. of the Int. Semantic Web Conf.*, Sardinia, Italy, pp. 264–278, June 2002.

[38] Hodge, V.J. & Austin, J., Hierarchical word clustering – automatic thesaurus generation. *Neurocomputing*, **48(1–4)**, pp. 819–846, 2002.

[39] Tang, T.Y. & McCalla, G., Smart recommendation for an evolving e-learning system. *Proc. of the 11th Int. Conf. on Artificial Intelligence in Education (AIED)*, pp. 699–710, 2003.

CHAPTER 3

Data mining for the analysis of content interaction in web-based learning and training systems

C. Pahl

Dublin City University, School of Computing, Dublin, Ireland.

Abstract

Data mining is based on the detection and extraction of knowledge from a database. Web usage mining is a special form of data mining to address behavior in web sites. Web usage mining shall be proposed as the central, non-intrusive and objective evaluation technique for the analysis of the usage of web-based learning and training systems and in particular of the interaction with educational content in these systems. We will introduce and illustrate a number of mining techniques that were developed specifically for the educational context. The behavior of learners in learning and training technology systems, in particular when a variety of interactive learning and training features is offered, needs to be analyzed and evaluated in order to show the effectiveness and to improve, if necessary, the instructional design. We look at techniques to determine the goals of learning sessions, the detailed interaction with content, and the changing of learning behavior over time.

1 Introduction

The use of computer-supported learning and training environments to enhance or replace traditional forms of learning and training has increased over the past years. In particular the World Wide Web has gained the status as the predominant platform for these environments. First generation web-based educational environments succeeded due to their advantage of easy access to educational resources. Recently, the focus has been on supporting a wider range of educational activities, thus enhancing the learning experience for the user through improved interactivity and engagement of the learner. Traditional knowledge-based learning is complemented by skills-oriented training activities. In web-based environments, the interaction between learners and content supporting knowledge acquisition and skills training is central [1, 2]. On the technical level, interaction is a reflection of learning activities and strategies. The evaluation of learning and training behavior needs to be based on the analysis of content interaction in these environments.

Learning behavior in learning and training environments, however, is currently not well understood. In contrast to traditional classroom-based learning and training, the learning strategies and behavior are more determined by the learner's own decisions how to organize learning and training [3]. Additionally, often several educational features are available at the same time, allowing competent learners to choose their own approach of combining resources and features. Consequently, the analysis and evaluation of learning and training behavior is of central importance [4]. A general understanding of effective and preferred learning styles and behavior is required for authors and instructional designers to improve the design of learning content. Instructors require feedback on usage to improve the delivery of web-based educational resources. Supporting both summative and formative evaluation is therefore our aim, whereby, due to the novelty of the application, formative evaluation integrated in an incremental design and development process is the more crucial aspect.

A framework for the analysis and evaluation of learning and training behavior and interaction in web-based educational systems needs to support a variety of techniques:

- the detection and discovery of learning and training interaction from sources such as web access logs;
- the explicit capture and representation of interaction behavior abstracted from the interaction and access requests recorded in the logs;
- the analysis and interpretation of behavior within the educational context using an analytic model.

Traditionally, direct observation and surveys are used to determine the learning behavior in classroom-based learning and training, but with the emergence of computer-supported, and in particular web-supported learning and training environments, there is now another option. Learners leave traces of their activities and behavior in computer supported systems. In web-based systems, access logs are automatically generated by web servers that handle user requests. Data mining [5–7], in the application to behavior in web-based environments called web usage mining, can here be deployed to make this latent knowledge explicit.

Data mining is about the discovery, extraction, and analysis of data from large databases. Data mining aims to make implicitly represented information explicit. The special form of web usage mining aims to extract behavior in web sites from access logs. Web usage mining is an observation-oriented evaluation technique suitable for learning behavior analysis [8–11]. Despite some limitations, it offers a non-intrusive form of observation that can contribute substantially to reliable and accurate evaluation results for educational applications.

Our objectives here are to introduce central web usage mining techniques and to illustrate their benefits using a case study. While web usage mining has been applied in various domains, we will focus here on techniques that are specific to the educational context and content interaction in particular.

2 Interaction and behavior

2.1 Learning and training interaction

Supporting design and formative evaluation is the main goal behind the deployment of web usage mining. The design of learning and training systems requires a suitable methodology. An abstract model of learning and training can form part of the foundations for the instructional design that can also act as an analytic model for evaluations. In particular, the notion of interaction plays a central role in such a model.

Interaction can be characterized in different ways. A common classification is by role [12]: learner–content interaction, learner–instructor interaction, and learner–learner interaction. Learner–content interaction is at the core, according to Ohl [13]. In particular behavior in web-based educational environments is often an expression of learner–content interaction, as the Web has been predominantly used to provide access to learning resources. In the web context, the notion of interaction is, however, overloaded. It has a meaning in the context of education, but also as part of the computer environment. These different views can be reconciled through an abstract interaction model [14].

2.2 Implementing interaction

Learning and training has to be mapped to, or implemented by, a learning technology system [15]. On the technology side, two aspects have to be considered in particular: the human–computer interface from a more general perspective [16] and educational media and services in particular [17] as components of the learning technology system. These two aspects add two additional layers to the learning and training interaction, with different notions of interaction in all three of them. The interaction between the learner and the system (which provides content and educational services) needs to be designed and implemented.

- The learner needs to be characterized in terms her or his behavior at the human–computer interface, i.e. in terms of cognitive aspects, the learning goals and tasks, and linguistic aspects.
- The system needs to be described in terms of a technically oriented interaction language for the educational services implementation and media.

As we can see, the notion of interaction is central – but interpreted differently in different contexts. The interaction of a learner in educational systems can be traced on the implementation level, translated into human–computer interactions, and analyzed in the context of learning and training interaction. This characterizes the layered abstract interaction model for our design and evaluation approach based on web usage mining.

2.3 An abstract model of content interaction

Interaction is a term that is used in different contexts. Different meanings of interaction can be distinguished at levels of abstraction for interaction and behavior:

- *Learning and training interaction* refers to interaction between learners, instructors, and content in the context of education.
- The *human–computer interface* aspect relates human activities to the software and interface features of the computer system.
- *Multimedia* and *service interaction* deals with processes and formats of interaction at the technical level.

These three layers are the essential elements of an abstract conceptual model that defines and structures notions of interaction.

In instructional design, we need to relate learning and training interaction to system-level interaction at the multimedia and services interface [18]. In the web mining process we need to look in the other direction: system-level interaction activities extracted from the web logs need to be related to and interpreted in the learning and training context.

The formative evaluation is our major objective. Due to the novelty of web-based learning and training, development methodologies focusing on interaction and supported by data mining are sought. The support of incremental instructional design and its implementation is, however, only one goal. Web usage mining is a tool that allows the constant monitoring of learners in an educational technology system. For instance, the approach can be used to identify weak learners through their behavior. These are, for instance, often characterized by erratic behavior.

2.4 The interactive database learning environment

In order to illustrate the education-specific mining techniques and the benefits of these techniques for the analysis and evaluation of learning and training interaction, we refer to the interactive database learning environment (IDLE) [19]. IDLE is a support environment for a third-level undergraduate computing course – an introduction to databases. IDLE can be characterized as follows in terms of its educational objectives:

- IDLE implements a virtual apprenticeship approach, considering the learner as a (virtual) apprentice who has to be trained to self-reliantly perform subject-specific tasks under the guidance of a (virtual) master.
- IDLE aims to seamlessly integrate various educational services (lectures, tutorials, labs) in one environment and to enhance the practical aspects by a realistic learning and training environment.

A virtual lecture component in IDLE is based on a synchronized delivery of audio and visual material. IDLE tutorial services make use of animation and simulation techniques in order to demonstrate practical aspects of the course content. A lab feature aims to support the practical coursework (consisting of database development and programming) within the learning environment. Some especially interesting components for web mining applications are the tutorial and lab training services. These aim at skills training by supporting a range of active learning features. Learners interact with IDLE to learn about and train graphical database design and database programming. IDLE plays here the role of the virtual master interacting with a virtual apprentice.

The IDLE environment has been developed over a period of several years. As a result of the novelty of the technology, an incremental, prototyping-based development approach was taken. System prototypes were developed, used in the course, and evaluated; the formative evaluation results were integrated in consecutive improvement and extension steps. Web usage mining has played an essential role in this process. It allowed the determination and evaluation of learner behavior in order to improve the system and the instructional design. In addition, the possibility to constantly monitor the class has helped the instructor in running the course.

3 Data and web usage mining

The aim of *data mining* is the discovery and extraction of latent knowledge from a database [5]. This knowledge is classified into rules and patterns in order to support analysis and decision making processes. Classical uses of data mining include decision support systems for the business context and analysis tools for scientific applications. It can be used in a predictory (decision making), generative (create new or improved designs), and explanatory (scientific analysis) style.

3.1 Web usage mining in the educational context

Web usage mining is a specific form of data mining, focusing on the analysis of user behavior in web-based systems (Fig. 1). The database in the web context is the access log created by web servers. A web log entry includes the requestor (or the respective URL), the requested resource, and the date and time of the request. If the content and purpose of the resource is known, we can deduce the corresponding activities from the log entries. For instance, audio files and some HTML-pages in the IDLE system support lecture participation as the activity. Web usage mining is different from data mining in general since only activities and behavior are looked at. Web usage mining has been used widely in e-commerce application to monitor and analyze shopping behavior [5–7]. Customer relationship management is the ultimate objective in the e-commerce context, which is achieved through optimization and personalization of the shopping processes based on usage mining results.

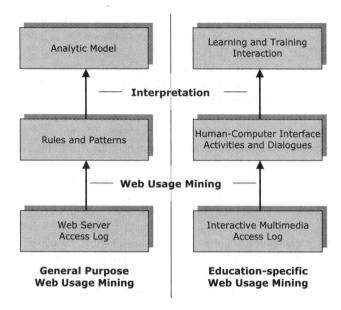

Figure 1: Web usage mining in the educational context.

We propose web usage mining here as a similar tool to design and manage the relationship between the learner and the educational environment, aiming at an improved learning experience. We can classify data mining techniques [20–24] in general into three broad categories that are of relevance to the educational context [8–11]: basic statistics (of usage), static relationships, and dynamic relationships.

3.2 Data and web mining techniques

Basic quantitative usage attributes are often looked at first, although *usage statistics* are usually not considered as data mining techniques. However, they often form the starting point of evaluations. For web-based systems, usage is captured in simple measures such as total number of visits, number of visits per page, and so forth. Tracking features of most learning technology systems and most web log analyzers are based on these measures.

Static relationships refer to relationships between objects of interest at one moment in time or within a given period of time.

- *Classification* and *prediction* are related techniques. Classification predicts class labels, whereas prediction predicts continuous-valued functions. A model is used to analyze a sample. The result of this learning step is then applied. Regression is a typical form of prediction.
- *Clustering* groups are mutually similar data items. In contrast to classification, the class labels are not pre-given. The learning process is called unsupervised here. Pattern recognition is a typical example.

- *Association rules* are interesting relationships discovered among the set of data items. A typical example is purchasing analysis, which can identify item pairs frequently purchased together.

Dynamic relationships refer to changes or changing patterns in the database under consideration.

- *Sequential pattern* analysis is applied if events are captured in a database over a period of time. Frequently occurring patterns of events are extracted. Web usage or sales transaction patterns are typical examples.
- *Time series*, which refers to the analysis of the variance of patterns and rules over time, are important since they allow an analyst to evaluate changing and varying behavior.

The implementation of data mining techniques through software tools can be distinguished into three phases – cleaning, extraction, and interpretation. During cleaning, irrelevant entries such as images can be removed. Extraction is based on the mining techniques, such as the ones we have introduced above, to determine patterns and rules. Finally, the results from the extraction phase have to be interpreted in the context of the application domain.

Despite its potential and benefits, web usage mining has also some limitations [6, 7]. These are, for instance, connected to the fact that not necessary all interactions are recorded in web logs. Web browsers use caching as a mechanism to avoid network traffic as a consequence of repeated loading of pages. In this case, the usage picture provided through data mining would be distorted. However, problems of this kind can be circumvented if pages are created dynamically, which is standard practice in commercial web sites.

3.3 Education-specific web usage mining

A number of aspects need to be considered if data mining shall be deployed in the educational context. The mining focus is on learning behavior. Some of the presented mining techniques for standard case are not targeted enough for the educational context to extract meaningful results. Some domain-specific techniques – mainly variations of the standard techniques – shall therefore be introduced. Learning and training interaction is the context in which the mining results have to be interpreted – this shall be captured through an analytic model of interaction. As a consequence of these considerations, we have developed the following education-specific techniques:

- *Session statistics* are based on simple quantitative measurements – the purpose is a quantitative overview of the usage.
- *Session classification* is based on the classification technique – the purpose is learning goal identification.
- *Behavioral patterns* extend and generalize the sequential pattern technique – the purpose is activity identification.

- *Time series* are based on the time series technique – their purpose in the educational context is strategy identification.

We will illustrate these techniques in the next sections using the case study.

Languages play a central role in the mining and interpretation process. The interaction behavior has to be captured. While web logs are an expression of behavior, reflecting the interaction between the learner and content resources, a more abstract language is required to capture these interactions closer to the context of the interpretation and the interaction model. An intermediate level is the multimedia interface and service interaction protocol. Interactivity in the learning context can be expressed through a learning activity language that captures navigation behavior and allows the interpretation in a learning and training interaction model. The language needs to capture the interaction topology consisting of nodes and arcs between nodes:

- *Nodes* represent the system's *resources* ranging from static content objects to active services. Nodes are named resources, typed for instance based on the activities and topics they support.
- *Arcs* between the nodes represent the user's *activities* – navigation and selection of activities. Activity combinations such as sequences, choices, concurrent activities, and iterations can be expressed.

Given the nodes (resources) *Exercise1*, *Exercise2*, and *Exercise3*, the expression

$$(Exercise1;(Exercise2 \mid Exercise3))^*$$

means that repeatedly (iteration operator '*') *Exercise1* is addressed before (sequence operator ';') either (choice operator '|') *Exercise2* or *Exercise3* is addressed. This language can be a tool for design and implementation.

4 Session statistics

A *session* is a central notion in computer-mediated learning and training. A session is technically a sequence of web log entries that reflects the interaction behavior of a learner in a period of active study.

Session statistics is about basic quantitative measures that can help to answer questions about *which resources are used* and the *investment of time* for a given learning activity, often based on sessions as the basic unit. Any of the results can be compared against the expectations of the instructional designer. Explicitly formulated expectations form part of the analytic model. There are other statistical measures that might result in useful insights. The total number of requests by interval or total numbers ranked by resource provide relevant information based on simple measures. Table 1, for instance, shows that about half the students that have looked at the chapter overview pages also looked at the chapter content and the number actually finishing the chapter is lower than the number starting the chapter.

For instance, a student submitted in average 239 requests for resources to the IDLE system per term (after the cleaning, i.e. irrelevant resources requests were

Table 1: Access statistics for IDLE Chapter 1
material for a one-week period.

Resource	Number of requests
ch1-lectov.html	396
ch1-lect1.html	224
ch1-lect2.html	218
ch1-lect3.html	207
ch1-lect4.html	198

filtered out). Looking at the ranked total number of requests per resource, the course notes ranked first (initially a surprising result, but a more detailed later analysis showed that students use the course notes online during each session), followed by interactive lab features. A high total number of requests for interactive lab features, where students submit their solutions to given problems, shows a high investment of time for this part. These measures, however, give more an idea about 'what' resources are used than 'how' they are used.

5 Session classification

The objective of *session classification* is to *extract* and *identify the main learning goals* and *higher-level learning tasks* from a session log [25]. Typically, a learner focuses on one or two main activities in a session. Using a *classification* approach we can identify the main learning objectives by looking at the predominant types of interaction with the system.

The media resources of a course web site can be classified, i.e. a number of classes $C_1, \ldots, C_N$ are created where each class C_i is a set $\{U_{i1}, \ldots, U_{iM}\}$ of URLs. This corresponds to the nodes and their types of our learning activity language. Each class C_i is associated to a type of system-level interaction that facilitates a particular knowledge-level learning activity, such as attending a virtual lecture or working on lab exercises. If a learner spends substantial session time on a particular activity or submits a high number of requests for these resources and activities, then this activity is a manifestation of a particular goal. The requests of pages of the individual classes are counted. In the following example the class names such as *Lectures* or *Tutorials* represent the activities connected to the resources, see Table 2.

For each session, a *ranking* $C_{i1} \leq \cdots \leq C_{iN}$ of main learning goal(s) represented by learning activity classes is produced based on the number of requests for each class, which gives us some insight into the students' learning goals and their implementation. The classification for the sample activities results in

$$Lectures \leq Labs \leq Tutorials \leq Downloads \leq Look\ Up$$

as the ranking based on Table 3.

Table 2: Resource and activity classification.

Class	URLs	Activity
Lectures	{ch1-lectov.html, ch1-lect1.html, ch1-lect2.html, …}	Attending virtual lectures
Tutorials	{ch3-anim1.html, ch5-anim1.html, …}	Participating in a virtual tutorial
Labs	{ch6-sql1.html, ch6-sql2.html, …}	Practicing and training in a virtual lab
Downloads	{CourseNotes.pdf, ProjectSpec.pdf, …}	Downloading resources
Look up	{Schedule.html, Results.html, …}	Look up of course-related information

Table 3: Session classification.

Class	Percentage of requests
Lectures	33
Labs	26
Tutorials	21
Download	12
Look Up	8

This session classification can be generalized for all sessions of a learner or for groups of learners. It gives an instructor a high-level overview of the system usage.

The technique can be used in an iterative evaluation process. Initial classifications might turn out too unspecific and can be refined into more fine-granular classifications, identifying more specific activities, tasks, and goals; thus providing more detailed and meaningful analysis results. While our distinction in our example was by learning activity type, we found it useful in a refined classification to look at the topics as a sub-classification, e.g. by chapter resulting in classes such as *LecturesCh1*, *LecturesCh2*, etc. or *TutorialCh1*, *TutorialsCh2*, etc. This is a typical form of a drill-down approach to data mining usage, which gives a more detailed picture of learner activity.

6 Behavioral patterns

The goal identification through session classification that we looked at in the previous section is a tool on an abstract level that ignores the time dimension, i.e. the sequencing of different activities is ignored. Often, however, a closer look at interactions at a lower, fine-granular level is necessary in order to investigate learning activities in detail.

The objective of the *behavioral pattern mining* technique is to *extract behavioral interaction patterns* from the log file. Irrelevant activities – students might look up other pages, even leave the system temporarily – can be discarded. The filtered sequences are candidates for *sequential patterns*. In order to find out what patterns learners follow, the sequences are subjected to some threshold control – another filter to discard too uncommon ones.

Behavioral patterns encompass more than sequences – learners repeat elements, choose between options, or work on several course elements in parallel. A model of the course topology – navigation infrastructure and interactive elements abstracted by nodes and arcs – underlies behavioral patterns. The navigation along these topologies can be expressed using the *learning activity language* – in particular the expressions on the connections of the topology. A *behavioral pattern* is an expression of a learning activity language that describes potential or actual learning as interactions with an educational multimedia system.

$$(Lecture1 \mid Tutorial1^*) \; ; \; (Lecture2 \mid Tutorial2^*) \; ; \ldots$$

In this example, *Lecture1* and *Tutorial1* are activities. The expression specifies that the learner can use either lectures or tutorials (the | -operator). The tutorial might be attended repeatedly (the * -operator), before the next lesson is looked at (the ; -operator). These expressions can also be represented in a graphical form, see Fig. 2, which visualizes in the learning activity language.

$$Home \; ; (TableOfContents \; ;$$
$$(Lecture1 \; ; \; Lecture2 \; ; \; Lecture3 \mid Tutorial1 \; ; \; Tutorial2 \,))^*$$

The learning activity language we used here to describe these patterns is an integral part of the analysis model that is used to interpret mining results. Therefore, we need to relate these behavioral patterns with the sequential patterns extracted from the web log. As explained earlier on, activities can be associated with the transitions between the nodes (URLs) reflected in the log. The behavioral pattern expressions can be a reflection of the instructor's intended use (a design instrument) or an abstraction of the learner's behavior (an evaluation instrument) gained through web usage mining. Two applications can be distinguished:

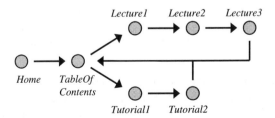

Figure 2: A behavioral pattern (visualized as a graph).

- *Verification of expected behavior*: The aim is to compare abstract behavioral patterns specified by the instructor with the actual sequential patterns of learner–content interactions. This only needs sequential pattern extraction to be implemented as a mining technique. For instance, we found that the expected behavioral pattern for a specific lab feature (specified by the instructor) had been met in 85% of all lab sessions (extracted from the web logs as sequential patterns). Sequential patterns are compared with behavioral patterns by checking for instance the choice and iterations that were allowed according to the behavioral pattern. We used a simulation relation here to determine matching between behavioral and sequential patterns [9]. In order for a sequential pattern to satisfy (or simulate) a behavioral pattern, the following sequential pattern expressions are permitted:

  - actual repetitions P ; …; P are allowed if $P*$ is specified,
  - choices $P1$ or $P2$ can be made if $P1 \mid P2$ is specified.

  Sequences and parallel uses of resources have to be followed, if required. Alternative definitions that would loosen the simulation constraint could also allow deviations from the required path.

- *Extraction of actual behavior*: Actual behavior is extracted in the form of behavioral patterns. The difficulty with this approach is that there is no unique solution. In particular, iterations and concurrent use are difficult to determine, even if the overall topology with its navigation links is known. The extraction of the pattern is the first step; the second is the determination of the support of the pattern by the class. Two patterns can be compared if the distance between them is calculated; this is based on the sequence alignment method [22] where the comparison is based on the extent of deviation from the joint path.

While this technique offers interesting results, the potential has not been fully exploited; more research is required here. More advanced results can be achieved if for example the time spent on each activity and other properties are included in the evaluation [26]. The time spent on an activity can tell us about the actual usage of the resource (and not only the presumed activity based on the intended usage).

7 Time series

Time series are sequences of measurements over a period of time. These measurements can include results from any of the mining techniques presented so far. The purpose is here the *detection of change in learning behavior*, which is often a reflection of the overall learning strategy over the duration of a course. This is important for two reasons.

- First, change might be intended by the instructional designer and the actual occurrence of change needs to be verified. An example for this case is an evaluation of scaffolding features through behavioral pattern analysis. Fading use of scaffolds – features that support students in becoming self-reliant and competent

Table 4: Time series (by week) based on the results of session
classification.

	Lecture	Tutorial	Lab	Download	Look Up
Week 1	35	22	13	19	11
Week 2	29	22	33	9	7
Week 3	20	27	40	5	8
Week 4	42	33	10	9	6

in a topic – is an essential characteristic that is expected to happen in an effective scaffolding implementation.

- Second, unexpected changes need to be detected. Web mining-based time series evaluations allow the detection and constant monitoring of student activity changes. Apart from behavior change, changes of learning strategies have also been observed in the case study. Early patterns often show single-goal use, but later patterns show a concurrent, integrated usage of different educational services. Time series of usage patterns can illustrate the evolution of student learning from web logs. This was initially an unexpected change in our case study.

The example in Table 4 illustrates the change in behavioral patterns over a period of four weeks (the first four weeks of term). Initially, learners have predominantly focused on online lectures and have downloaded course material. Over the next weeks, the tutorial and lab elements have been used more frequently – which in the case study reflects the start of the practices and courseware in weeks two and three of the term.

8 Conclusions

Both the design and the evaluation of web-based learning and training techno-logy systems poses problems due to the novelty of these systems, in particular when different learning and training activities are integrated in highly interac-tive environments. In this context, the learning behavior of learners and their interaction with content in particular are central for both design and evaluation activities.

Web usage mining geared towards the specifics of the educational domain can provide access to latent knowledge hidden in access logs for web-based systems. We have used web usage mining for different purposes:

- In an *explanatory* style to understand student learning in a novel environment. Mining techniques have been used to clarify the understanding of the learner's goals and task hierarchies. Mining techniques have been used to investigate the sequential and concurrent use of features. This analysis formed the starting point for the design of a multi-feature learning environment.

- In a *predictive* style to confirm expectations and validate designs. Learning styles and strategies and their change over time were analyzed. An example is the design of lab and scaffolding usage support, which has been validated through predicted learning behavior based on mining data.
- In a *generative* style to improve the design. The instructor's expectations of student learning behavior were expressed in a learning activity language and compared with actual behavior. The navigation features and the course topology have been gradually improved using this technique.

The explanatory and generative use of web usage mining techniques supports the incremental development of web-based learning technology systems. We have focused our discussion here on three central usage mining techniques for learning behavior extraction and analysis. Other applications of web usage mining in this context are possible. For instance, learner types – or learning styles – could be identified. Kolb's learning style inventory is an example of a learner classification, which suggests concrete experiences, reflective observation, analytic conceptualization, and active experimentation as four activity dimensions. Based on the preferred activity type, learner types are identified. We could relate these activity types to the activities supported by the case study features: tutorials provide concrete experiences, labs support active experimentation. A classification of learner activities – see session classification – results in a ranking of activities. Variations from the standard pattern can be interpreted as expressions of a particular learning style.

In addition to more substantial analyses that were carried out at the end of term, we also used mining as a tool to constantly monitor students throughout the term, which created a form of immediate feedback for the instructor. While web usage mining provides useful insights into learner behavior, it should be combined with other evaluation methods such as surveys to broaden the evaluation.

Education-specific mining techniques can help us to improve the instructional design and also to confirm delivery-related decisions that were made. It has supported instructors in our case study in providing quality instruction and in achieving a better learning experience for learners. In a wider sense, it allows the instructor or author to stay in touch with the learners' activities and to maintain the relationship by reacting to unforeseen events and necessary changes. Mining results can act as a medium of communication between the actors involved in web-based learning and training systems.

Acknowledgments

The author would like to thank the School of Computing and the Teaching and Learning Fund at Dublin City University for their support. The author is also greatly indebted to Dave Donnellan and Lei Xu for their work on the mining techniques described here.

References

[1]   Sims, R., Interactive learning as 'emerging' technology: A reassessment of interactive and instructional design strategies. *Australian Journal of Educational Technology*, **13(1)**, pp. 68–84, 1997.

[2]   Weston, T.J. & Barker, L., Designing, implementing, and evaluating web-based learning modules for University students. *Educational Technology*, **41(4)**, pp. 15–22, 2001.

[3]   Northrup, P.A., Framework for designing interactivity into web-based instruction. *Educational Technology*, **41(2)**, pp. 31–39, 2001.

[4]   Oliver, M. (ed.), Special Issue on Evaluation of Learning Technology. *Educational Technology & Society*, **3(4)**, pp. 20–30, 2000.

[5]   Chang, G., Healey, M.J., McHugh, J.A.M. & Wang, J.T.L., *Mining the World Wide Web – An Information Search Approach*. Kluwer Academic Publishers: Boston, 2001.

[6]   Scime, A., *Web Mining: Applications and Techniques*. Idea Group Inc.: Hershey, 2004.

[7]   Spiliopoulou, M., Web usage mining for web site evaluation. *Communications of the ACM*, **43(8)**, pp. 127–134, 2000.

[8]   Zaïane, O.R., Web usage mining for a better web-based learning environment. *Proc. of the Conf. on Advanced Technology for Education CATE'2001*, pp. 60–64, 2001.

[9]   Pahl, C. & Donnellan, D., Data mining for the evaluation of web-based teaching and learning environments. *Proc. of E-Learn 2002 World Conference on E-Learning in Corporate, Government, Healthcare, & Higher Education*, AACE, 2002.

[10] Zaïane, O.R. & Luo, J., Towards evaluating learners' behaviour in a web-based distance learning environment. *Proc. of the Int. Conf. on Advanced Learning Technologies ICALT'01*, IEEE, 2001.

[11] Xu, L., Pahl, C. & Donnellan, D., An evaluation technique for content interaction in web-based teaching and learning environments. In *Proc. of the Int. Conf. on Advanced Learning Technologies ICALT 2003*, IEEE Press: Los Alamitos, CA, 2003.

[12] Moore, M.G., Three types of interaction. *The American Journal of Distance Education*, **3(2)**, pp. 1–6, 1992.

[13] Ohl, T.M., An interaction-centric learning model. *Journal of Educational Multimedia and Hypermedia*, **10(4)**, pp. 311–332, 2001.

[14] Pahl, C., A conceptual architecture for interactive educational multimedia (Chapter 5) *Web-based Intelligent e-Learning Systems: Technologies and Applications* ed. J. Ma, Idea Group Inc.: Hershey, 2005.

[15] Jonassen, D.H. & Mandl, H. (eds), *Designing Hypermedia for Learning*, Springer-Verlag: Berlin, 1990.

[16] Dix, A., Finlay, J., Abowd, G. & Beale, R., *Human-Computer Interaction*, Prentice Hall: London, 1993.

[17]   Elsom-Cook, M., *Principles of Interactive Multimedia,* McGraw-Hill: London, 2001.

[18]   Hirami, A., The design and sequencing of e-learning interactions: a grounded approach. *International Journal on E-Learning,* **1(1)**, pp. 19–27, 2002.

[19]   Pahl, C., Barrett, R. & Kenny, C., Supporting active database learning and training through interactive multimedia. *Proc. of the Int. Conf. on Innovation and Technology in Computer Science Education ITiCSE'04,* ACM, 2004.

[20]   Agrawal, R. & Srikant, R., Mining Sequential Patterns. *Proc. of the 11th Int. Conf. on Data Engineering ICDE,* Taipei, Taiwan, 1995.

[21]   Cooley, R., Tan, P.-N. & Srivastava, J., Discovery of interesting usage patterns from web data. *Proc. Web-based Knowledge Discovery and Data Mining WEBKDD'99,* London: Springer-Verlag, pp. 163–182, 1999.

[22]   Hay, B., Wets, G. & Vanhoof, K., Clustering navigation patterns on a website using a sequence alignment method. *Proc. 7th International Joint Conference on Artificial Intelligence IJCAI'2001,* 2001.

[23]   Mullier, D., Hobbs, D. & Moore, D., Identifying and using hypermedia browsing patterns. *Journal of Educational Multimedia and Hypermedia,* **11(1)**, pp. 31–50, 2002.

[24]   Srivastava, J., Cooley, R., Deshpande, M. & Tan, P.-N., Web usage mining: discovery and applications of usage patterns from web data. *SIGKDD Explorations* **1(2)**, pp. 12–23, 2000.

[25]   Donnellan, D., *User Session Classification Tool for the Analysis of Web Server Logs,* MSc Dissertation, Dublin City University, School of Computing, 2002.

[26]   Xu, L., *Analysis of Behavioural Patterns using Web Mining,* MSc Dissertation, Dublin City University, School of Computing, 2003.

CHAPTER 4

On using data mining for browsing log analysis in learning environments

F. Wang
Department of Computer Science and Information Engineering,
Ming Chuan University, Taiwan, R.O.C.

Abstract

Recently, the rapid progress of Internet technology has triggered the widespread development of web-based learning environments in the educational world. As compared with conventional CAI systems, web-based learning environments are able to accumulate a huge amount of learning data. As a result, there is an urgent need for analyzing methods of discovering useful knowledge from the huge log database for improving instructional/learning performance. In this chapter, I will present some models and methods of analyzing the browsing log data to construct a browsing behavioral model that is helpful in supporting e-learning applications. For example, teachers can investigate the model to identify some interesting or unexpected learning patterns in student's browsing behavior, which might therefore provide knowledge for teachers to reorganize their content structure in a more effective manner. Alternatively, another model can be used as a reference model by which personalized content recommendation could be made. To serve these purposes, a set of tools based on data mining techniques such as clustering, and association mining, combined with collaborative filtering techniques, are developed. The effectiveness of these methods is investigated on a real database collected from web-based courses. Through the case studies, some revelations are presented and some future research directions are discussed.

1 Introduction

Web-based learning environments have been the main trend for technology-enhanced education in the last decade. In this new era of web-based education technology, the Internet and the World Wide Web have been exploited as a vast repository of information, playing the role of providers of educational resources. In web-based learning environments, teachers could conduct many kinds of instructional/learning activities such as online material browsing, exercise practicing, group discussion, online testing and so on. However, one of the prevailing issues in such a learning environment is that it is not easy to monitor students' learning behavior. Nevertheless, as compared with conventional CAI systems, web-based learning environments are able to keep track of most learning behavior of the students, and hence are able to provide a huge amount of learning profiles. As a result, there is an urgent need of analyzing methods to discover useful information for improving instruction/learning performance from the huge log database. These learning profiles provide teachers a valuable data source to observe and analyze students' learning processes and performance [1, 2].

Data mining in e-learning has been receiving more and more attention from researchers in various learning aspects. For example, Tang *et al.* [3] proposed a technique to construct personalized courseware based on data mining. Abramowicz *et al.* [4] used data mining techniques to support the creation of topic map so that distributed content resources could be shared and reused more efficiently. Zaiane exploited web access logs and advanced data mining techniques to extract useful patterns that can help instructors evaluate and interpret online course activities to assess the learning process and measure web course structure effectiveness [5, 6]. Personalized e-learning through delivering personalized content has been one of the main focus of research and has receiving many interesting results [7–10].

While there are several kinds of online learning activities, this chapter focuses on the online material browsing behavior. Traditionally, online materials are divided into units of topics that are organized and structured by some semantic relations among themselves [11]. Analyzing browsing behavior of students in a web-based learning environment might reveal some insights into the true structure required of the online material for being helpful to student learning. Such knowledge about the dynamic browsing structure would be an important reference base in designing effective online educational materials. It may also be helpful to the design of adaptive navigation guiders and/or personalized recommenders. Therefore, this chapter proposes a research framework in which browsing log can be dealt with in such a way that the aforementioned e-learning applications can be improved. Specifically, a set of browsing models to describe useful browsing patterns are proposed, and analysis tools based on web mining technique [12] to discover those patterns from the historical browsing database will be presented.

Finally, applications of the analysis methods are conducted on a real database collected from three web-based courses at Ming Chuan University, Taiwan. Three classes of the Expert System course had been conducted for a semester at Ming Chuan University, Taiwan; two of the courses were open to daytime students and the third to on-job students. Students were grouped and they were required to do a term project of building an expert system. During the semester, students had to work collaboratively in a web-based virtual classroom, in which their interactions and activities such as online material browsing were recorded in a back-end database for both evaluation and investigation purposes. The analysis results illustrate the potential capability of the methods to reveal useful browsing knowledge as a basis for investigation and comparison of student's learning behavior.

2 Data mining

Data mining, which is also referred to as knowledge discovery in database, is a process of non-trivial extraction of implicit, previously unknown and potentially useful information (such as knowledge rules, constraints, regularities) from data in database [13]. The data mining algorithms can be divided into three major categories based on the nature of their information extraction: predictive modeling (also called classification or supervised learning), clustering (also called segmentation or unsupervised learning), and frequent pattern extraction [14]. In the following, we briefly review some of the mining methods and applications that are relevant to our research.

2.1 Association mining

Association mining is one of the most well studied mining methods in data mining [13–16]. It serves as a useful tool for discovering correlations among items in a large database. It explores the probability that when certain items are present, which other items are also present in the same affairs. An association rule is a condition of the form $X \Rightarrow Y$ where X and Y are two sets of items. An interpretation of the association rule in a business trade situation is when a customer buys items in X, the customer will also buy items in Y.

There are two important threshold values used in mining association rules: *support* and *confidence*. Support indicates the frequencies of the occurring patterns in the rule. In the minimum support approach, association rules are generated by discovering *large itemsets*. A set of items X is called a large itemset if the support rate of X, with respect to a transaction database, meets the minimum support requirement. Confidence denotes the strength of the implication of the association rule. If the confidence is higher, the rule is more reliable.

2.2 Clustering

Clustering is a useful technique for discovering interesting data distributions and patterns in the underlying data. It is a process of grouping physical or abstract objects into classes of similar objects. Clustering analysis helps construct meaningful partitioning of a large set of objects based on a 'divide and conquer' methodology which decomposes a large scale system into smaller components to simplify design and implementation [13]. The principle of clustering is maximizing the similarity inside an object group and minimizing the similarity between the object groups.

The most well-known and commonly used partitioning methods are k-means, k-medoids, and their variations [16]. In the k-means algorithm, cluster similarity is measured in regard to the mean value of the objects in a cluster, which can be viewed as the cluster's center of gravity. The k-means method, however, can be applied only when the mean of a cluster is defined. This may not be the case in some applications, such as when data with categorical attributes are involved. Besides, it is sensitive to outliers since an object with an extremely large value may substantially distort the distribution of data. On the other hand, instead of taking the mean value of the objects in a cluster as a reference point, the k-medoids method use the medoid, which is the most centrally located object in a cluster. Therefore, the k-medoids method takes advantage over the k-means in the aspects of versatileness and outlier insensitivity. However, the necessity of both methods for users to specify k, the number of clusters, in advance can be seen as a common disadvantage.

2.3 Web usage mining

In the World Wide Web context, web sites are generating a great amount of web usage data that contain useful information about users' behavior. The term 'web usage mining' was introduced by Cooley *et al.* [12], in 1997, in which they define web usage mining as the 'automatic discovery of user access patterns from web servers'. Web usage mining has gained much attention in the literature as a potential approach to fulfilling the requirement of web personalization [12, 17–21]. The discovered knowledge indicating users' navigational behavior is useful for the system to personalize the web site according to each user's behavior and profile. The data mining methods that are employed including association rule mining, sequential pattern discovery, clustering and classification. In this chapter we focus on the association mining method, which is a widely used data analysis method in web usage mining [7, 8, 17, 22].

3 Recommendation systems

In a large-scale distributed network environment like the Internet, the popularization of computers and the Internet have resulted in an explosion in the amount of digital information. As a result, it becomes more important and difficult to retrieve proper information adapted to user preferences. Therefore, personalized recommendation systems are in need to provide proper recommendations based on users' requirements and preferences [21, 23] In general, there are two types of recommendation systems, the content-based filtering systems and the collaborative filtering systems [20, 24].

3.1 Content-based filtering systems

Content-based filtering techniques are based on content analysis of target items. For examples, the technique of term frequency analysis for text document and its relation to the user's preferences is a well-known content analysis method. In content-based filtering systems, recommendations are provided for a user based solely on a profile built up by analyzing the content of items that the user has rated in the past and/or user's personal information and preferences. The user's profile can be constructed by analyzing the responses to a questionnaire, item ratings, or the user's navigation information to infer the user's preferences and/or interests. However, a pure content-based filtering system has several shortcomings and critical issues remained to be solved, including that only a very shallow analysis of specific kinds of content (text documents, etc.) are available and that users can receive only recommendations similar to their earlier experiences and the sparseness problem of item rating information [22, 25].

3.2 Collaborative filtering systems

In collaborative filtering, items are recommended to a particular user when other similar users also prefer them. The definition of 'similarity' between users depends on applications. For example, similarity may be defined as users having similar ratings of items or users having similar navigation behavior. This kind of recommendation system is the first that uses the artificial intelligence technique to do the personalized job [23]. A collaborative filtering system collects all information about users' activities on the web site and calculates the similarity among the users. If some users have similar behavior, they will be categorized to the same user group. When a user logins into the web site again, the system will first compute the group most similar to the user using methods like the k-nearest neighborhood, and then recommend items that the members of the group prefer to the user. A pure collaborative filtering system also has several shortcomings and critical issues, including that the coverage of item ratings could be very sparse, hence yielding poor recommendation efficiency; and that it is difficult to provide services for users who have unusual tastes, and the user clustering and classification problems for users with changing and/or evolving preferences [26]. Table 1 shows a brief comparison between the two filtering methods.

3.3 Recommendation systems based on association rules mining technologies

As data mining techniques become more and more mature, researchers have explored their applications in recommendation systems in the last decade, trying to improve the efficiency and the effectiveness of the recommendation systems. Among those efforts, Fu et al. [19] try to integrate the collaborative filtering method and association mining technology to develop a recommendation system called SurfLen that recommends web pages on the web site. Their research reorganized the web pages collected from the 'Yahoo!' search engine, and experimented on the influence of the noise upon the recommendation effectiveness [19]. Besides, Lee et al. [22] integrate the collaborative filtering method and association mining technology to develop a recommendation system to recommend movies for the audiences on the MovieLens web site (http://www.movielens.umn.edu).

Table 1: Comparison between content-based filtering and collaborative filtering systems [9].

	Content-based filtering	Collaborative filtering
Advantage	1. A user can receive proper recommendations without help from other users.	1. A user may have a chance to receive items that s/he never contacted before, but may be of his/her potential interest.
	2. It is more feasible to tackle the problems of multiple user interests and interest transference by monitoring the change and evolving of user profiles.	2. Facilitate the sharing of knowledge and/or experiences among users having similar interests.
Limitation	1. Some types of items (e.g. multimedia) are not easy to analyze.	1. It is hard to provide recommendations for users who have unusual preferences.
	2. A user can just receive items that are similar to his/her past experiences.	2. It is hard to cluster and classify users with changing and/or evolving preferences.

4 The research framework

Due to the rapid growth of e-learning applications on the Internet, the complexity of the tasks such as content structure design, LMS server design, and content navigation design has increased along with this growth. To handle these complex tasks, we need knowledge about user behavior characteristics. This section presents a research framework that integrates data mining techniques to extract knowledge for specific e-learning applications from user's historical activity, in particular for intelligent personalized services.

As shown in Fig. 1, the research framework consists of six research tasks that have to be dealt with properly. The first is learning activity design, which deals with the problem of designing learning tasks that a researcher is interested. For example, material browsing is a common learning task that in the literature researchers have been most interested. The design of learning activity depends on the purposes of the specific e-learning applications. For example, to facilitate the design of proper material structure, dynamic document browsing model could be constructed from the browsing history data such that the browsing patterns can be reflected in an improved content structure. Another example of e-learning application is the matching of a student with some other well-performing group of users that share

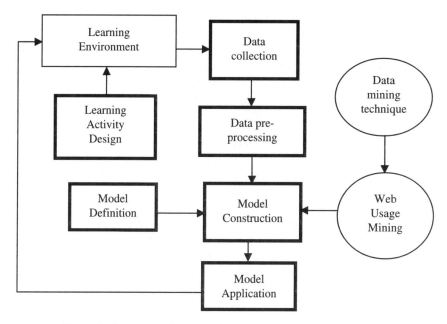

Figure 1: A research framework for data mining and e-learning.

similar activity characteristics such that their behavior can be referenced to give proper suggestions to the student. User browsing model could be constructed from logged user browsing data that could reflect the real browsing behavior of well-performing users. In summary, what learning activities are provided to students need to be decided first before we can go on to the next step.

Data tracking is required to facilitate the data collection for the interested learning tasks. A designer of data tracking needs to select proper tracking attributes such as the user id, the date and time period of the learning task a user performed, and so on. For example, in the aforementioned example of matching a student with some other well-performing group of users that share similar activity characteristics, the categories of activities performed by a student and their performance results are both required to be tracked for further analysis.

Data pre-processing is one of the important research tasks in this field. Data has to be cleaned and transformed properly before it can be analyzed. In some situations where user sessions are not easy to identify, several heuristic methods have been explored to decide user sessions from the logged access history (often logged in an http server). In some other cases where registered user login operation is required, user session determination is not a problem. Nevertheless, determination of meaningful user sessions is still a challenging problem. Besides, since it often happens that students may navigate documents back and forth, we need a way to handle a tree-structured browsing behavior such that the user's meaningful intentions in a browsing session can be identified. Some researchers have proposed heuristic methods to divide a user session into a set of shorter meaningful sub-sessions. These sub-sessions are the real sessions fed into the next step of model construction using data mining techniques.

The next step is the model definition and construction. Researchers have to define a behavior model that reflects the real topics or issues they are interested. For example, a browsing model that depicts the real browsing behavior can be defined in terms of the association and sequential browsing patterns that occur often in the history. These models can be used by teachers to identify some interesting or unexpected learning patterns in student's browsing structure, and therefore might provide knowledge for teachers to reorganize their content structure in a more effective manner. After the model definition, efficient and effective methods to construct the model are to be derived next. In this chapter, I will focus on web usage mining and collaboration filtering techniques that can be of help in this phase. Finally comes the model application phase to investigate the fitness and effectiveness of the devised model. Some evaluation metrics have to be defined. In the following, I will present two cases studies of our previous work based on this research framework. One is for content structure model construction [9], and the other is for navigation guidance by personalized recommendation [27].

5 Construction of browsing content structure

Traditionally, web materials are divided into units of topics that are organized and structured by some semantic relations among themselves [11]. However, the organization of online content does not necessarily meet the individual needs of students. On the other hand, as the content volume increases with time, maintenance of the content structure may become an uneasy load for designers. Analyzing browsing behavior of students might reveal some insights into the real content structure for being helpful to student learning. Such knowledge about the dynamic browsing structure would be an important reference base for designing more effective online materials. This section presents a browsing model to describe useful browsing patterns, and develops analysis tools based on data mining technique to discover those patterns from the historical browsing log.

5.1 Data pre-processing

The data analysis process consists of the following five stages: (1) data filtering, (2) data transformation, (3) frequency analysis, (4) co-reference mining of document clusters, and (5) sequence mining, as shown in Fig. 2. Since this study focuses on the browsing activities, all other unrelated data are filtered out, including those browsing records with short stay-time, e.g. reference pass-by pages. To validate long-stay-time records, a client program could be deployed to monitor users' interactions with the computer. Besides, the raw data has to be reconfigured for each student's browsing session. First, all the browsing records are sorted with the student id as a major key and start time as a minor key in an ascendant manner.

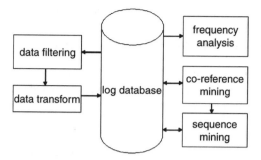

Figure 2: The data analysis process of content-structuring browsing model.

Then, browsing records picked up between two successive 'login' records are grouped into a browsing-session record. As it often happens that students navigate documents back and forth, we need a way to handle such a tree-structured browsing behavior [28]. This study adopts the pre-order scan approach [25] for converting student's tree-structured navigation paths so that a maximal number of ordered browsing sequences could be obtained.

Frequency analysis is helpful for instructors to get an overview of the usage of various categories of materials. Two kinds of frequency analysis may be performed: (1) the hit rate analysis of the material, and (2) the summary hit rate analysis of the material categories. Co-reference clustering and sequence mining are then performed to construct the content structuring model.

5.2 Model definition and construction

The patterns we are interested here include the co-referenced document clusters and sequences between the clusters. A document cluster indicates a set of documents that students often study together (i.e. the co-referenced knowledge units), while the sequence rules between the document clusters reflect students' knowledge construction sequence in a specific target domain, which also reflects possible prerequisite relations between the documents. Associative mining technique can be applied to find document clusters. Content documents can be bound together with different strength. By adopting different support rates, the documents form a hierarchical cluster structure so that teachers can investigate document clusters in different grain size (i.e. association strength). Then a sequence mining (of length 2) can be applied to find the binary sequence patterns between document clusters.

The following definitions are adapted from [27] to describe the content structure model formally. First, a learning session is the duration when a student logs into the system until he/she leaves the system. Since we are only interested in browsing activity, each session retains only browsing activities by removing other learning activities present in it.

Definition 1 (Co-reference relation): For any documents P_1 and P_2, we say P_1 is co-referenced with P_2 if and only if P_1 and P_2 are 'frequently' browsed in a learning session without 'observable' ordering between P_1 and P_2.

Definition 2 (Sequence relation): For any documents P_1 and P_2, we say P_1 precedes P_2 if and only if P_1 and P_2 are 'frequently' browsed together and there is 'observable' ordering between P_1 and P_2.

Definition 3: Given a pair of documents (P_1, P_2), define the 'sequence strength' of $P_1 \rightarrow P_2$ as $\|P_1 - P_2\| = \max\{\text{SEQ}(P_1, P_2) - \text{SEQ}(P_2, P_1)/N(P_1, P_2), 0\}$, where $N(P_1, P_2)$ is the number of session records containing both P_1 and P_2, and SEQ (P_i, P_j) denotes the number of session records where P_i precedes P_j.

Definition 4: Given a document cluster C of size n, the intra-cluster sequence strength of C is $\|C\| = \max\limits_{i=1,...,n, j=i+1,...,n} \|P_i - P_j\|$, where $P_i, P_j \in C$.

Definition 5: Given a set of cluster C of n documents $\{P_1, P_2, ..., P_n\}$, the support rate of cluster C, $\sup(C) = N(P_1, P_2, ..., P_n)/T$, where $N(P_1, P_2, ..., P_n)$ is the count of session records containing $P_1, P_2, ..., P_n$, and T is the total number of session records.

Definition 6: A document cluster C is a valid co-reference cluster if and only if $\sup(C) \geq \beta$ and $\|C\| \leq \delta$, where β is a given support rate threshold, and δ is an intra-cluster sequence strength threshold.

Definition 7: Given two document clusters C_1 and C_2, define the *support* of the sequence rule $C_1 \rightarrow C_2$ as $\sup(C_1 \rightarrow C_2) = N(C_1 \rightarrow C_2)/T$, where $N(C_1 \rightarrow C_2)$ is the number of sessions containing the pattern of $C_1 \rightarrow C_2$, and T is the total number of sessions.

Definition 8: Given two document clusters C_1 and C_2, define the *confidence* of the sequence rule $C_1 \rightarrow C_2$ as $|\sup(C_1 \rightarrow C_2)|/|\sup(C_1)|$.

Consider the browsing log shown in Table 2. Set the minimum support rate and maximum intra-cluster distance to 0.5 and 0.1, respectively. The co-reference mining proceeds as follows. Initially, all 1-clusters (i.e. the large 1-itemsets) with sufficiently large supports are calculated, resulting in four clusters $\{P_1\}$, $\{P_2\}$, $\{P_3\}$ and $\{P_4\}$. Next, the mining proceeds to discover clusters of size 2. All candidates of 2-clusters are generated by combining pair-wisely the 1-clusters, and then each checked the validity by computing its support and intra-cluster sequence strength. The resulting clusters are listed in Table 3. However, by checking both the minimum support and the maximum sequence strength constraints, only the two clusters $\{P_1 P_2\}$ and $\{P_3 P_4\}$ are valid. Continuing this process, a new candidate cluster $\{P_1 P_2 P_3 P_4\}$ is produced with support 0.66 and intra-cluster sequence strength 1.

Table 2: An example log of browsing sessions.

Session #	Browsing path
1	$P_1P_2P_3P_4$
2	P_4P_2
3	$P_2P_1P_4P_3$
4	P_3P_1
5	$P_2P_1P_4P_3$
6	$P_1P_2P_3P_4$

Table 3: Support rates and intra-cluster sequence strength of 2-clusters for the log of Table 2.

Cluster	Support rate	Cluster distance
P_1P_2	0.66	0
P_1P_4	0.66	1
P_2P_3	0.66	1
P_3P_4	0.66	0
P_1P_3	0.83	0.2
P_2P_4	0.83	0.6

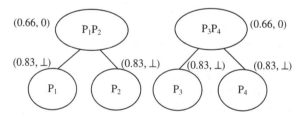

Figure 3: Hierarchical clustering of co-reference documents with (support rate, intra-cluster sequence strength).

However, it is not valid due to its intra-cluster sequence strength. As a result, the final co-referenced clusters are $\{P_1P_2\}$ and $\{P_3P_4\}$.

The co-referenced clusters $\{P_1P_2\}$ and $\{P_3P_4\}$ form a hierarchical clustering of documents with different levels of support rates, as shown in Fig. 3. A hierarchical sequence rule structure can be derived by composing the clusters in $\{P_1P_2\}$ and $\{P_3P_4\}$. An efficient lattice-product algorithm was devised that outputs all feasible sequence rules in the form of a lattice hierarchical structure [27], as shown in Fig. 4. By 'feasible' rules we mean those rules with sufficient support and confidence (say, with a minimum support and confidence constraint, say 0.5 and 0.8, respectively). Note that a link from a lower node X to its upper parent node Y indicates

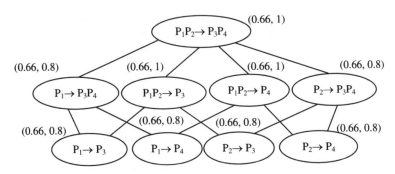

Figure 4: Hierarchical sequence rules generated from clusters in $(\{P_1P_2\}, \{P_3P_4\})$ with (support rate, confidence).

that the rule corresponding to node X is a generalizer of the one corresponding to node Y. For example, the rule $\{P_1\} \to \{P_3P_4\}$ is a generalized rule of the rule $\{P_1P_2\} \to \{P_3P_4\}$.

5.3 Model application

The aforementioned analysis process is performed in three web-based classes of the Expert System course at Ming Chuan University, Taiwan. A total of 172711 browsing records are stored in the log database. The minimum threshold of browsing time is 10 s and the minimum support is 0.03. A total of 22846 sessions are left after the cleaning process and 960 browsing sessions are attained after the transforming process. The total number of material documents is 96.

Through frequency analysis it was found that students in all three classes spent more efforts in browsing material of the Design category, which might have something to do with the term projects that are required in all classes. As to the Theory and Demo Systems categories, both daytime classes prefer studying the Demo System category than the Theory one. On the contrary, the on-job class prefers studying the Theory category than the Demo System. Finally, all three classes reveal similar browsing patterns of material in the Design category; i.e. the most on 'Language', then the 'Operations', and the least on 'Samples'. This implies that the original intention of providing samples to help students lean the design task more efficiently is not effectively fulfilled, and it deserves more investigation to explore the reason why.

To improve the reliability of the mining results by increasing the amount of historical data, sessions of the three classes are collected for the co-reference and sequence rule mining tasks. The thresholds of the support rate, intra-cluster sequence strength and cluster support rate are set to 0.03, 0.2 and 0.1, respectively, and the sequence strength threshold is set to 0.2. The results show that 23 clusters are found with the largest cluster being of size 3. Among these clusters, it is found that 'Theory' and 'Demo Systems' categories are often browsed together, and 'Demo System' and

'Language' categories are also often browsed together. This implies that the goal of encouraging cross-references of the materials in 'Demo System' and 'Language' was effectively achieved.

On the other hand, most of the sequence rules meet the instructor's expectations. Nevertheless, some interesting sequence patterns are also found. For example, the sequence rule ([Backward-chaining ES], [Inference Engines]) → ([CLIPS Language]) with confidence 0.3 reveals that some students misunderstood the 'CLIPS language' (a tool for designing forward-chaining expert systems) as a candidate design language for backward-chaining expert systems. This knowledge of phenomena could be used by instructors to clarify the usage of expert tools in future courses.

5.4 Summary statements

In this case study, a content structure modeling process is presented, and a tool for analyzing the historical browsing data is presented. There is more work worth further pursuit. For example, there is still a lack of more effective mining tools for analyzing other kinds of learning information, such as the behavior of 'thinking order' in a web-based online discussion context, and also those tools for helping teachers to explore the relationships between the various learning patterns and the learning outcomes [29]. Teachers could then answer the questions such as 'what are the behavioral characteristics of students tending to good learning outcomes?'

6 Personalized recommendation based on association mining

Personalized recommendation by predicting user-browsing behavior using association mining technology has gained much attention in web personalization research area [11, 21, 22, 30, 31]. In particular, it can be a potential way to create personalized e-learning applications [2, 3, 9, 20, 31, 32]. However, the association patterns did not perform well in prediction of future browsing patterns due to the low matching rate of the association rules against users' browsing behavior. According to the evaluation results of [17], the accuracy and coverage rate of the association mining technique is usually quite low. Also note that their results showed that though the sequence mining method produced higher accuracy than association mining did, it produced much lower coverage. Besides, Wang and Thao [8] applied the association mining on the whole navigation sessions to establish a knowledge model to predict users' next request in an e-learning web site. However, their results also revealed similar evidences to this fact. This drawback of applying pure association mining shows the potential limitation of the prediction knowledge built through conventional association mining technique.

Instead of performing association mining on users' navigation sessions as a whole, which might eliminate the visibility of important access patterns due to the large population, users are clustered elaborately by sampling the navigation

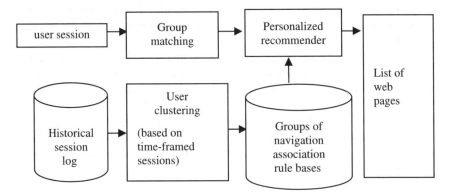

Figure 5: The personalized recommendation mechanism based on association mining and time-framed user session clustering.

sessions in a specific time frame. Wang and Shao [9] found that by clustering users properly according to their browsing behavior within specific time intervals, the recommendation effectiveness could be improved significantly. The case study presented as follows is adapted from the work of [9].

The framework of the personalized recommendation of [9] based on association mining and time-framed user session clustering is shown in Fig. 5. Users are clustered based on so-called time-framed navigation sessions, and then access patterns are discovered for each user by the association mining technique. To produce personalized recommendations for a user, the group most similar to the user's navigation sessions is first selected, and then the recommender applies the prediction rules in the corresponding rule base to generate the item recommendation list that sorts the items in terms of relevance.

6.1 Model definition and construction

Historical navigation sessions for each user are divided into frames of sessions based on a specific time interval. Selection of a good time interval is an elaborative decision that depends on the characteristics of the applications. For example, in this case study, candidate time intervals may be a 'week' or a 'semester', which coincides with the teaching/learning schedule of the testing courses.

The different impacts of the chosen time frame size are depicted as below. A long time interval, such as a 'semester', provides a macro view of a user's navigation behavior embedded with richer long-term access information, but it may be hard to generalize the navigation rules in such a macro behavior view. On the other hand, a shorter time interval provides a micro view on a user's navigation behavior with more focused access information, but it may lose long-term access information such that it is harder to perform a trend analysis.

6.1.1 User browsing similarity in time-framed navigation sessions

As mentioned above, users' navigation sessions are grouped into session frames according to a pre-specified time interval. Consider two time-framed navigation sessions from different users U_i and U_j, as shown below, respectively,

$$U_i : TF_u(U_i) = \{S_{i1}, S_{i2}, \ldots, S_{in}\}, \text{the } u\text{th time - framed sessions,}$$

$$U_j : TF_v(U_j) = \{S_{j1}, S_{j2}, \ldots, S_{jm}\}, \text{the } v\text{th time - framed sessions,}$$

where session S_k is a collection of web pages that the users have visited during a session at specific time interval. Then two users are said to be similar to each other in two time intervals if the two users have similar navigation behavior during the two time intervals (may be the same time interval). Specifically, define the similarity of two session records, S_{is} and S_{jt}, as follows:

$$\text{Sim}(S_{is}, S_{jt}) = \frac{\mid S_{is} \cap S_{jt} \mid}{\mid S_{is} \cup S_{jt} \mid}, \quad 1 \leqq s \leqq n, \quad 1 \leqq t \leqq m. \tag{1}$$

Next, define the similarity of two time-framed sessions $TF(U_i)$ and $TF(U_j)$ as:

$$\text{Sim}(TF_u(U_j), TF_v(U_j)) = \min(\overline{S}_{ij}, \overline{S}_{jt}), \tag{2}$$

where $\overline{S}_{ij} = \text{Avg} \, s = 1, \ldots, n \, (\max t = 1, \ldots, m \, \{\text{Sim}(S_{is}, S_{jt})\})$ and $\overline{S}_{ji} = \text{Avg} \, t = 1, \ldots, m \, (\max s = 1, \ldots, n \, \{\text{Sim}(S_{is}, S_{jt})\})$. Actually, for the two time intervals u and v, $\overline{S}_{ij}$ indicates the average degree to which user i is similar to user j, while $\overline{S}_{ji}$ is the average degree to which user j is similar to user i, and $\text{Sim}(TF_u(U_i), TF_v(U_j))$ is the mutual similarity between the two users in the two time intervals.

6.1.2 The HBM clustering algorithm

A clustering method, called hierarchical bisecting medoids (HBM) algorithm was developed to cluster users within time intervals based on the time-framed navigation similarity. One feature of this algorithm is that it avoids the common problem of requiring users to pre-specify on the number of clusters by using a hierarchical clustering technique. The algorithm combines features of the k-medoids and hierarchical clustering. Interested readers could refer to [9].

6.1.3 Mining association rules

The purpose of mining association rules is to find out which web pages are usually visited together in a session. Operated on the clusters of time-framed navigation sessions, the association rules discovered for each user session cluster will characterize the navigation patterns of specific user groups. As a result, these clustered association rules can serve as the knowledge models to predict the next navigation requests for future similar users.

6.2 Model application

6.2.1 User classification

The clustered association rules can serve as the knowledge base to give suggestion for future similar users. To achieve this purpose, a user classification method is needed to identify the cluster of navigation patterns to which the current user is most similar. Recall that each cluster of timed-framed sessions has a medoid, which is a frame of navigation sessions from some user. The medoid in some sense represents a typical user navigation pattern for users from that cluster. For a specific user, the session cluster to which the user is most similar can be selected by choosing the medoid to which the user's current behavior is most similar. The similarity computation is similar to the aforementioned similarity except that in this case we do not need to calculate the degree a medoid is similar to the user. That is, while the user's current behavior may be very similar to (or part of) that of the selected medoid, the medoid's behavior may have little similarity to the user's current behavior. As a result, we do not consider the mutual similarity between a medoid and the user, as its value may be very low due to the incompleteness of the user's current frame sessions.

A recommendation process is started right after a user has made his/her first request to a web site. After classifying user k as similar to a cluster, the association rules in the corresponding knowledge model of the cluster can be used to match the pages in the current session S_n of user k. Those rules matched with sufficient confidence (greater than a confidence threshold) will be fired, and the predicted items are added into the recommendation list in a sorted manner according to their decreasing confidence values. Furthermore, items that are suggested by more than one rules will be added to list only once with the highest confidence value.

However, it happens quite often that the current session of the user matches no association rules at all. So we need a recommendation mechanism that can provide reasonable suggestions when facing such a situation. Wang and Thao [9] proposed the following two mechanisms for this purpose.

6.2.2 The window-sliding method

This method uses a sliding window technique to control the number of session pages to be matched against the association rules. Let $S_n = [p_1, p_2, ..., p_k]$ be the user's current session. Initially, the window covers all pages in S_n, and hence all pages $(p_1, p_2, ..., p_k)$ in the current session are used to match against the association rules. If no matched association rules can be found, the window will slide one position to the right, leaving the pages $p_2, ..., p_k$ for rule matching. While the sliding actions will lose more and more information about the user's navigation behavior, it does preserve the most recent information as possible as it can. The sliding process will repeat until at least one rule is matched or the window coverage becomes empty. For the latter case, we say that the user cannot receive the recommendation service under his/her current navigation session.

6.2.3 The maximal-matching method

In contrast to using a sliding window method to preserve only the most recent session information for the matching work, the maximal-matching method preserves as much session information as possible for the matching work. This is achieved by finding all maximal subsets of the session pages that match successfully against the association rules. Given a set P of session pages, any subset M of P is called maximal if it matches at least one of the association rules, and no proper upper-set of M, which is also a subset of P, can find a matching rule. An efficient graph-based algorithm was implemented to find all the maximal-matching subsets of a page set given a set of association rules. To achieve this purpose, a lattice structure was used to store large itemsets discovered in the association-mining phase. Again, if no maximal-matching itemsets could be found, we say that the user cannot receive the recommendation service under his/her current navigation session.

6.3 Summary statements

Several factors have an impact on the performance of the recommendation method. They include: the time frame, the user classification method, the recommendation policies, the confidence threshold of recommendation, and the amount of training data. Historical navigation data was collected from three classes (classes A, B and C) of a virtual classroom course ('Expert System') for one semester. The experimental results show that the best average weighted precision rate is 0.6, average weighted recall rate is 0.7 and average service rate is 0.5, respectively. The results showed that the method is better in precision and recall rates than the conventional non-clustering one, and is comparable in the service coverage rate. The results also suggest that the recommendation method uses a shorter frame size such as a week for clustering user navigations and mining association rules, because a shorter frame size could track more flexibly the changes of users' traversal behavior. As to the recommendation policies, the results show that the maximal-matching policy is significantly better than the window-sliding one.

7 Concluding remarks

Data mining in e-learning is still in its nascent stage and needs much more research endeavor to make it of practical use for instructors and learners. There is more work worth further pursuit. For example, there are more effective mining tools for analyzing other kinds of learning activities, such as the behavior of 'thinking order' in a web-based online discussion context, and also those tools for helping teachers to explore the relationships between the various learning patterns and the learning outcomes [6, 29]. Teachers can analyze the stored student learning data to answer the questions such as 'what are the behavior characteristics of students tending to good learning outcomes?'

Besides, one limitation of current data association mining in e-learning is the inherent problem caused by the low supports of web page navigations, making it harder to build appropriate knowledge models. This is often solved by choosing appropriately low support values used to mine the association rules, as is adopted in this research. Other association mining techniques [32] could be applied to avoid the low-support problem. Another area of work is to probe the effect of the knowledge model built by combining framed session clustering with mining sequential patterns.

A recent development has been in the use of learning objects which are cohesive pieces of learning material. With the emerging techniques of e-learning standards, instructors are able to disseminate their contents in the form of organized learning objects, instead of hyperlinked contents. Leaning objects represent learning experiences from instructors in a more compact representation form than the hyperlinked ones. Applying data mining on the usage analysis of learning objects is also an important research direction.

Finally, while data mining technology enables the provision of 'limited' personalized e-learning services, educational domain knowledge may be the key to make it really practical. For example, domain constraints might exist that could be used to confine the search space of data mining. Furthermore, content usage mining based on learning outcome will be able to give positive learning suggestions to learners. Pedagogical domain knowledge (such as educational thresholds, constraints, taxonomies and knowledge [33]), when integrated with the data mining technique, might be able to generate more flexible, efficient, contextualized and adapted learning environments. We need a mechanism of modeling and integrating the educational domain knowledge and data mining techniques to realize the dream of effective and efficient personalized e-learning.

References

[1] Arter, J.A., *Portfolios for Assessment and Instruction*, ERIC Clearinghouse on Counselling and Student Services: Greensboro, NC, 1995.

[2] Zaiane, O.R., Xin, M. & Han, J., Discovering web access patterns and trends by applying OLAP and data mining technology on web logs. *Proc. of Advances in Digital Libraries Conf. (ADL'98)*, Santa Barbara, CA, pp. 19–29, 1998.

[3] Tang, C., Lau, R.W.H., Li, Q., Yin, H., Li, T. & Kilis, D., Personalized courseware construction based on web data mining. *Proc. of WISE Conf.*, pp. 204–211, 2000.

[4] Abramowicz, W., Kaczmarek, T. & Kowalkiewicz, M., Supporting topic map creation using data mining techniques. *Australian Journal of Information Systems*, **10**, pp. 63–78, 2004.

[5] Zaiane, O.R., Web usage mining for a better web-based learning environment. *Proc. of Conf. on Advanced Technology for Education*, pp. 60–64, 2001.

[6] Zaiane, O.R. & Luo, J., Towards evaluating learners' behaviour in a web-based distance learning environment. *Proc. of IEEE Int. Conf. on Advanced Learning Technologies (ICALT01)*, pp. 357–360, 2001.

[7] Mor, E. & Minguillon, J., E-learning personalization based on itineraries and long-term navigational behaviour. *Proc. WWW2004*, pp. 264–265, 2004.

[8] Wang, F.H. & Thao, S.M., A study on personalized web browsing recommendation based on data mining and collaborative filtering technology. *Proc. of National Computer Symp.*, Taiwan, pp. 18–25, 2003.

[9] Wang, F.-H. & Shao, H.-M., Effective personalized recommendation based on time-framed navigation clustering and association mining. *Expert Systems with Applications*, **27(3)**, pp. 365–377, 2004.

[10] Zaiane, O.R., Building a recommender agent for e-learning systems. *Proc. of the Int. Conf. on Computers for Education*, pp. 1203–1212, 2002.

[11] Barker, F.B., *Computer Managed Instruction: Theory and Practice*, Educational Technology Publications: Englewood Cliffs, NJ, pp. 4–10, 1979.

[12] Cooley, R., Mobasher, B. & Srivastava, J., Web mining: information and pattern discovery on the World Wide Web. *Proc. of IEEE Int. Conf. Tools with AI*, pp. 558–567, 1997.

[13] Chen, M.S., Han, J. & Yu, P.S., Data mining: an overview from a database perspective. *IEEE Trans. Knowledge and Data Engineering*, **8(6)**, pp. 866–883, 1996.

[14] Agrawal, R., Imielinski, T. & Swami, A., Mining association rules between sets of items in large databases. *Proc. of ACM SIGMOD*, pp. 207–216, 1993.

[15] Agrawal, R., & Srikant, R., Fast algorithm for mining association rules. *Proc. of The VLDB Conf.*, pp. 487–499, 1994.

[16] Han, J. & Kamber, M., Cluster analysis (Chapter 8). *Data Mining, Concepts and Techniques*. Morgan Kaufmann: San Francisco, CA: 2001.

[17] Gery, M. & Haddad, H., Evaluation of web usage mining approaches for user's next request prediction. *Proc. of the Fifth ACM int. workshop on Web Information and Data Management*, pp. 74–81, 2003.

[18] Eirinaki, M. & Vazirgiannis, M., Web mining for web personalization. *ACM Transactions on Internet Technology*, **3(1)**, pp. 1–27, 2003.

[19] Fu, X., Budzik, J. & Hammond, K.J., Mining navigation history for recommendation. *Proc. of the Fifth Int. Conf. on Intelligent User Interfaces*, pp. 106–112, 2000.

[20] Mobasher, B., Cooley, R. & Srivastava, J., Automatic personalization based on web usage mining. *Communications of the ACM*, **43(8)**, pp. 142–151, 2000.

[21] Mulvenna, M.D., Anand, S.S. & Buchner, A.G., Personalization on the net using Web mining. *Communications of the ACM*, **43(8)**, pp. 123–125, 2000.

[22] Lee, C.H., Kim, Y.H. & Rhee, P.K., Web personalization expert with combining collaborative filtering and association rule mining technique. *Expert Systems with Applications*, **21**, pp. 131–137, 2001.

[23] Riecken, D., Personalized views of personalization. *Communications of the ACM*, **43(8)**, pp. 27–28, 2000.

[24] Nichols, D.M., Implicit rating and filtering. *Proc. of the Fifth Workshop on Filtering and Collaborative Filtering*, pp. 31–36, 1997.

[25]   Kashihara, A., Suzuki, R., Hasegawa, S. & Toyoda, J., A learner-centered navigation path planning in web-based learning. *Proc. of ICCE/ICCAI*, pp. 1385–1392, 2000.

[26]   Kuo, C.-C., A data mining approach to auto-extraction of browsing structures of web materials. MD Thesis, Graduate School of Information Management, Ming Chuan University, Taiwan, 2001.

[27]   Wang, F.-H., On analysis and modelling of student browsing behaviour in web-based asynchronous learning environments. *Lecture Notes in Computer Science*, **2436**, pp. 69–80, 2002.

[28]   Breese, J.S., Heckerman, D. & Kadie, C., Empirical analysis of predictive algorithms for collaborative filtering. *Proc. of the Fourteenth Conf. on Uncertainty in Artificial Intelligence*, pp. 43–52, 1998.

[29]   Liu, C.-C., Chen, G.-D., Ou, K.-L., Lee, C.-H. & Lu, C.-F., An instrument for on-line learning performance analysis by using decision tree technology on Web-based Portfolios. *Proc. of Int. Conf. on Computers in Education*, Japan, 1999.

[30]   Chen, Z., Lin, F., Liu, H., Liu, Y., Ma, W.Y. & Wenyin, L., User intention modelling in web applications using data mining. *World Wide Web: Internet and Web Information Systems*, **5**, pp. 181–191, 2002.

[31]   Lu, J., A personalized e-learning material recommender system. *Proc. of the 2nd Int. Conf. on Information Technology for Application (ICITA 2004)*, pp. 374–379, 2004.

[32]   Wang, K., He, Y. & Han, J., Pushing support constraints into association rules mining. *IEEE Transactions on Knowledge and Data Engineering*, **15(3)**, pp. 642–658, 2003.

[33]   Buchner, A.G. & Patterson, D., Personalized e-learning opportunities, call for a pedagogical knowledge model, *DEXA Workshops*, pp. 410–414, 2004.

PART 2

Case studies and experiences of applying data mining techniques in e-learning systems

CHAPTER 5

Recommender systems for e-learning: towards non-intrusive web mining

O.R. Zaïane

Department of Computing Science, University of Alberta, Edmonton AB, Canada.

Abstract

Recommender systems are software agents that recommend options to users. They are becoming very popular in e-commerce applications to recommend the online purchase of some products. These agents can be very useful in an e-learning environment to recommend actions, resources or simply links to follow. However, most approaches to develop these intelligent agents are based on data explicitly collected from users to build profiles such as rankings, opinions and the like. This can be considered intrusive and a distraction by online learners. In this chapter we discuss methods to build recommender systems for e-learning that are non-intrusive and true to the choices of users.

1 Introduction

Using electronic and digital means to deliver courses is a very common trend, whether for distance learning courses or even for typical face-to-face courses as enhancements or supplements to what is delivered in classrooms. Today, there are many comprehensive online course management systems, some commercial and some distributed under the open-source license agreement. Typical web-based learning environments, such as Virtual-U [1, 2] and WebCT [3], include course content delivery tools, synchronous and asynchronous conferencing systems, polling and quiz modules, virtual workspaces for sharing resources, white boards, grade reporting systems, logbooks, assignment submission components, etc. These systems are commonly used to provide supplementary course material for typical classroom lectures or to implement student-centered learning approaches such as problem-based or evidence-based learning allowing sustained interaction between learners.

E-learning is becoming a reality with more and more learners and educators becoming versed with technology. However, the majority of current course management systems and web-based learning systems are closed learning environments [4]. Courses and learning materials are fixed for all learners and do not adapt to individuals. The course content and its delivery is static. Only the organization of the online material is sometimes dynamic. While it is widely recognized that learners have different preferred learning styles and learning paces, very few course management systems accommodate any dynamic component that can follow learners' progress, build intelligent profiles and provide contextual individual help.

With the advent of the World Wide Web, research in e-learning and web-based delivery of course material has gained attention. But again, very few course management systems incorporate intelligent agents that would allow to personalize the course delivery system or individualize the suggested learning material. Similar applications in business have flourished. The personalization of online catalogues and virtual stores to enhance the online buying experience, limit churning, entice purchase and attract new customers has been the focus of many research studies in computing science, business, communication and psychology. Today, many such applications are commercialized and are becoming popular. For example, some web sites may present customized product catalogues that would contain mainly items that are similar to the customer's previous likings or with high probability to be purchased based on the customer's profile avoiding annoying the user with lengthy and useless lists. Other commercial sites may provide automatic suggestions for products based on the current purchase and the likings and 'tastes' of the customer and the collective choices. The typical example is the recommender agent for books: 'Other people who bought this book also bought books A and B. Would you like to purchase them too?' Similar recommender systems exist to suggest music CDs, movies, clothes, and even jokes.

One natural question is, could such software agents be used in e-learning applications? The major difference between recommender systems in e-commerce and in e-learning is that the goals are different and are certainly not measured the same way. The obvious goal of recommender systems in e-commerce is to increase profit. Profit is tangible and can be measured in terms of amount of money, number of customers and customer loyalty. The money aspect is certainly the driver in these sophisticated implementations. In e-learning, the goals of a recommender system appear clear too: improving the learning. However, this goal is more subjective and is too subtle to be measured. Moreover, while querying a user and requesting opinions about products and rankings of products is somewhat acceptable in an e-commerce application to receive in return a better service, explicit surveys are considered intrusive and distracting in a learning environment.

In this chapter, we discuss the usefulness of recommender systems and how to design them as non-intrusive intelligent agents in the context of e-learning.

2 Collaborative filtering: how most systems work

Most recommender systems adopt the collaborative filtering approach [5, 6]. This approach is relatively simple and effective. Many variations of this algorithm exist but the principles are the same. User profiles are built based on past experience. The set of all user profiles constitutes the collective. When a user needs suggestions or a software agent is about to generate recommendations to a given user, the profile of the user is compared to the collective to find similar profiles. A selection from these similar profiles is used to produce recommendations. This is what is called collaborative filtering. Profiles collaborate to produce appropriate recommendations. The various approaches vary in the way profiles are built and modeled, in the way similarity between profiles is measured, in the way similar profiles are selected, and, finally, in the way recommendations are produced and ranked for presentation to the user. In general, user profiles are modeled in a vector space where each vector constitutes the ratings of a given user. Ratings are normalized numbers representing the opinion of the user vis-à-vis a given product (or object). Similarity between profiles could be measured in different ways using a variety of measures such as the cosine measure, correlations, Jaccard coefficient. Let us illustrate this approach with an example. Suppose we have an online recommender system for a library or a bookstore. Figure 1 shows the profiles for four people with regard to seven books. The matrix contains the ratings from the users for all books they read. These ratings are measured from 5 (high) to 1 (low). Empty cells mean an absence of opinion. We need to recommend a book to Jane. Using the correlation measure we find that Jane's ratings are highly correlated with Duncan's. Since Duncan read two books that Jane did not and book 7 was highly appreciated by Duncan, book 7 is the selected one to be recommended to Jane. This is obviously a imaginary situation. In reality more books could be selected (from different highly correlated profiles) and a ranking of these suggestions is necessary. Different criteria could be used for this ranking.

Collaborative filtering is commonly used in e-commerce applications to give suggestions. It is effective despite its simplicity. However, it has a significant drawback.

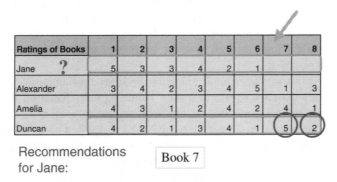

Ratings of Books	1	2	3	4	5	6	7	8
Jane ?	5	3	3	4	2	1		
Alexander	3	4	2	3	4	5	1	3
Amelia	4	3	1	2	4	2	4	1
Duncan	4	2	1	3	4	1	5	2

Recommendations for Jane: Book 7

Figure 1: An example of collaborative filtering.

Building profiles necessitates the collection of opinions. The matrix of ratings needs to be large enough and trusted to be able to generate good recommendations. In reality, users do not take the effort to go back to the system to enter their opinions and if they do, the ratings they enter may not necessarily reflect their real opinion. In practice, the rating matrix ends up being very sparse and ineffective.

Can collaborative filtering be used in e-learning? Yes, but selectively. This is because without good and trusted ratings entered by the learners, the recommendations become useless and untrustworthy. Moreover, ratings may never be entered by the online learners as entering ratings could be considered intrusive and biased. To recommend learning activities, learning objects or simply online links to resources, it is better to use real past activities (history logs) by users as input for their profiles. This is not only non-intrusive but reflects the real choices of uses. Then again, collaborative filtering can still be used in an e-learning context. For example a software agent acting as an academic advisor recommending courses to take could rely on collaborative filtering if opinions of learners are collected after a course is taken. Constraints such as course prerequisites and requested curriculum paths in a program taken by a learner could be taken into account in the selection of courses to recommend. Another type of recommendation in the case of e-learning systems is the recommendation of research papers [7] or citations of papers [8].

3 Desired recommender systems in an online learning environment

In addition to the previously described course recommender system for which ratings are envisaged and intrusiveness is acceptable, other recommender systems can be foreseen in a web-based learning environment. These two types of recommender systems do not require any rating input. We refer to these as shortcut recommenders and action recommenders. Recommending shortcuts consists of providing to a learner a list of resources, typically Internet addresses (i.e. URL), that allows the user to directly 'jump' to the desired resource without having to look for it in the maze of hyperlinks in the sometimes complicated learning sites. In a site with a deep topology, a good and effective shortcut recommender system can save significant time and directly provide the needed learning resources. These resources, again, could be a web page, an applet, an image, a video, a simulation, or any learning object.

Figure 2A illustrates an example of recommendation for shortcuts. The software agent analyzes the click-stream of a user, builds a profile based on these initial visited pages, and compares this activity with actions in sessions of other users. This allows the prediction of pages to be visited by the current user. A model can be built based solely on previous history using the web access logs, or complemented, as we shall see later, by the connectivity in the site and even the content of the pages. In the example of Fig. 2A, the content is taken into account and the subject of interest in predicted before text web pages (modules) or simulations are suggested in a database security course web site.

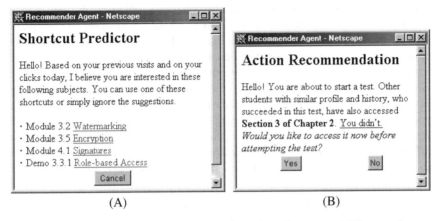

Figure 2: Recommender system suggesting (A) a shortcut and (B) an action.

An action recommender system also suggests resources or learning objects, but often acts upon triggers. Typically, in web mining and web analytics, the canonical event is a click or request of a page. In e-learning the canonical event is an action such as the completion of polling, the answering of a quiz question, the execution of a simulation, the request of a text chapter for reading. The granularity and resolution of these actions could depend on a concept hierarchy previously defined by the educator. The recommendation of actions is triggered by other actions. The start of a test, the answering of a quiz question, the successful termination of a simulation, the incorrect response at an assessment stage, or the request of a module of a new chapter, all constitute good examples for actions that could trigger the action recommender system. Once the software agent is activated for suggestions, the recommender system not only considers past activity but other semantically significant information about successes and failures of the learner to build a profile. The profile is matched with a subset of other profiles of successful learners and constrained with desirable behavior imposed by the educator. Figure 2B shows an example of an action recommender activated by the request to start an online test. The action 'accessing Section 3 of Chapter 2' is suggested because the action is taken before the test by successful learners at the concerned test and probably not by the less successful ones.

4 Non-intrusive methods for recommendation

Since we do not have ratings for course material, and it is not desired to survey learners about their evaluations of the different learning objects and modules since we opt for a non-intrusive approach, collaborative filtering is not applicable for devising an accurate recommender agent for e-learning activities. We will build our models only based on logged online activities.

In recent years there has been an increasing interest in applying web usage mining techniques to build web recommender systems [9–12]. Web usage recommender systems take web server access logs as input, and make use of data mining techniques such as *association rule* and *clustering* to extract implicit, and potentially useful navigational patterns, which are then used to provide recommendations. Web server access logs record user browsing history, which contains plenty of hidden information regarding users and their navigation. They could, therefore, be a good alternative to the explicit user rating or feedback in deriving user models. In web usage recommender systems, navigational patterns are generally derived as an offline process. A significant cleaning and transformation phase needs to take place so as to prepare the information for data mining algorithms [13, 14].

4.1 E-learning recommender with association rules

Association rules are one of the typical rule patterns that data mining tools aim at discovering. They are very useful in many application domains, but are mainly applied in the business world as in market-basket analysis. In a transactional database where each transaction is a set of items bought together, association rules are rules associating items that are frequently bought together. A rule consists of an antecedent (left-hand side) and a consequent (right-hand side). Example: $I_1, I_2, \ldots, I_n \Rightarrow I_\alpha, I_\beta, \ldots, I_\gamma$. The intersection between the antecedent and the consequent is empty. If items in the antecedent are bought then there is a probability that the items in the consequent would be bought as well at the same time. An efficient algorithm to discover these association rules was first introduced in [15]. The algorithm constructs a candidate set of frequent itemsets of length k, counts the number of occurrences, keeps only the frequent ones, then constructs a candidate set of itemsets of length $k + 1$ from the frequent itemsets of smaller length. It continues iteratively until no candidate itemset can be constructed. In other words, every subset of a frequent itemset must also be frequent. The rules are then generated from the frequent itemsets with probabilities attached to them indicating the likelihood (called support) that the association occurs.

This idea of association rules is often used to train a recommender agent to build a model representing the web page access behavior or associations between online learning activities.

A recommender system suggests possible actions or web resources based on its understanding of the user's access. To do so the entries in the web log have to be translated into either known actions (i.e. learning activities such as accessing a course notes module, posting a message on the forum, doing a test, trying a simulation) or URLs of a web resource. This mapping is a significant processing phase that in itself presents a considerable challenge [16, 17]. Moreover, these identified actions and URLs are grouped into sessions which is yet another difficult and delicate task [13]. These sessions are then modeled into transactions as sets of actions and URLs. The association rule mining technique is applied on such transactions to discover associations between actions, associations between URLs and associations between actions and URLs, as well as associations between sequences of

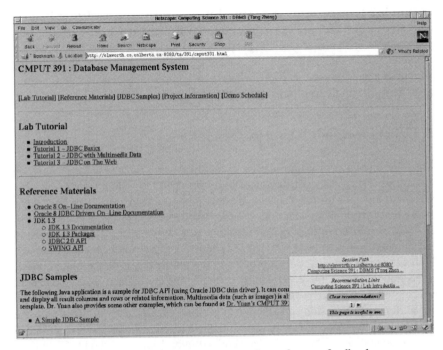

Figure 3: Recommender system using reference feedback.

actions and/or URLs. This process usually leads to a very large number of association rules. A sophisticated pruning and filtering phase is required [18]. When the recommender agent is activated, the association rules are consulted to check for matches between the triggering event, or sequence of events, with the rule antecedents. When a match is found, the consequent of the rule is suggested. If more matches are found, the suggestions are ranked and only a small set (highest ranked) is displayed. The ranking is often based on some interestingness measures such as confidence. However, in some cases input from the user can interactively improve these measures. Figure 3 shows a prototype of a recommender system for pages in an online database course at the University of Alberta where the user rates the recommendation by reference feedback. This feedback adjusts the weights on the rules used for future recommendations.

4.2 A model with clustering

While using association rule mining is popular in building non-intrusive recommender systems [19, 20], clustering is also an accepted approach although not as effective. Indeed there are myriad clustering techniques not all as capable [21]. Clustering consists of grouping objects based on similarity or dissimilarity (i.e. distance function) by maximizing similarity between objects in a group and maximizing dissimilarity between objects in different groups. In the context of recommender systems in e-learning, the objects are either pages with their content (or learning objects) or sequences of clicks representing navigational behaviors. In both cases, page content or sequence of clicks, are modeled in a vector space. When the recommendation agent is activated, the current page (action or learning object) or the current sequence of event is compared to its neighbors in its cluster. The k-nearest neighbors are simply recommended to the user.

5 Hybrid methods for recommendations

Most non-intrusive recommendation agents rely either on access usage only, on content of visited pages or on connectivity between the visited pages. Very few combine these information channels. We have proposed a model to combine all these information channels [22] and showed the effectiveness in different contexts [23].

A few combined or hybrid web recommender systems have been proposed in the literature [24, 25]. The work in [24] adopts a clustering technique to obtain both site usage and site content profiles in the offline phase. In the online phase, a recommendation set is generated by matching the current active session and all usage profiles. Similarly, another recommendation set is generated by matching the current active session and all content profiles. Finally, a set of pages with the maximum recommendation value across the two recommendation sets is presented as recommendation. This is called a *weighted* hybridization method [26]. In [25], Nakagawa and Mobasher use association rule mining, sequential pattern mining, and contiguous sequential mining to generate three types of navigational patterns in the offline phase. In the online phase, recommendation sets are selected from the different navigational models, based on a localized degree of hyperlink connectivity with respect to a user's current location within the site. This is called a *switching* hybridization method [26].

5.1 Architecture of a hybrid recommender system

As most web usage recommender systems, our system is composed of two modules: an offline component, which pre-processes data to generate users' navigational models, and an online component which is a real-time recommendation engine. Figure 4 depicts the general architecture of our system.

Entries in a web server log are used to identify users and visit sessions, while web pages or resources in the site are clustered based on their content. These clusters of web documents are used to scrutinize the discovered web sessions in order to identify what we call *missions* [23]. A mission is a sub-session with a consistent goal. These missions are in turn clustered to generate navigational patterns, and augmented with their linked neighborhood and ranked based on resource connectivity, using the *hub* and *authority* idea [27]. These new clusters (i.e. augmented navigational patterns) are provided to the recommendation engine. When a visitor starts a new session, the session is matched with these clusters to generate a recommendation list.

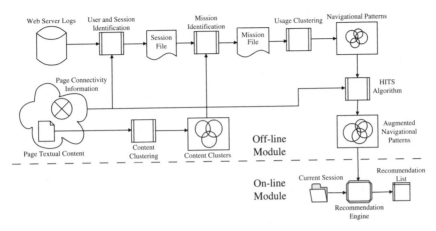

Figure 4: System architecture with all three channels available.

5.2 User and visit session identification

A web log is a text file which records information regarding users' requests to a web server. A typical web log entry contains a client address, the requested date address, a time-stamp, and other related information.

For any web access log data, several pre-processing tasks have to be performed before applying data mining techniques for pattern discovery. The pre-processing tasks usually include user identification, visit session identification, and transaction identification. We use similar pre-processing techniques as in [14] to identify individual users and sessions. To sessionize log entries, we chose an idle time of 30 min. Session-based access logs, however, like for a password protected e-learning system, logs have entries identified by users since the users have to login, and sessions are already identified since users may also have to logout.

5.3 Visit mission identification

The last data pre-processing step proposed in [14] is transaction identification, which divides individual visit sessions into transactions. Two transaction identification approaches are proposed: *reference length* approach and *maximal forward reference* approach, both of which have been widely applied in web mining. Rather than dividing sessions into arbitrary transactions, we identify sub-sessions with coherent information needs. We call these sub-sessions missions. We assume that a visitor may have different information needs to fulfill during a visit, but we make no assumption on the sequence in which these needs are fulfilled. In the case of transactions in [14], it is assumed that one information need is fulfilled after the other. A mission would model a sub-session related to one of these information needs, and would allow overlap between missions, which would represent a concurrent search in the site.

Now how do we identify missions? The first approach we proposed to identify missions is based on web content [22]. While in the transaction-based model, pages are labeled as *content* pages and *auxiliary* pages, and a transaction is simply a sequence of auxiliary pages that ends with a content page, in the mission-based model we propose, the identified sequence is based on the real content of pages. Indeed, a content page in the transaction-based model is identified simply based on the time spent on that page, or on backtracking in the visitor's navigation. We argue that missions could better model users' navigational behavior than transactions. In our model, users visit a web site with concurrent goals, i.e. different information needs. For example, a user could fulfill two goals in a visit session: a, b, c, d, in which pages a and c contribute to one goal, while pages b and d contribute to the other. Since pages related to a given goal in a visit session are generally supposed to be content coherent, whether they are neighboring each other or not, we use page content to identify missions within a visit session.

All web site pages are clustered based on their content, and these clusters are used to identify content coherent clicks in a session. Let us give an example to illustrate this point. Suppose the text clustering algorithm groups web pages a, b, c, and e, web pages a, b, c, and f, and web pages a, c and d into three different content clusters (please note that our text clustering algorithm is a soft clustering one, which allows a web page to be clustered into several clusters). Then for a visit session: a, b, c, d, e, f, our system identifies three missions as follows: mission 1: (a, b, c, e); mission 2: (a, b, c, f); and mission 3: (a, c, d). As seen in this example, mission identification in our system is different from transaction identification in that we can group web pages into one mission even if they are not sequential in a visit session. We can see that our mission-based model subsumes the transaction-based model, since missions could become transactions if visitors fulfill their information needs sequentially.

To cluster web pages based on their content, we use a modified version of the DC-tree algorithm [28]. Originally, the DC-tree algorithm was a hard clustering approach, prohibiting overlap of clusters. We modified the algorithm to allow web pages to belong to different clusters. Indeed, some web pages could cover different topics at the same time. In the algorithm, each web page is represented as a keyword vector, and organized in a tree structure called the DC-tree. The algorithm does not require the number of clusters to discover as a constraint, but allows the definition of cluster sizes. This was the appealing property which made us select the algorithm. Indeed, we do not want either too large or too small content cluster sizes. Very large clusters cannot help capture missions from sessions, while very small clusters may break potentially useful relations between pages in sessions.

The missions we extracted and clustered to generate navigational patterns are primarily based on the sessions from the web server logs. These sessions exclusively represent web pages or resources that were visited. It is conceivable that there are other resources not yet visited, even though they are relevant and could be interesting to have in the recommendation list. Such resources could be, for instance, newly added web pages or pages that have links to them not evidently presented due to bad design. Thus, these pages or resources are never presented in the missions previously discovered. Since the navigational patterns, represented by the clusters of pages in the missions, are used by the recommendation engine, we need to provide an opportunity for these rarely visited or newly added pages to be included in the clusters. Otherwise, they would never be recommended. To alleviate this problem, our general system model expands the clusters to include the connected neighborhood of every page in a mission cluster. The local neighborhood of a page, obtained by tracing a small number of links from the originating page, is a good approximation to the 'semantic neighborhood' of the page [29]. In our case, the connected neighborhood of a page p is the set of all the pages directly linked from p and having similar content of p, and all the pages that directly link to p also with similar content. In detail, this approach of expanding the neighborhood is performed as follows: we consider each previously discovered navigational pattern (i.e. a cluster of content coherent and visitation cohesive missions) as a set of seeds. Each seed is supplemented with pages it links to and pages that link to it as well as having similar content. The result is what is called a connectivity graph which now represents our augmented navigational pattern. This process of obtaining the connectivity graph is similar to the process used by the HITS algorithm [27] to find the authority and hub pages for a given topic. The difference is that we do not consider a given topic, but start from a mission cluster as our set of seeds.

Moreover, it was shown in [30] that HITS, using pure connectivity analysis, introduces a problem known as 'topic drift'. We eliminate this problem in our case by computing relevance weights of all supplementary pages. The relevance weight of a page equals the similarity of the page content to the corresponding mission cluster, which is represented by the cosine normalization of web pages and mission clusters keyword vectors. We then prune nodes with relevance weights below a threshold from the connectivity graph. For simplicity, we use *median weight* (i.e. the median of all relevance weights) as the pruning threshold [30]. The pruning process avoids augmenting the navigational patterns with pages that focus on other topics and guarantees that the augmented patterns are still coherent and focused. After expanding and pruning the clusters representing the navigational patterns, we also augment the keyword vectors that label the clusters. The new keyword vectors that represent the augmented navigational patterns have also the terms extracted from the content of the augmented pages.

We take advantage of the built connectivity graph by cluster to apply the HITS algorithm in order to identify the authority and hub pages within a given cluster. These measures of authority and hub allow us to rank the pages within the cluster. This is important because at real time during the recommendation, it is crucial to rank recommendations, especially if they are numerous. Long recommendation lists are not advisable.

Authority and hub are mutually reinforcing [27] concepts. Indeed, a good authority is a page pointed to by many good hub pages, and a good hub is a page that points to many good authority pages. Since we would like to be able to recommend pages newly added to the site, in our framework, we consider only the hub measure. This is because a newly added page would be unlikely to be a good authoritative page, since not many pages are linking to it. However, a good new page would probably link to many authority pages; it would, therefore, have the chance to be a good hub page. Consequently, we use the hub value to rank the candidate recommendation pages in the online module.

When a visitor starts a new session in the web site, we identify the navigation pattern after a few clicks and try to match on-the-fly with already captured navigational patterns. If they were matched, we recommend the most relevant pages in the matched cluster.

5.4 Evaluating hybrid recommenders

To demonstrate the effectiveness of the hybrid approach using all three information channels, usage, linkage and content, to build an effective recommender system for shortcuts and activities, we present herein a test using a generic web access log from the computing science department web site. The collected web access log is divided into months each averaging about 200,000 hits accessing on average more than 40,000 unique pages with on average 150,000 hyperlinks between them. Successively, each month is used to train a recommender system and the subsequent month is used to evaluate it.

We devised a methodology to assess the recommender system [23]. The evaluation is based on *recommendation accuracy* and *shortcut gain*. The recommendation accuracy $(RA = [\Sigma_s| \cup_p (T(p) \cap R(p))|/| \cup p\, R(p)|]/S$ where S is the visit session in the log, s is a given session, p is a page in s, $R(p)$ is the generated recommendation list from p, and $T(p)$ the tail (suffix) of s after p) is the ratio of correct recommendations among all recommendations, and the correct recommendation is the one that appears in the suffix of a session from which the prefix triggers the recommendation. The shortcut gain $(SG = [\Sigma_s|s| - |s'|/|s|]/S$ where s is the original session and s' is the improved session after the jump) measures how many clicks the recommendation allows users to save if the recommendation is followed. In addition, we compute the *coverage* of a recommender system, which measures the ability of a system to produce all pages that are likely to be visited by users $(RC = [\Sigma_s| \cup_p (T(p) \cap R(p))|/| \cup_p T(p)|]/S)$. The concept is similar to what is called *recall* in information retrieval.

We first evaluated the performance of our system on the UofA CS web server dataset. Our first experiment varies the coverage to see the tendency of the recommendation accuracy, as depicted in Fig. 5A. For the purpose of comparison, we also implement an *association rule recommender system*, the most commonly used approach for web mining based recommender systems, and record its performance in the same figure. As expected, the accuracy decreases when we increase coverage. However, our system was consistently superior to the association rule system by at least 30%.

We next varied the coverage to test the shortcut gain, both with our system and with the association rule system, as illustrated in Fig. 5B.

From Fig. 5B, we can see that in the low boundary where the coverage is lower than 8%, the shortcut gain of our system is close to that of the association rule system. With the increase of the coverage, however, our system can achieve

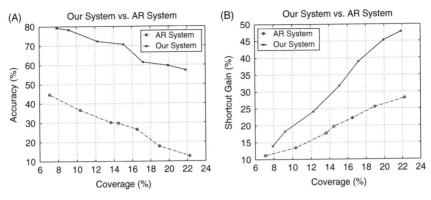

Figure 5: Performance comparison: our system vs. association rule Recommender System. (A) Recommendation accuracy; (B) shortcut gain.

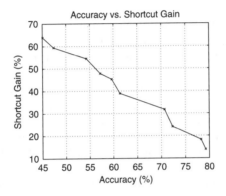

Figure 6: Accuracy vs. shortcut gain.

an increasingly superior shortcut gain than the latter, although the performance of both systems continues to improve.

Figure 6 depicts the relationship of recommendation accuracy and shortcut gain in our system. It shows that recommendation accuracy is inversely proportional to the shortcut gain. Our study draws the same conclusion from the association rule recommender system. We argue that this is an important property of a usage-based web recommender system, and therefore, how to adjust and balance between the accuracy and shortcut gain for a web recommender system to achieve the maximum benefit is a question that should be investigated. Some web sites, e.g. those with high link density, may favor a recommender system with high accuracy, while some others may favor a system with high shortcut gain.

In the above tests, the three distinctive information channels – usage, content, and structure – are provided to and used in our system. In a second battery of tests we measured the effect of the individual information channels. We first compared three recommender systems, one using all channels, one using only usage and

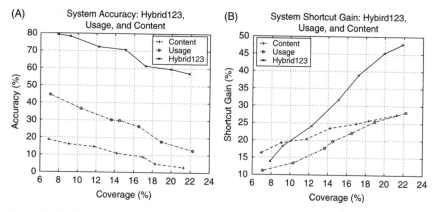

Figure 7: Hybrid123, Usage, and Content. (A) Recommendation accuracy; (B) shortcut gain.

one using only content. We refer to our recommender using the three channels as *Hybrid123*. For this comparison, we implemented an association rule-based usage recommender system as in the previous tests (referred to as *Usage*), as well as a web recommender system based purely on content similarity (referred to as *Content*). The Usage system works as follows: an efficient association rule algorithm [31] is applied to the access logs to generate a set of rules. Whenever the pages in the antecedent of an rule have appeared in the user's current session, those pages in its consequence are recommended. For the Content system, all pages in the web site are extracted and grouped into clusters solely based on their textual content similarity, using a high-quality content clustering algorithm [32]. If one or more pages in a cluster have been visited, the pages in the same clusters are selected to be recommended. The recommendation accuracy and shortcut gain of the three systems are depicted in Fig. 7. In the experiment, we varied the coverage to test the trend and consistency of the system quality.

Figure 7A shows the recommendation accuracy of the three contenders. As expected, the accuracy decreases when we increase coverage. However, Hybrid123 is consistently the best among the three systems, superior to Usage by at least 30% – while Usage always ranks second.

From Fig. 7B, we can see that in the low boundary, the shortcut gain of Content is the best of the three systems, and the other two are close. With the increase of coverage, the shortcut gain of all three systems continues to improve, but in different degrees. Hybrid123 can achieve an increasingly superior shortcut gain to that of Usage, and exceeds Content after coverage is larger than about 10%. The major reason that the shortcut gain improvement of Content is lowest is that with the increase of coverage, more and more pages containing only the same terms, but without any logical relationship are selected to be recommended.

In our next experiment, we illustrate the advantage of incorporating web content and web structure information in our system. To do so, we implemented additional two recommender prototypes. The first is similar to Hybrid123 but is stripped

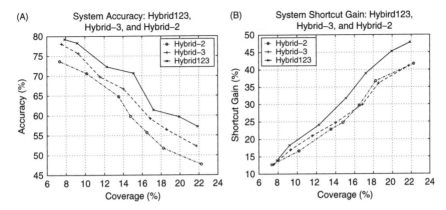

Figure 8: Hybrid123, Hybrid-3, and Hybrid-2. (A) Recommendation accuracy; (B) Shortcut gain.

from its connectivity information channel. That is, we do not make use of linkage information to augment and improve the navigational patterns built on usage and content information. We name this hybrid system *Hybrid-3*. The second is also a similar system to Hybrid123 but does not make use of content information to identify a mission. Rather, the navigational patterns in the system is built upon traditional transactions identified according to the approach in [14]. Then, the patterns are improved with structure information, as with Hybrid123. This hybrid system is called *Hybrid-2*. The recommendation accuracy and shortcut gain of the three systems are depicted in Fig. 8.

Figure 8A shows the recommendation accuracy of the three systems. The consistently best performance of Hybrid123 illustrates the validity of content and connectivity information to improve recommendations in our hybrid system, and also indicates that content is more useful for recommendation accuracy improvement. The shortcut gains of the three systems are depicted in Fig. 8B. We notice that with the increase of coverage, Hybrid123 can achieve an increasingly superior shortcut gain compared to both Hybrid-3 and Hybrid-2, while the two systems keep similar performance in terms of shortcut gain. This figure verifies our justification for using distinctive information channels in building a hybrid recommender system, and shows that content and structure information make a similar contribution to the improvement in shortcut gain in our system.

In summary, this experiment shows that our system can significantly improve the quality of web site recommendation by combining the three information channels, while each channel included contributes to this improvement.

6 Conclusion

Most recommender systems rely on ratings from users. We argue that this is intrusive and quickly loses effectiveness in an e-learning setting. Non-intrusive methods relying on web access logs are true to the real learning behavior of a user. A web usage-based recommender system which focuses solely on access history has its own problems:

- *Incomplete information problem*: One restriction with web server logs is that the information in them is very limited. Thus, a number of heuristic assumptions have to be made to identify individual users, visit sessions, and transactions in order to apply any data mining algorithm. One such assumption is that user information needs are fulfilled sequentially while in practice they are often in parallel.
- *Incorrect information problem*: When web site visitors are lost, the clicks made by them are recorded in the log, and may mislead future recommendations. This becomes more problematic when a web site is badly designed and more people end up visiting unsolicited pages, making them seem popular.
- *Persistence problem*: When new pages are added to a web site, because they have not been visited yet, the recommender system may not recommend them, even though they could be relevant. Moreover, the more a page is recommended, the more it may be visited, thus making it look popular and boost its candidacy for future recommendation.

To address these problems, we proposed a hybrid web recommender system, which attempts to use three information channels to model user navigational behavior: web access logs, the structure of a visited web site, and the content of visited web pages. In particular, the approach uses the terms within visited web pages to partition visit sessions into overlapping sub-sessions, called missions. Our preliminary experiments demonstrate that combining the different information channels has great potential for improving the quality of non-intrusive recommendation.

References

[1] Virtual-U, http://www.elearningsolutionsinc.com/productsvu.htm
[2] Groeneboer, C., Stockley, D. & Calvert, T., Virtual-U: a collaborative model for online learning environments. *Second Int. Conf. on Computer Support for Collaborative Learning*, Toronto, Canada, 1997.
[3] WebCT, http://www.webct.com
[4] Tang, T. & McCalla, G., Smart recommendation for an evolving e-learning system: Architecture and experiment. *International Journal on E-Learning*, **4(1)**, pp. 105–129, 2005.
[5] Chee, S., Han, J. & Wang, K., RecTree: an efficient collaborative filtering method. *3rd Int. Conf. on Data Warehousing and Knowledge Discovery (DAWAK 2001)*, Springer Verlag: Munich, Germany, LNCS 2114, pp. 141–151, 2001.
[6] Melville, P., Mooney, R. & Nagarajan, R., Content-boosted collaborative filtering for improved recommendation. *18th National Conf. on Artificial Intelligence (AAAI'02)*, Edmonton, Canada, pp. 187–192, 2002.

[7]   Tang, T.Y. & McCalla, G., Towards pedagogy-oriented paper recommendation and adaptive annotations for a web-based learning system. *Workshop on Knowledge Representation and Automated Reasoning for E-Learning Systems (in IJCAI'03)*, Acapulco, Mexico, 2003.

[8]   McNee, S., Alberta, I., Cosley, D., Gopalkrishnan, P., Lam, S., Rashid, A., Konstan, J. & Rield, J., On the recommending of citations for research papers. *ACM Int. Conf. on Computer Supported Collaborative Work (CSCW'02)*, pp. 116–125, 2002.

[9]   Srivastava, J., Cooley, R., Deshpande, M. & Tan, P.N., Web usage mining: Discovery and applications of usage patterns from web data. *SIGKDD Explorations*, **1(2)**, pp. 12–23, 2000.

[10] Fu, X., Budzik, J. & Hammond, K.J., Mining navigation history for recommendation. *Intelligent User Interfaces*, pp. 106–112, 2000.

[11] Lin, C., Alvarez, S. & Ruiz, C., Collaborative recommendation via adaptive association rule mining, 2000.

[12] Yi-Hung Wu, A.L.C., Yong-Chuan Chen, Enabling personalized recommendation on the web based on user interests and behaviors. *11th Int. Workshop on Research Issues in Data Engineering*, 2001.

[13] Zaïane, O.R., Web usage mining for a better web-based learning environment. *Proc. of Conf. on Advanced Technology for Education*, Banff, AB, pp. 60–64, 2001.

[14] Cooley, R., Mobasher, B. & Srivastava, J., Data preparation for mining world wide web browsing patterns. *Knowledge and Information Systems*, **1(1)**, pp. 5–32, 1999.

[15] Agrawal, R., Imielinski, T. & Swami, A., Mining association rules between sets of items in large databases. *Proc. 1993 ACM-SIGMOD Int. Conf. Management of Data*, Washington, DC, pp. 207–216, 1993.

[16] Zaïane, O.R., Xin, M. & Han, J., Discovering web access patterns and trends by applying OLAP and data mining technology on web logs. *Proc. Advances in Digital Libraries ADL'98*, Santa Barbara, CA, USA, pp. 19–29, 1998.

[17] Zaïane, O.R. & Luo, J., Towards evaluating learners' behaviour in a web-based distance learning environment. *Proc. of IEEE Int. Conf. on Advanced Learning Technologies (ICALT01)*, Madison, WI, pp. 357–360, 2001.

[18] Zaïane, O.R., Building a recommender agent for e-learning systems. *Int. Conf. on Computers in Education*, 2001.

[19] Lin, W., Alvarez, S.A. & Ruiz, C., Efficient adaptive-support association rule mining for recommender systems. *Data Mining and Knowledge Discovery*, **6(1)**, pp. 83–105, 2002.

[20] Spertus, E. & Stein, L.A., A hyperlink-based recommender system written in squeal. *Proc. ACM CIKM'98 Workshop on Web Information and Data Management (WIDM'98)*, Washington, DC, pp. 1–4, 1998.

[21] Zaïane, O.R., Foss, A., Lee, C.H. & Wang, W., On data clustering analysis: Scalability, constraints and validation. *Sixth Pacific-Asia Conf. on Knowledge Discovery and Data Mining (PAKDD'02)*, Taipei, Taiwan, Lecture Notes in AI (LNAI 2336), pp. 28–39, 2002.

[22] Li, J. & Zaïane, O.R., Combining usage, content, and structure data to improve web site recommendation. *5th Int. Conf. on Electronic Commerce and Web Technologies (EC-Web 2004)*, 2004.

[23] Li, J. & Zaïane, O.R., Using distinct information channels for mission-based web recommender system. *Sixth ACM SIGKDD Workshop on Webmining and Web Analysis (WebKDD 2004)*, Seattle, WA, USA, pp. 35–46, 2004.

[24] Mobasher, B., Dai, H., Luo, T., Sun, Y. & Zhu, J., Integrating web usage and content mining for more effective personalization. *EC-Web*, pp. 165–176, 2000.

[25] Nakagawa, M. & Mobasher, B., A hybrid web personalization model based on site connectivity. *Fifth WebKDD Workshop*, pp. 59–70, 2003.

[26] Burke, R., Hybrid recommender systems: Survey and experiments. *User Modeling and User-Adapted* Interaction, 2002.

[27] Kleinberg, J.M., Authoritative sources in a hyperlinked environment. *Journal of the ACM*, **46(5)**, pp. 604–632, 1999.

[28] Wong, W. & Fu, A., Incremental document clustering for web page classification, 2000.

[29] Lieberman, H., Autonomous interface agents. *Proc. of the ACM Conf. on Computers and Human Interface, CHI-97*, Atlanta, Georgia, 1997.

[30] Bharat, K. & Henzinger, M.R., Improved algorithms for topic distillation in a hyperlinked environment. *Proc. of SIGIR-98, 21st ACM Int. Conf. on Research and Development in Information Retrieval*, Melbourne, AU, pp. 104–111, 1998.

[31] Chen, M.S., Park, J.S. & Yu, P., Efficient data mining for path traversal patterns. *IEEE Transactions on Knowledge and Data Engineering*, **10(2)**, pp. 209–221, 1998.

[32] Pantel, P. & Lin, D., Document clustering with committees. *The 25th Annual Int. ACM SIGIR Conf. on Research and Development in Information Retrieval*, 2002.

CHAPTER 6

Active, context-dependent, data-centered techniques for e-learning: a case study of a research paper recommender system

T. Tang[1,2] & G. McCalla[2]
[1]*Department of Computing, Hong Kong Polytechnic University, Hung Hom, Kowloon, Hong Kong.*
[2]*ARIES Laboratory, Department of Computer Science, University of Saskatchewan, Saskatoon, Saskatchewan, Canada.*

Abstract

In this chapter we discuss an e-learning system that recommends research papers to students wishing to learn an area of research. Recommender systems in the e-learning domain have specific requirements not present in other domains, most importantly the need to take into account pedagogical aspects of the learner and the system (such as the learning goals of each) and the need to recommend sequences of items in a pedagogically effective order. First, the architecture and some of the basic methodologies of the system are presented. Then, two studies are presented showing some of the 'pedagogical' characteristics affecting recommendations and comparing two recommendation algorithms: one that is content-based and the other that employs hybrid content-collaborative filtering and clustering techniques. We then generalize from the recommender system to discuss a general approach to the design of an e-learning application called the *ecological approach*, which is centered on finding patterns in learners' interactions with learning objects and using these to actively compute information relevant to the application that is sensitive to the current end use context, especially to characteristics and goals of the learner. The ecological approach holds the promise of overcoming many problems in e-learning that have made systems controlling and unresponsive.

1 Introduction

The general problem of managing repositories of learning objects in order to support students who wish to learn about a domain is now being actively studied in artificial intelligence in education (AIED) and other e-learning research areas [1, 2]. We are working on a specialized instance of the general problem: recommending papers from a research paper repository to learners who wish to learn about a research area. The target audience for our experiments into the paper recommender system is graduate students and senior undergraduate students who wish to learn about the domain of data mining, although the approach is not restricted to this domain.

Most research in recommender systems have not been in e-learning domains, but instead in domains such as e-commerce or the most studied domain: movie recommendations [3–6]. There is, however, some specific research in tracking and recommending research papers. Basu *et al.* [7] define the paper recommendation problem as: 'Given a representation of my interests, find me relevant papers.' Their goal is to assign conference paper submissions to reviewing committee members. Reviewers do not need to key in their research interests as they usually do; instead, a novel autonomous procedure is incorporated in order to collect reviewer interest information from the web. Bollacker *et al.* [8] refine CiteSeer, through an automatic personalized paper-tracking module that retrieves each user's interests from well-maintained heterogeneous user profiles. Woodruff *et al.* [9] discuss an enhanced digital book with a spreading-activation mechanism to make customized recommendations for readers with different types of background and knowledge. McNee *et al.* [10] investigate the adoption of collaborative filtering techniques to recommend papers for researchers. They do not address the issue of how to recommend a research paper, but rather, how to recommend additional references for a target research paper. In the context of an e-learning system, additional readings in an area cannot be recommended purely through an analysis of the citation matrix of the target paper.

Our research has a different focus from these other projects. We assume there is a pre-existing repository of relevant papers, rather than the open web (although we would eventually like to automatically retrieve papers from web sources). We also assume the goal is to put together a whole sequence of papers, in a broader e-learning context. In such an e-learning context:

- User interest is not the only relevant metric. Items liked by learners might not be pedagogically suitable for them, and vice versa. For example, a learner without prior background knowledge of the techniques of web mining may only be interested in knowing the state-of-the-art of web mining in e-commerce. Then, it should be recommended that he/she read some review papers, for example, an editorial article by two of the leading researchers in this area [11], although there are also many high quality technical papers related to his/her interest. On the other hand, for the learner coming from industry with some prior knowledge who wants to know how web mining can be utilized to solve e-commerce problems, should be recommended, because the paper is the KDD-Cup 2000 organizers' report on how web mining can support business decision making for a real-life e-commerce vendor, and it points out challenges as well as lessons learned from the competition, which can benefit both researchers and industry practitioners. In other domains, recommendations are made based purely on users' interests.

- More than one item must be returned and it is important to organize these items in a sequence specifically tailored to the learner [12]. This is because there are pedagogically relevant dependencies (e.g. prerequisite relationships) among learning objects that mean one object should be 'consumed' by the learner before another, for example an introductory paper on data mining before more technical papers outlining various techniques. In contrast, in the movie domain normally only one movie is recommended at a time, and in e-commerce domains it is usually preferred to leave the list of recommended items unordered to avoid leaving the impression that a specific recommendation is the best choice [13].

Thus, in making recommendations to learners two things are of paramount importance: individualization to particular learners and the incorporation of pedagogical aspects into the recommendation algorithms.

In this chapter we will explore these issues further. We start with an overview of our research paper recommender system architecture, and show how data clustering techniques play a significant role. In Section 3 we discuss two studies we have undertaken: (i) an empirical study of actual learners and their preferences and goals that sheds some light on important versus not so important pedagogical goals and learner characteristics that we must take into account in the design of the research paper recommender system; and (ii) a study with simulated learners that sheds light on the trade-offs between two different recommender system techniques, content-based filtering and a hybrid content-collaborative technique. Then, in Section 4 we discuss an approach to the design of e-learning systems called the *ecological approach* which is a synthesis of ideas that has emerged from our work on the research paper recommender system and various other investigations in the ARIES laboratory at the University of Saskatchewan. Fundamental to the ecological approach is data mining, thus making this an appropriate culmination for a chapter in this book, although there is a brief concluding section that forms our official denouement to the chapter.

2 A research paper recommender system

We can state the goal for our paper recommender system as follows:

Given a collection of papers and a model of the learner, recommend and deliver a set of pedagogically suitable papers in an appropriate sequence, so as to meet the learner's pedagogical needs as well as to be consistent with the learner's background and other characteristics.

Ideally, the system will maximize a learner's utility such that the learner gains a maximum amount of knowledge and is still highly motivated in the end.

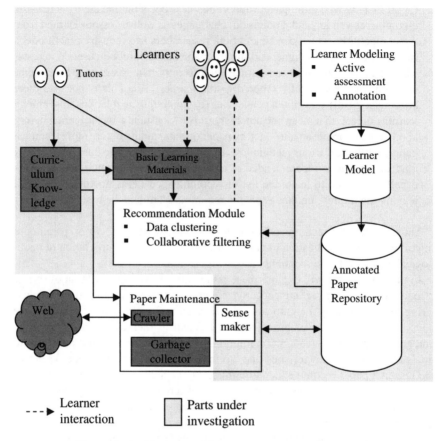

Figure 1: Architecture of the paper recommender system.

Figure 1 shows the architecture of our research paper recommender system (for more detailed descriptions of each module see [14]). The system is primarily intended as a support tool in an e-learning system for senior undergraduate or first year graduate students who want to read pedagogically useful papers that may help them either in their class projects or future studies. The darkened part in the figure is the part that we are actively exploring, i.e. the modules that make the actual recommendations. It is a longer-term goal to develop the paper maintenance module to have the ability to automatically update the paper repository with new papers through a web crawler browsing CiteSeer or other such external sources to retrieve relevant new papers; however, we have not actively explored this yet.

The paper repository is where papers related to the course are actively maintained through the paper maintenance module. Papers must currently be added and removed manually, by tutors or learners, since the crawler and garbage collector modules are not currently being explored. Any explicit metadata must also be added by hand at this time. Learners are responsible for giving ratings and other assessments after interacting with a paper, and these are also kept as annotations with the paper in the repository.

The sense-maker module is responsible for filtering out loosely related papers and clustering them into their appropriate topical categories. The sense making here is adaptively performed based on the collective learning behaviors and interests of users instead of an individual learner. For instance, the majority of learners might find the paper to be highly technical which requires more extensive background knowledge. Therefore, each paper's technical tag evolves according to the collective usage and ratings of its learners. As discussed in Section 4, in the long run we think it is promising to consider annotating the papers with full learner models of each learner after they have interacted with a learning object such as a paper, and then mining these learner models to find patterns of end use relevant to various pedagogical goals. This is the basis of the so-called ecological approach to e-learning promoted there.

It is through the recommendation module that personalized recommendations are made. The recommendation module consists of two sub-modules: the data clustering module and the focused collaborative filtering module. The data clustering module clusters learners into a sub-class according to the purpose of the recommendation, while the focused collaborative filtering module will find the closest neighbor(s) of a target learner and recommend paper(s) to him/her according to the ratings by those closest neighbor(s). Tutors are responsible for setting up the curriculum and providing the basic learning materials. Based on this information, the system can select a set of papers for a learner.

Assume a learner L wants papers with content C, arranged in an appropriate sequence. There are two paper recommendation processes: content-based filtering and collaborative filtering. In content-based filtering, the idea is to find a cluster of papers with related content to C through content annotations attached to the papers in the repository. Information about the type of similarity between two papers can be useful in deciding which papers to include in the cluster and, later, how to order the papers. For example, one paper may be a version (e.g. an update or refinement) of another paper, one paper may take a different approach to the same topic as another, one paper may explore the same technique in a different context from another paper, one paper may be of the same level of difficulty as another paper, and so on. The recommender system could stop with this content-based filtering, but it is often useful to go further and apply collaborative filtering (CF) techniques to select a subset of other learners who have read papers in this content cluster who also have similar learner models to L (a learner cluster), and then uses learner cluster's opinions to choose which papers to recommend to L. This hybrid-CF technique is explored further in Section 3.2.

Once a set of papers has been selected through one of these techniques, the set must be ordered according to various heuristics. The similarity metrics, above, can be useful. Other ordering heuristics can also be used, for example ordering according to technical difficulty (easy to hard), length, level of abstraction, prestige of publications (most prestigious to least), or date of publication. The ordering decisions can be affected by information in L's learner model, for example taking into account other papers L has read or experience recorded there about the kinds of papers L has liked or disliked or found useful (drawing on techniques from the instructional planning area [15]). In this way individualization can happen in both the selection of the papers (through CF) and their sequencing.

The recommendation process requires considerable information in the content annotations associated with the papers. As discussed above these annotations can be explicit 'pedagogical' and content metadata attached by experts like tutors, or, more interestingly, information explicitly or implicitly added by the learners as they have interacted with the papers. Such learner annotations can provide an increasingly sophisticated repository of data about actual end use experience of the learners, and potentially allow ever more refined decisions about which papers are relevant to which learners in which contexts.

This is a very brief overview of the recommendation process. More technical details and a formal description can be found in [16], and a discussion of learner clustering based on learners' browsing behavior can be found in [17]. In the next section we will look at two experiments we have undertaken, one a human subject experiment with real learners, and the other a study with simulated learners, to explore the implications of pedagogical recommender systems.

3 Two experiments in paper recommendation

3.1 What learners want: a survey

The first experiment is a human subject study to determine some of the various factors affecting learners when they select papers. Results from this experiment have helped us to understand the relevant 'pedagogical' features we need to incorporate into the recommender system. We provided a questionnaire (see Appendix A) to 28 people and received 26 responses. The subjects were graduate students and alumni from computer science and engineering departments in Canada, Hong Kong, and China. The following learning scenario was introduced in the questionnaire: 'Assume that you are taking a graduate-level class where you need to read several papers (as what we usually did). For each topic taught in the class, you are required to read 2 or more items (journal paper, workshop paper, etc.) recommended by the professor or your classmates.' Then, 10 questions were asked that can be categorized into three groups: questions about learner preferences about different items, questions about content, and questions about delivery methods.

The results of the survey are shown in Fig. 2. The upper-left chart shows the learner preferences for type of paper, assuming the learner was interested in the topic being taught, while the lower-left chart shows the preferences if the learner was not interested in the topic. The vertical axis in these charts represents the number of respondents who liked/disliked the type of item shown below the horizontal axis. The upper-right chart shows learners' preferences regarding the presentation of the paper. The lower-right chart tracks answers to various questions in the survey, showing learner preferences for various kinds of papers and recommendations.

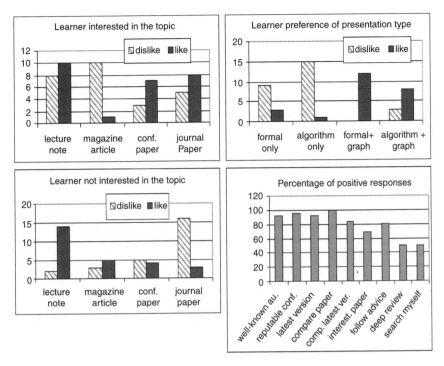

Figure 2: Some results of the survey.

The results show that magazine articles were the least popular items for learners who are interested in the topic being taught, but journal papers were least popular for learners who aren't that interested in the topic. In either case learners would rely heavily on lecture notes.

Learners preferred graphical presentations in preference to papers with formal models or algorithms only. And, as shown in the first three bars of the lower-right chart, most of them preferred papers by well-known authors, from reputable conferences, and with up-to-date results or the latest version of the research being reported (Q6 of Appendix A). On the delivery issue (bar four in the lower-right chart), respondents preferred to know more about various approaches to solving a similar problem rather than learning a single approach repetitively, which indicates their enthusiasm for in-breadth exploration. For similar papers by the same authors, most of the respondents preferred up-to-date work (third answer of Q7 in Appendix A) rather than earlier versions. Respondents who preferred the earlier version of a paper (second answer of Q7) believed that the earlier version was less 'distilled' and thus easier to read (even though we explicitly stated in the question that both earlier and later-versions have a similar technical level). But they would read the up-to-date version, as well, if they found the topic to be interesting enough to pursue. The majority of respondents preferred to read an interesting but unimportant paper before they proceeded to read an important but uninteresting one (see bar 6).

An even bigger majority (bar 7) of respondents were still willing to eventually read that important, yet uninteresting, paper, however. This finding substantiates our claim that uninteresting, yet pedagogically valuable papers should be recommended. Bar 8 in the lower-right chart shows a balance between learners who preferred deep review paper(s) (with many technical aspects) to shallow review paper(s) (with many interesting presentations/application descriptions). In comments made on the survey, three respondents said that they would be willing to read both papers if they were interested in the topic being reviewed and two of them stated that they would skim the shallow review paper first before going deeply into the other one. When asked about whether they would follow a link to rich resources maintained by well-known researchers or research groups, half of the learners (bar 9) preferred the recommender system to provide more specific information before they would follow the link. A solution to this problem is to provide additional annotations so as to make recommendations more personalized and specific. A more detailed analysis of this study is available in [18].

From the above analysis, a number of factors are seen to be important in making recommendations. Some of these factors are more or less independent of individual differences in learners (for example the dislike of approaches that are only formal, and the preference for papers from well known authors in reputable conferences). However, many of the recommendations are affected by individual differences among learners, most importantly the goals and motivations of the learners and their level of interest in the topic. This study thus provides further evidence that personalization is important. Since it is already well known in the AIED literature that other individual differences (e.g. in the level of knowledge of the learners) are also of great importance in helping learners access appropriate content and keeping learners engaged, this confirms the requirement to be able to incorporate individualization techniques into the paper recommender system.

3.2 Evaluating pedagogy-oriented hybrid collaborative filtering

In the previous section our study reinforced the importance of individual differences in learner motivation and knowledge (among other things) in making recommendations. In Section 2 we discussed two recommendation techniques: pure content-based filtering and a hybrid content-collaborative filtering technique. In this section we describe a simulation experiment to compare these two techniques to determine how the papers each recommends may affect the knowledge and motivation of the learner after the paper is 'consumed'. We provide only a brief overview: fuller details can be found in [16].

3.2.1 Simulation setup

For the purpose of the simulation, we first generated 500 artificial learners and used 50 papers related to data mining as the main learning materials. A pure content-based recommender system then delivered recommendations of 15 papers to each learner according to each individual learner model. Each artificial learner rated these papers according to their properties. After that, we generated 100 additional artificial learners, who became the target learners. Then, two recommendation techniques were applied for these target learners in order to evaluate their differences as well as performances. The first technique was the same pure content-based technique used with the first 500 artificial learners. The second technique used the hybrid-CF recommendation technique (content-based with collaborative filtering) described in Section 2.

3.2.2 Evaluation metrics and control variables

Normal metrics used in the recommender system community (e.g. the receiver operating characteristic (ROC), [4]) are not too relevant in recommending papers to learners. Metrics such as ROC are mainly adopted to test the 'satisfaction' of users in terms of item interestingness. However, in e-learning the most critical thing is to facilitate learning (not just to provide 'interesting' items). Therefore, we propose two new metrics:

- average learner *motivation* after recommendation.
- average learner *knowledge* after recommendation.

These should both go up if the recommended paper was appropriately chosen. In our simulation, we compared the percentage differences on these metrics between content-based recommendation and hybrid-CF recommendation.

We needed some way to simulate a variety of changes in motivation and knowledge after an artificial learner reads a paper. We also needed to capture the fact that some papers are more important (authoritative) than others. We thus created three control variables: x, representing the motivation change of a learner after reading a paper; and the pair (w_1, w_2), representing the knowledge gained by the learner after reading authoritative and non-authoritative papers. These were assigned differentially to different artificial learners to capture their different learning styles. There were four different levels of motivation change assigned to different artificial learners: $x = 1$ for fast motivation change (FMC), $x = 0.3$ for moderate (MMC), $x = 0.1$ for slow (SMC), and $x = 0$ for no change (NMC). Artificial learners could have one of eight pairs of knowledge change variables (w_1, w_2): $(1, 0)$; $(U[0, 1], 0)$; $(U[0, 0.3], 0)$; $(1, U[0, 0.3])$; $(U[0, 1], U[0, 0.3])$; $(U[0, 0.3], U[0, 0.3])$; $(1, U[0, 1])$; $(U[0, 1], U[0, 1])$; $(1, 1)$, where $U[0, y]$ means a random value generated from a uniform distribution between the two end points. For example, $(1, 0)$ indicates that only authoritative papers can fully increase a learner's knowledge of the content of a paper they have 'read'; $(1, 1)$ indicates that both authoritative and non-authoritative papers are equally weighted and can fully increase a learner's knowledge of the content of the paper; and $(U[0, 0.3], U[0, 0.3])$ means that for both authoritative and non-authoritative papers, the knowledge increases somewhere between 0 and 0.3 after a paper is 'read' (randomly generated in this range for each paper). The various conditions were divided equally among the artificial learners. Each group of experiments was repeated thirty times for statistical analysis.

3.2.3 Experimental results and discussion

Table 1 shows the results of the experimentation. The value shown in each cell is the pair of numbers representing the percentage difference between content-based recommendation and the hybrid-CF technique in terms of average learner knowledge and motivation gained (or lost). A negative value indicates that the content-based recommendation technique is better (on the metric being measured) than hybrid-CF. And a positive value represents the reverse situation. For example, the pair value (**0.65; 2.93**) represents that using hybrid-CF is 0.65% and 2.93% better than using content-based in terms of the average learner knowledge and motivation respectively. All results are checked by t-test for equal mean hypothesis (assuming different variance). A value in italics inside the table shows that the null hypothesis is not rejected (for $\alpha = 0.05$), or the difference between content-based and hybrid-CF is not statistically significant. If we exclude zero and italic values in Table 1, then there are 14 and 6 negative values for the difference of learner knowledge and motivation respectively, with the lowest value equal to -1.05% and -5.68%, respectively. And there are 8 and 12 positive values for the difference of learner knowledge and motivation, with the highest value equals to 1.20% and 19.38%, respectively.

These results are not that conclusive, but we can say that using hybrid-CF overall results in a lower performance in terms of learner average knowledge. However, since hybrid-CF usually needs lower computational cost than content-based recommendation and the performance loss is not big, hybrid-CF is still promising in an e-learning system. The results also shed some light on individual differences, so that if we know something about the motivation and knowledge changes likely for a particular real learner, we may be able to choose the recommendation technique most appropriate for him or her.

A final note on the usefulness of computer simulation in these circumstances is in order. Computer simulation and artificial learners have long been valuable assets in shedding light on issues in intelligent tutoring systems [17, 19, 20]. Although a simulation can only model aspects of an environment with real learners, it can

Table 1: The differences between content-based and hybrid-CF recommendation techniques (in percentage %).

(w_1, w_2)	FMC	MMC	SMC	NMC
$(1, 0)$	**0.59; 2.77**	$-0.70; -0.06$	$-0.77; -0.42$	$-0.43; 0.00$
$(U[0, 1], 0)$	**0.98; 7.97**	$-0.28; 3.85$	$0.21; -0.32$	**0.54; 0.00**
$(U[0, 0.3], 0)$	$-0.47; 15.15$	$-0.52; 0.75$	$0.33; -5.42$	**1.09; 0.00**
$(1, U[0, 0.3])$	$-0.57; 1.61$	$-1.05; -1.05$	$-0.76; -0.90$	$-0.29; 0.00$
$(U[0, 1], U[0, 0.3])$	$0.30; 8.09$	$-0.44; 3.41$	$0.22; -0.01$	**0.69; 0.00**
$(U[0, 0.3], U[0, 0.3])$	$-0.85; 19.38$	$-0.69; -0.19$	$0.06; -5.68$	**1.20; 0.00**
$(1, U[0, 1])$	**$-0.52; 1.13$**	$-0.96; -0.8$	$-0.82; -0.84$	$-0.27; 0.00$
$(U[0, 1], U[0, 1])$	**0.96; 7.36**	$-0.15; 4.68$	$0.16; -0.06$	**0.88; 0.00**
$(1, 1)$	$-0.34; 1.47$	$-0.69; -1.31$	$-0.47; -0.81$	$-0.43; 0.00$

provide a powerful tool for gaining insights in complex settings. Therefore, the simulation discussed here can provide guidance to our future work. In fact, we have designed a human subject study, which looks at some of the same issues we have studied here, focused on human rather than artificial learners. Details of this study can be found in [21]. Further studies are planned.

4 The ecological approach

The recommender system architecture and empirical studies we have discussed in this chapter illustrate the need to be sensitive to the unique characteristics of an e-learning domain, in particular the need to take into account pedagogical aspects, such as the learner's knowledge state, learning objectives, and motivational level, and the need to provide an appropriate sequencing of the papers recommended to the learner. Strong learner modeling is necessary, including the modeling of learner characteristics and goals, as well as the capture and interpretation of learner feedback about the papers they have read. It is also important to understand the relationship of the papers to each other and to determine how they relate to these pedagogical issues. Various techniques have been discussed in this chapter including annotating papers with explicit metadata provided by experts like tutors, attaching to papers opinions and feedback provided by learners, and using clustering techniques to find clusters of like-minded learners or similar papers. Data mining techniques also have a strong role to play: usage mining to find patterns in learner interactions, text mining to help categorize the papers according to actual contents, and possibly even web mining if the paper recommender system were embedded in a larger e-learning environment that included links to web resources.

The research paper recommender system has been one of the core inspirations for the ecological approach, an architecture recently proposed by Mc Calla [22] for the design of learner centered, adaptive, reactive e-learning systems. Generalizing from the goal of recommending papers for one learner from a paper repository, in the ecological approach the basic e-learning environment is assumed to possibly have many learners, many tutors, a large number of learning objects (papers, web pages, online exercises, quizzes, etc.), and a number of different applications that support learners including learning object recommenders (similar to the paper recommender), help or helper finders, tutoring systems, and so on.

In the ecological approach the e-learning system keeps a learner model for each learner, tracking characteristics of the learner and information about the learner's interactions with the learning objects each encounters. After a learner has interacted with a learning object, the learning object is 'tagged' with an instance of the learner model. The information in such a learner model instance can include:

- information about the learner, including cognitive, affective, and social characteristics and most importantly their goal(s) in accessing the content;
- information about the learner's perspectives on the content itself, including the learner's feedback on the content, the learner's knowledge of the content

(as determined, for example, by a test administered during the learner's interactions with the learning object);
- information about how the learner interacted with the content, including observed
  metrics such as dwell time, number of learner keystrokes, patterns of access;
- information about the technical context of use, including characteristics of the
  learner's software and hardware environment;
- information about the social context of use, including links to the learner model
  instances attached to learning objects previously encountered by the learner.

Over time, each learning object thus slowly accumulates learner model instances
that collectively form a record of the experiences of all sorts of learners as they have
interacted with the learning object. The collected learner model instances can then
be 'mined' for patterns about how learners interacted with the learning object, for
example that learners whose knowledge has been evaluated as weak did not have
long dwell times, or that learners with certain cognitive characteristics did well.
The sequence of learner model instances for a particular learner forms a 'learning
trail' through the learning object repository, and this trail can also reveal interesting
patterns of success and failure for the learner.

To illustrate this diagrammatically, Fig. 3 shows a learning object repository
with six learning objects and four learners who have been interacting with the
learning objects. As can be seen, each learning object is annotated with the learning
model instances of these various learners, sometimes two different instances for a
particular learner attached to the same object, representing two different times that
this learner has interacted with the same learning object. Within these instances, of
course, would be all the information the e-learning system had about the learner
and their interactions with the learning object. The sequence of learning object
instances for a particular learner would also be captured.

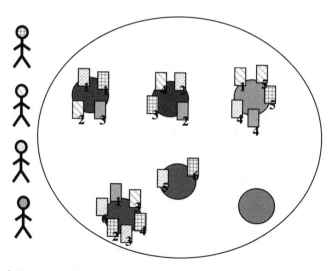

Figure 3: Learning object repository annotated with learner model instances.

There are, of course, a potentially huge number of patterns that can be found when mining learner behavior in these learner model instances. The key to finding meaningful patterns is the purpose (in the sense of [23]) for which the patterns are sought. Each such purpose places its own particular constraints on what patterns are meaningful, how to look for these patterns, and how to use what these patterns reveal in order to achieve the purpose. Thus, if the purpose is to recommend a specific learning object to a particular learner, this may require comparing this learner to other learners on important characteristics and then looking at how similar learners have evaluated (or been evaluated on) the content (and, moreover, the characteristics considered to be important are themselves determined by the learner's own goals). This is similar to the hybrid-CF technique that seems preferred for the paper recommender system discussed in Sections 2 and 3. On the other hand, if the purpose is to determine whether a learning object is now obsolete, this may require an examination of all learners' evaluations of the content, trying to extract temporal patterns in the evaluations that show how recent learners like or dislike the content. The key point is that it is the purpose that determines what information to use and how it is to be used. An ideal for a real time e-learning system is that this determination be made actively (in the sense of [24]) at the time the purpose is invoked, so that no a priori interpretation needs to be given to the information; however, time constraints on executing the data mining algorithms may mitigate against such real time computation in many circumstances.

In sum, then the ecological approach promotes the notion that information gradually accumulates about learning objects, the information is about the use of the learning object by real learners, and this information is interpreted only in the context of end use. The approach is ecological because over time the system is populated with more and more information, and something like natural selection based on purposes determines what information is useful and what is not. The ecological approach, with its emphasis on end-use context thus has a focus on pragmatics, rather than semantics. Dealing with pragmatics issues is a key to the usability of any system, and pragmatics is likely to be a major focus of research as semantic web research starts to move beyond the current focus on content towards usability and understanding the social context.

One of the difficulties in the ecological approach is getting information about learners to stock the learner models. Fortunately, experience in all sorts of learning environments (electronic and otherwise) have proven learners to be more willing to provide information to systems that will help them to learn than they have been to be so open with standard application systems, aimed at commercial profit for others, especially if they think that such information will make the e-learning system more effective and responsive to their own needs. They are also more likely to be willing to be monitored and evaluated, including to allow the testing of their knowledge and the diagnosis of their misconceptions. A learner's learning goals can be explicitly known because he or she will tell the e-learning system directly or they can be implicitly determined from the very fact that the learner is interacting with this particular e-learning system. For example a learner may want to learn about some subject, to find content relevant to a particular issue, to get help to overcome an impasse, and so on. E-learning systems themselves can also have explicit pedagogical goals that can be known and used in doing the purpose-based computations.

There are many possible applications for the ecological approach in e-learning. In addition to learning object recommender systems, such as the paper recommender discussed in this chapter or the educational recommender system discussed in [25], the ecological approach could underlie the design of:

- a group formation tool, to suggest to the learner a group of other learners relevant to solving a particular task or learning about a particular subject;
- a help seeker, to find another learner who can help the learner solve a problem he or she has encountered (as in I-Help [26]);
- a reminder system, to keep a learner updated with new information, say from the web, that is relevant to the learner's goals;
- an evaluation and assessment tool, to allow learners' interactions with an e-learning system to be studied by instructional and cognitive scientists, in particular to look at the experiences of all learners or particular types of learners with some educational content;
- an end-use learning object annotation system, to automatically derive educational content annotations from pre-established ontologies based on the experiences of the actual users of the content, and that can be parameterized by end use variables such as type of learner, success/failure of the educational content for each type of learner. A variant of this is possibility is the ability to refine, modify, or change pre-assigned metadata based on inferences from end use;
- an 'intelligent' garbage collection system, to determine the on-going relevance of educational content and, if necessary, to suggest modifications or even that it be deleted as no longer being useful to learners (e.g. as discussed in [27]).

Most of these applications would involve a large amount of purpose-based data mining of the learner model instances attached to the learning objects in the learning object repository.

The ecological approach is still more of research proposal than a proven architecture, and it stimulates the need to resolve many deep and interesting educational and computer science issues. In the ARIES Laboratory we are exploring some of these issues. Following up on the initial inspiration provided by the paper recommender system discussed in this chapter, we have a number of other projects underway that fit the ecological framework. In one of these projects we have developed the MUMS middleware [28] that allows the designers of the e-learning system to tailor modeling processes to look for particular kinds of patterns in raw data collected about learner interactions with learning objects in the repository. These patterns can then be fed into the higher-level applications that need information about the learners to make their decisions. We have collected detailed raw data about learner interactions with two fully online computer science courses (and the associated I-Help open peer forum used by learners to find help as they took the courses) over a couple of offerings of the courses. In one experiment with MUMS we then created MUMS modelers to mine this data so as to inform a proof of concept 'open modeling' prototype system that displays information about learners' progress to their instructors at several levels of time granularity [29].

We have also explored in [30] how to capture learner goals in 'purpose hierarchies' that provide 'purpose clichés' for doing active learner modeling. Such an approach to representing learner goals is highly useful, since the purpose cliché is not just a label but is a full-fledged procedure for actually using the goal information appropriately in the application. When this procedure is executed, all of the relevant information about the end-use context will be available and can be factored appropriately into the processing, and the purpose itself can make tough decisions about what is relevant or not to its goals.

Perhaps our most ambitious exploration of the ecological approach is within our University of Saskatchewan theme 3 of the LORNET project, a multi-pronged, multi-situated Canadian research project to develop sophisticated techniques for supporting learning object repositories [2]. In LORNET theme 3 we are exploring the application of artificial intelligence techniques to the design of e-learning tools to support learners interacting with a learning object repository. In particular we are looking at making learning objects into agents, and also adding into the learning object repository personal agents representing learners and tutors. These extended learning object repositories are thus distributed systems where the learners and tutors (through their proxy agents) and learning objects (now agents) all co-exist and carry out interactions with each other in support of the e-learning application and the learners and tutors using the application. Such large-scale distributed computation will allow the e-learning applications to be more reactive to the end-use context (since the agents will carry out their computations 'just in time' within this context). Such context-sensitivity is exactly the goal of the ecological approach and the active modeling perspective. Work is still relatively new on this vision for LORNET theme 3, although the MUMS system is an early spin-off.

5 Conclusion

In conclusion, many of the investigations underway in the ARIES Laboratory are exploring learner-centric e-learning systems, with a strong need for data mining of actual learner use of the systems. As shown in this chapter through the paper recommender system 'case study', this data mining must be able to make sense of learner behavior in context, preferably actively as the context evolves and changes. Knowledge of goals, both learner goals and the explicit or implicit pedagogical goals of the application doing the data mining, is critical to determining which patterns to look for. Knowledge of various pedagogical aspects of the learners, accessed through their learner models, provides further constraints on the data mining algorithms. The ecological approach outlined in the previous section *may* provide a unifying architecture in which to explore such active, context-dependent, data centered techniques for e-learning. But, there is much left to do before this hypothesis is proven.

Acknowledgments

We would like to acknowledge the Canadian Natural Sciences and Engineering Research Council for their financial support of this research, both through an on-going discovery grant to the second author and through their funding of the LORNET Network of Centres of Excellence. We also thank our colleagues at Hong Kong Polytechnic University and in the ARIES Laboratory at the University of Saskatchewan who have influenced our ideas substantially.

References

[1] Wiley, D.A. (ed.), *The Instructional Use of Learning Objects*, Agency for Instructional Technology and Association for Educational Communications of Technology: Bloomington, IN, 2002.

[2] Paquette, G., *The Learning Object Repository Network*, NSERC Networks of Centres of Excellence Research Proposal, Montréal, QC, 2003.

[3] Basu, C., Hirsh, H. & Cohen. W.W., Recommendation as classification: using social and content based information in recommendation. *Proc. of the Fifteenth National Conf. on Artificial Intelligence (AAAI/IAAI 1998)*, pp. 714–720, 1998.

[4] Herlocker, J.L., Konstan, J.A., Borchers, A. & Riedl, J., An algorithmic framework for performing collaborative filtering. *Proc. of the 22nd Annual Int. ACM SIGIR Conf. on Research and Development in Information Retrieval (SIGIR'99)*, Berkley, USA, pp. 230–237, 1999.

[5] Schein, A., Popescul, A., Ungar, L. & Pennock, D., Methods and metrics for cold-start recommendations. *Proc. of the 25th Annual Int. ACM SIGIR Conf. on Research and Development in Information Retrieval (SIGIR'02)*, Tampere, Finland, August 2002.

[6] Melville, P., Mooney, R. & Nagarajan, R., Content-boosted collaborative filtering for improved recommendations. *Proc. of the 18th National Conf. on Artificial Intelligence (AAAI-2002)*, Edmonton, Canada, July 2002, pp. 187–192, 2002.

[7] Basu, C., Hirsh, H., Cohen, W. & Nevill-Manning, C., Technical paper recommendations: a study in combining multiple information sources. *Journal of Artificial Intelligence Research*, **1**, pp. 231–252, 2001.

[8] Bollacker, K.D., Lawrence, S. & Giles, C.L., A system for automatic personalized tracking of scientific literature on the web. *Proc. ACM Conf. on Digital Libraries (DL-1999)*, pp. 105–113, 1999.

[9] Woodruff, A., Gossweiler, R., Pitkow, J., Chi, E. & Card, S.K., Enhancing a digital book with a reading recommender. *Proc. ACM CHI-2000*, pp. 153–160, 2000.

[10] McNee, S.M., Albert, I., Cosley, D., Gopalkrishnan, P., Lam, S.K., Rashid, A.M., Konstan, J.A. & Riedl, J., On the recommending of citations for research papers. *Proc. of ACM Int. Conf. on Computer Supported Collaborative Work (CSCW'02)*, pp. 116–125, 2002.

[11] Kohavi, R. & Provost, F., Applications of data mining to electronic commerce (Editorial of the special issue of Data Mining on Electronic Commerce). *Data Mining and Knowledge Discovery*, **5(1/2)**, 2001.

[12] Kobsa, A., Koenemann, J. & Pohl, W., Personalized hypermedia presentation techniques for improving online customer relationships. *The Knowledge Engineering Review*, **16(2)**, pp. 111–155, 2001.

[13] Schafer, J.B., Konstan, J.A. & Riedl, J., Electronic commerce recommender applications. *Data Mining and Knowledge Discovery*, **5(1/2)**, pp. 115–152, 2001.

[14] Tang, T. & McCalla, G., Smart recommendation for an evolving e-learning system. *Proc. Workshop on Technologies for Electronic Documents for Supporting Learning, Int. Conf. on Artificial Intelligence in Education (AIED-2003)*, Sydney, Australia, 2003.

[15] Vassileva, J. & Wasson, B., Instructional planning approaches: from tutoring towards free learning. *Proc. of European Conf. on Artificial Intelligence in Education*, Lisbon, Portugal, pp. 1–8, 1996.

[16] Tang, T.Y. & McCalla, G., Smart recommendation for an evolving e-learning system: architecture and experiment. *International Journal on E-Learning*, **4(1)**, pp. 105–129, 2005.

[17] Tang, T.Y. & Chan, K.C.C., Feature construction for student group forming based on their browsing behaviors in an e-learning system. *PRICAI 2002, Springer LNCS*, **2417**, pp. 512–521, 2002.

[18] Tang, T.Y. & McCalla, G., On the pedagogically guided paper recommendation for an evolving web-based learning system. *Proc. of FLAIRS-2004*, AAAI Press, 2004.

[19] Chan, T. & Baskin, A.B., Learning companion systems. *ITS 1990*, pp. 6–33, 1990.

[20] VanLehn, K., Ohlsson, S. & Nason, R., Application of simulated students: an exploration. *International Journal of Artificial Intelligence in Education*, **5(2)**, pp. 135–175, 1994.

[21] Tang, T.Y. & McCalla, G., Utilizing artificial learners to help overcome the cold-start problem in a pedagogically-oriented paper recommendation system. *Proc. of AH 2004: Int. Conf. on Adaptive Hypermedia and Adaptive Web-Based Systems*, pp. 245–254, 2004.

[22] McCalla, G., The ecological approach to the design of e-learning environments: purpose-based capture and use of information about learners. *Journal of Interactive Media in Education*, **(7)**, Special Issue on the Educational Semantic Web, 2004.

[23] Vassileva, J., McCalla, G. & Greer, J., Multi-agent multi-user modeling in I-Help. J. *User Modeling and User-Adapted Interaction*, Vol. 13, Kluwer Academic Publishers: Netherlands, pp. 179–210, 2003.

[24] McCalla, G., Vassileva, J., Greer, J. & Bull, S., Active learner modeling. *Proc. of ITS-2000: Intelligent Tutoring Systems*, Montréal, QC, Canada, Springer-Verlag: Berlin, Germany, pp. 53–62, 2000.

[25] Recker, M. & Wiley, D., A non-authoritative educational metadata ontology for filtering and recommending learning objects. *Interactive Learning Environments Journal: Special Issue on Metadata*, pp. 1–17, 2001.

[26] Greer, J., McCalla, G., Cooke, J., Collins, J., Kumar, V., Bishop, A. & Vassileva, J., The intelligent helpdesk: supporting peer-help in a university course. *Proc. of ITS 1998: Fourth Int. Conf. on Intelligent Tutoring Systems*, August, San Antonio, TX, Springer-Verlag: Berlin, Germany, pp. 494–503, 1998.

[27] Bannan-Ritland, B., Dabbagh, N. & Murphy, K., Learning object systems as constructivist learning environments: related assumptions, theories and applications. *The Instructional Use of Learning Objects* (online version), section 2.1, ed. D. Wiley, Association for Instructional Technology and Association for Educational Communications and Technology (AIT/AECT), 2000.

[28] Brooks, C., Winter, M., Greer, J. & McCalla, G., The massive user modelling system (MUMS). *Proc. of the Int. Conf. on Intelligent Tutoring Systems (ITS-04)*, Maceió, Brazil, pp. 635–645, 2004.

[29] Webster, A., Visual models of MUMS' events. Report on Senior Course Project, Department of Computer Science, University of Saskatchewan, Saskatoon, SK, 2005.

[30] Niu, X., McCalla, G. & Vassileva, J., Purpose-based expert finding in a portfolio management system. *Computational Intelligence*, **20(4)**, pp. 548–561, 2005.

Appendix A: Questionnaire used in the study in Section 3.1

Thank you for taking your time to participate in this short survey.

The purpose of this survey is to collect information about recommendations (research papers, tutorials, survey papers, magazine papers, resource links, etc.) for e-learning.

The scenario is as follows:

Assume that you are taking a graduate-level class where you need to read several papers (as what we usually did). For each topic taught in the class, you are required to read 2 or more reading materials (journal paper, workshop paper, etc.) recommended by the professor or your classmates.

Q1. Please number your preference in reading those materials if you are VERY interested in the topic being taught (please number with '1' for the most preferred one and '4' for the most disliked one):
( ) lecture note (power point slide)   ( ) related magazine article
( ) conference paper (5 to 10 pages)   ( ) journal paper (30 to 60 pages)

Q2. Please number your preference in reading those materials if you are NOT interested in the topic being taught (please number with '1' for the most preferred one and '4' for the most disliked one):
( ) lecture note (power point slide)   ( ) related magazine article
( ) conference paper (5 to 10 pages)   ( ) journal paper (30 to 60 pages)

Q3. Please number your preference in reading the same material with different presentations as follows (please number with '1' for the most preferred one and '4' for the most disliked one):
( ) paper with formal model only (theorem/equation)
( ) paper with algorithm only
( ) formal model + graphs/diagrams only   ( ) algorithm + graphs/diagrams only

Q4. Assume there are two papers with the same topic, same technical level and same length. The first paper was written by a well-known author and the other was written by an unknown author. Which one will you read first? (please mark 'X' on your choice)
( ) Paper by well-known author   ( ) Paper by unknown author

Q5. Assume there are two papers with the same topic (e.g. multi-agent planning) and the same technical level. The first paper was presented in a reputable international conference and the other was presented in an unknown local conference. Which one will you read first?
( ) Paper in a reputable conference   ( ) Paper in an unknown conference

Q6. Assume there are two related papers written by the same author with the same topic and technical level. The first paper was presented in a conference in 1998 and the second one is the revised version with some improvements and was presented in a similar conference in 2002. Which one will you read first?
( ) Paper in 1998   ( ) Paper in 2002

Q7. Assume your professor recommends three papers with the same technical level and the same topic. He/she asks you to read 2 papers only. Papers 1 and 2 solve the problem using method X. Paper 2 is a refined version of paper 1 with minor improvements. Paper 3 solves the problem by method Y (written by a different author and substantially different from X). Which two will you read?
( ) Papers 1 and 2   ( ) Papers 1 and 3   ( ) Papers 2 and 3

Q8. Assume your professor recommends an important but uninteresting paper. Besides, he/she also recommends an interesting paper, whose work is based on the first one. How will you read them?
( ) Read the interesting one and followed by the boring/important one
( ) Read the boring/important one and then read the interesting one
( ) Read the interesting one and then skim (read quickly) the boring/important one

Q9. Assume your professor recommends two review papers. Which one will you read?
( ) Deep review paper with many technical aspects
( ) Shallow review paper, yet with many interesting
    examples/illustrations/applications

Q10. Assume your professor recommends several important resources links (containing papers, conference presentations, tutorial slides, etc.) maintained by some 'big name' researchers in the area, which one of the following do you like?
( ) just list those links and you want to explore
    them by yourself
( ) you do not want to explore them by yourself, you hope to receive
    a more specific recommendation

CHAPTER 7

Applying web usage mining for the analysis of behavior in web-based learning environments

K. Becker, M. Vanzin, C. Marquardt & D. Ruiz
*Faculdade de Informática, Pontifícia Universidade
Católica do RS, Brazil.*

Abstract

The extraction of students' navigation patterns can be an invaluable tool to evaluate the design and effectiveness of web-based learning environments. Web usage mining (WUM) addresses the application of data mining techniques over web data in order to identify navigation patterns. WUM is a complex process composed of three core phases: data pre-processing, data mining, and pattern analysis. In this chapter, we describe the key issues and challenges involved in each of these phases, illustrating them in a case study developed at the distance education department of our university. We then describe two tools we have developed to address key problems faced in this experience. LogPrep is an extensible and customizable pre-processing tool. It provides operators that automate typical tasks performed in this phase, and which are easily combined according to the mining goals using a visual language. O3R provides functionality to support the retrieval and interpretation of navigation patterns, based on the use of a domain ontology. O3R associates semantics to patterns dynamically, as they are analyzed. The combination of these tools with traditional mining algorithms have presented good results, simplifying and speeding up the WUM process, and allowing domain-related people to assume a pro-active role.

1 Introduction

Web-based distance education requires the development of proper learning environments that organize a set of individual and group activities, together with the necessary resources. A web-based Learning Environment (WBLE) is designed as a set of pages, through which the course is delivered and knowledge is shared among students and instructors. Web-based course management infrastructures (e.g. WebCT [1], ATutor [2]) provide a collection of resources to compose a WBLE. Common functionality includes content management, communication (e.g. email, chat), assignment submission, and various accessories (e.g. blackboard, calendar, and quiz). WBLEs establish a distributed and virtual interaction model, which makes difficult the observation and evaluation of how learning resources available in the site are actually explored by students. Typical monitoring functionality includes access statistics, recently accessed pages, and participation in communication tools. However, the evaluation of WBLE adequacy and effectiveness in the learning process is hard and subjective. Thus, monitoring functionality is limited for analyzing students' perception of the WBLE and usage tendency.

The extraction of students' navigation patterns can be an invaluable tool to evaluate the design and effectiveness of a WBLE. Web usage mining (WUM) addresses the application of data mining techniques over web data in order to identify navigation patterns [3]. Large volumes of data are collected from daily operations, and recorded automatically by Web servers. The analysis of this data can reveal how the site is actually being used, providing insights on how to arrange contents and services to better fit its users' needs. WUM is an iterative and complex process, which includes the execution of specific phases, namely data pre-processing (used to select, clean and prepare the log raw data), data mining (application of mining algorithms), and pattern analysis (retrieval and interpretation of yielded patterns to seek for unknown and useful information). WUM has been extensively applied in e-commerce [4–7] and its benefits are being extended to other domains such as distance education [8–10].

WUM allows various types of analysis over the learning process and/or the learning environment, which can be roughly classified into two classes of behavior: usage and navigation. Usage behavior focuses on how resources are used to perform learning activities. It allows the characterization of students' learning processes and models, based on the set of contents they study, tools they use, and how these resources are combined to accomplish goals or acquire competences. The navigation behavior allows investigating (un)frequently used paths, groups of students with similar access characteristics, disorientation, among others. It should be pointed out, however, that applying WUM for the analysis of WBLE effectiveness is even harder than in the e-commerce domain [4]. In the e-learning context, objectives and site effectiveness cannot be easily defined, nor measured. Distinct students may reach a same learning goal by accessing different resources, with distinct frequencies and in a different order. Hence, learning site analysis and evaluation cannot be performed independently of learning process evaluation.

In this chapter, we describe the key issues and challenges involved in each WUM phase, illustrating them in a case study developed at PUCRS-Virtual, the distance education department of our university. We then describe two tools we have developed based on the lessons learned from this practical experience. LogPrep [11] is an extensible and customizable pre-processing tool, which provides operators that automate typical tasks performed in this phase. A visual language allows combining these operators easily in order to pre-process raw data according to mining goals. O3R [12] provides functionality to support the retrieval and interpretation of navigation patterns, based on the use of a domain ontology. O3R associates semantics to patterns dynamically, as they are analyzed. The combination of these tools with traditional mining algorithms have presented good results, simplifying and speeding up the WUM process, and allowing the active involvement of domain-related people.

The remainder of this chapter is structured as follows. Section 2 discusses each phase of the WUM process, and briefly describes some supporting environments. Section 3 describes the challenges faced in a real case study, and summarizes the lessons learned. The tools LogPrep and O3R are described in Sections 4 and 5, respectively. Section 6 discusses the contributions of these tools. Section 7 presents conclusions and future work.

2 The process of WUM

2.1 Pre-processing phase

Pre-processing involves performing several tasks with the aim of creating a user clickstream (i.e. sequence of page accesses), to be used as input in the data mining phase. The main data sources for that purpose are the Web server logs, which record all page accesses according to some standard format [13]. Typical information includes URL requested, IP that originated the request, request time-stamp, possibly user identification, etc. Pre-processing is the most difficult and laborious phase of the process due to the low quality of the available data, which is a consequence of missing data and disorganization [3, 13].

Moreover, there is a huge semantic gap between the events occurred in the site and how these are translated and recorded in the logs as a set of URLs [14]. When a user requests a page, actually several requests are issued to the server. These requests involve files (e.g. text, pictures, and style sheets) and programs that, together, compose the user's view of the page (i.e. page-view). Proxies, caching, dynamic pages and frame-based systems add additional difficulties [5].

Pre-processing tasks and challenges involved are thoroughly discussed in [13], and summarized below:

- *Data cleaning*: removes from the log the entries that are accessories to compose the page-views (e.g. graphics, style sheets).
- *User identification*: associates a URL request with the corresponding user. Most e-commerce applications are anonymous, thus requiring heuristics for inferring accesses of a same user.
- *Session identification*: groups all page references of a given user and breaks them up into user sessions (clickstream), according to time-oriented or referrer-based heuristics.
- *Path completion*: fills in page references that are missing due to caching.

- *Transaction identification*: breaks down sessions into smaller units, referred to as transactions or episodes. Various criteria are used, such as maximal forward reference, content transactions, auxiliary/content transactions, etc.
- *Data enrichment and integration*: consists in providing meaning to page references contained in the log, possibly by the integration of data from heterogeneous sources (e.g. various types of logs, organizational database, page contents, site topology, user data).

2.2 Data mining phase

Well-known mining techniques have been extensively applied in WUM to extract usage patterns [3, 7]. *Association rules* relate pages that most often are referenced together in a user session. In the WBLE domain, they can reveal which contents students tend to access together, or which combination of tools they explore during their learning processes. *Sequential patterns* describe related accesses in a specific order. It could reveal which content motivated the access to other contents, or how tools and contents are entwined in the learning process. *Clustering* groups together a set of items having similar characteristics. It is suitable for finding pages with similar contents, users with similar navigation behavior, or similar navigation sessions. *Classification* allows characterizing the properties of a group (e.g. user profiles, similar pages, learning sessions).

Most works in WUM do not focus on new mining techniques, but rather on how to efficiently combine existing techniques to explore new applications (e.g. adaptive sites and recommendation systems [7], site evaluation [4]).

2.3 Pattern analysis phase

An interesting pattern is valid, new, useful and simple to understand [15]. Pattern retrieval and pattern interpretation are the key issues in this phase. Mining techniques (e.g. association, sequence) typically yield a huge number of patterns, most of which are incomprehensible or uninteresting to users [16]. Pattern retrieval deals with difficulties involved in managing a large set of patterns. Pattern interpretation deals with pattern interestingness and relevance in regard to the domain. In the context of WUM, pattern interpretation challenges address the semantic gap between URLs and user events [10, 14].

Filtering is a common pattern retrieval approach. A filter defines the properties that patterns must present in order to fit in the analyst's current interest and search space. Filtering mechanisms can be applied in both mining and pattern analysis phases [16]. In the mining phase, the filter is embedded into the mining algorithm, restricting its output. In the analysis phase, it is used to interactively focus the search on potentially (un)interesting patterns, without having to re-mine data.

A filter can express statistical, conceptual and structural properties. Support and confidence are examples of objective statistical filters [17], which aim at reducing the number of rules yielded by mining algorithms. Beliefs expressing domain knowledge [5, 16] are examples of subjective statistical measures. The use of conceptual and structural properties in filtering is presented in [4, 18].

Conceptual properties in WUM are related to domain events, i.e. contents and services offered by a site, which are represented syntactically by URLs. There is an urge for approaches to provide semantics to these URLs. Semantic is most frequently provided by data enrichment performed in the pre-processing phase (e.g. [6, 19]). This approach is static, in the sense that a new perspective about the patterns may imply re-preprocessing data to enrich it differently. The Semantic Web opens new perspectives for this challenge [14, 20].

2.4 Support environments

Websift (formerly known as Webminer [5, 13]) and the environment named *WUM* [4, 6] are examples of dedicated suites for developing WUM applications. They provide the core pre-processing techniques discussed in Section 2.1. *Websift* offers various mining algorithms, whereas the environment *WUM* is restricted to a specific sequence technique. Both provide functionality for pattern analysis, based on visualization techniques and filtering mechanisms. The environment *WUM* includes MINT, a mining (filtering) language, and visualization functionality for navigation paths. *Websift* supports comparing patterns with domain beliefs about page contents and site structure. WUM can also be developed with the support of generic KDD (Knowledge Discovery on Databases) suites. Commercial and academic suites (e.g. Clementine [21], Intelligent Miner [22], Amadea [23] and Weka [24]) provide generic pre-processing functionality, which have to be complemented or extended by other applications for WUM purposes. They offer various mining algorithms, and filtering and visualization techniques for pattern interpretation.

3 WUM challenges in practice: a case study

This section describes a project developed at PUCRS-Virtual [9]. WebCT is the main infrastructure for the development of learning sites and management of distance courses at PUCRS-Virtual. The project focused on understanding WUM potential for analyzing the effectiveness of WBLEs. The goal was to model this problem as a WUM application, and to explore abstractions and types of patterns that could help in the analysis of site usage. The subject of study was an intensive extracurricular course, which lasted 11 days and involved 15 students, represented by a log containing 15,953 records.

We established a framework for interpreting page accesses in terms of the learning processes that motivate them. The framework helped us to understand the mapping of the learning environment into the technological infrastructure, the specifics of the course at hand and its site, as well as WebCT functionality. Emphasis was settled on how the learning resources were distributed and accessed in the site. This particular course was organized as a set of predefined activities (e.g. learning a concept). For each activity, the use of different resources was recommended or at least expected (e.g. learning objects, quiz, and communication tools). The web site was designed aiming that all required resources were conveniently accessible for the ensemble of planned activities.

Our framework also defines a paradigm for the search of navigation patterns. It focuses on the actions taken by students over the technological resources available to perform each planned activity. Hence, each planned learning activity is used as a unit for guiding and orienting the WUM process.

This application was exploratory, and the various tasks performed are described in next sections in terms of WUM phases. The lessons learned, which motivated the development of new tools to support WUM, close this section.

3.1 Pre-processing phase

In this phase, we basically applied over the web server log the techniques presented in [13] according to the defined framework. However, specific types of analyses demanded adaptation of these techniques, such as the concept of learning session [8, 9], and different types of transactions. For instance, a *learning session* includes all accesses underlying the execution of one learning activity, representing a time span that ranges from minutes to days, possibly implying that students logged in and out several times. Pre-processing techniques were employed with the support of the Intelligent Miner (IM) suite, in combination with specific purpose applications we developed using embedded SQL and Java.

Enriching data with semantics was the most difficult task of this phase. In the WebCT, most page accesses actually correspond to script executions. URLs are incomprehensible and do not provide any hint about their relationship to learning resources. Classical techniques for capturing site topology and content (e.g. crawler, information retrieval) could not be employed. We manually mapped each URL to the corresponding event. We also developed a taxonomy of events. For example, *send-email* and *read-email* were generalized as *email*, which was generalized as *communication*. This taxonomy was explored in subsequent phases of the process.

Pre-processing techniques were combined differently to produce various datasets, according to the analysis goals established. For instance, if the goal is to find correlation of contents in an activity, we can employ the learning session technique, and divide sessions using the content transaction technique. On the other hand, if the goal is to evaluate the paths between correlated resources, we can use a conventional session technique, without breaking sessions into transactions.

3.2 Data mining phase

Association and sequence mining techniques were employed with the support of the IM suite. According to the activity-oriented approach, we applied filters constraining the presence of specific resources, which were either expected or unexpected. We also sought for generalized patterns [25] (e.g. *Hypertext.pdf* → *Communication* is the generalized pattern of *Hypertext.pdf* → *Chat*, if the taxonomy defines *Communication* as the generalization of *Chat*).

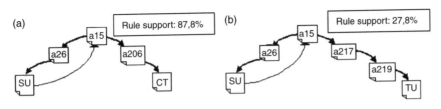

Figure 1: Pattern examples.

Several experiments were run using datasets pre-processed differently, and for different activities. Figure 1 illustrates two sequential patterns extracted for examining site design in terms of available paths among commonly used resources. These patterns represent sequences of accesses that include WebCT submission functionality (SU). This page is reached after accessing two auxiliary pages (pages that provide links for other pages), depicted in the picture using numbered labels (a15, a26). After that, they return to auxiliary page a15.

In Pattern (a) students then proceed to a chat page (CT), whereas in Pattern (b), they head towards the submission tutorial (TU). These patterns possibly reveal a problem related to the submission functionality. Because students have difficulty on its use, very frequently they cancel the submission and seek for help (chat or tutorial). The stronger support of Pattern (a) suggests it represents the most common behavior. Pattern (b) shows a more autonomous behavior with regard to the same problem. However, from a site design perspective, there is no indication of the existence of such a tutorial in the submission page. So perhaps students became aware of its existence by discussing through the chat, or browsing in the site. This is an example of how difficult it is to separate design and learning issues.

3.3 Pattern analysis phase

The goal of this project was to illustrate extractable patterns, and to understand their power if used as an instrument for site usage analysis. Hence, developing this phase to produce real knowledge was beyond the scope of this project. We limited pattern analysis to various discussions with a domain expert. At each interaction, we would show preselected rules yielded by our experiments. Based on her extensive knowledge of the course at hand and WebCT infrastructure, the expert would suggest possible pattern interpretations, such as the ones provided for the patterns in Fig. 1. To aid her comprehension, we would show at first generalized patterns, and when an interesting pattern was identified, we would search for more specific related patterns and deepen the discussion. IM did not provide adequate support for these tasks. Moreover, frequently questions raised by the expert would imply in running new experiments, producing new rules to be validated.

It should be pointed out that the distance education department staff was excited about the results, and willing to participate in a more thorough evaluation. However, there was no available domain expert who could dedicate the time required, particularly given the huge number of patterns.

3.4 Lessons learned

The project yielded very interesting results, but confirmed that in practice the extraction of interesting patterns is hard. Most difficulties were related to pre-processing and pattern analysis. The main lessons learned are described below.

3.4.1 Pre-processing issues
Although most e-commerce techniques could be transposed to the education domain, different approaches were also necessary (e.g. learning session). WUM-dedicated environments provide the core techniques summarized in [13], and implementing variations is not necessarily easy, if possible. KDD suites are difficult to extend to include WUM specific algorithms, and imply a lot of programming.

This application was exploratory: different types of analysis were interactively defined and for each of them, the process was developed according to the goals settled. A key issue was the alignment of mining goals with a set of pre-processing techniques that organize raw data such that intended type of patterns were extractable. Combining all required techniques with the support of different, non-integrated applications was very time-consuming, and resulted in a difficulty for creating and managing the data sets.

The structure and content of a site is a critical input to overcome the semantic gap between site events and URLs. WebCT is mostly based on dynamic pages, and its internal structure makes very difficult to add semantics to URLs. Moreover, the developed framework enabled to considered not only the site itself, but also the characteristics of the overall learning process that guides students' actions. All this knowledge was used to semantically enrich the clickstream, in a laborious, time consuming and error-prone process. However, it was implicitly embedded in the dataset, and could not be explored in the subsequent phases.

3.4.2 Pattern analysis issues
Pattern interpretation can only be performed if the meaning of patterns is intuitive. This problem is typically addressed using static enrichment, performed in the pre-processing phase. In practice, however, very frequently the result of a certain phase suggests new ways of enriching data or new types of analysis. This may imply a return to the pre-processing phase to produce new data sets. The limitations of static semantic enrichment is a major lesson learned.

The overwhelming number of rules yielded by the chosen algorithms is another key issue. This problem was worsened by the use of a taxonomy to produce generalized patterns. Each experiment yielded thousands of rules, most of them redundant or representing domain common sense. Raising the support threshold reduced the size of output, as much as its interest. Explicitly represented domain knowledge is invaluable for filtering rules that are potentially relevant for interpretation.

Filtering reduced the number or rules, by focusing on certain resources (un)-planned for each activity, but with a number of disadvantages. First, this strategy requires knowledge about course planning. Second, there was a lot of redundancy among patterns yielded by different filtering, and the suite adopted provided no support for consolidating the results. Explicit domain knowledge could support filtering definition and the integration of results.

Providing rules at different abstraction levels revealed itself invaluable for establishing a closer dialog with domain experts. However, the KDD suite lacked support to relate generalized rules with their corresponding specific ones, as well as to establish other types of relationships.

We interacted with the staff of PUCRS-Virtual during the whole project, but carried out most tasks of the process ourselves. After an initial project set-up for understanding the domain and business goals, the only interaction with PUCRS-Virtual staff was during pattern analysis tasks. Each of these interactions would trigger another cycle of the process. The knowledge of the domain-related people is essential for all WUM phases, and they should be given the proper means to be as actively involved as possible.

4 LogPrep: a customizable pre-processing tool

From the lessons learned, we derived a set requirements for designing LogPrep. It should: (1) support the automation of pre-processing tasks; (2) provide alternative operators, corresponding to different techniques used to accomplish a same task; (3) be extensible and customizable in terms of the provided operators; (4) support the easy combination of operators to prepare data according to different mining goals; and (5) support the active involvement of domain-related people by providing appropriate concepts and means to manipulate them. By domain-related people we refer to people with knowledge about the domain (in our case, the learning environment, such as designers, instructors), and a few skills on WUM-related issues.

LogPrep supports the visual definition, reuse and execution of configurations of pre-processing operators. An *operators' configuration* defines a sequence of pre-processing tasks to be applied over the data, where each operator defines a specific technique to execute a task. An operator is an algorithm that implements a technique proposed in the literature for a task (e.g. time-based session) or a new approach (e.g. learning session). The operators' configuration concept allows addressing pre-processing as the activity of combining task-oriented techniques in accordance with mining goals. Consider the examples provided in Fig. 2. Each configuration is suitable for attaining specific mining goals, and the difference between them is simply how the transaction identification task is performed (auxiliary transaction vs. content transaction operators).

A visual language addresses usability and user-friendliness issues related to the definition and execution of operators' configurations. It allows users to intuitively regard the pre-processing phase as a simple visual configuration of task-level operators. Hence, LogPrep does not require advanced skills or extensive training from users. Since each operator automates a task, users can experiment different configurations and observe extracted patterns. If results are not satisfactory, the configuration can be easily altered (add/change/remove operators), resulting in a significant reduction of time and effort. It should be stressed that users are not guided in

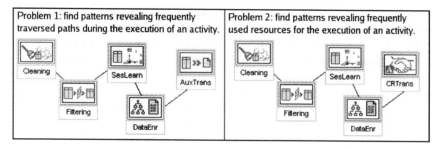

Figure 2: Configuration examples.

the configuration activity, given that expressing knowledge that precisely characterizes a class of problems is not trivial [26]. Nevertheless, LogPrep contributes to this problem in two ways. First, it highlights all tasks that can be applied and combined, with their variance in terms of operators. Second and more important, successful configurations can be documented and made available for later reuse through the concept of *configuration template*. By selecting and refining a configuration template that addresses goals similar to the ones of the problem at hand, users can easily prepare data for the extraction of potentially interesting patterns.

The remainder of this section summarizes the striking features of the current prototype, developed in Java. Further details can be found in [11].

4.1 Configuration language and configuration template

Figure 3 illustrates the user interface of the prototype. The visual configuration language supports all functionality related to the definition and execution of operators' configurations by direct manipulation of operators in the *Configurations Area*. It is a graph-based language, where the nodes represent the operators and the links, the flow of data execution. Hence, each node represents an execution unit that receives a dataset as input, processes data according to its role and parameters, and outputs a transformed dataset. This approach can be found in tools such as Clementine and Amadea. The visual language allows users to: (1) define an operators' configuration, which includes the operators, their parameters and their order; (2) load various types of inputs (e.g. log, enrichment data); and (3) export data. Operators are selected from the ones available in the *Tasks Area*. Two execution modes are provided for a defined configuration: *complete*, where all operators are applied in the defined sequence and a final dataset is produced; or *step-by-step*, where the transformed dataset can be inspected right after each operator is applied.

An operators' configuration can be saved as a template. A configuration template represents successful pre-processing for a well-defined problem class, a procedure for a specific type of analysis, etc. The *Templates Area* allows documenting, searching, inspecting and retrieving templates. The user loads a selected template in the Configurations Area and edit it to create a new configuration.

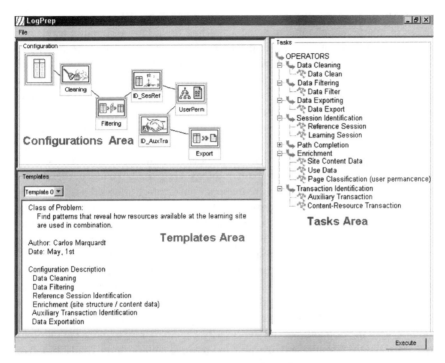

Figure 3: LogPrep user interface.

4.2 Customization features

The extension and customization of LogPrep must be in charge of someone with technical programming skills, referred to as the tool administrator. Operators are executable components that have to be programmed in a compatible language (e.g. Java). The tool administrator customizes LogPrep using a set-up file describing in XML: (1) the tasks, their respective operators, and the components that implement them; (2) rules establishing valid connections and execution flows between operators. When LogPrep is launched, it reads this set-up file and loads the operators, displaying them in the Tasks Area. This mechanism allows the inclusion of new operators for the development of other pre-processing tasks (or the execution of tasks according to different techniques), or even a complete set of operators, targeted at the domain at hand.

5 OR3: ontology-based rule rummaging and retrieval tool

O3R focuses on support for the pattern analysis phase, according to the following requirements: (1) it should support both pattern retrieval and pattern interpretation in an integrated manner; (2) patterns analysis should be based on domain events, disregarding their syntactical representation in terms of URLs; (3) events should be easily interpreted and manipulated according to various abstraction levels and dimensions of interest, without implying re-processing raw data or re-mining it; (4) it should be possible to establish and maintain various types of relationships between related patterns; (5) domain knowledge should be explicitly represented and exploited by both tool functionality and user; and (6) it must support the active involvement of domain-related people.

O3R functionality encompasses *pattern rummaging*, *pattern filtering* and *pattern clustering*. The former is targeted at pattern interpretation, whereas the later two focus on pattern retrieval. The striking feature of O3R is that all functionality is based on the availability of the domain ontology, composed of concepts describing domain events, into which URLs are mapped. This feature allows the retrieval and interpretation of conceptual patterns, i.e. patterns formed of concepts, in opposition to physical patterns, composed of URLs. Hence, users can interactively explore pattern semantics during analysis activities, according to distinct abstraction levels and dimensions of interest. This approach enables to overcome the limitations of static semantic enrichment. All functionality is based on direct manipulation of visual representations of conceptual patterns and ontology, thus enabling a pro-active involvement of domain users with minimal training and limited technical skills. Since the ontology makes the domain knowledge explicit, users are expected to be familiar with the domain, but not necessarily experts. Users explore the ontology to learn about the domain, and interpret and retrieve patterns more easily, based on domain characteristics.

Current implementation of O3R is limited to sequential patterns extracted according to the sequential algorithm described in [25]. It assumes that these patterns were extracted from a dataset resulting from a typical pre-processing phase. Due to the availability of the domain ontology, no particular data enrichment is assumed for this data set in the pre-processing phase. For the same reason, the mining algorithm should not generate generalized patterns.

5.1 Ontology representation

O3R assumes the representation of domain events in two levels: conceptual and physical. At the physical level, events are represented by URLs. The conceptual level is represented by the domain ontology. The ontology is composed of concepts, representing either a content of a web page, or a service available through a page. Concepts are related to each other through hierarchical or property relationships. A hierarchical relationship connects a descendant concept to an ascendant one. Two types of hierarchical relationships are considered: *generalization*, in which the generalized concept is ascendant of a specialized one; and *aggregation*, in which the ascendant represents the whole assembly and the descendent represents one of its parts. Every concept has at most one ascendant. Property relationships represent arbitrary associations that connect a subject to an object.

URLs are mapped into ontology concepts according to two dimensions: service and content. An URL can be mapped into one service, one content or both, in which

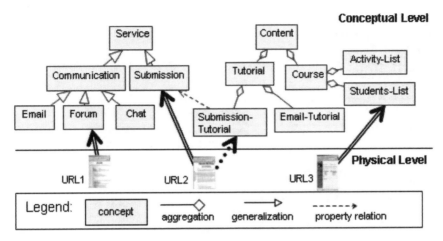

Figure 4: Mapping URLs to semantic concepts.

case the predominant dimension must be defined. A same concept can be used in the mapping of various URLs. Figure 4 illustrates this ontology structure by describing the semantics of a WBLE. Services include chat, email, submission, authentication, etc. Content is related to the material available in the site, or the subject related to some service. In Fig. 4, *URL1* was mapped to the service concept *Forum*; *URL2* was mapped to both service *Submission-Tutorial* and content *Submission* concepts, where service dimension was defined as predominant; and *URL3* was mapped to the content concept *Students-List*.

5.2 Conceptual pattern representation

Since no semantic enrichment is assumed in the pre-processing phase, mined patterns are sequences of URLs. O3R uses the mapping between the physical and conceptual events to present these physical patterns as a sequence of the corresponding concepts, i.e. the *conceptual patterns*. Users manipulate conceptual patterns using the provided functionality. For their analyses, users always have to establish a *dimension of interest*, which can be *content*, *service* or *content/service*. Considering the ontology of Fig. 4, the physical pattern *URL1 → URL2* corresponds to the conceptual pattern *Forum → Submission* according to the both service dimension and content/service dimension (where the predominant dimension is used). The physical pattern *URL2 → URL3*, according to content dimension, corresponds to *Submission-Tutorial → Students-List*.

Conceptual patterns can be interpreted according to different abstraction levels by exploring the hierarchical relationships. For example, the pattern *URL2 → URL3* can be interpreted as *Submission-Tutorial → Students-List, Tutorial → Students-List, Tutorial → Course, Content → Content*, and so on.

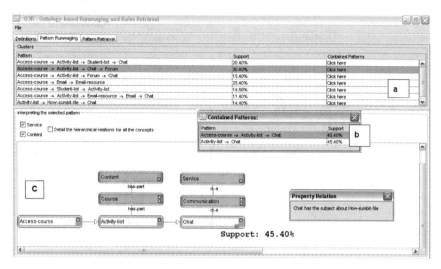

Figure 5: Pattern rummaging interface.

5.3 Pattern rummaging

Interpretation activities are supported through concept-oriented interactive rummaging. Rummaging explores the ontology to: (1) represent patterns in a more intuitive form, thus reducing the gap between URLs and site events; (2) allow pattern analysis according to different dimensions of interest and abstraction levels; (3) establish different relationships between patterns. Figure 5 displays the pattern rummaging interface, in which various representations of conceptual patterns are depicted. This interface is divided into three areas: *Clustering* (Figure 5a), *Contained Patterns* (Figure 5b) and *Rummaging* (Figure 5c). To rummage around a pattern in the Rummaging area, the user chooses a pattern (from the Clustering area, Contained Patterns area, or Filtering Interface), and defines a dimension of interest. In the example, the user has selected the service/content dimension, thus resulting in the conceptual pattern *Access.course → Activity-list → Chat*. By changing the dimension of interest to service, this same pattern would be visualized as *Access.course → Visualize-Information → Chat*.

Two groups of operations allow to explore ontology relationships: *detailing* and *drill*. Figure 5c illustrates the resultant pattern after using detailing operations to better understand the events represented by the pattern. The user related pattern concepts *Activity-List* and *Chat* to their respective generalizations, and queried a property relationship of which *Chat* is the subject.

Drill operations are similar to roll-up and drill-down in online analytical processing, and they are a means to establish relationships among patterns in different abstraction levels. Roll-up is used to obtain a generalized pattern, whereas drill-down finds the specific related patterns. Figure 6 illustrates a generalized pattern obtained by rolling up the pattern of Fig. 5c (concept *Chat* was rolled up to

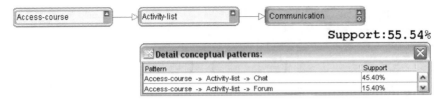

Figure 6: Generalized and specific conceptual patterns.

Communication), with the respective support. Figure 6 also presents a window displaying the patterns found using drill-down. This approach can be contrasted with the generation of generalized rules during the mining phase [25], which results in the generation of a huge set of unrelated rules. In our approach, generalized rules are created on-demand, and it is always possible to relate them to the respective specific rules. Further details can be found in [12].

5.4 Pattern clustering

Retrieval functionality is targeted at managing large volumes of rules. The basic idea is to reduce the interpretation search space by finding sets of related rules. Clustering groups related rules in different sets, such that the analyst can set focus for further inspection on a whole set of rules (or discard them all), as depicted in the Fig. 5. Hence, clustering and rummaging are closely integrated. O3R prototype is currently limited to the maximal sequence criterion to group rules that are subsequences of a maximal sequence [25], but criteria are possible.

5.5 Pattern filtering

Filtering is another mechanism in O3R to manage the elevated number of rules, establishing a relationship among rules that match a same filter. Users have the support of the ontology to understand the domain and establish event-based filters. Filters are quite expressive, in that it is possible to define conceptual, structural and statistical constraints. Users are not required to learn any complicated syntax, because filters are defined visually by direct manipulation of domain concepts and structural operators. Two filtering mechanisms are provided, referred to as *equivalence filtering* and *similarity filtering*. Filtering and rummaging are closely integrated: users choose a filtered pattern to rummage around, which possibly leads to a new filter definition, and so on.

5.5.1 Filter definition
Conceptual constraints define the interest on patterns involving specific domain events, at any abstraction level. Structural constraints establish an order among events (i.e. start, end, and be followed by). Statistical constraints refer the support of sequential rules. Figure 7 shows O3R filtering interface. The domain ontology

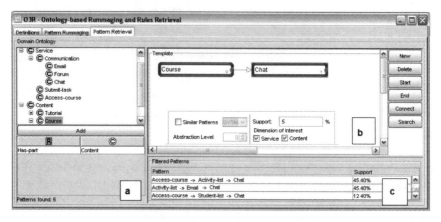

Figure 7: Pattern retrieval interface.

is represented graphically on the left most window (Fig. 7a), which displays all concepts and relationships. To establish conceptual constraints, the user chooses concepts from the ontology and places them at the *Filter Definition* area (Fig. 7b). He then uses the structural operators (buttons at the right of the Filter Definition area) to organize concepts. In the example, the user is interested in sequential rules involving any event classified as *Course*, (immediately or not) followed by the *Chat* event, with at least 5% of support.

5.5.2 Equivalence filtering
The filtering mechanism examines all conceptual patterns, verifying whether each one of them meets the statistical, conceptual and structural constraints of the filter. The statistical constraint is verified by comparing the pattern support with the support threshold. A conceptual constraint states all concepts that must appear in a rule. In the equivalence filtering, a concept is contained in a conceptual pattern either if it explicitly composes the pattern, or one of its descendants does. Structural constraints verify whether these concepts are in the correct order. Figure 7c illustrates possible patterns according to the equivalence filtering mechanism.

5.5.3 Similarity filtering
Similarity filtering extends equivalence filtering. Similarity is defined in terms of the distance between concepts in the ontology, considering the hierarchical relationships [27]. The user must provide the *minimum similarity threshold* and the *ancestor scope level* (ASL), i.e. the farthest common ancestor in the hierarchy to be considered for similarity. In the example of Fig. 7, if ASL is defined as 1, *Communication* is the farthest common ancestor of *Chat*, and therefore, *Forum* is a similar concept. Each filtered pattern has a similarity measure, calculated according to the similarity of individual concepts and structural constraints. Figure 8 exemplifies

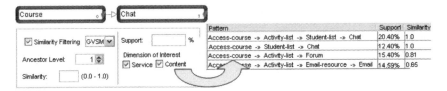

Figure 8: Similarity filtering.

similarity filtering. Patterns with similarity equal to 1 are equivalent to the filter, whereas the others are similar in some degree.

6 Discussions

LogPrep and O3R have been used in combination with traditional mining algorithms for developing WUM applications in our research group. We are also developing experimental evaluations with the staff of PUCRS-Virtual to confirm our claim that these tools are suitable for domain-related people.

LogPrep was tested by seven users with background in computers in education and mathematics. As a preparation, we gave them a 30 min talk about WUM and pre-processing, and developed two training exercises. Then, they were given five mining goals statements, for which they had to develop the corresponding configurations. They were able to establish these five rather complex configurations by themselves, without a single mistake. They all also recognized that two exercises involved slightly different mining goals, and that they could develop a configuration by modification of a previously developed one. They highlighted as advantages: the user friendliness of the visual language, the easiness of structuring the configuration at task level, and the possibility of reusing configuration templates.

LogPrep is suitable for both exploratory and plan-based applications. In exploratory applications, users add, change and remove operators to try out different results, and reapply it over the same data set. Plan-based applications can benefit from configuration templates, which can be applied with the same purpose over different data, possibly with different parameters. Table 1 summarizes the advantages of LogPrep in accordance with the design requirements it meets.

O3R evaluation is currently limited to the demonstration of its functionality to the same expert who participated in the previous experience (Section 3.3). For that purpose, we developed the domain ontology, reproduced one of the experiments yielding a set of sequential patterns, and enacted a typical interaction occurred at that time. We started by showing the clusters, from which the expert selected a rule for rummaging. She detailed the pattern, changed the dimension of interest, rolled the pattern up to generalize it, and then drilled it down to find related patterns, which she selected again for rummaging, and so on. From the insight gained through rummaging, she showed interest on patterns with specific properties, which were filtered with the support of the ontology. She then selected some filtered patterns

Table 1: LogPrep advantages.

Requirement	Advantage
Automation of pre-processing tasks	Reduction of the time and effort spent in pre-processing, as well as errors.
Combination of operators at task level	Easier alignment of mining goals and required data pre-processing.
Alternative operators to accomplish a same task	Flexibility for preparing data as required.
	Easier creation and management of data sets due to the use of a single tool.
Extensibility and customization	Environment can be fully adapted to different contexts and domains.
Active involvement of domain-related people	Direct translation of WBLE evaluation goals into data pre-processing requirements.

Table 2: O3R advantages.

Requirement	Advantage
Close integration of interpretation and retrieval	Support for exploratory and hypothesis-based analysis.
Event-based analysis	Pattern intuitiveness.
	Easiness for identifying interesting patterns.
Interpretation of events according different perspectives	Dynamic enrichment of data.
	No re-execution of previous phases.
Support for various types of relationships among patterns	Reduced number of rules.
	Identification of rules with similar properties.
	Ability to relate generalized and specific patterns.
	Easy identification of redundant patterns.
Explicit domain knowledge representation	Support for developing analysis tasks.
	Deeper insight of the domain.
Active involvement of domain-related people	Direct identification of useful and interesting patterns for the domain.

and rummaged them, leading to the definition of new filters, exploring all the inter-activity provided by O3R. In comparison with her previous experience, for which almost no support was provided, the expert highlighted the following advantages: interactivity, intuitive pattern representation, visualization of patterns according to various perspectives, ability to establish various types of relationships, and support provided by domain ontology to perform analysis. An empirical validation with a larger sample of users is under definition. Table 2 summarizes O3R advantages in accordance with its design requirements.

O3R supports both exploratory and hypothesis-based pattern analysis. The for-mer is suitable when the expert does not know what to expect and wishes to explore relationships among concepts and among patterns to identify interesting patterns. In exploratory analysis, filtering is most frequently a consequence of the insight pro-vided by rummaging. Hypothesis-based analysis focuses on filtering for defining hypotheses, and rummaging for interpreting results.

7 Conclusions and future work

In this chapter, we discussed and illustrated in a real case study the challenges of applying WUM in the WBLE domain. We then described two tools developed in response to critical issues faced in that experience. A common characteristic of these tools is that they are aimed at allowing an active involvement of domain-related people in different phases of WUM. Preliminary results display evidences that this requirement was suitably achieved. This is a crucial feature if WUM is to be used in complement with monitoring functionality to understand and evaluate students' behavior.

Our goal is to integrate these tools in a complete framework targeted at identi-fying learning processes and models, understanding of site usage, and evaluating WBLE effectiveness. For that purpose, the framework must support the applica-tion of various mining techniques (with the corresponding pre-processing) and analysis of yielded models. Currently we are extending and evaluating O3R and studying various issues involved in the application of clustering to understand stu-dents' behavior. O3R can be easily extended to support other mining techniques (e.g. association), as well as other algorithms for sequential patterns (e.g. [6]). Other limitations of O3R must be addressed, particularly the constraints upon the ontology structure and on the semantic mapping of URLs. Currently, Log-Prep is being extended to include pre-processing tasks and operators required for clustering. Domain-ontology is considered for two purposes: defining sim-ilarity between learning behaviors and for the easy interpretation of learning clusters.

Future research includes, among others, the definition of the integration archi-tecture for the framework, semantic enrichment through the semantic web as well as additional mining techniques (e.g. classification).

References

[1] WebCT, http://www.webct.com

[2] ATutor, http://www.atutor.ca

[3] Srivastava, J., Cooley, R., Deshpande, M. & Tan, P.N., Web usage mining: Discovery and applications of usage patterns from web data. *SIGKDD Explorations*, **1(2)**, pp. 12–23, 2000.

[4] Spiliopoulou, M., Web usage mining for web site evaluation. *Communications of the ACM*, **43(8)**, pp. 127–134, 2000.

[5] Cooley, R., The use of web structure and content to identify subjectively interesting web usage patterns. *ACM Transactions on Internet Technology*, **3(2)**, pp. 93–116, 2003.

[6] Berendt, B. & Spiliopoulou, M., Analysis of navigation behaviour in web sites integrating multiple information systems. *VLDB Journal*, **9(1)**, pp. 56–75, 2000.

[7] Mobasher, B., Web usage mining and personalization (chapter 15). *Practical Handbook of Internet Computing*, ed. M.P. Singh, Chapman Hall/CRC/ Press: Boca Raton, FL, 2004.

[8] Zaïane, O.R., Web usage mining for a better web-based learning environment. *CATE: Proc. of the Conf. on Advanced Technology for Education*, Banff, Alberta, pp. 60–64, 2001.

[9] Machado, L. & Becker, K., Distance education: A web usage mining case study for the evaluation of learning sites. *ICALT: Proc. of the Int. Conf. on Advanced Learning Techs*, IEEE Computer Society, pp. 360–361, 2003.

[10] Becker, K. & Vanzin, M., Discovering interesting usage patterns in web-based learning environments. *Proc. of the Int. Workshop on Utility, Usability and Complexity of e-Information Systems*, pp. 57–72, 2003.

[11] Marquardt, C.G., Becker, K. & Ruiz, D.D.A., A pre-processing tool for web usage mining in the distance education domain. *IDEAS: Proc. of the 8th Int. Database Engineering and Applications Symposium*, pp. 78–87, 2004.

[12] Vanzin, M. & Becker, K., Exploiting knowledge representation for pattern interpretation. *Proc. of the Workshop on Knowledge Discovery and Ontologies – KDO*, Pisa, Italy, pp. 61–71, 2004.

[13] Cooley, R., Mobasher, B. & Srivastava, J., Data preparation for mining world wide web browsing patterns. *Knowledge and Information Systems*, **1(1)**, pp. 5–32, 1999.

[14] Berendt, B., Hotho, A. & Stumme, G., Towards semantic web mining. *ISWC: Proc. of the First Int. Semantic Web Conference on The Semantic Web*, Springer-Verlag: London, UK, pp. 264–278, 2002.

[15] Fayyad, U., Piatetsky-Shapiro, G. & Smyth, P., The kdd process for extracting useful knowledge from volumes of data. *Communications of the ACM*, **39(11)**, pp. 27–34, 1996.

[16] Silberschatz, A. & Tuzhilin, A., What makes patterns interesting in knowledge discovery systems. *IEEE Transactions on Knowledge and Data Engineering*, **8(6)**, pp. 970–974, 1996.

[17]   Hipp, J. & Güntzer, U., Is pushing constraints deeply into the mining algorithms really what we want?: an alternative approach for association rule mining. *SIGKDD Explorations*, **4(1)**, pp. 50–55, 2002.

[18]   Klemettinen, M., Mannila, H., Ronkainen, P., Toivonen, H. & Verkamo, A.I., Finding interesting rules from large sets of discovered association rules. *CIKM: Proc. of the Third Int. Conf. on Information and Knowledge Management*, ACM Press, pp. 401–407, 1994.

[19]   Dai, H. & Mobasher, B., Using ontologies to discover domain-level web usage profiles. *2nd Semantic Web Mining Workshop at ECML/PKDD*, 2002.

[20]   Oberle, D., Berendt, B., Hotho, A. & Gonzalez, J., Conceptual user tracking. *AWIC: Proc. of the Web Intelligence, First Int. Atlantic Web Intelligence Conf.*, pp. 155–164, 2003.

[21]   Clementine, http://www.spss.com/clementine/

[22]   Miner, I., http://www-3.ibm.com/software/data/iminer/fordata/index.html

[23]   Amadea, http://alice-soft.com/html/prod_amadea.htm

[24]   Weka, http://www.cs.waikato.ac.nz/ml/weka/

[25]   Srikant, R. & Agrawal, R., Mining sequential patterns: Generalizations and performance improvements. *EDBT: Proc. of the 5th Int. Conf. on Extending Database Technology*, pp. 3–17.

[26]   Bernstein, A. & Provost, F., An intelligent assistant for the knowledge discovery process. *Proc. of the Workshop on Wrappers for Performance Enhancement in KDD*, Seattle, WA, 2001.

[27]   Ganesan, P., Garcia-Molina, H. & Widom, J., Exploiting hierarchical domain structure to compute similarity. *ACM Transactions on Information Systems*, **21(1)**, pp. 64–93, 2003.

CHAPTER 8

Association analysis for a web-based educational system

B. Minaei-Bidgoli[1], P. Tan[2], G. Kortemeyer[3] & W.F. Punch[2]
[1]*Computer Engineering Department, Iran University of Science and Technology, Iran.*
[2]*Computer Science & Engineering Department, Michigan State University, USA.*
[3]*Lyman Briggs School of Science, Michigan State University, USA.*

Abstract

An important goal of data mining is to discover the unobvious relationships among the objects in a data set. Web-based educational technologies allow educators to study how students learn (descriptive studies) and which learning strategies are most effective (causal/predictive studies). Since web-based educational systems collect vast amounts of student profile data, data mining and knowledge discovery techniques can be applied to find interesting relationships between attributes of students, assessments, and the solution strategies adopted by students. This research focuses on the discovery of interesting contrast rules, which are sets of conjunctive rules describing interesting characteristics of different segments of a population. In the context of web-based educational systems, contrast rules help to identify attributes characterizing patterns of performance disparity between various groups of students. We propose a general formulation of contrast rules as well as a framework for finding such patterns. Our research provides a new algorithm for mining contrasting rules that can improve web-based educational systems for both teachers and students – allowing for greater learner improvement and more effective evaluation of the learning process. We apply this technique to an online educational system developed at Michigan State University called LON-CAPA. A larger advantage of developing this approach is its wide application in any other data mining application.

1 Introduction

Many web-based educational systems with different capabilities and approaches have been developed to deliver online education in an academic setting. In particular, Michigan State University (MSU) has pioneered systems to provide an infrastructure for online instruction. The research presented in this study was part of the latest online educational system developed at MSU called the *Learning Online Network with Computer-Assisted Personalized Approach* (LON-CAPA) [1, 2].

LON-CAPA involves three types of large data sets: (1) educational resources such as web pages, demonstrations, simulations, and individualized problems designed for use on homework assignments, quizzes, and examinations; (2) information about users who create, modify, assess, or use these resources; and (3) activity log databases which log actions taken by students in solving homework assignment and exam problems.

This research investigates methods for finding interesting rules based on the characteristics of groups of students or assignment problems. More specifically, our research is guided and inspired by the following questions: Can we identify the different groups of students enrolled in a particular course based on their demographic data? Which attribute(s) best explain the performance disparity among students over different sets of assignment problems? Are the same disparities observed when analyzing student performance in different sections or semesters of a course?

We address the above questions using a technique called contrast rules. Contrast rules are sets of conjunctive rules describing important characteristics of different segments of a population. Consider the following toy example of 200 students who enrolled in an online course. The course provides online reading materials that cover the concepts related to assignment problems. Students may take different approaches to solve the assignment problems. Among these students, 109 students read the materials before solving the problems while the remaining 91 students directly solve the problems without reviewing the materials. In addition, 136 students eventually passed the course while 64 students failed. This information summarized in a 2 × 2 contingency table as shown in Table 1.

The table shows that there are interesting contrasts between students who review the course materials before solving the homework problems and students who do not review the materials. The following contrast rules can be induced from the contingency table shown in Fig. 1 (where s and c are the support and confidence

Table 1: A contingency table of student success vs. study habits for an online course.

	Passed	Failed	Total
Review materials	95	14	109
Do not review	41	50	91
Total	136	64	200

of the rules [3]). These rules suggest that students who review the materials are more likely to pass the course. Since there is a large difference between the support and confidence of both rules, the observed contrast is potentially interesting. Other examples of interesting contrast rules obtained from the same contingency table are shown in Figs 2 and 3.

Not all contrasting rule pairs extracted from Table 1 are interesting, as the example in Fig. 4 shows.

The above examples illustrate some of the challenging issues concerning the task of mining contrast rules:

1. There are many measures applicable to a contingency table. Which measure(s) yield the most significant/interesting contrast rules among different groups of attributes?
2. Many rules can be extracted from a contingency table. Which pair(s) of rules should be compared to define an interesting contrast?

We present a general formulation of contrast rules and propose a new algorithm for mining interesting contrast rules. The rest of this study is organized as follows: Section 2 provides a brief review of related work. Section 3 offers a formal definition of contrast rules. Section 4 gives our approach and methodology to discover the contrast rules. Section 5 describes the LON-CAPA data model and an overview of our experimental results.

$$
\begin{array}{ll}
\text{Review materials} \Rightarrow \text{Passed,} & s = 47.5\%, \ c = 87.2\% \\
\text{Review materials} \Rightarrow \text{Failed,} & s = 7.0\%, \ c = 12.8\%
\end{array}
$$

Figure 1: A contrast rule extracted from Table 1.

$$
\begin{array}{ll}
\text{Passed} \Rightarrow \text{Review materials,} & s = 47.5\%, \ c = 69.9\% \\
\text{Failed} \Rightarrow \text{Review materials,} & s = 7.0\%, \ c = 15.4\%
\end{array}
$$

Figure 2: A contrast rule extracted from Table 1.

$$
\begin{array}{ll}
\text{Passed} \Rightarrow \text{Review materials,} & s = 47.5\%, \ c = 69.9\% \\
\text{Passed} \Rightarrow \text{Do not review,} & s = 20.5\%, \ c = 30.1\%
\end{array}
$$

Figure 3: A contrast rule extracted from Table 1.

$$
\begin{array}{ll}
\text{Do not review} \Rightarrow \text{Passed,} & s = 20.5\%, \ c = 45.1\% \\
\text{Do not review} \Rightarrow \text{Failed,} & s = 25.0\%, \ c = 54.9\%
\end{array}
$$

Figure 4: A contrast rule extracted from Table 1.

2 Background

In order to acquaint the reader with the use of data mining in online education, we present a brief introduction of association analysis and measures for evaluating association rules. Next, we explain the history of data mining in web-based educational systems. Finally, we discuss previous work related to contrast rules.

2.1 Association analysis

Let $I = \{i_1, i_2, ..., i_m\}$ be the set of all items and $T = \{t_1, t_2, ..., t_N\}$ the set of all transactions where m is the number of items and N is the number of transactions. Each transaction t_j is a set of items such that $t_j \subseteq I$. Each transaction has a unique identifier, which is referred to as TID. An *association rule* is an implication statement of the form $X \Rightarrow Y$, where $X \subset I$, $Y \subset I$, and X and Y are disjoint, that is, $X \cap Y = \emptyset$. X is called the antecedent while Y is called the consequence of the rule [3, 4].

Support and confidence are two metrics, which are often used to evaluate the quality and interestingness of a rule. The rule $X \Rightarrow Y$ has support, s, in the transaction set, T, if $s\%$ of transactions in T contains $X \cup Y$. The rule has *confidence*, c, if $c\%$ of transactions in T that contains X also contains Y. Formally, support is defined as shown in eqn (1),

$$s(X \Rightarrow Y) = \frac{s(X \cup Y)}{N},$$

(1)

where N is the total number of transactions, and confidence is defined in eqn (2)

$$c(X \Rightarrow Y) = \frac{s(X \cup Y)}{s(X)}.$$

(2)

Another measure that could be used to evaluate the quality of an association rule is presented in eqn (3)

$$RuleCoverage = \frac{s(X)}{N}.$$

(3)

This measure represents the fraction of transactions that match the left hand side of a rule.

Techniques developed for mining association rules often generate a large number of rules, many of which may not be interesting to the user. There are many measures proposed to evaluate the interestingness of association rules [5, 6]. Silberschatz and Tuzhilin suggest that interestingness measures can be categorized into two classes: objective and subjective measures [7].

An objective measure is a data-driven approach for evaluating interestingness of rules based on statistics derived from the observed data. In the literature different objective measures have been proposed [8]. Examples of objective interestingness measure include support, confidence, correlation, odds ratio, and cosine.

Subjective measures evaluate rules based on the judgments of users who directly inspect the rules [7]. Different subjective measures have been addressed to discover the interestingness of a rule [7]. For example, a rule *template* [9] is a subjective technique that separates only those rules that match a given template. Another example is *neighborhood*-based interestingness [10], which defines a single rule's interestingness in terms of the supports and confidences of the group in which it is contained.

2.2 Data mining for online education systems

Recently, several researchers have worked on the application of data mining to examine or classify students' problem-solving approaches within web-based educational systems. For example, we previously developed tools for predicting the student performance with respect to average values of student attributes versus the overall problems of an online course [2]. Zaïane [11] suggested the use of web mining techniques to build an agent that recommends online learning activities in a web-based course. Ma *et al.* [12] focused on one specific task of using association rule mining to select weak students for remedial classes. This previous work focused on finding association rules with a specific rule consequent (i.e. a student is weak or strong). Herein, we propose a general formulation of contrast rules as well as a framework for finding such patterns.

2.3 Related work

An important goal in data mining is the discovery of major differences among segments of population. Bay and Pazzani [13] introduced the notion of contrast sets as a conjunction of attributes and values that differ 'meaningfully' in their distribution across groups. They used a chi-square test for testing the null hypothesis that contrast-set support is equal across all groups. They developed the STUCCO (search and testing for understandable consistent contrast) algorithm to find significant contrast sets. Our work represents a general formulation for contrast rules using different interestingness measures. We show that alternative measures allow for different perspectives on the process of finding interesting rules.

Liu *et al.* [14] have also used a chi-square test of independence as a principal measure for both generating the association rules and identifying non-actionable rules. Below, we briefly discuss the chi-square test of independence and one of its shortcomings.

Chi-square testing is used as a method for verifying the independence or correlation of attributes. The chi-square test compares observed frequencies with the corresponding expected frequencies. The greater the difference between observed and expected frequencies, the greater is the power of evidence in favor of dependence and relationship. Let CT be a contingency table with K rows and L columns. The chi-square test for independence is shown in eqn (5), where $1 \leq i \leq K$ and $1 \leq j \leq L$, and the degree of freedom is $(K-1)(L-1)$.

Table 2: A contingency table proportional to
Table 1.

	Passed	Failed	Total
(a)			
Male	40	49	89
Female	60	51	111
Total	100	100	200
(b)			
Male	400	490	890
Female	600	510	1110
Total	1000	1000	2000

$$\chi^2 = \sum_i \sum_j \frac{(O_{ij} - E_{ij})^2}{E_{ij}}. \qquad (4)$$

However, a drawback of this test is that the χ^2 value is not invariant under the *row–column scaling* property [8]. For example, consider the contingency table shown in Table 2(a). If χ^2 is higher than a specific threshold (e.g. 3.84 at the 95% significance level and degree of freedom 1), we reject the independence assumption. The chi-square value corresponding to Table 2(a) is equal to 1.82. Therefore, the null hypothesis is accepted. Nevertheless, if we multiply the values of that contingency table by 10, a new contingency table is obtained as shown in Table 2(b). The χ^2 value increases to 18.2 (>3.84). Thus, we reject the null hypothesis. We expect that the relationship between gender and success for both tables as being equal, even though the sample sizes are different. In general, this drawback shows that χ^2 is proportional to N.

3 Contrast rules

In this section, we introduce the notion of contrast rules. Let A and B be two itemsets whose relationship can be summarized in a 2×2 contingency table as shown in Table 3.

Let Ω be a set of all possible association rules that can be extracted from such a contingency table (Fig. 5).

We assume that B is a target variable and A is a conjunction of explanatory attributes. Let μ be a set of measures that can be applied to a rule or contingency table. Examples of such measures include support, confidence, chi-square, odds ratio, correlation, cosine, Jaccard, and interest [8]. In Fig. 6, we provide a formal definition of 'contrast rule'.

Table 3: A contingency table for the binary case.

	B	$\overline{B}$	Total
A	f_{11}	f_{12}	f_{1+}
$\overline{A}$	f_{21}	f_{22}	f_{2+}
Total	f_{+1}	f_{+2}	N

$$A \Rightarrow B \ , \ A \Rightarrow \overline{B} \ , \ \overline{A} \Rightarrow B \ , \ \overline{A} \Rightarrow \overline{B}$$
$$B \Rightarrow A \ , \ \overline{B} \Rightarrow A \ , \ B \Rightarrow \overline{A} \ , \ \overline{B} \Rightarrow \overline{A}$$

Figure 5: Set of all possible association rules for Table 3.

Definition (General Formulation of Contrast Rules):

A contrast rule, *cr*, is a 4-tuple $<br, \upsilon(br), M, \Delta>$ where:

1. $br \subset \Omega$, is the base rule,
2. $\upsilon(br) \subset \Omega$ is a neighborhood to which the base rule *br* is compared,
3. $M=<m_{base}, m_{neighbor}>$ is an ordered pair of measures where m_{base}, $m_{neighbor}$ $\in \mu$, and m_{base} measures the rules in br and $m_{neighbor}$ measures the rules in $\upsilon(br)$,
4. $\Delta(m_{base}(br), m_{neighbor}(\upsilon(br)))$ is a comparison function between $m_{base}(r)$ and $m_{neighbor}(\upsilon(br))$.

A contrast rule, *cr*, is interesting if and only if $\Delta(m_{base}(br), m_{neighbor}(\upsilon(br))) \geq \sigma$, where σ is a user defined threshold, which implies that there is a large difference between *br* and its neighborhood with respect to *M*.

Figure 6: Formal definition of a contrast rule.

As shown in Fig. 6, the contrast rule definition is based on a paired set of rules, base rule *br* and its neighborhood $\upsilon(br)$. The base rule is a set of association rules with which a user is interested in finding contrasting association rules. Below are some examples that illustrate the definition.

3.1 Example 1: cr_1 (difference of confidence)

The first type of contrast rules examines the difference between rules $A \Rightarrow B$ and $A \Rightarrow \overline{B}$. An example of this type of contrast was shown in Fig. 1. Let confidence be the selected measure for both rules. Let absolute difference be the comparison function. We can summarize this type of contrast as follows:

- br: $\{A \Rightarrow B\}$
- $\upsilon(r)$: $\{A \Rightarrow \overline{B}\}$
- M: $\langle$confidence, confidence$\rangle$
- Δ: absolute difference.

The evaluation criterion for this example is shown in eqn (5). This criterion can be used for ranking different pairs of contrast rules.

$$\Delta = |c(r) = c(\upsilon(r))|$$
$$= |c(A \Rightarrow B) - c(A \Rightarrow \overline{B})|$$
$$= \left| \frac{f_{11}}{f_{1+}} - \frac{f_{12}}{f_{1+}} \right| = \left| \frac{f_{11} - f_{12}}{f_{1+}} \right|, \tag{5}$$

where f_{ij} corresponds to the values in the ith row and jth column of Table 3. Since $c(A \Rightarrow B) + c(A \Rightarrow \overline{B}) = 1$, therefore,

$$\Delta = |c(A \Rightarrow B) - c(A \Rightarrow \overline{B})|$$
$$= |2c(A \Rightarrow B) - 1|$$
$$\propto c(A \Rightarrow B).$$

Thus, the standard confidence measure is sufficient to detect an interesting contrast of this type.

3.2 Example 2: cr_2 (difference of proportion)

An interesting contrast could be considered between rules $B \Rightarrow A$ and $\overline{B} \Rightarrow A$. An example of this contrast was shown in Fig. 2. Once again, let confidence be the selected measure for both rules. Let absolute difference be the comparison function. We can summarize this type of contrast as follows:

- br: $\{B \Rightarrow A\}$
- $\upsilon(br)$: $\{\overline{B} \Rightarrow A\}$
- M: ⟨confidence, confidence⟩
- Δ: absolute difference.

The evaluation criterion for this example is shown in eqn (6), where Δ is defined as follows:

$$\Delta = |c(r) - c(\upsilon(r))|$$
$$= |c(B \Rightarrow A) - c(\overline{B} \Rightarrow A)|$$
$$= \left| \frac{f_{11}}{f_{+1}} - \frac{f_{12}}{f_{+2}} \right| = \left| \rho(A \Rightarrow B) - \rho(A \Rightarrow \overline{B}) \right|, \tag{6}$$

where ρ is the rule proportion [15] and is defined in eqn (7)

$$\rho(A \Rightarrow B) = \frac{P(AB)}{P(B)} = c(B \Rightarrow A). \tag{7}$$

3.3 Example 3: cr_3 (correlation and chi-square)

Correlation is a broadly used statistical measure for analyzing the relationship between two variables. The correlation between A and B in Table 3 is measured as follows:

$$corr = \frac{f_{11}f_{22} - f_{12}f_{21}}{\sqrt{f_{1+}f_{+1}f_{2+}f_{+2}}}. \tag{8}$$

The correlation measure compares the contrast between the following set of base rules and their neighborhood rules:

- br is $\{A \Rightarrow B, B \Rightarrow A, \overline{A} \Rightarrow \overline{B}, \overline{B} \Rightarrow \overline{A}\}$
- $\upsilon(br)$ is $\{A \Rightarrow \overline{B}, \overline{B} \Rightarrow A, \overline{A} \Rightarrow B, B \Rightarrow \overline{A}\}$
- M: $\langle$confidence, confidence$\rangle$,
- Δ: the difference in the square root of confidence products [see eqn (9)]

$$\Delta = \sqrt{c_1 c_2 c_3 c_4} - \sqrt{c_5 c_6 c_7 c_8}, \tag{9}$$

where $c_1, c_2, c_3, c_4, c_5, c_6, c_7$, and c_8 correspond to $c(A \Rightarrow B)$, $c(B \Rightarrow A)$, $c(\overline{A} \Rightarrow \overline{B})$, $c(\overline{B} \Rightarrow \overline{A})$, $c(A \Rightarrow \overline{B})$, $c(\overline{B} \Rightarrow A)$, $c(\overline{A} \Rightarrow B)$, and $c(B \Rightarrow \overline{A})$, respectively. Equation (10) is obtained by expanding eqn (9)

$$\Delta = \sqrt{\frac{P(AB)}{P(A)} \frac{P(AB)}{P(B)} \frac{P(\overline{A}\,\overline{B})}{P(\overline{A})} \frac{P(\overline{A}\,\overline{B})}{P(\overline{B})}}$$

$$- \sqrt{\frac{P(A\overline{B})}{P(A)} \frac{P(A\overline{B})}{P(\overline{B})} \frac{P(\overline{A}B)}{P(\overline{A})} \frac{P(\overline{A}B)}{P(B)}}, \tag{10}$$

$$\Delta = \frac{P(AB)P(\overline{A}\,\overline{B}) - P(A\overline{B})P(\overline{A}B)}{\sqrt{P(A)P(B)P(\overline{A})P(\overline{B})}}. \tag{11}$$

Equation (11) is the correlation between A and B as shown in eqn (8). Chi-square measure is related to correlation in the following way:

$$corr = \sqrt{\frac{\chi^2}{N}}. \tag{12}$$

Therefore, both measures are essentially comparing the same type of contrast.

3.4 Contrast rules and interestingness measures

Different measures have different perspectives on finding interesting rules. Specifically, each measure defines a base rule and a neighborhood of rules from which interesting contrast rules can be detected. In our proposed approach a user can choose a measure and detect the corresponding contrast rules. In addition, the user has flexibility to choose a base rule/attribute according to what he or she is interested in. Then he or she selects the neighborhood rules as well as the measures to detect the base rule and its neighborhood. This is similar to rule template approaches (see 2.1). We implemented examples 1–3 for LON-CAPA data sets, which will be explained in Section 5.

4 Algorithm

In this section we propose an algorithm to find surprising and interesting rules based on the characteristics of different segments of students/problems. The difficulty with algorithms such as Apriori is that when the minimum support is high, we miss many interesting but infrequent patterns. On the other hand if we choose a minimum support that is too low the Apriori algorithm will discover so many rules that finding interesting ones becomes difficult.

Herein, we propose an automatic rule miner to discover hidden patterns amongst the contrast elements, even those with low support. We call this the mining contrast rules (MCR) algorithm shown in Fig. 7.

In order to employ the MCR algorithm, several steps must be taken. During the pre-processing phase, we remove items whose support is too high. For example, if 95% of students pass the course, this attribute will be removed from the itemsets so that it does not overwhelm other, more subtle, rules. Then we must also select the target variable of the rules to be compared. This allows the user to focus the search space on subjectively interesting rules. If the target variable has C distinct

---

Mining Contrast Rules (MCR) Algorithm:

Input: D – Input set of N transactions

B – Target variable, the basis of interesting contrasts

σ – Minimum (very) low support

m – A measure for ranking the rules

k – Number of the most interesting rules

Divide data set D based on the values of the target variable

foreach j in B

  Select $D(j)$, a subset of transactions including j

  Find the set of closed frequent itemsets, $L(j)$ within $D(j)$

  foreach $\ell \in L(j)$

    Generate rule $\ell \Rightarrow j$

    Compute measure $m(\ell \Rightarrow j)$

  end

end

Find common rules among the different groups of rules

foreach br and $\upsilon(br)$ pair compute difference in measures, Δ

Sort the rules with respect to Δ

Select top k rules

return R

Figure 7: MCR algorithm for discovering interesting candidate rules.

values, we divide the data set, D, into C disjoint subsets based on the elements of the target variable, as shown in Fig. 7. For example, in the case where gender is the target variable, we divide the transactions into male and female subsets to permit examination of rule coverage.

Using Borgelt's implementation (the code for this program is available at http://fuzzy.cs.uni-magdeburg.de/~borgelt/apriori.html) of the Apriori algorithm (version 4.21), we can find closed itemsets employing a simple filtering approach on the prefix tree [16]. A closed itemset is a set of items for which none of its supersets have exactly the same support as itself. The advantage of using closed frequent itemsets for our purposes is that we can focus on a smaller number of rules for analysis, and larger frequent itemsets, by discarding the redundant supersets.

We choose a very low minimum support to obtain as many frequent itemsets as is possible. Using perl scripts, we find the common rules between two contrast subsets. Finally, we rank the common rules with all of the previously explained measures, and then the top k rules of the sorted ranked-rules are chosen as a candidate set of interesting rules. Therefore an important parameter for this algorithm is minimum support, σ; the lower the σ, the larger the number of common rules. If the user selects a specific ranking measure, m, then the algorithm will rank the rules with respect to that measure.

5 Experiments

In this section we first provide a general model for data attributes, data sets and their selected attributes, and then explain how we handle continuous attributes. Finally, we discuss our results and experimental issues.

5.1 Data model and attributes

In order to better understand the interactions between students and the online education system, a model is required to analyze the data. Ideally, this model would be both descriptive and predictive in nature. The model is framed around the interactions of the two main sources of interpretable data: students and assessment tasks (problems). Figure 8 shows the actual data model, which is frequently called an entity relationship diagram (ERD) since it depicts categories of data in terms of entities and relationships.

The attributes selected for association analysis are divided into four groups within the LON-CAPA system:

1. *Student attributes*: These are fixed for any student. Attributes such as ethnicity, major and age were not included in the data out of necessity – the focus of this work is primarily on the LON-CAPA system itself, so the demographics of students is less relevant. As a result, the following three attributes are included:

   - *GPA*: is a continuous variable that is discretized into eight intervals between zero and four with a 0.5 distance.
   - *Gender*: is a binary attribute with values Female and Male.

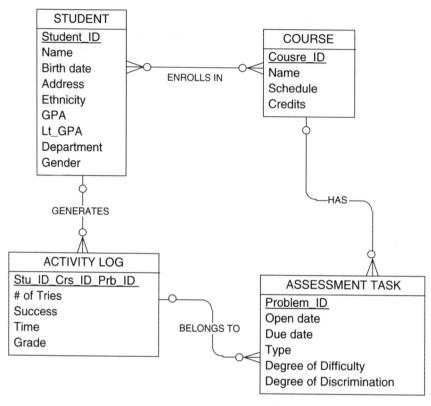

Figure 8: ERD for a LON-CAPA course.

- *LtGPA* [Level Transferred (i.e. High School) GPA]: measured the same as GPA.

2. *Problem attributes*: These are fixed for any problem. Among several attributes for the problems we selected the four following attributes:

   - *DoDiff* (degree of difficulty): This is a useful factor for an instructor to determine whether a problem has an appropriate level of difficulty. DoDiff is computed by the total number of students' submissions divided by the number of students who solved the problem correctly. Thus, DoDiff is a continuous variable in the interval [0,1] which is discretized into terciles of roughly equal frequency: easy, medium, and hard.
   - *DoDisc* (degree of discrimination): A second measure of a problem's usefulness in assessing performance is its discrimination index. It is derived by comparing how students whose performance places them in the top quartile of the class score on that problem compared to those in the bottom quartile. The possible values for DoDisc vary from −1 to +1. A negative value means that students in the lower quartile scored better on that problem than those in the upper. A value close to +1 indicates the higher achieving students

(overall) performed better on the problem. We discretize this continuous value into terciles of roughly equal frequency: negatively discriminating, non-discriminating, and positively discriminating.

- *AvgTries* (average number of tries): This is a continuous variable which is discretized into terciles of roughly equal frequency: low, medium, and high.

3. *Student/problem interaction attributes*: We have extracted the following attributes per student per problem from the activity log:

- *Succ*: Success on the problem (YES, NO).
- *Tries*: Total number of attempts before final answer.
- *Time*: Total time from first attempt until the final answer is derived.

4. *Student/course interaction attributes*: We have extracted the following attributes per student per course from the LON-CAPA system.

- *Grade*: Student's grade, the nine possible labels for grade (a 4.0 scale with 0.5 increments). An aggregation of 'grade' attributes is added to the total attribute list.
- *Pass–Fail*: Categorize students with one of two class labels, 'Pass' for grades above 2.0 and 'Fail' for grades less than or equal to 2.0.

5.2 Data sets

For this study we selected three data sets from the LON-CAPA courses as shown in Table 4. For example, the second row of the table shows that BS111 (Biological Science: Cells and Molecules) integrated 235 online homework problems, and 382 students used LON-CAPA for this course. BS111 had an activity log with approximately 239 MB of data. Though BS111 is a larger course than LBS271 (first row of the table), a physics course, it is much smaller than CEM141 (third row), general chemistry I. This course had 2048 students enrolled and its activity log exceeds 750 MB, corresponding to more than 190k transactions of students attempting to solve homework problems.

For this research we focus on two target variables, gender and pass–fail grades, in order to find the contrast rules involving these attributes. A constant difficulty in

Table 4: Characteristics of three MSU courses which used LON-CAPA in the fall semester 2003.

Data set	Course title	No. of students	No. of problems	Size of activity log (MB)	No. of Transactions
LBS 271	Physics_I	200	174	152.1	32,394
BS 111	Biological Science	382	235	239.4	71,675
CEM141	Chemistry_I	2048	114	754.8	190,859

using any of the association rule mining algorithms is that they can only operate on binary data sets. Thus, in order to analyze quantitative or categorical attributes, some modifications are required – binarization – to partition the values of continuous attributes into discrete intervals and substitute a binary item for each discretized item. In this study, we mainly use equal-frequency binning for discretizing the attributes.

5.3 Results

This section presents some examples of the interesting contrast rules obtained from the LON-CAPA data sets. Since our approach is an unsupervised case, it requires some practical methods to validate the process. The interestingness of a rule can be subjectively measured in terms of its actionability (usefulness) or its unexpectedness [6, 17–19, 20].

One of the techniques for mining interesting association rules based on unexpectedness. Therefore, we divide the set of discovered rules into three categories:

1. *Expected and previously known*: This type of rule confirms user beliefs, and can be used to validate our approach. Though perhaps already known, many of these rules are still useful for the user as a form of empirical verification of expectations. For our specific situation (education) this approach provides opportunity for rigorous justification of many long-held beliefs.
2. *Unexpected*: This type of rule contradicts user beliefs. This group of unanticipated correlations can supply interesting rules, yet their interestingness and possible actionability still requires further investigation.
3. *Unknown*: This type of rule does not clearly belong to any category, and should be categorized by domain-specific experts. For our situations, classifying these complicated rules would involve consultation with not only the course instructors and coordinators, but also educational researchers and psychologists.

The following rule tables present five examples of the extracted contrast rules obtained using our approach. Each table shows the coded contrast rule and the 'support' and 'confidence' of that rule. Abbreviations are used in the rule code, and are summarized as follows: *Succ* stands for success per student per problem, *LtGPA* stands for transfer GPA, *DoDiff* stands for degree of difficulty of a particular problem, and *DoDisc* stands for degree of discrimination of a problem. In our experiments, we used three measures to rank the contrast rules.

5.3.1 Difference of confidences
The focus of this measure is on comparing the confidences of the contrast rules ($A \Rightarrow B$ and $A \Rightarrow \bar{B}$). Therefore, top rules found by this measure have a high value of confidence ratio (c_1/c_2). Contrast rules in Table 5 suggest that students in LBS 271 who are successful in homework problems are more likely to pass the course, and this comes with a confidence ratio $c_1/c_2 = 12.7$.

Table 5: LBS_271 data set, difference of confidences measure.

Contrast rules	Support and confidence
(Succ = YES) ⇒ Passed	$(s = 86.1\%, c = 92.7\%)$
(Succ = YES) ⇒ Failed	$(s = 6.8\%, c = 7.3\%)$

Table 6: CEM_141 data set, difference of confidences measure.

Contrast rules	Support and confidence
(Lt_GPA = [1.5,2)) ⇒ Passed	$(s = 0.6\%, c = 7.7\%)$
(Lt_GPA = [1.5,2)) ⇒ Failed	$(s = 7.1\%, c = 92.3\%)$

Table 7: BS_111 data set, difference of proportion measure.

Contrast rules	Support and confidence
Male ⇒ (Lt_GPA = [3.5,4] & Time > 20_hours)	$(s = 0.1\%, c = 26.3\%)$
Female ⇒ (Lt_GPA = [3.5,4] & Time > 20_hours)	$(s = 0.6\%, c = 89.7\%)$

This rule implies a strong correlation among the student's success in homework problems and his/her final grade. Therefore, this rule belongs to the first category; it is a known, expected rule that validates our approach.

Contrast rules in Table 6 could belong to the first category as well; students with low transfer GPAs are more likely to fail CEM 141 ($c_2/c_1 = 12$). This rule has the advantage of actionability; so, when students with low transfer GPAs enroll for the course, the system could be designed to provide them with additional help.

5.3.2 Difference of proportions

The focus of this measure is on comparing the rules ($B \Rightarrow A$ and $\overline{B} \Rightarrow A$). Contrast rules in Table 7 suggest that historically strong students who take long periods of time between their first (incorrect) solution attempt and subsequent attempts tend to be female. This rule could belong to the second category. We found this interesting contrast rule using the difference of confidences to discover the top significant rules for BS 111. Though the support of the rules is low, that is the result for an interesting rule with low support.

Table 8: CEM_141 data set, chi-square measure.

Contrast rules	Support and confidence
(Lt_GPA = [3,3.5) & Sex = Male & Tries = 1) $\Rightarrow$ Passed	($s = 4.4\%, c = 82.7\%$)
(Lt_GPA = [3,3.5) & Sex = Male & Tries = 1) $\Rightarrow$ Failed	($s = 0.9\%, c = 17.3\%$)

Table 9: LBS_271 data set, difference of confidences measure.

Contrast rules	Support and confidence
(DoDiff = medium & DoDisc = non_discriminating & Succ = YES & Tries = 1) $\Rightarrow$ Passed	($s = 28.9\%, c = 94.1\%$)
(DoDiff = medium & DoDisc = non_discriminating & Succ = YES & Tries = 1) $\Rightarrow$ Failed	($s = 1.8\%, c = 5.9\%$)

5.3.3 Chi-square

It is a well-known condition in chi-square testing for contingency tables that cell expected values need to be above 5 to guarantee the veracity of the significance levels obtained [16]. We do pruning if this limitation is violated in some cases, and this usually happens when the expected support corresponding to f_{11} or f_{12} in Table 3 is low.

Contrast rules in Table 8 suggest that students with transfer GPAs in the range 3.0–3.5 who were male and answered homework problems on the first try were more likely to pass the class than to fail ($c_1/c_2 = 4.8$). This rule could belong to the second category. We found this rule using the chi-square measure for CEM 141.

Contrast rules in Table 9 show more complicated rules for LBS 271 using difference of proportion ($c_1/c_2 = 15.9$); these rules belong to the third (unknown) category and further consultation with educational experts is necessary to determine whether or not they are interesting.

6 Conclusion

LON-CAPA servers are recording students' activities in large logs. We proposed a general formulation of interesting contrast rules and developed an algorithm to discover a set of contrast rules investigating three different statistical measures. This tool can help instructors to design courses more effectively, detect anomalies, inspire and direct further research, and help students use resources more efficiently.

An advantage of this developing approach is its broad functionality in many data mining application domains. Specifically, it allows for contrast rule discovery with very low minimum support, therefore permitting the mining of possibly interesting rules that otherwise would go unnoticed.

More measurements tend to permit discovery of higher coverage rules. A combination of measurements should be employed to find out whether this approach for finding more interesting rules can be improved. In this vein, we plan to extend our work to analysis of other possible kinds of contrast rules.

Acknowledgments

We thank the National Science Foundation for grants supporting this work through the Information Technology Research (ITR 0085921) and the Assessment of Student Achievement (ASA 0243126) programs. During the earlier years of this project support was also received from the Alfred P Sloan and Andrew W Mellon Foundations. We are grateful to our own institution, Michigan State University and to its administrators for over a decade of encouragement and support.

References

[1]   Kortemeyer, G., Bauer, W., Kashy, D.A., Kashy, E. & Speier, C., The LearningOnline Network with CAPA Initiative. *Proc. of IEEE conf. on Frontiers in Education*, Vol. 31, 2001. See also http://www.loncapa.org

[2]   Minaei-Bidgoli, B., Kashy, D.A., Kortemeyer, G. & Punch, W.F., Predicting student performance: an application of data mining methods with an educational web-based system. *IEEE conf. on Frontier In Education FIE 2003*, Boulder, November 2003.

[3]   Agrawal, R., Imielinski, T. & Swami, A., Mining associations between sets of items in massive databases. *Proc. of the ACM-SIGMOD 1993 Int. Conf. on Management of Data*, Washington, DC, May 1993.

[4]   Agrawal, R. & Srikant, R., Fast Algorithms for Mining Association Rules. *Proc. of the 20th Int. Conf. on Very Large Databases*, Santiago, Chile, September 1994.

[5]   Freitas, A.A., On rule interestingness measures. *Knowledge-Based Systems Journal*, **12(5–6)**, pp. 309–315, 1999.

[6]   Meo, R., *Replacing Support in Association Rule Mining,* Rapporto Tecnico RT70-2003, Dipartimento di Informatica, Università di Torino, April 2003.

[7]   Silberschatz, A. & Tuzhilin, A., On subjective measures of interestingness in knowledge discovery. *Proc. of KDD*, pp. 275–281, 1995.

[8]   Tan, P.N., Kumar, V. & Srivastava, J., Selecting the right objective measure for association analysis. *Information Systems*, **29(4)**, pp. 293–313 2004.

[9]   Fu, Y. & Han, J., Meta-rule-guided mining of association rules in relational databases. *Proc. 1995 Int. Workshop on Knowledge Discovery and Deductive and Object-Oriented Databases (KDOOD'95)*, pp. 39–46, December 1995.

[10]   Dong, G. & Li, J., Interestingness of discovered association rules in terms of neighborhood-based unexpectedness. *Proc. of Pacific Asia Conf. on Knowledge Discovery in Databases (PAKDD)*, pp. 72–86. Melbourne, 1998.

[11]   Zaïane, O.R., Web usage mining for a better web-based learning environment. *Proc. of Conf. on Advanced Technology for Education*, Banff, Alberta, pp. 60–64, June 27–28, 2001.

[12]   Ma, Y., Liu, B., Kian, C., Wong, Yu, P.S. & Lee, S.M., Targeting the right students using data mining. *Proc. of the ACM SIGKDD Int. Conf. on Knowledge Discovery & Data Mining (KDD-2000, Industry Track)*, Boston, USA, August, 2000.

[13]   Bay, S.D. & Pazzani, M.J., Detecting Group Differences: Mining Contrast Sets. *Data Mining and Knowledge Discovery*, **5(3)**, pp. 213–246, 2001.

[14]   Liu, B., Hsu, W. & Ma, Y. Identifying Non-Actionable Association rules. *Proc. of the Seventh ACM SIGKDD Int. Conf. on Knowledge Discovery and Data Mining(KDD-2001)*, San Francisco, USA, 2001.

[15]   Agresti, A., *Categorical Data Analysis*. 2nd edition, Wiley: New York, 2002.

[16]   Borgelt, C., Efficient implementations of Apriori and Eclat: *Workshop of Frequent Item Set Mining Implementations* (FIMI), 2003.

[17]   Piatetsky-Shapiro, G. & Matheus. C.J., The interestingness of deviations. *Proc. of the AAAI-94 Workshop on Knowledge Discovery in Databases*, pp. 25–36, 1994.

[18]   Liu, B., Hsu, W., Mun, L.F. & Lee, H., Finding interesting patterns using user expectations. *IEEE Transactions on Knowledge and Data Engineering*, **11(6)**, pp. 817–832, 1999.

[19]   Silberschatz, A. & Tuzhilin, A., What makes patterns interesting in Knowledge discovery systems. *IEEE Transactions on Knowledge and Data Engineering*, **8(6)**, pp. 970–974, December, 1996.

[20]   Minaei-Bidgoli, B., Tan, P.-N. & Punch, W.F., Mining interesting contrast rules for a web-based educational system. *Proc. of ICMLA'04*, Louisville, KY, pp. 320–327, December 2004.

CHAPTER 9

Data mining in personalizing distance education courses

W. Hämäläinen, T.H. Laine & E. Sutinen
Department of Computer Science, University of Joensuu, Finland.

Abstract

The need to personalize distance education courses stems from their ultimate goal: the need to serve an individual student independently of time, place, or any other restrictions. This means that a distance education system should be served by a data mining system (DMS) to monitor, intervene in, and counsel the teaching–studying–learning process. Compared to intelligent tutoring systems or adaptive learning environments where a teacher has only an occasional role, a DMS emphasizes the role of an expert, in this case the teacher, to interpret the findings obtained from analyzing the data retrieved from the course. A DMS was designed and implemented to analyze the study records of two programming courses in a distance curriculum of computer science. Various data mining schemes, including the linear regression and probabilistic models, were applied to describe and predict student performance. The results indicate that a DMS can help a distance education teacher, even in courses with relatively few students, to intervene in a learning process at several levels: improving exercises, scheduling the course, and identifying potential dropouts at an early phase.

1 Introduction

The need to personalize distance education courses stems from their ultimate goal: the need to serve an individual student independently of time, place, or any other restrictions. This means that a distance education system should be served by a data mining system (DMS) to monitor, intervene in, and counsel the teaching–studying–learning process. Compared to current intelligent tutoring systems (ITSs) or adaptive learning environments where a teacher has only an occasional role, a DMS emphasizes the role of an expert, in this case the teacher, to interpret the findings obtained from analyzing the data retrieved from the course.

ViSCoS (Virtual Studies of Computer Science) is a distance education program intended originally for high school students interested in continuing later at university with computer science (CS) as their major subject [1]. The reasons for the Department of CS at the University of Joensuu to initiate the program in 2000 were threefold: to recruit high school student to study CS at university, particularly in Joensuu; to design an experimental platform with real learners to explore the opportunities of technology in education; and to attract young people to choose information and communication technology as their future career. One could call these interests recruiting, academic, and industrial ones, respectively. Therefore, the success of the ViSCoS program could be measured by the fulfillment of the three expectations, and to some extent, data mining could be used for analyzing and supporting at least purposes one and three. In this chapter, we focus on how data mining techniques can contribute to better student performance, also benefiting our recruiting purpose.

An important part of recruiting the students via ViSCoS is to have them to complete their studies in a due manner. However, as in many distance education courses in almost any if not every academic field and in almost any programming course, face-to-face or distance, the problem has been the large proportion of dropouts [2]. It seems to be that at least part of the students could be supported, if their learning process were traced and analyzed for a sufficiently early intervention – either by course tutors or an ITS. This, however, requires a predictive model of their future performance, given the data from their previous study outcomes, like assignment and exercise points collected this far.

Instead of picking up an ad hoc model – which is common manner in educational field – our main motive has been to construct models from real data. This requires interaction between *descriptive* and *predictive modeling* – or data mining and machine learning. In the following, we will first consider the general paradigms for such data-driven modeling. Then we will describe our datasets and the models constructed from this data. We will introduce four simple modeling paradigms for analyzing the dynamics of different factors in two distance learning courses. As a result, we construct two descriptive–predictive model pairs, namely correlation analysis followed by linear regression models and association rules followed by naive Bayes models. These paradigms were selected for their simplicity, easy interpretation and suitability to small data sets. The emphasis is in descriptive modeling and selecting the most promising modeling paradigms and model structures for future ITSs. The predictive accuracy of the selected models will be compared by cross-validation. Finally we will conclude our results and make suggestions for future research.

2 General paradigms for ITSs

The idea of ITSs [3–7] is to adapt the teaching according to individual skills, knowledge, and needs, and give personal feedback just in time. The core of the system is a *tutoring module*, which is responsible for selecting suitable actions like generating tests and exercises, giving hints and explanations, suggesting learning topics, searching learning material and collaborative partners.

The main idea of ITS is that they should be *adaptive* – i.e. adapt to the individual student's needs, but so far the current ITSs are far from real adaptivity. Rather, the current systems are very stable: they are either based on a fully deterministic rule-based system [8] or even if some uncertain rules are used, they are predefined by experts [9–11]. A typical ITS consists of a predefined learning path, which a student proceeds by studying a concept and passing a test before entering the next topic. If the student fails in tests, s/he is advised to study more. In so-called Bayesian learning models [12, 13], the model structure is also fixed and teachers have assigned probabilities for passing a test, if the concepts are actually not known. The only Bayesian thing in such models is the method of updating probabilities by Bayes rule. For example, the *SModel* [14] offers a general framework for Bayesian ITS, which the teacher can tailor for her/his own course setting by assigning the desired parameters.

A better approach would be to learn the model from real data, but only few experiments have been done on this direction. Kotsiantis *et al.* [15] have done a pioneer work in predicting dropouts by machine learning techniques. The data consisted of detailed personal data (including family and occupation obligations) and course activity in the beginning of course. In the comparison of six modeling paradigms – naive Bayes model, decision trees (C4.5), back-propagation neural networks, support vector machines, 3-nearest neighbors algorithm and logistic regression – the naive Bayes model and back-propagation performed best with over 80% prediction accuracy in the middle of course. Shin and Kim [16] have analyzed the most influencing factors for course grades by logistic regression. In their experiment, the data was collected by a query, which contained questions about job load, social integration, willingness to study, amount of study time etc. The analysis revealed important factors, but they were not used further for prediction.

The unwillingness to use data mining and machine learning techniques in educational context is partly due to domain-specific problems. The data sets are typically very small (size of a class) and very often the courses change every year. Thus, we can accurately learn only very simple (and less informative) models, with decreased number of attributes and small domains to prevent over-fitting. Still, it is likely that even the training error is quite large, because students do not behave deterministically. Special care should also be given for model validation, but in the educational setting it is not straightforward: two classes never represent the same population, because even the smallest changes in material, tutors, assessment practices etc. affect the measured learning.

In this chapter, we clarify general modeling paradigms for developing truly adaptive ITSs and test the suitability of certain techniques with real course data. In contrast to previous approaches, we do not suppose any background data, but try to analyze and predict course outcomes based on the data available during the course. We suppose that suitable prerequisite queries would improve the results, but students are usually not willing to fill any queries.

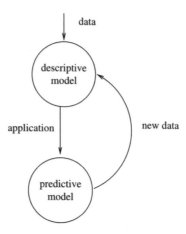

Figure 1: The iterative process of descriptive and predictive modeling.

We have adopted a dual principle of descriptive and predictive modeling [17], which combines classical paradigms of data mining and machine learning (Fig. 1). The idea is that in the descriptive phase, we analyze the previous year course data and search for local patterns like correlations and association rules. These results guide in selection of suitable modeling paradigm and especially in determining the model structure for predictive models. In the predictive phase, the modeling paradigm or paradigms (e.g. linear regression, Bayesian networks) are fixed and we define the model structure (variables and their relations). Then the model parameters are learnt from data. The resulting models are applied in the next course and updated in the light of new evidence. This is also the final test for validity of the model and guides the construction process in the next cycle.

In this framework, we can evaluate the descriptive and predictive power of models separately. For descriptive models, we can use the standard statistic measures like χ^2-test and F-values. In the search for associative rules, this can be taken into account beforehand, by determining the minimum frequency thresholds according to χ^2-test values. These evaluations confirm that we have found statistically exceptional dependencies, but their utility in prediction is harder to validate. In educational setting, the testing itself affects on course results, either directly (if the test is transparent, as recommendable) or indirectly, through tutors and/or test setting. Cross-validation with the current data set gives good guidelines on how well the model generalizes to new data, supposing that the future course setting stays quite stable.

3 Data description

In model construction we used the course records from two programming courses, (*Prog.1* and *Prog.2*), which are taught under ViSCoS distance learning program. The course records contained student identifiers, gender, exercise task points for

19 weeks, exam task points, total points, and grades. The exercise tasks were divided into six categories, according to topics covered (Table 1).

The data was collected during the academic years 2001–2002 and 2002–2003. Since the course has remained unchanged during both years, we simply combined both records after some normalization. The resulting data sets were divided into two parts: *viscos1*, which contained all students (122 rows), and *viscos2*, which contained only those students, who had passed *Prog.1* course (91 rows).

The selected attributes, their domains and descriptions are presented in Table 2. In the original data set, all attributes were numerical, but for association rules and probabilistic models we converted them to binary-valued qualitative attributes. In exercise categories $A, \ldots, F$, we simply split the numeric domain in two: $little = \{0, \ldots, max/2\}$, $lot = \{max/2 + 1, \ldots, max\}$. However, in total points, $max/2 = 15$ is the passing limit, and we were interested in students, who had passed the *Prog.1* course. Thus, we defined that the binary value is *little*, when $TP < 23$, and *lot*, otherwise.

Table 1: Exercise task categories.

Category	Description
A	Basic programming structures (*Prog.1*, weeks 1–3)
B	Loops and arrays (*Prog.1*, weeks 4–6)
C	Applets (*Prog.1*, weeks 7–9)
D	Object-oriented programming (*Prog.2*, weeks 1–3)
E	Graphical applications (*Prog.2*, weeks 4–8)
F	Error handling (*Prog.2*, weeks 9–10)

Table 2: Selected attributes, their numerical domain (NDom), binary-valued qualitative domain (QDom), and description.

Attribute	NDom	QDom	Description
G	0, 1	F, M	Student's gender
A	$\{0, .., 12\}$	$\{little, lot\}$	Exercise points in A
B	$\{0, .., 14\}$	$\{little, lot\}$	Exercise points in B
C	$\{0, .., 12\}$	$\{little, lot\}$	Exercise points in C
D	$\{0, .., 8\}$	$\{little, lot\}$	Exercise points in D
E	$\{0, .., 19\}$	$\{little, lot\}$	Exercise points in E
F	$\{0, .., 10\}$	$\{little, lot\}$	Exercise points in F
TP1	$\{0, .., 30\}$	$\{little, lot\}$	Total points of *Prog.1*
TP2	$\{0, .., 30\}$	$\{little, lot\}$	Total points of *Prog.2*
FR1	$\{0, 1\}$	$\{fail, pass\}$	Final result of *Prog.1*
FR2	$\{0, 1\}$	$\{fail, pass\}$	Final result of *Prog.2*

4 Correlations and linear regression models

We started the research by (Pearson) correlation analysis to find the most strongly correlating attributes. The emphasis was to identify the most important factors for predicting final results *FR1* and *FR2*. The results are presented in Table 3.

It can be recognized that the exercise points in *B* category correlate strongly with the amount of total points, especially in *Prog.1* (*TP1*), but also in *Prog.2* (*TP2*) course. The latter correlation can be partially reduced to the correlation between *B* and *E*, which suggests that skills in loops and arrays are important prerequisites for graphical applications. However, the exercise points in *A* category have only a weak correlation with the total points of the courses. This may be due to the fact that the tasks in *A* were the easiest and nearly all students solved a lot of them.

Another interesting observation is that the exercise points in category *E* have a very strong correlation to the amount of total points on *Prog.2* course. These results suggests that the students' performance in the middle of the course has a strong impact on the outcomes.

The strong correlation between *TP1* and *TP2* can either describe the general learning tendency or prove the importance of managing basic programming skills before proceeding to more difficult topics.

Gender (*G*) was excluded from the correlation table, because it did not have any significant correlations with other attributes. For example, the correlation coefficients between *gender* and *TP1/TP2* were only approximately 0.16.

The natural complement of correlation in predictive modeling is *linear regression* (see e.g. [18]). In our research, we used a multiple linear regression model, in which the predicted variable can depend on several factors. Formally we define:

Definition 1 *Let $X_1, \ldots, X_k$ and Y be discrete variables, where X_is are independent (explanatory) variables and Y is a dependent (response) variable. Then the expected value $\hat{Y}$ of Y can be predicted by linear equation*

$$\hat{Y} = \alpha + \beta_1 X_1 + \beta_2 X_2 + \cdots + \beta_k X_k.$$

in which α and $\beta_1, \ldots, \beta_k$ are real-valued regression coefficients.

Table 3: Correlation coefficients between the attributes.

corr(A, TP1)	0.61	*corr(D, E)*	0.59
corr(B, C)	0.69	*corr(D, F)*	0.42
corr(B, E)	0.61	*corr(D, TP2)*	0.60
corr(B, TP1)	0.75	*corr(E, F)*	0.73
corr(B, TP2)	0.54	*corr(E, TP2)*	0.73
corr(C, D)	0.51	*corr(F, TP2)*	0.61
corr(C, TP1)	0.69	*corr(TP, TP2)*	0.61

We constructed several linear regression models for the selected attributes that proved to have meaningful correlations in the first phase of our study. Analyses concentrated on predicting the final results of both courses ($FR1$ and $FR2$), with emphasis on predicting the outcome of *Prog.2*. Actually, the linear regression model predicted the total points ($TP1$ and $TP2$), and the final results ($FR1$ and $FR2$) were obtained by rule: $FR = 1$, if $TP \geq 15$, and $FR = 0$, otherwise.

The constructed models, with some validation measures, are presented in Table 4. The model name indicates which attributes were used as independent variables to predict the final results ($FR1$ or $FR2$). *True positive* and *true negative* values indicate the classification accuracy, i.e. the rate of correctly predicted outcomes from all passed/failed students. *F-significance* indicates the significance level of the F-value for the whole model, i.e. the probability that such model would appear by chance. All the F-values are much less than 0.001, which means that the dependencies are very significant (there is much less than 0.1% probability that they would occur by chance).

Models $A, B \Rightarrow FR1$ and $A, B, C \Rightarrow FR1$ were constructed from the *viscos1* data set and the rest of the models from *viscos2* data set.

Validation measures of regression models suggest that each of these models can be used to predict quite reliably either success or failure of a student. Some models, like $TP1, D, E, F \Rightarrow FR2$, require information from the end of the other course (exercise category F particularly) in order to be usable. On the other hand model $B \Rightarrow FR2$ can already make good predictions for the outcomes of the second programming course based on the information on the exercise category B. Models where exercise category E has been used yield particularly good results for both success and failure predictions. This indicates great significance of E and therefore it could be used for instance to predict examination failure beforehand in order to provide a student with help to pass the course. We see also that attribute F has no effect in the model as predictions from $TP1, D, E, \Rightarrow FR2$ equal to predictions from $TP1, D, E, F \Rightarrow FR2$, thus influence of F to course outcome is minimal.

Table 4: Verification measures of regression models.

Model	True positive	True negative	F-Significance
$A, B \Rightarrow FR1$	0.978	0.333	$5.92e-19$
$A, B, C \Rightarrow FR1$	0.989	0.167	$1.70e-20$
$TP1 \Rightarrow FR2$	0.860	0.641	$6.94e-9$
$B, E \Rightarrow FR2$	0.840	0.845	$1.15e-9$
$B \Rightarrow FR2$	0.820	0.560	$2.70e-6$
$TP1, D \Rightarrow FR2$	0.840	0.744	$1.08e-10$
$TP1, D, E \Rightarrow FR2$	0.920	0.872	$6.76e-13$
$TP1, D, E, F \Rightarrow FR2$	0.920	0.872	$2.53e-12$

5 Association rules and probabilistic models

Association rules offer a good way to model non-linear dependencies between attributes. Generally, association rules are of form $X \Rightarrow Y$, where X is a set of attributes and Y a single attribute. The *confidence* of the rule, $cf(X \Rightarrow Y)$, indicates how strong the rule is, and the *frequency* or support of the rule, $fr(X \Rightarrow Y)$, indicates the coverage of the rule (i.e. the portion of dataset it covers). Formally we define:

Definition 2 *Let $R = \{A_1, \ldots, A_k\}$ be a set of binary-valued attributes, and $r \in R$ a relation in R. The confidence and frequency of rule $X \Rightarrow Y$, $X \subseteq R$, $Y \in R$, $Y \notin X$ are defined by*

$$cf(X \Rightarrow Y) = \frac{P(X, Y)}{P(X)} = P(Y|X) \ and$$

$$fr(X \Rightarrow Y) = P(X, Y).$$

Given the user-defined thresholds $min_{cf}, min_{fr} \in [0, 1]$, we say that the rule is confident, if $cf(X \Rightarrow Y) \geq min_{cf}$, and frequent, if $fr(X \Rightarrow Y) \geq min_{fr}$.

For example, an association rule '$B = lot, E = lot, F = lot \Rightarrow FR2 = 1$' with confidence $cf = 0.956$ and frequency $fr = 0.516$ indicates that about 96% of students who have done a lot of tasks in categories B, E and F have passed *Prog.2* course. In addition, the frequency indicates that the rule covers about 52% of the students.

In *viscos* data we have found several interesting association rules. In Table 5 we have listed all frequent rules for predicting the final results of *Prog.1* and *Prog.2* courses. The minimum frequency thresholds min_{fr} were defined according to χ^2-test to catch only those rules, which are statistically significant on level 0.01 (Table 6). This decision is critical (compared to user-defined, constant frequency thresholds), because for small datasets with few attributes the frequencies have to be really high, before the rules have any statistical value. In addition, the thresholds decrease fast, when the number of attributes grows. For minimum confidence threshold we used value $min_{cf} = 0.7$.

The association rules can already be used for prediction. For example, we can predict that students who have done a lot of A and B tasks will pass the *Prog.1* course with 92% probability. However, the frequent rules cover only some subsets of students, and a more general model would be needed. For this purpose we have constructed simple naive Bayes models, *NB1* and *NB2*, for both *Prog.1* and *Prog.2* courses. The model structures are presented in Fig. 2 and the parameters are given in Table 7.

In the naive Bayes model, we make the *naive Bayes assumption* that the leaf nodes depend only on the root node. In reality this assumption very seldom holds good, but in practice the naive Bayes model has proved to work well. In fact, Domingos *et al.* [19] have shown that this is only a sufficient, but not necessary, condition for optimality of the naive Bayes classifier. Our experiments suggest that a more accurate condition might be that the attributes are not correlated, i.e. they are not linearly dependent.

Table 5: The strongest frequent rules, and their frequencies and confidences for predicting final results for *Prog.1* and *Prog.2*. The min_{fr} values were selected according to χ^2-test to guarantee significance on level 0.01. min_{cf} was 0.7.

Rule	fr	cf
$A = lot, B = lot, C = lot \Rightarrow FR1 = 1$	0.270	1.000
$A = lot, B = lot \Rightarrow FR1 = 1$	0.582	0.922
$A = lot \Rightarrow FR1 = 1$	0.697	0.773
$TP1 = lot, D = lot, E = lot, F = lot \Rightarrow FR2 = 1$	0.121	0.846
$TP1 = little, E = little, F = little \Rightarrow FR2 = 0$	0.198	0.947
$TP1 = lot, D = lot, E = lot \Rightarrow FR2 = 1$	0.275	0.926
$TP1 = lot, D = lot \Rightarrow FR2 = 1$	0.363	0.846
$TP1 = lot, E = lot \Rightarrow FR2 = 1$	0.363	0.943
$A = lot, B = lot, F = lot \Rightarrow FR2 = 1$	0.473	0.956
$B = lot, E = lot, F = lot \Rightarrow FR2 = 1$	0.516	0.959
$B = lot, F = lot \Rightarrow FR2 = 1$	0.473	0.956
$C = little, D = little \Rightarrow E = little$	0.407	0.974
$D = little, E = little, F = little \Rightarrow FR2 = 0$	0.308	0.824
$D = little, F = little \Rightarrow FR2 = 0$	0.363	0.744
$E = little, F = little \Rightarrow FR2 = 0$	0.404	0.720

Table 6: min_{fr} values for association rules $X \Rightarrow Y$, based on χ^2-values on 0.01 significance level. That is, we demand that the probability that the rule holds by chance is less than 1%. Values are calculated for both datasets used.

$|X, Y|$	$n = 122$	$n = 91$
2	0.656	0.676
3	0.348	0.363
4	0.188	0.198
5	0.103	0.109

In our model, the root nodes indicate the probability of passing/failing the course and the leaf nodes are used to update the probabilities, when exercise task points are gathered. Actually, the exercise task points in different categories depend on each other, but this is not taken into account.

In *NB1*, the prior probability of passing the course is simply assigned to 0.5. In *NB2*, we can use *TP1* as a background variable, and define the prior probability of passing the course given that the student has got a lot/little of total points in *Prog.1*. This proved to be the most frequent rule for predicting *FR2* according to *Prog.1* performance. The conditional probabilities have been simply calculated

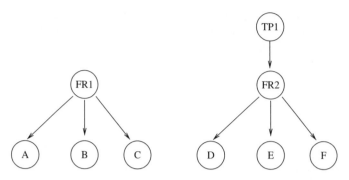

Figure 2: Naive Bayes models for predicting final results of *Prog.1* course, given the task points in *A*, *B* and *C* (left), and final results of *Prog.2* course, given the task points in *D*, *E* and *F* (right). *TP1* (total points of *Prog.1*) has been used as a background variable, which defines the prior probability distribution of *FR2*.

Table 7: Probabilities for naive Bayes models *NB*1 and *NB*2.

$P(FR1 = 1)$	0.500	$P(FR2 = 1 \mid TP1 = little)$	0.080
$P(A = little \mid FR1 = 0)$	0.167	$P(FR2 = 1 \mid TP1 = lot)$	0.727
$P(A = little \mid FR1 = 1)$	0.045	$P(D = little \mid FR2 = 0)$	0.732
$P(B = little \mid FR1 = 0)$	0.833	$P(D = little \mid FR2 = 1)$	0.300
$P(B = little \mid FR1 = 1)$	0.180	$P(E = little \mid FR2 = 0)$	0.829
$P(C = little \mid FR1 = 0)$	0.917	$P(E = little \mid FR2 = 1)$	0.320
$P(C = little \mid FR1 = 1)$	0.584	$P(F = little \mid FR2 = 0)$	0.878
		$P(F = little \mid FR2 = 1)$	0.660

from the data with rule $P(Y|X) = P(X, Y)/P(X)$. The complement probabilities can be derived by rule $P(X = lot) = 1 - P(X = little)$.

When the course proceeds, the prior probabilities are updated in the light of new evidence (exercise points in *A*, *B*, *C*, *D*, *E* and *F*) by *Bayes rule*:

$$P(FR|X) = \frac{P(FR) \times P(X|FR)}{P(X)}.$$

The predictions by naive Bayes models after each new evidence are presented in Table 8. In the beginning of *Prog.1* course, nearly all students have done many exercises and thus they are predicted to pass the course. However, when exercise points in *B* category are known, the predictions are already very good, both for passing and failing. *C* points do not improve the results much, because only few students had done a lot of those tasks.

In *Prog.2* course, we can predict the outcomes already before the course has begun, based on *Prog.1* outcomes. These predictions are already surprisingly good – better than *Prog.1* predictions, when *A* points were known. The predictions improve

Table 8: Predictions by naive Bayes models $A \Rightarrow FR1$, $A, B \Rightarrow FR1$, $A, B, C \Rightarrow FR1$, $TP1 \Rightarrow FR2$, $TP1, D \Rightarrow FR2$, $TP1, D, E \Rightarrow FR2$, and $TP1, D, E, F \Rightarrow FR2$.

Model	True positive	True negative
$A \Rightarrow FR1$	0.96	0.30
$A, B \Rightarrow FR1$	0.82	0.80
$A, B, C \Rightarrow FR1$	0.82	0.84
$TP1 \Rightarrow FR2$	0.96	0.56
$TP1, D \Rightarrow FR2$	0.96	0.56
$TP1, D, E \Rightarrow FR2$	0.82	0.85
$TP1, D, E, F \Rightarrow FR2$	0.80	0.78

fast, when D and E points are known. With F points we recognize a strange phenomenon: the classification accuracy decreases, even if we have got more evidence! This is totally correct, because F and E are highly correlating and thus the naive Bayes assumption is clearly violated. This is the only case, when we have met restrictions of naive Bayes model, and in practice these last predictions (when the course is over) are not so important. However, this demonstrates that naive Bayes should be used with care, when attributes are correlated. A better approach might be a general Bayesian network with dependencies between attributes, as well. Friedman *et al.* [20] suggest that the best accuracy can be achieved by letting each attribute depend on at most one other attribute. Dempster–Shafer theory [21] offers another alternative: we can update the beliefs with only strong association rules (e.g. $F = lot \rightarrow FR2 = 1$), but leave the other predictions untouched.

6 Evaluating the predictive power by cross-validation

Cross-validation is a standard way to evaluate the predictive power of a model, when no new test data is available. The idea is that the original data set of size n is divided k times to a training set and a test set of sizes $n - n/k$ and n/k. Each time a new model is learnt from the training set and tested with the test set. Finally the classification rates are summed to get the total (average) classification rates.

In our experiment, we divided our original data set into 10 training set–test set pairs. We constructed the corresponding linear regression and naive Bayes models for the following model structures:

1. $A, B \Rightarrow FR1$
2. $TP1, D \Rightarrow FR2$
3. $TP1, D, E \Rightarrow FR2$

These model structures were selected, because they allow us to predict potential failure even by in the middle of course. At the end of course (when all task points

Table 9: Comparison of prediction accuracy of linear regression and naive Bayes models. All models were evaluated by cross-validation and the classification rates on all test sets were summed.

Model structure	Linear regression rates		Naive Bayes rates	
	True positive	True negative	True positive	True negative
1	0.91	0.79	0.80	0.82
2	0.78	0.85	0.92	0.55
3	0.75	0.90	0.82	0.76

are known), the predictions are of course more accurate, but it is not of such benefit any more.

Each model was tested with corresponding test set and the classification rates were calculated. For naive Bayes models, the student's status was classified as *passing*, if the passing probability was ≥ 0.5, and *failing*, otherwise. The actual probabilities contain of course more information, but it was not used is this comparison. The average classification rates are presented in Table 9.

The most interesting and encouraging result is that both modeling paradigms were able to predict course performance for more than 80% of students, when the course was still on. This is especially surprising in the first test, when no previous information was available, and the predictions were totally based on exercise points. In test cases 2 and 3 the *Prog.1* performance was already known. Test 2 gives especially valuable information, because dropout and failing are bigger problem in *Prog.2* course and these models are able to predict the outcomes when only three weeks of the course has passed.

When we compare the models, we see that *the linear regression* model gives more 'pessimistic' predictions, i.e. it predict failing better than passing, while the naive Bayes model is more 'optimistic'. The general classification rate is also better in the linear regression model. This is mainly due to the naive Bayes's simpler model structure – the attributes contained only binary-valued information (whether student has got a little or a lot of points in a given category). However, if we consider only the general classification rates, we see that the naive Bayes model can utilize the new information (E points in test 3) better than the linear regression model. The naive Bayes model is also more general and we expect it to adapt better in a new course setting with different tasks and maximum points.

According to our initial tests with those students, who had filled the course prerequisite query, we expect even better classification accuracy in the future. Currently only 60% of students had filled the query, but we could find strong dependencies between the previous programming skills and course performance in both courses. Another important factor that should be queried is the student's knowledge in mathematics, which is known [22, 23] to have a strong correlation with programming skills.

7 Conclusions

In this chapter, we have introduced a general paradigms for tackling ITSs. We have focused on predicting the course performance in a distance learning setting, when only some of the exercise points are known. As an example, we have introduced two descriptive–predictive model pairs, correlations–linear regression and association rules–Bayes model. Both descriptive models have revealed statistically significant dependencies, which can be used to construct predictive models. In addition, when the predictive power of the models was tested by cross-validation, both predictive models were able to predict the outcomes with more than 80% accuracy during the course.

The applicability of both predictive modeling paradigms depends on some assumptions, which are revealed in the descriptive modeling. The linear regression models presuppose strong correlations between numeric attributes. Exercise points and total points satisfy this condition very well, but it should be noticed that the model can over-fit easily, if the attribute values vary between different classes. To minimize this variance we recommend to group similar attributes, in our case exercise tasks on similar topics.

The naive Bayes models do not catch only linear dependencies, but any conditional dependencies. They can be easily applied to any discrete data, but to restrict model complexity and thus over-fitting, we transformed all continuous attribute values to binary (*little/lot*). This makes the model very general, but on the other hand the naive Bayes model does not fit as well as the linear regression. An important issue is the naive Bayes assumption that attributes should be independent given the class. It has been shown that this condition is only sufficient but not necessary for optimality of the naive Bayes classifier, but our experiments suggest that the model suffers for strong correlations (i.e. linear dependencies). This situation occurs very often with course data, where certain topics are prerequisite for new topics, and managing former is reflected by latter. That is why we are currently studying suitability of other similar paradigms like general Bayesian networks and Dempster–Shafer theory. Another interesting question is whether the lack of correlation is generally a sufficient condition for naive Bayes optimality.

In the current research, we have simply tried to predict dropouts and failing as early as possible, but both proposed models can also be easily generalized to predict talented students who might desire more challenges. In addition, it might be useful to distinguish dropouts and those who fail in the exam, because they may need a different kind of tutoring.

Before implementing the ITS, we will carry on some more experiments to fully utilize all usable data. For example, our aim is to design a good prerequisite query, which all students should answer before the course. Other surveys [15, 16, 24] have reported that such prerequisite queries can predict the dropout at an early stage. In particular, the 'locus of control' – whether the student believes that she/he has control over performance in her/his hands or not – has proved to be the most important factor affecting dropout [24, 25]. This could be further divided into three factors, which are asked in the query: motivation, self-esteem and taking responsibility of one's own learning.

To summarize, the results from our experiments show the feasibility of data mining in order to personalize distance education courses. The data mining approach can also open the black box used in many adaptive or ITSs or learning environments. It is important for everyone in the teaching–studying–learning process to understand the explicit models used for description or prediction. For learners, this develops their meta-cognitive skills to observe, analyze and improve their learning process. For teachers, a model helps to understand and interpret the ongoing course at two levels: those of the whole learning group and of an individual learner. Therefore, data mining schemes can help the whole educational technology research community to move into the direction of semi-automation from a somewhat simplistic idea to automate the whole learning process.

References

[1]   Haataja, A., Suhonen, J., Sutinen, E. & Torvinen, S., High school students learning computer science over the web. *Interactive Multimedia Electronic Journal of Computer-Enhanced Learning*, **3(2)**, pp. 1–6, 2001.

[2]   Meisalo, V., Sutinen, E. & Torvinen, S., Choosing appropriate methods for evaluating and improving the learning process in distance programming courses. *Proc. of 33rd ASEE/IEEE Frontiers in Education Conference*, 2003.

[3]   Du Boulay, B., Can we learn from ITSs? *Fifth Int. Conf. on Intelligent Tutoring Systems*, pp. 9–17, 2000.

[4]   Kabassi, K. & Virvou, M., Personalized adult e-training on computer use based on multiple attribute decision making. *Interacting with Computers*, **16**, pp. 115–132, 2004.

[5]   Chou, C.Y., Chan, T.W. & Lin, C.J., Redefining the learning companion: the past, present, and future of educational agents. *Computers & Education*, **40**, pp. 255–269, 2003.

[6]   Wasson, B., Advanced educational technologies: the learning environment. *Computers in Human Behavior*, **13(4)**, pp. 571–594, 1997.

[7]   Weber, G., Episodic learner modeling. *Cognitive Science*, **20(2)**, pp. 195–236, 1996.

[8]   Cheung, B., Hui, L., Zhang, J. & Yiu, S., SmartTutor: an intelligent tutoring system in web-based adult education. *The Journal of Systems and Software*, **68**, pp. 11–25, 2003.

[9]   Ioannis, H. & Prentzas, J., Using a hybrid rule-based approach in developing an intelligent tutoring system with knowledge acquisition and update capabilities. *Expert Systems with Applications*, **26**, pp. 477–492, 2004.

[10]   Vos, H., Contributions of minmax theory to instructional decision making in intelligent tutoring systems. *Computers in Human Behavior*, **15**, pp. 531–548, 1999.

[11]   Hwang, G.J., A conceptual map model for developing intelligent tutoring systems. *Computers & Education*, **40**, pp. 217–235, 2003.

[12]   Mislevy, R. & Drew, H., The role of probability-based inference in an intelligent tutoring system. *User-Mediated and User-Adapted Interaction*, **5**, pp. 253–282, 1996.

[13]   Butz, C., Hua, S. & Maguire, R., Web-based intelligent tutoring system for computer programming. *Web Intelligence and Agent Systems: An International Journal*, **4(1)**, 2006 (in press).

[14]   Zapata-Rivera, J.D. & Greer, J., Inspectable Bayesian student modelling servers in multi-agent tutoring systems. *International Journal of Human-Computer Studies*, **61(4)**, pp. 535–563, 2004.

[15]   Kotsiantis, S., Pierrakeas, C. & Pintelas, P., Preventing student dropout in distance learning using machine learning techniques. *KES*, eds. V. Palade, R. Howlett & L. Jain, Springer, *Lecture Notes in Computer Science*, **2774**, pp. 267–274, 2003.

[16]   Shin, N. & Kim, J., An exploration of learner progress and drop-out in Korea National Open University. *Distance Education*, **20(1)**, pp. 81–95, 1999.

[17]   Hämäläinen, W., General paradigms for implementing adaptive learning systems. *Proc. of IADIS Virtual Multi Conference on Computer Science and Information Systems (MCCSIS)*, 2005. (http://www.cs.joensuu.fi/~wham alai/articles/paradigm.pdf).

[18]   Draper, N. & Smith, H., *Applied Regression Analysis*, Wiley: New York, 1981.

[19]   Domingos, P. & Pazzani, M., On the optimality of the simple Bayesian classifier under zero-one loss. *Machine Learning*, **29(2–3)**, pp. 103–130, 1997.

[20]   Friedman, N., Geiger, D. & Goldszmidt, M., Bayesian network classifiers. *Machine Learning*, **29(2–3)**, pp. 131–163, 1997.

[21]   Shafer, G., *A Mathematical Theory of Evidence*, Princeton University Press: New Jersey, 1976.

[22]   Page, R., Software is discrete mathematics. *ACM SIGPLAN Notices*, **38(9)**, pp. 79–86, 2003.

[23]   Devlin, K., Why universities require computer science students to take math. *Communications of the ACM*, **46(9)**, pp. 37–39, 2003.

[24]   Parker, A., A study of variables that predict dropout from distance education. *International Journal of Educational Technology*, **1(2)**, pp. 36–43, 1999.

[25]   Dille, B. & Mezack, M., Identifying predictors of high risk among community college telecourse students. *The American Journal of Distance Education*, **5(1)**, pp. 24–35, 1991.

CHAPTER 10

Rule mining with GBGP to improve web-based adaptive educational systems

C. Romero, S. Ventura, C. Hervás & P. González
Department of Computer Sciences and Numerical Analysis,
University of Cordoba, Spain.

Abstract

In this chapter we describe how to discover interesting relationships from student's usage information to improve adaptive web courses. We have used AHA! to make courses that adapt both the presentation and the navigation depending on the level of knowledge that each particular student has. We use data mining methods for providing feedback to courseware authors. The discovered information is presented in the form of prediction rules since these are highly comprehensible and they show important relationships among the presented data. The rules will be used to improve courseware, specially Adaptive Systems for Web-based Education. We propose to use grammar-based genetic programming (GBGP) with multi-objective optimization techniques as the rule discovery method. We have developed a specific tool named EPRules (Education Prediction Rules) to facilitate the knowledge discovery process for non-experts users in data mining.

1 Introduction

In the past, we have seen an exponential growth in the use of web-based technology in distance learning systems. At the same time, different artificial intelligence techniques have been applied to these systems to improve students' learning, leading to what is known as intelligent tutoring systems. The union of web-based learning with intelligent tutors has given rise to the current web-based educational hypermedia adaptive systems [1] that allow adapting the teaching to each individual student through the Internet. But the methodology used for its construction is static. Once the construction of a course is concluded and it is published on the Web for its use, the system logs information about the users' interaction with the course. However, teachers only use this information for student evaluation. We propose a dynamic construction methodology that uses the system usage information to discover information that will allow the teacher to improve the course. The application of knowledge discovery techniques and data mining in web-based education systems is a very novel and promising research area [2]. The same idea has been successfully used for a long time in e-commerce systems [3]. But whereas the e-commerce objective is to guide clients in making purchase decisions, the e-learning objective is to guide students in learning. Currently there are a lot of tools, both commercial and freeware, to carry out data mining tasks, and mainly rule discovery. Among all these, DBMiner [4] and Weka [5] stand out because they are very popular public domain systems and they have an integrated graphic environment that lets them carry out almost all data mining tasks. The main inconvenience is that these tools can be difficult to use for a non-expert in data mining (teachers are typically not experts in data mining). In addition they are of a general-purpose nature, so they cannot carry out a specific treatment of domain knowledge. In particular they do not contain features that are specific to the area of Adaptive Systems for Web-based Education (ASWEs) [1]. To resolve these problems we have developed a specific tool that has been denominated EPRules (Education Prediction Rules), to simplify the process of discovering prediction rules [6]. We have used AHA! [7] to make courses that adapt both the presentation and the navigation depending on the level of knowledge that each particular student has. We have performed several modifications in AHA! to specialize it and power it in the educational area. Our objective is to discover relations from the gathered usage data (reading times, difficulty levels and test results) from student executions and show the most interesting ones to the teacher so that he can carry out the suitable modifications in the course to improve it.

In the following, we start describing the use of rule mining techniques in e-learning systems. Next we show the process of discovering information, implemented in EPRules, and the proposed grammar-based genetic programming (GBGP) for rule discovery. Then, EPRules tool and the performed tests are described and some instances of the discovered rules are presented. Finally we present the main conclusions and future work.

2 Data mining in e-learning systems

Data mining is a knowledge discovery process to find previously unknown, potentially useful and non-trivial patterns from large repositories of data [4]. Web mining is the application of data mining techniques to extract knowledge from web data. There are three web mining categories: web content mining, web structure mining and web usage mining [3]. Web usage mining is the more relevant technique for e-learning systems. Web usage mining generally refers to the application of data mining techniques on web logs and metadata. Frequently used methods in web usage mining are:

- *Association rules:* Associations between web pages visited.
- *Sequence analysis:* Analyzing sequences of page hits in a visit or between visits by the same user.
- *Clustering and classification:* Grouping users by navigation behavior, grouping pages by content, type, access, and grouping similar navigation behaviors.

Association rules are interesting relationships discovered among data items [8]. The typical example is purchasing analysis, which can identify item pairs frequently purchased together. The use of rule mining in education is not new but was already successfully employed in several web-based educational systems. In a pioneering article, Zaïane [2] proposes the use of web mining techniques to build an agent that could recommend online learning activities or shortcuts in a course web site based on learner's access history to improve course material navigation as well as assist the online learning process. In other research, Wang [9] describes a set of tools for analyzing browsing log files based on data mining techniques such as association mining and collaborative filtering. Related research has been carried out by Yu *et al.* [10], who use data mining technology to find incorrect student behavior. They modify traditional web logs and apply fuzzy association rules to find out the relationships between each pattern of learner behavior, including time spent online, numbers of articles read, number of articles published, number of questions asked, etc. In other research, Ha *et al.* [11] propose to use web page traversal path analysis for customized education and web page associations for virtual knowledge structures. Finally, Minaei-Bidgoli and Punch [12] introduce an approach for predicting student performance using clustering web-based assessment resources and discover interesting association rules within a web-based educational system. They use genetic algorithms to optimize a combination of multiple classifiers by weighing feature vectors.

All these current approaches use the visited pages as input to the search, and hence the discovered information describes relations between pages. In contrast, our proposed method also searches for relations between concepts and chapter units of web-based courses, and not only between pages. We are going to propose a methodology that uses evolutionary algorithms as association rule mining method for discovering interesting relationships in student's usage data to improve adaptive systems for web-based education [13]. Four main steps are distinguished in our methodology there are:

1. *Construction of the course:* The teacher builds the hypermedia adaptive course providing information of the domain model, the pedagogic model and the interface module. An authoring tool is usually used to facilitate this task. Once the teacher finishes the elaboration of the course, all the contents may be published on a web server.

2. *Execution of the course:* Students execute the course using a web navigator and the usage information is picked up in a transparent way and stored on the server in the log file of each student.

3. *Rule discovery:* After the log files have been transferred to a database, the teacher can apply evolutionary algorithms to discover important relationships among the gathered data. We want to discover relationships between knowledge levels, times and scores. The teacher can use our specific mining tool (EPRules) in order to facilitate this task.

4. *Improving the course:* The teacher can use the discovered relationships in order to perform the modifications that he believes are more appropriate to improve the performance of the course. For example, he can modify the course's original structure (joining concepts, changing concepts from level or chapter, etc.) and content (eliminating or improving bad questions, bad pages, etc.). To do this, he uses an authoring tool again.

3 Students' usage data

The usage information we have used to carry out the prediction rule discovery is the usage information captured from a Linux operating system course. We have developed the Linux course using AHA! [7] because apart from being a generic adaptive hypermedia system, it captures all the user's usage information, and its source code is available so we can (and are allowed to) modify it. We have modified AHA! in order to increase its adaptation power in education [14]. More precisely, we wanted to adapt or personalize the system to each particular student depending on his knowledge level. To do it, we have modified: the user model, the domain model and the adaptation engine of AHA!:

- *Domain model:* A course consists of several chapters with several concepts, but the concepts and the questions related with these concepts are divided in three levels of difficulty (high, medium or low).
- *User model:* The student's knowledge for each concept, initial test or final test can be only one of these values: 0 (not yet read), 10 (low), 50 (medium) and 100 (high).
- *Adaptation engine:* Before studying a new chapter the students have to do an initial adaptive test to discover their initial knowledge level. The system then presents them only the concepts with this level. Each concept has an activity to evaluate the student's knowledge about this specific concept. When the students have visited all the concepts they have to do a final (multiple-choice) test to evaluate their knowledge about the chapter at this level. If they obtain a medium or high level in the final test they can go to a higher level. If they are in the highest level already they can go to the next chapter. In each chapter everything starts again (see Fig. 1): initial test, studying pages and doing activities and then the final test.

In Fig. 2 the Introduction chapter of the Linux course is shown at two different difficulty levels (beginner and expert). Each version has a different concept explanation that is suited to the respective knowledge level that it is expressed by the background color of the page and the text label: Grado 0 (beginner), Grado 1 (normal) and Grado 2 (expert).

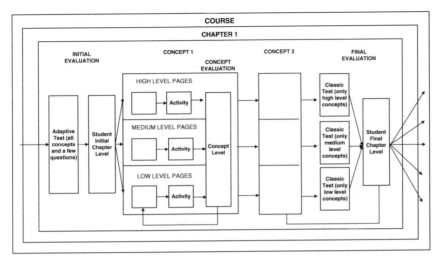

Figure 1: Modified AHA!.

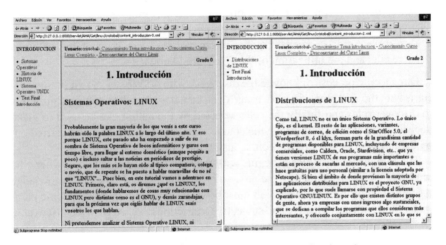

Figure 2: Two different levels of the Linux Introduction chapter.

The AHA! system stores the usage information in two web log files (logs and model files) in which the information about user navigation and user knowledge is respectively stored. In addition, we have used another log file (test file) to store the scores of the questions (activities and tests). The specific usage information used for data mining is the data logged for each student's interaction with the Linux course:

- *Times:* It is created from the log files and it contains information about the Web pages (contents, questions, etc.) and the time in which the student has accessed to them.

- *Levels:* It is created from the model file and it contains information about the knowledge level (high, medium, low) that the student has in each concept.
- *Success:* It is created from the test file and it contains information about the success or failure of the students in the questions (tests or activities).

Before applying rule mining algorithms we have transformed and moved all the log information to a relational database. This made (repeated) data extraction easier and increased the speed of the algorithms. During this process we have carried out the following pre-processing tasks [15]: attribute selection, data cleaning, discretization of continuous attributes and data integration.

4 Knowledge discovery process

The typical knowledge discovery process is shown in Fig. 3.

As we can see data mining is only one step of the full process of knowledge discovery [16] that consists of:

Pre-processing: It consists of the data gathering, data cleaning, discretization of continuous data, attribute selection, data integration, etc.

Data mining: It consists of the application of a data mining task: classification, regression, clustering, rule discovery, etc.

Post-processing: It consists of the interpretation, evaluation of the obtained results and the utilization of the discovered knowledge.

Our specific process of knowledge discovery with ASWEs is shown in Fig. 4. It starts with the selection of course usage data, then it applies data mining algorithms to discover rules and finally the rules selected by the author can be used to make decisions about how to improve the course. All these processes can be carried out by the teacher or author of the course, using the EPRules tool [13].

The rule discovery process begins with the selection of the database where the pre-processed usage data of the course to be used are stored. Then the knowledge discovery algorithms to be applied must be selected as well as their specific parameters and both the objective and subjective restrictions that we want the discovered

Figure 3: Typical knowledge discovery process.

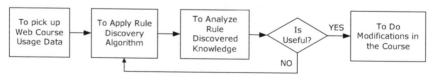

Figure 4: Specific knowledge discovery process.

rules to fulfill. After the algorithm execution is completed, the group of discovered prediction rules is displayed: the elements of the rule antecedent and consequent as well as the evaluation measures of each rule are shown, and it is determined if the group of discovered rules are interesting or not. This depends on the number of rules, on their quality with respect to the different measures, and on their semantic meaning. Then it is decided which of the discovered rules are sufficiently interesting to use them to take decisions on possible modifications to the course. If the rules are not considered sufficiently interesting the algorithm is applied again, with different parameters and restrictions, in order to discover a more interesting group of rules.

4.1 Rule discovery with GBGP

IF–THEN rules are one of the most popular forms of knowledge representation, due to its simplicity, comprehensibility and expressive power [4]. There are different types of rules depending on the knowledge they store. They are referred to as: decision rules, association rules, classification rules, prediction rules, causal rules, optimization rules, etc. The types of rules we will use are the prediction rules and Table 1 shows the precise format of the rules in (EBNF) Extended Backus Naur Form.

The objective of prediction rules [17] is to predict an objective attribute depending on the values of another group of attributes. Although the syntax of prediction rules is similar to classification rules that have only one condition in the consequent, any of the attributes can appear in the consequent of the rule as it occurs in association rules. We are going to discover prediction rules, doing for that a dependence modeling task. This data mining task consists of the prediction of relationships among attributes specified (or not) by the user [15]. Prediction rules are very popular in data mining because they usually represent discovered knowledge at a high level of abstraction and it can be used directly in the decision making process. Dependence modeling can be considered like a generalization of discovering classification rules [18] or a specialization of association rules [8].

Table 1: IF–THEN rule format in EBNF.

\<rule\>	::=	IF\<antecedent\>THEN\<consequent\>
\<antecedent\>	::=	\<antecedent\>AND\<condition\> | \<condition\>
\<consequent\>	::=	\<condition\>
\<condition\>	::=	\<level-attribute\> = \<level-value\> |
		\<time-attribute\> = \<time-value\> |
		\<success-attribute\> = \<success-value\>
\<level-attribute\>	::=	LEVEL.Name of a valid level attribute
\<time-attribute\>	::=	TIME.Name of a valid time attribute
\<success-attribute\>	::=	SUCCESS.Name of a valid success attribute
\<level-value\>	::=	BEGINNER | NORMAL | EXPERT
\<time-value\>	::=	HIGH | MEDIUM | LOW
\<success-value\>	::=	YES | NO

The rule discovery is carried out by GBGP [19] using multi-objective optimization techniques [20] which let us use several criteria to assess the quality of the rules. GBGP is a genetic programming paradigm in which individuals are represented by trees derived from a grammar defined by the user to specify the solutions of the problem, in our case all the possible prediction rules. This paradigm has been chosen because it allows a high expressive power which is going to simplify the interaction with the user, restricting the grammar so the requested rules will be the only ones generated. There are plenty of metrics to evaluate the quality of the rules [21, 22], each one centered on some (different) aspects of quality. However, there is no any metric which clearly surpasses the others in all application domains. For this reason this problem has been set out like a multi-objective optimization problem [20]. In this case there would not be a single attitude function associated to a metric, but several functions to perform the optimization at the same time. There are several ways to deal with the multi-objective optimization problem using evolutionary algorithms: the first one uses the 'aggregation function', while the second one uses the Pareto Front concept. In the Pareto Front (which is the one we use) there is a vector of objectives to optimize within each individual, and the purpose of the algorithms is to make the solution for the individual converge towards the group of the best solutions (in terms of all objectives together and not in any specific objective) [23].

The evolutionary algorithm we have used consists of the following steps (Michalewicz, 96). The first step is Initialization, next Evaluation, Selection and Reproduction steps are repeated until the Finalization condition is fulfilled.

- Initialization consists of generating a group of initial rules specified by the user. They are generated from the most frequent values in the database. We use a Michigan approach in which each individual (chromosome) encodes a single rule. We use encoding scheme value in which a rule is a linear string of conditions, where each condition is a variable-value pair. The size of the rules depends on the number of elements in antecedent and the last element always represents the consequent. The generic format of the rules we are going to discover in Backus Naur Form is shown in Table 1.
- Evaluation consists in calculating the fitness of the current rules. The fitness function used is made up of a three-valued vector in which each value measures one of the three main aspects of the discovered knowledge using a data mining algorithm [15], that is, comprehensible, interestingness and accuracy. The metrics selected as partial objectives are the ones named certainty factor measure [24], interestingness measure [22] and simplicity measure [25].
- Selection chooses rules from the population to be parents to crossover or mutate. We use rank-based selection that first ranks the population and then every rule receives fitness from its ranking. The worst will have fitness 1, second worst 2, etc., and the best will have fitness N (number of rules in population). Parents are selected according to their fitness. With this method all the rules have a chance to be selected.

- Reproduction consists of creating new rules, mutating and crossing over current rules (rules obtained in the previous evolution step). Mutation consists of the creation of a new rule, starting from an older rule where we change a variable or value. We randomly mutate a variable or values in the consequent or antecedent. Crossover consists of making two new rules, starting from the recombination of two existent rules. In recombination the antecedent of a rule is joined to the consequent of another rule in order to form a new rule and vice versa (the consequent of the first rule is joined to an antecedent of the second).
- Finalization is the number of steps or generations that will be applied to the genetic process. We could also have chosen to stop when a certain number of rules are added to the final rule vector.

5 EPRules tool

The EPRules tool [6] is a visual tool to discover prediction rules and it is oriented to be used by the teacher or author of the course. It has been implemented in the Java programming language and its main characteristic is its specialization in education through attributes, filters and specific restrictions for the ASWE domain. Furthermore, it is a dynamic tool, because it lets the (advanced) user add new rule-discovering algorithms and new rule-evaluation measures, by modifying only some configuration files (Java properties files) and by selecting the new types in the algorithm directory or the new evaluation measures. The graphic interface of the EPRules application consists of four main windows:

- *Data input:* In this window (Fig. 5) you can either open an existing database with the usage data of a course or create a new one and add new students to it.

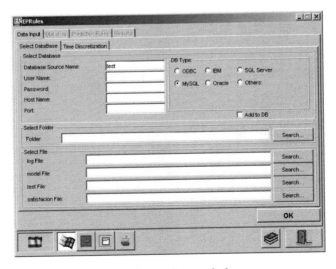

Figure 5: Data input window.

The course usage files (students' log files) must be selected in order to be pre-processed and integrated into a relational database. We have also transformed continuous attributes into discrete attributes using one of the following unsupervised global methods: equal-width method, equal-frequency method and manual method (in which you have to specify the cut-off points). We have only done discretization of the time attribute, assigning three values: HIGH, MEDIUM and LOW.

- *Data view:* If a course database has been opened from this window all students' pre-processed usage data can be visualized. These data are about the access times, correct answers and knowledge levels obtained by students for the different web pages (activities and contents) that make up the course. You can select either visualizing all students' data or a specific student's data, or just about a particular chapter of the course or about a specific concept of the chapter, or the visibility and difficulty level of a particular chapter (high, normal, low), or a type of particular information (time, level or correct answers).

- *Rule discovery:* This is the most important part of the tool because this is where the different algorithms for rule discovery are applied. The implemented algorithms are algorithms for decision-tree building like ID3 [18], an algorithm for association rule discovery like Apriori [8], an algorithm for induction rules like Prism [26] and different versions of evolutionary algorithms, specifically the GBGP algorithm with or without multi-objective optimization (Pareto). You can select the algorithm to use and its particular parameters of execution (Fig. 6) and also the subjective restrictions that the rules have to fulfill (Fig. 7), so that the rules finally shown to the user are really interesting for him.

- *Results:* This window appears automatically after the algorithm execution is completed and lets us visualize all the discovered prediction rules (Fig. 8).

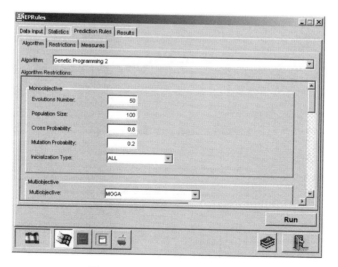

Figure 6: Algorithms window.

For each discovered prediction rule the conditions of the rule antecedent and consequent are shown and then all the values for each rules evaluation measure [21, 22] (certainty factor, interestingness, simplicity, confidence, support, interest, gini, laplace, etc., currently 40 different available measures). In a predetermined way, they appear ordered from the first discovered one to the last one, but they can be rearranged taking into account a condition or the value of any measure by simply clicking the desired column.

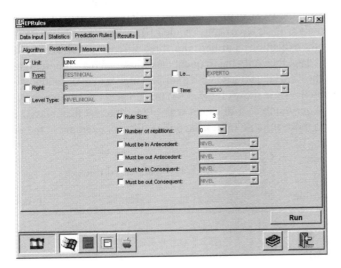

Figure 7: Restrictions window.

CONSEQUENT	SUPPORT	CONFIDENCE	CERTAINTY F	INTEREST	GINI	
ACIERTO.HISTORIA_INTRODUCCION-BAJA(0)=N	0.22222222	0.6666666	0.52631575	0.3964024	0.47668034	0
NIVEL.SSOO_INTRODUCCION-BAJA=EXPERTO	0.44444445	0.7058824	0.43277314	0.5989648	0.704543	0
ACIERTO.TESTF_INTRODUCCION-BAJA(2)=5	0.44444445	0.7058824	0.43277314	0.5989648	0.704543	0
ACIERTO.TESTF_INTRODUCCION-BAJA(3)=5	0.5185185	0.8235294	0.6334842	0.6859649	0.5718632	0
NIVEL.SSOO_INTRODUCCION-BAJA=EXPERTO	0.37037036	0.6666666	0.35714278	0.51500267	0.7277091	0
NIVEL.SSOO_INTRODUCCION-BAJA=EXPERTO	0.37037036	0.71428573	0.44897962	0.52396256	0.6551953	0
ACIERTO.TESTF_INTRODUCCION-BAJA(5)=N	0.37037036	0.5882353	0.3051471	0.5204245	0.8815461	0
ACIERTO.TESTF_INTRODUCCION-BAJA(4)=5	0.4074074	0.64705884	0.4044118	0.5724669	0.7730493	0
ACIERTO.TESTF_INTRODUCCION-BAJA(0)=5	0.4074074	1	1	0.5724669	0.5497257	0
ACIERTO.TESTF_INTRODUCCION-MEDIA(0)=5	0.5925926	0.94117653	0.7731095	0.7170813	0.39214888	0
ACIERTO.TESTF_INTRODUCCION-MEDIA(4)=5	0.44444445	0.7058824	0.2780749	0.56866586	0.6843784	0

Figure 8: Results window.

6 Experimental results

To carry out the tests we have used the log information of 50 students of Computer Science Engineering at the Cordoba university taking a course about the LINUX operating system. The course was developed with (and served through) the AHA! system [7]. Different tests have been carried out in order to compare the results that each implemented algorithm produces in the task of knowledge discovery. The objective is to compare the number of discovered rules in each case and the quality of them based on the previously set out measures about accuracy, interestingness and comprehensibility. Because evolutionary algorithms are not deterministic, the evolutionary algorithms have been executed 10 times, and we have used the average values of all the executions. Furthermore, three different tests have been carried out: first using all data, then only the frequent data (those with a support higher than 0.5) and finally, the range data (those with a support higher than 0.2 and lower than 0.9).

The obtained results show (Tables 2–4) that, in general, evolutionary algorithms generate a lower number of rules but with higher interest than classic algorithms, making them more suitable to be used online, like for example in the extraction of

Table 2: Number of discovered rules.

Algorithm	All	Range	Frequent
ID3	474	131	89
Prism	657	172	62
Apriori	5960	491	70
AE-GBGP	198	162	51

Table 3: Percentage of exact rules.

Algorithm	All	Range	Frequent
ID3	46.0	51.9	60.3
Prism	71.9	53.7	91.9
Apriori	84.3	90.0	93.0
AE-GBGP	76.5	86.1	96.3

Table 4: Percentage of interesting rules.

Algorithm	All	Range	Frequent
ID3	1.5	7.6	15.6
Prism	2.5	11.6	49.3
Apriori	3.6	7.9	53.1
AE-GBGP	21.9	60.4	76.6

knowledge in an adaptive system of education. Classic algorithms, and specially Apriori, produce very exact rules, but fail when generating rules with a higher interest and, furthermore, the length of the produced rules makes these rules difficult to understand. In addition, when we use all data (this could happen when the user wants to extract global information about the system without applying any type of restriction over the group) it generates a group of rules so large that it becomes impossible to exploit the rules later. The obtained results using the proposed evolutionary algorithms show that, in general, these algorithms produce a lower number of rules than classic algorithms. Moreover, the use of algorithms based on Pareto Front (MOGA and NSGA) let us optimize the three objectives at the same time, producing in all the executions the higher proportion of accurate, comprehensible and interesting rules.

6.1 Description of the discovered information

The main objective of our work is to discover a group of useful and interesting rules and to present them to the teacher so that he can easily take decisions about how to improve the course. Semantically, the discovered rules express the following relationships:

```
IF Level|Time|Success AND ...
THEN Level|Time|Success
```

Where Level, Time and Success are expressions referring to users' attained knowledge state (BEGINNER, NORMAL, EXPERT), the reading time for pages (HIGH, MEDIUM, LOW), and to information on students' successes and failures in the test and activities questions (YES, NO). Taking the discovered rules as a basis the teacher can decide which of the expressed relationships are desirable or undesirable, and what can be done to strengthen or weaken them (namely changing or modifying the contents, structure and adaptation of the course). The discovered rules show different types of relationships depending on which attributes are in the rule consequent:

- *Time:* It shows which attributes (in the rule antecedent) have an influence on the time (attribute of the rule consequent).
- *Level:* It shows which attributes (in the rule antecedent) have an influence on the level (attribute of the rule consequent).
- *Success:* It shows which attributes (in the rule antecedent) have an influence on the success (attribute of the rule consequent).

These relationships can make reference to chapters (levels obtained in initial and final tests) or to concepts (times, successes and levels obtained in exposition content pages and evaluation activities) of web-based adaptive courses. Using these discovered relations a teacher can make decisions about which modifications in the course are the most appropriate in order to increase the relationship (if he considers it to be desirable) or on the contrary to eliminate the relationship (if he considers it not to be desirable), changing or modifying the contents, the structure or the adaptation of the course.

Next we are going to describe the meaning and the possible use of several discovered rules.

```
IF LEVEL.interface-network-high = EXPERT THEN
LEVEL.tcpip-telnet-medium = EXPERT
(Interest=0.57, Factor Certainty=0.75, Simplicity=1)
```

This rule shows that the knowledge level obtained in the evaluation activities of the two mentioned concepts have been simultaneously very high (EXPERT). This indicates that the concepts (NETWORK, with HIGH difficulty level in the INTER-FACE chapter, and TELNET, with MEDIUM difficulty level in the TCPIP chapter) may be related to each other. In this case, the teacher should check the presentation content of both concepts and try to find what the reason of the relationship is. And he should then decide if merging both concepts into a single concept, putting both concepts in the same chapter, setting them to the same level of difficulty, correcting the rules that assign levels, or any other modification is most appropriate. In this particular rule example we have considered that both concepts should have the same level of difficulty. But if the levels refer to initial or final test instead of activities, it can be concluded that the chapters are related. Then the teacher can join the chapters, or put them one after the other, or on the contrary, create more distance between them.

```
IF SUCCESS.characteristic-introduction-high(2) = NO AND
TIME.characteristic-introduction-high(2) = HIGH THEN}
LEVEL.characteristic-introduction-high = EXPERT
(Interest=0.65, Factor Certainty=0.87, Simplicity=0.5)
```

This second rule shows that students, evaluated as EXPERT in the concept CHARACTERISTIC in the INTRODUCTION chapter at the HIGH difficulty level, fail question number two of the activity of this concept, and they also need a HIGH time to answer that question. So, this rule shows that something is wrong with this question (bad or not clear enunciate, several or no correct answers, etc.) and the teacher should review that question to see what happen.

7 Conclusions and future work

In this paper we have introduced a visual tool to discover knowledge in the form of prediction rules in order to help teachers to improve adaptive web-based courses. Particularly, we have proposed the use of GBGP with multi-objective techniques. The quality of the results, depending on the number of rules obtained and their interestingness, accuracy and comprehensible factor of the rules, is higher than for a number of classic algorithms that use only one measure or a composition of some of them to evaluate the rules. Regarding the usability of the discovered rules for taking decisions about the modifications to be carried out in ASWEs, the different types of rules, and the usefulness that they can have to improve the course have been described and illustrated using specific instances of the discovered rules in a Linux course. A specific tool, named EPRules, has been developed in order to simplify the whole process of knowledge discovery. This tool lets us carry out the pre-processing of usage data in web courses, the selection of restrictions on the type of information to be discovered as well as the application of data mining algorithms to extract the rules and to show them. Currently we are working on the following issues:

- Complete automation of the knowledge discovery process in ASWEs, so that the discovered rules can be applied directly to the course, without manual intervention by the teacher or author of the course, except for accepting or rejecting the changes proposed by the rules.
- Use other metrics related to the subjective interest of professionals in the discovered rules. Some work has been done using evolutionary algorithms [27] in which there is no aptitude function but individuals are assessed by an expert in each cycle of the algorithm.
- Use parameter-free rule mining algorithms [28]. In this way, we don't need to ask to the courseware authors for the specific values of the algorithm's parameters, and they don't need to understand what is the role of these parameters in the data mining process.

Acknowledgment

The authors gratefully acknowledge the financial support provided by the Spanish Department of Research of the Ministry of Science and Technology under TIC2002-04036-C05-02 Projects.

References

[1] Brusilovsky, P., Adaptative educational systems on the world-wide-web: A review of available technologies. *Int. Conf. on Intelligent Tutoring System*, 1998.

[2] Zaïane, O.R., Web usage mining for a better web-based learning environment, Technical report, 2001.

[3] Spiliopoulou, M., Web usage mining for web site evaluation. *Communications of the ACM*, **43(8)**, pp. 127–134, 2000.

[4] Klosgen, W. & Zytkow, J., (eds.), *Handbook of Data Mining and Knowledge Discovery*, Oxford University Press: New York, 2001.

[5] Witten, I.H. & Frank, E., *Data Mining. Practical Machine Learning Tools and Techniques with Java Implementations*, Morgan Kaufmann: San Franciso, CA, 1999.

[6]   Romero, C., Ventura, S. & de Bra, P., Discovering prediction rules in AHA! courses. *9th Int. Conf. on User Modeling*, Johnstown, PA, USA, pp. 25–34, 2003.

[7]   de Bra, P. & Ruiter, J., AHA! adaptive hypermedia for all. *Proc. of the WebNet Conference*, pp. 262–268, 2001.

[8]   Agrawal, R., Imielinski, T. & Swami, A., Mining association rules between sets of items in large databases. *ACM SIGMOD Int. Conf. on Management of Data*, 1993.

[9]   Wang, F., On analysis and modeling of student browsing behavior in web-based asynchronous learning environments. *International Conference on Web-based Learning*, Hong Kong, pp. 69–80, 2002.

[10] Yu, P., Own, C. & Lin, L., On learning behavior analysis of web based interactive environment. *International Conference ICCEE*, Oslo, 2001.

[11] Ha, S., Bae, S. & Park, S., Web mining for distance education. *APAN Conference*, Beijing, 2000.

[12] Minaei-Bidgoli, B. & Punch, W., Predicting student performance: an application of data mining methods with the educational web-based system LON-CAPA. *IEEE Frontiers in Education*, pp. 1–6, 2003.

[13] Romero, C., Ventura, S. & de Bra, P., Knowledge discovery with genetic programming for providing feedback to courseware author. *User Modeling and User-Adapted Interaction: The Journal of Personalization Research*, **14(5)**, pp. 425–465, 2005.

[14] Romero, C., de Bra, P., Ventura, S. & de Castro, C., Using knowledge levels with AHA! for discovering interesting relationship. *World Congress ELEARN*, Montreal, 2002.

[15] Freitas, A.A., *Data Mining and Knowledge Discovery with Evolutionary Algorithms*, Springer-Verlag: Berlin, 2002.

[16] Mitraa, S., Pal, S.K. & Mitra, P., Data mining in soft computing framework: a survey. *IEEE Transactions on Neural Networks*, **13(1)**, pp. 3–14, 2002.

[17] Noda, E., Freitas, A. & Lopes, H.S., Discovering interesting prediction rules with a genetic algorithm. *Conf. on Evolutionary Computation*, 1999.

[18] Quilan, J.R., Generating production rules from decision trees. *Proc. of IJCAI-87*, 1987.

[19] Whigham, P.A., Grammatically-based genetic programming. *Proc. of the Workshop on Genetic Programming*, pp. 33–41, 1995.

[20] Coello, C., Veldhuizen, D. & Lamount, G., *Evolutionary Algorithms for Solving Multi-Objective Problems*, Kluwer: New York, 2002.

[21] Lavrac, N., Flach, P. & Zupan, B., Rule evaluation measures: A unifying view. *ILP-99*, Berlin, Heidelberg, 1999.

[22] Tan, P. & Kumar, V., Interesting measures for association patterns, Technical Report TR00-036, Department of Computer Science, University of Minnesota, 2000.

[23] Fonseca, C.M. & Fleming, P.J., Genetic algorithms for multiobjective optimization: formulation, discussion and generalization. *Conf. on Genetic Algorithms*, San Mateo, CA, 1993.

[24]   Shortliffe, E. & Buchanan, B., A model of inexact reasoning in medicine. *Mathematical Biosciences*, **23**, pp. 351–379, 1975.

[25]   Liu, J.L. & Kwok, J.T., An extended genetic rule induction. *Conf. on Evolutionary Computation*, 2000.

[26]   Cendrowska, J., Prism: an algorithm for inducing modular rules. *Journal of Man-Machine Studies*, **27**, pp. 349–370, 1987.

[27]   Williams, G.J., Evolutionary hot spots data mining: an architecture for exploring for interesting discoveries. *Conf. on Knowledge Discovery and Data Mining*, 1999.

[28]   Keogh, E., Lonardi, S. & Ratanamahatana, C., Towards parameter-free data mining. *ACM SIGKDD Int. Conf. on Knowledge Discovery and Data Mining*, Seattle, WA, pp. 22–25, 2004.

CHAPTER 11

Identifying gifted students and their learning paths using data mining techniques

S. Bae[1], S.H. Ha[2] & S.C. Park[3]
[1]*Department of Industrial & Management Engineering,*
HANBAT National University, Korea.
[2]*School of Business Administration, Kyungpook National University,*
Korea.
[3]*Department of Industrial Engineering, Korea Advanced Institute of*
Science and Technology (KAIST), Korea.

Abstract

Today, educating the gifted and talented has become an important part of school education. School staff are increasingly aware of this. They develop special programs for the identification of gifted students and create a curriculum for them. In addition, existing gifted education pays too much attention to curriculum with methods such as a curriculum compacting, acceleration, and ability clustering. Currently, the identification of gifted students depends mainly on a simple identification test based on their age. But, the test results do not reveal all the potentially gifted students. In this chapter, we propose a neural network model for identification of gifted students and a framework for web mining in distance education to provide their learning path. With a specially designed questionnaire, we measure the implicit capabilities of giftedness and cluster the students with similar characteristics. The neural network and data mining techniques are applied to extract a type of giftedness, their characteristics, and their learning path.

1 Introduction

At present, formal education provided in schools is structured on the assumption of age-related development and intellectual homogeneity [1]. It further assumes that student's intellectual, emotional and social development depends on age. It denies the real existence of difference in intellectual, social and emotional development of students of similar chronological age. Also, gifted education has not been recognized as an important part of education.

In general, gifted education is only limited to a few gifted students because the frequency of its occurrence in the population is very low. Also, the most serious barrier to gifted education is the negative attitudes of teachers, parents of students who are not gifted, and the education policy for a homogenous education system. But, today, these negative situations are slowly changing. As mentioned before, all school staff have increased awareness and knowledge about gifted education and most parents of gifted children want to get a special school program for their children.

Thus, gifted education starts with the identification of potentially gifted students. Traditionally, to identify gifted students, a paper-based test was taken. The participants of the test would solve difficult and complex problems. But the 'real' gifted students might not pass the test due to the students' immature intellectual ability. A big chance is lost.

To avoid this, we developed an easy and simple test for measuring the implicit capabilities of giftedness and built a model for distinguishing gifted students from other students using neural network and data mining techniques. In addition, we identified a giftedness feature and classified the type of giftedness. Then, based on these results, we suggest how to design educational programs considering the type of giftedness and how to provide the feature of giftedness to potentially gifted students.

2 Data mining in education

2.1 Gifted education: a short review

In general, gifted education is composed of three parts. The first part is awareness and knowledge, the next is the identification of gifted students, and the third part refers to implementation of gifted programs, a supportive environmental and differentiated curriculum [1].

Research to identify gifted students is divided into two categories: an explicit approach and an implicit approach [2]. In the explicit approach, researchers gather and analyze a large amount of data from a participant group. They define characteristics of giftedness under the assumption that the group has specific characteristics of giftedness. In addition, it measures a degree of giftedness with the number of questions a student answers correctly. On the other hand, the implicit approach identifies characteristics of giftedness which are not measured from traditional IQ tests by investigating and analyzing implicit things which the general population has. Contents for explaining characteristics of giftedness are easy and simple. However, it is difficult for the approach to be used for measuring characteristics of giftedness because of reliability.

In Queensland, Australia, almost all schools are using identification procedures which include the UNICORN model of identification published by Education Queensland. The model uses the 'bubble-up' method. The UNICORN model is composed of four stages [3]. However, it needs a teacher's observation of the student and well-designed checklists which are hard to develop. Michael Sayler developed the Gifted and Talented Checklist for Teachers and Parents. It is the recommended identification tool for Australian state schools [4].

In a gifted education program, five components are considered commonly: thinking, curriculum compacting, subject acceleration, ability clustering, and extension activities [1]. Thinking, which is used for curriculum planning, enables differentiation in content and strategies to match the different abilities and learning styles of individual students. Curriculum compacting is a process used to streamline the regular curriculum. Subject acceleration occurs when a student takes a single subject 1 or 2 years earlier. Ability clustering is used to build ability classes for specific subjects. Lastly, extension activities include various programs such as individual program, think fest, and so on.

2.2 Web mining

Web mining has been used in three distinct ways, such as web content mining, web usage mining, and web structure mining [14]. Of them, web content mining is the process of information discovery from sources across the Web. In recent years it has prompted researchers to develop more intelligent tools for information retrieval, such as intelligent web agents, and to extend data mining techniques to provide a higher level of organization for semi-structured data available on the Web.

Web usage mining is the process of the automatic discovery of user browsing and access patterns from web servers. Organizations, which run distance education sites, collect large volumes of data, generated automatically by web servers and collected in server access logs. Other sources of user information include referrer logs that contain information about the referring pages for each page reference, and user registration or survey data. Analyzing such data can help organizations determine the thinking styles of learners, cross studying patterns across subjects, and effectiveness of a web site structure. It can also provide information on how to restructure a web site to create a more effective web site presence, and shed light on more effective management of collaborative study group communication and web server infrastructure.

Web structure mining discovers the link structures of the Web. They are discovered on the basis of the topology of the hyperlinks. These structures can be used to categorize web pages and are useful to generate information such as the similarity and relationship between different web sites. Web structure mining can be used to discover authority sites for specific subjects and to discover overview sites for the subjects that point to many authorities.

3 Identification of gifted students using neural network and data mining

As mentioned before, identification of gifted students plays an important role in gifted education. Existing methods of identifying gifted students only reveal the

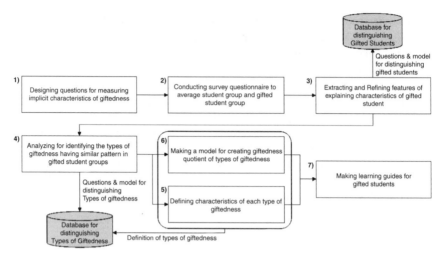

Figure 1: Identification of gifted students.

degree of giftedness. But, today, the degree of giftedness – such as IQ – is not enough. Other measures of giftedness such as EQ are proposed by many pedagogues and psychologists. In this section we propose a framework for identification of gifted students based on data mining techniques to classify their type of giftedness and each group's characteristics, as depicted in Fig. 1.

The proposed questionnaire measures various implicit capabilities of giftedness such as scientific attitude, leadership, morality, creativity, challenge, and motivation of achievement. In the third step, we compare gifted students' data with average students' data and extract and refine features that distinguish gifted students from average students. The questionnaire and analysis results are stored in the database.

After that, to identify the types of giftedness, we divide the students into several groups with similar characteristics such as interested fields and their capabilities. Next, we identify each group's features and patterns of each types of giftedness. When the type of giftedness is decided, we classify extracted features of each group into common and distinct features. With these results, we can define characteristics of each type of giftedness.

In the sixth step, we build a model to create a giftedness quotient of the type of giftedness. The giftedness quotient can be used as a measurement for evaluating similarity between students' characteristics and students' type of giftedness. In this manner, we could decide a student's type of giftedness by comparing each student's giftedness quotients. Finally, we can compile a pertinent learning guide by taking into consideration the giftedness features to develop capabilities of gifted students.

3.1 Design of questionnaire

For designing an easy and simple questionnaire for students, we investigated the implicit capabilities of giftedness. Implicit capabilities of giftedness are suggested by researchers such as Renzulli [5], Gardner [6], and Clark [7]. In the proposed questionnaire, we performed a pilot testing of the questionnaire to the measure implicit capabilities of giftedness.

For verifying each question's effectiveness, we randomly selected some students in the gifted students' group and average students' group and performed the identification test. With a one-way ANOVA test, we examined each question's power of discrimination. Based on this result, the final questionnaire was refined.

3.2 Clustering and classification of gifted students

The next step is clustering and classification. We divide the survey data into several clusters using the k-means clustering algorithm. The k-means clustering algorithm is a method for partitioning n objects into k clusters by measuring cluster similarity.

After that, we identify the characteristics of each cluster. In this step, we use a classification tool – C4.5 [8]. In general, classification tools are used to identify characteristics of each cluster and to build a model to predict clusters where unclassified data are classified. Decision-tree-based classification is obtained to a directed graph showing the possible sequences of questions, answers and classification. We can identify features and patterns for distinguishing a student's giftedness type from the others.

To realize the method, we must examine the most suitable number of type of giftedness as evaluating the k value which has a high intra-cluster similarity value and a low inter-cluster similarity value in the k-means algorithm. Also, with C4.5, we can select the features that distinguish one type of giftedness from another.

3.3 Creating a giftedness quotient using neural networks

A giftedness quotient can be a measurement for similarity between students' characteristics and their type of giftedness. That is, if a student has a high giftedness quotient, we can assume that the probability of the student belonging to the specific type of giftedness is high.

Creating a giftedness quotient using a neural network gives us two advantages. The first is that we can evaluate students' type of giftedness and distinguish excellent students. The second advantage is that we can measure a significant degree of features in the type of giftedness.

As shown as Fig. 2, we use a back-propagation neural network for creating giftedness quotient. A neural network is a set of connected input and output nodes where each connection has a weight associated with it. We build a neural network model which consists of n inputs for n questions, one output value between 1 and 100 and one hidden layer which has m hidden nodes. The hidden layer has $n \times m$ weight vectors which connect between each input and hidden node. The appropriate number of hidden nodes is known to double or triple the number of input nodes. In our model, a sigmoid function is used as the threshold activation function and the output node's activation function uses a linear function. The following is the procedure for building the neural network model for creating the giftedness quotient.

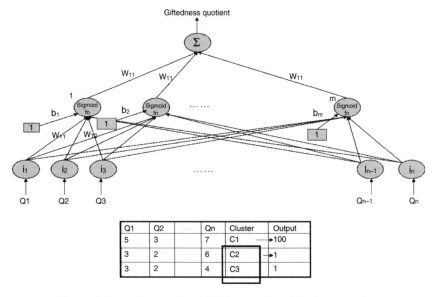

Figure 2: Neural network model for creating giftedness quotient.

We choose a specific type of giftedness in interested fields such as science, liberal art, and so on. Let us assume that we choose Type X in the science field.

1. We randomly select a part of the survey data and assign a target output value of 100 if the type of giftedness of the cluster that the selected data belongs to is Type X, otherwise 1. As depicted in Fig. 2, target output value for cluster C1 is 100 because the giftedness type of cluster C1 is Type X and that of the others are 1.

2. With a back-propagation algorithm, we reduce a difference between an output value and its target output value until the difference is less than a termination criteria.

3. When training is terminated, we can obtain the neural network model for creating the giftedness quotient. If the giftedness quotient of a student is close to 100, we can classify the student to Type C in a science field.

Based on our model, we can measure a significant degree of the features because we can calculate the variation of the output value when one question is increased or decreased in the input node.

3.4 Applications

To implement our neural network model, we developed an online identification system to distinguish gifted students and to identify their type of giftedness. In Fig. 3,

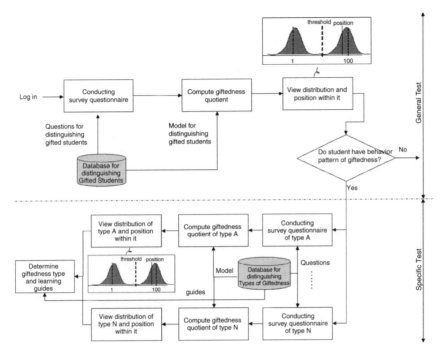

Figure 3: Online identification system composed of a general test and a specific test.

the proposed system performs two types of test; a general and a specific test of identification of gifted.

When a participant logs in the system, a general test of identification begins. Based on his or her answers, we compute a participant's giftedness quotient and view participant's position. If participant's giftedness quotient is more than a specific threshold value, we decide that a participant belongs to the gifted student group.

After the general test, the system gives various questionnaires retrieved in the database for identifying a participant's type of giftedness and computes a giftedness quotient for each giftedness type. Then, it shows characteristics of giftedness type and a learning guide. We applied our identification system to the two giftedness fields, a science and a liberal art field in Korea.

3.4.1 General and specific test: identifying of giftedness and their type

To extract the implicit capabilities of giftedness, we organized an advisory committee which consists of scientists, professors, teachers and parents of students. We chose seven implicit capabilities such as scientific attitude, leadership, motivation of achievement, morality, creativity, challenge and general ability. Based on that, we composed 77 questions for the measuring implicit capabilities of giftedness.

Then, we conducted the survey on 130 students in high school, 280 students in the science high school (science field) and 183 students in the foreign language high school (liberal art field). We identified features of ordinary type, features and patterns of all giftedness types related in each giftedness field. We obtained four giftedness types for each field and selected 34 features which explained giftedness types using clustering and classification techniques. We used k-means as the clustering algorithm and C4.5 as the classification tool.

We discovered eight giftedness types which have similar patterns (features and their values) and selected features identifying them. As shown in Fig. 4, we could present the pattern of giftedness types with seven feature sets. The ratio of each type means the number of gifted students, who belonged to each giftedness type, to the total number of gifted students in the given field. For example, in the science field, the giftedness Type C is the most common type of gifted students.

We defined eight giftedness types which have different values of feature sets. For example, Type D has high f2 (leadership) and f5 (creativity) values and low f1 (scientific attitude) and f7 (challenge) values. The others are zero.

With this result, we could provide a learning guide that could maximize their creativity and leadership. In addition, we could stimulate their scientific attitude and challenge and encourage their motivation of achievement, morality and general ability.

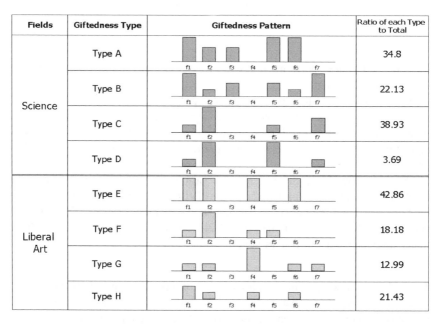

Figure 4: Characteristics and patterns of giftedness type (f1: scientific attitude, f2: leadership, f3: motivation of achievement, f4: morality, f5: creativity, f6: challenge, f7: general ability).

3.4.2 Evaluating the results of the identification test

To evaluate the results of the identification test, we compared average students and gifted students in the science field distinguished by our model. As shown in Table 1, the test category is composed of four types of capabilities – memorization, cognition, logic, and evaluation.

We perform a significance test to examine the difference between the gifted students group and the average students group using one-way ANOVA analysis. If the significance test is performed with $\alpha = 0.05$ and the p-value is less than 0.001, then the null hypothesis is not accepted. That is, we could say that there exists a significant difference between two groups.

Table 1 shows the results of the ANOVA analysis for the four types of capabilities. Because the p-values of the four capabilities are less than 0.001, we could confirm that the difference between the gifted students group and the average students group does exist. That is, it shows that gifted students distinguished by our model have more capabilities than average students in the fields of memorization, cognition, logic, and evaluation.

4 Web mining for extracting learning path

We have developed a framework for web usage mining in distance education, which is presented in Fig. 5. The framework starts with using web server logs and user login information, which is stored, maintained within a distance education system. Because the log cannot solely carry on the complete information for web mining and, therefore, include the difficulty in identification of unique learners as well as learner sessions or transactions, it is necessary to develop a framework to integrate any web information with back-end operational data, such as user login information [9]. Everyone who enrolls for distance education has to register in the system and his/her demographic information is stored in a user demographics database.

Before extracting the access histories of learners, on which the mining algorithms can be run, a number of data pre-processing issues, such as data cleaning and transaction identification, have to be addressed.

The major pre-processing task is data cleaning. Techniques to clean a server log, to eliminate irrelevant items, are of importance for this type of web log analysis. Elimination of irrelevant items can be reasonably accomplished by checking the suffix of a file name in the URL (uniform resource locator). We can remove all log entries with filename suffixes such as gif, jpeg, GIF, JPEG, which indicate graphic files. Identifying individual learners and their sessions can be done relatively easily because the system keeps login histories of each learner. For more details about the problem of transaction identification, refer to [10] and [11].

It is clear that the extracted access histories of each individual learner represent the physical layout of web sites, with web pages and hypertext links between pages, which are just given by distance educators (push-type knowledge structures). Once user access histories have been identified, there are several kinds of access pattern mining, such as path analysis, discovery of association rules and sequential patterns, and clustering and classification.

Table 1: Results of ANOVA analysis for four types of capabilities.

	Memorization			Cognition			Evaluation			Logic		
	Mean square	F	p-value	Mean square	F	p-value	Mean square	F	p-value	Mean square	F	p-value
Between groups	0.734	52	<0.001	1.371	122	<0.001	3.900	214	<0.001	0.974	67	<0.001
Within groups	0.014			0.011			0.018			0.015		

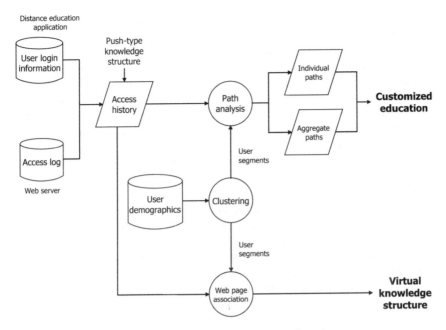

Figure 5: Web mining for distance education.

We perform web page traversal path analysis for customized education and web page associations for virtual knowledge structures, which could be formed by learners themselves as they navigate web pages.

4.1 Customized education

There are many different types of path analyses for customizing education. The most obvious is a graph representation [12], since a graph represents some relation defined on web pages; a graph with web pages as nodes and hypertext links between pages as directed edges, a graph with edges representing similarity between pages, or creating edges that give the number of users who go from one page to another.

Our work relating to path analysis involves determining most frequent traversal patterns from the physical layout of a web site.

The path analysis is performed from two points of view: aggregate and individual paths. The first part, aggregate paths, includes the process of clustering registered learners. A registration at the onset of learning can capture important personal information (gender, age, ZIP code, and education level) that can be enhanced and mined later on [13].

A web site database, which is especially created for user registration, can be segmented by one of the clustering techniques such as a self-organizing map, also known as a Kohonen feature map, to discover learners with similar characteristics. The resulting learner segments with access histories can be used to determine most frequently visited paths of learners in each segment in a web site (aggregate paths).

Examples of aggregate paths that can be discovered through path analysis are listed in Table 2.

The first aggregate path indicates 52% of learners in a segment with high educational level start at '/Information/DataMining/Classification' and proceed to a more advanced topic, such as '/Information/ArtificialIntelligence/NeuralNetwork'. The second aggregate path indicates that 65% of learners with low education, at first, study on a data structure of tree in a subject, 'Information'. But they go back to the data structures of stack and queue and list for acquiring background knowledge to better understand the tree structure.

The second part of path analysis is about discovering individual paths. It amounts to determining a set of frequently visited web pages accessed by a learner on his/her visits to the server during a certain period of time.

Discovering such aggregate and individual paths for learners engaged in distance education can help in the development of effective customized education. In addition, aggregate paths discovered from World Wide Web access logs can give an indication of how best to organize the educator organization's web space. The aggregate paths make suggestions on learning sequences to learners who belong to the same segment and share similar characteristics (e.g. education level). Later on, they can facilitate the development and execution of future web space design, such as dynamically changing a particular page (contents, hypertext links) for learners belonging in different segments.

Table 2: Aggregate paths of learners.

Count	Aggregate paths	Segment
52%	/Information/DataMining/Classification -> /Information/ArtificialIntelligence/ NeuralNetwork	High educational level learners
65%	/Information/DataStructure/Tree -> /Information/DataStructure/StackQueue -> /Information/DataStructure/List	Low educational level learners

Table 3: Association rules for discovering the virtual knowledge structure.

Correlation	Association rules	Segment
45%	(/Information/DataStructure, /Mathematics/Algorithm)	High educational level learners
53%	(/Mathematics/Derivative, /Help/Mathematics)	Low educational level learners
34%	(/Bulletin, /Chatting)	All learners

4.2 Virtual knowledge structure

Discovering association rules is to find all associations and correlations among web pages where the presence of one set of web pages in a transaction implies (with a certain degree of confidence and support) the presence of other pages. In doing so, we discover the correlations among references to various web pages available on the server by a given learner or learners in a specific segment. We can find correlations such as those shown in Table 3.

The first rule in the Table 3 shows that 45% of learners who belong to a high educational level segment and access '/Information/DataStructure' also access '/Mathematics/Algorithm'. The second rule states that 53% of learners in low education who access '/Mathematics/Derivative' make reference to '/Help/Mathematics'. The last rule indicates that 34% of all learners go around '/Bulletin' and '/Chatting' regardless of their educational levels.

The discovery of association rules in web server access logs allows web-based distance educators to identify virtual knowledge structures against push-type knowledge structures and helps in reorganizing web space based on these structures. We call it 'virtual knowledge structure' because it includes differences between the physical topology of web spaces and user access patterns.

4.3 Application of web mining to a web-based education system

The distance education system for KAIST, which deals with four principles (information, mathematics, physics, and chemistry), was developed by the KAIST educational center for science education. The system mainly aims at middle school and high school students. It took about a year to develop the system, and it has been fully operational from 1998 (Fig. 6).

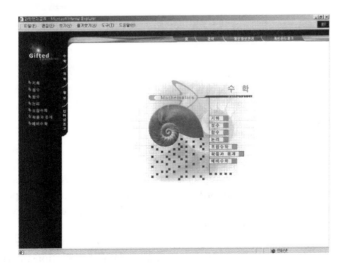

Figure 6: Mathematics and its sub-menus.

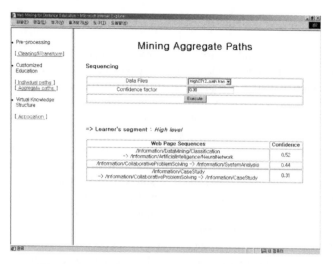

Figure 7: Aggregate paths for high-level learners.

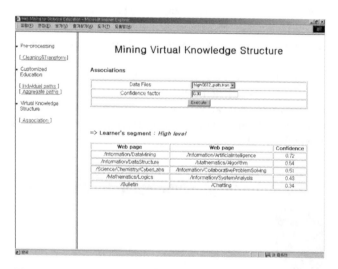

Figure 8: Virtual knowledge structure for high-level learners.

Figure 7 reveals several aggregate paths for high-level learners, as they frequently visit some web pages in order. The prototype system takes two parameters as an argument, such as an individual path file and confidence factor, with which sequential patterns discovered have to comply.

Figure 8 depicts the result of mining association rules among web pages for identifying a virtual knowledge structure. It also shows associations, correlations among web pages for the high-level learners.

5 Conclusions

In this paper, we have proposed a neural network model for giftedness identification and a learning path extraction in the distance learning environment using data mining techniques. We measured the implicit capabilities of giftedness with a specially designed questionnaire and classified the students with their types of giftedness. Data mining techniques such as clustering and classification were applied to extract the type of giftedness and their characteristics. The neural network was used to evaluate the similarity between characteristics of students and types of giftedness. The gifted quotient was gained from the trained neural network.

To evaluate our model's effectiveness, we applied our model to the science and the liberal art field in Korea. The evaluation test results showed that there are various types of gifted students and they have different characteristics. If we can exactly identify students' giftedness type, we can develop pertinent learning guides for maximizing their strong capabilities and encouraging their weak capabilities.

Discovering aggregate and individual paths for learners engaged in distance education could help in the development of effective customized education, and give an indication of how to best organize the educator organization's web space. The discovery of association rules could make it possible for web-based distance educators to identify virtual knowledge structures. In order to reveal the possibilities of application of web mining to distance education, we developed a prototype system for web mining, and showed the results of using web mining for educational purposes.

In the future, we will refine our identification model by using various data mining techniques and develop an intelligent learning-guide system actually for potentially gifted students.

References

[1]   Imison, K., *The Acceptance of Difference*, Report on the review of gifted and talented education in Queenslands state school, Education Queensland, 2001.

[2]   Renzulli, J.S. & Smith, L., Two approaches to identification of gifted students. *Exceptional Children*, **43(8)**, pp. 512–518, 1977.

[3]   Education Queensland Report, *A Model for Curriculum Provisions for Gifted Education and Talent Development*, Education Queensland, 2000.

[4]   Department of Education and Arts, *Framework for Gifted Education*, Queensland Government, 2004.

[5]   Renzulli, J.S., The identification and development of giftedness as a paradigm for school reform. *Journal of Science Education and Technology*, **9(2)**, pp. 95–114, 2000.

[6]   Gardner, H., *Intelligence Reframed: Multiple Intelligences for the 21st Century*, Basic Books: New York, 2000.

[7]   Clark, B., *Growing Up Gifted: Developing the Potential of Children at Home and at School*, Prentice Hall: New York, 2001.

[8]   Quinlan, J.R., *C4.5: Programs for Machine Learning*, Morgan Kaufmann: San Mateo, CA, 1993.

[9]   McNamara, J., Cleaning up web data. *DB2 Magazine*, Qtr 4, online edition, 1999.

[10] Chen, M.S., Park, J.S. & Yu, P.S., Data mining for path traversal patterns in a web environment. *Proc. of the 16th Int. Conf. on Distributed Computing Systems*, 1996.

[11] Cooley, R., Mobasher, B. & Srivastava, J., Grouping web page references into transactions for mining world wide web browsing patterns, Technical Report TR 97-021, University of Minnesota, Department of Computer Science, Minneapolis, 1997.

[12] Pirolli, P., Pitkow, J. & Rao, R., Silk from a sow's ear: extracting usable structures from the web. *Proc. of Conf. on Human Factors in Computing Systems*, Vancouver, Canada, 1996.

[13] Mena, J., Mining e-customer behaviour. *DB2 Magazine*, Qtr 4, online edition, 1999.

[14] Kosala, R. & Blockeel, H., Web mining research: a survey. *SIGKDD Explorations*, **2(1)**, pp. 1–15, 2000.

CHAPTER 12

Data mining to support tutoring in virtual learning communities: experiences and challenges

E. Gaudioso[1] & L. Talavera[2]
[1]*Departamento de Inteligencia Artificial UNED, Spain.*
[2]*Departamento de Llenguatges i Sistemes Informàtics*
Universitat Politècnica de Catalunya, Spain.

Abstract

Computers and the Internet are becoming widely used in educational contexts. Particularly, the wide availability of Learning Management Systems (LMSs) allows easy set up of virtual communities providing channels and workspaces to facilitate communication and information sharing. Most of these systems are able to track student interaction within the workspaces and store it in a database that can be analyzed later to assess student behavior. In this chapter we review some experiences using data mining to analyze data obtained from e-learning courses based upon virtual communities. We illustrate several issues that arise in this task, providing real world examples and applications, and discuss the challenges that must be addressed in order to integrate data mining technologies in LMSs.

1 Introduction

In recent years there has been a rising interest in using collaborative and communication tools in education. A new approach to e-learning has emerged with the concept of *virtual learning communities*. These are groups of people with common interests or goals that use Internet resources to improve their communication and coordination. In education, virtual communities share a common goal of learning and are usually monitored by a tutor. A simple but commonly used pedagogical model consists of making a tutor and a set of students members of a web-based workgroup with course materials available online (and possibly offline also) and one or several shared services. These groups are supported by the so-called *Learning Management Systems* (LMSs). These platforms offer a great variety of channels and workspaces to facilitate information sharing and communication between participants in a course and therefore enable collaborative learning.

Virtual learning communities offer a weaker form of collaborative learning than more structured interfaces that support collaboration, such as computer-mediated conversations through the use of dialog tags or sentence openers. However, there are two aspects that support our interest in this approach. First, although providing less elaborate support, educational virtual environments enable teachers to set up structured collaborative activities. Second, these sort of settings are rapidly becoming popular because of the availability of powerful open source LMSs allowing a relatively easy set up of the collaborative space and the flexibility they provide.

A number of key issues arise in the use of virtual learning communities. One concern is that students could need some guidance in order to take full advantage of the communication services provided by the community. In addition, tutors should be supported in order to manage the community and to monitor student interactions. While the first issue has received some attention by researchers, the latter has been largely neglected in the literature. However, supporting tutors is very important to make learning communities effective.

Although some platforms offer reporting tools, when there are a great number of students and a great diversity of interactions, it becomes hard for a tutor to extract useful information. Data mining techniques can build analytic models and uncover meaningful patterns from data. Usually, building data mining models require considerable expertise and cannot be done by regular course tutors. Therefore, achieving a seamless integration of these techniques into virtual learning platforms is a very desirable goal.

In this chapter, we describe the application of data mining techniques on data obtained from e-learning courses based upon virtual learning communities. First, we provide a general description of the data mining process. Next we present a real application example and then describe how each of the stages of the process is carried out. We illustrate several issues raised by these experiences, and we close with the lessons learned and the challenges we have identified in order to develop embedded data mining applications for virtual learning communities.

2 Data mining

Classical data analysis is hypothesis driven. The user starts from a question and explores the data to confirm the intuition. In a first level, we can have a set of predefined reports that reflect trends that are known to be of interest. In a more elaborate setting, we can use analysis technologies that enable interactive exploration of the data, such as OLAP tools.

While question-driven analytics can be a useful tool to understand data when a moderate number of factors are involved, it can be very difficult for the user to find more complex patterns that relate different aspects of the data.

An alternative to traditional data analysis is to employ an inductive approach to automatically discover significative patterns and tendencies. Data mining can provide these functionalities by building analytic models that summarize interesting patterns present in the data. From now on, we will refer to data mining not only as the analytical technique used to build models, but as the whole process that must be carried out in order to use these technologies in a real application. Therefore, data mining can be viewed as a cycle that consists of the following steps:

- *Identify a problem* where analyzing data can provide value.
- *Collect the data.*
- *Pre-process the data* to obtain a clean, mineable table.
- *Build a model* that summarizes patterns of interest in a particular representation form.
- *Interpret/evaluate* the model.
- *Deploy the results* incorporating the model into another system for further action.

It is widely recognized that successful data mining projects require a careful formulation of the problem and to understand how data mining is going to provide added value to the users. Although this step is commonly left implicit or neglected in some research literature, it is important in order to implement a closed-loop approach. We think that it is desirable to express the problem in terms of the particular domain, rather than in terms of the technological approach. Following [1] putting data mining into context contributes to determine three important aspects: the role of the final system, the scope and distribution of the inputs to which the system will be applied and the performance criterion and standards by which the system will be judged.

The application of data mining to educational problems and, particularly, to virtual learning communities is not very different than for any regular industrial application. For example, a definition such as 'a system to support the tutor in detecting and improving weak student performance' not only suggests the use of a predictive modeling technique but also determines the user of the system, the intended value that it is going to provide to the organization, how the results can lead to actions, and suggests that evaluation cannot be performed simply in terms of overall accuracy, since different situations may imply different prediction costs.

The primary infrastructure of a virtual learning community is based upon web and Internet technologies. Web-based environments can provide huge volumes of data about the user interactions through web server logs. There has been a significant amount of research on web usage mining from web logs [2] that unanimously recognizes the limits of this source of information. In the specific case of e-commerce it has been remarked a need to log higher-level events and not only page requests to better reflect user interaction in every particular context [3].

Although we focus on virtual learning performed through modern database-backed LMSs, we are not committing to any particular technological setting but only remarking on the general functionalities of LMSs that are of our interest. One important aspect that emanates from this setting is that we assume that in educational environments we are dealing with registered users. This has an important impact in the quality of the data gathered, since we remove the uncertainty associated to user identification when processing web logs. Second, we assume the existence of a tracking module that stores user interactions at a higher level than simple page accesses. Particularly, we assume that it is possible to gather detailed access and usage information on any of the services offered (forums, chats, file storage, etc.) by the LMS.

This structure is not uncommon in modern LMSs and provides a much more reliable source of data than web logs. This reduces the amount of work required in the data preparation stage, especially regarding cleaning and error or inconsistency detection. However, data transformations that summarize the information at the required level (e.g. student) are still needed. As happens with any other data mining application in which the data source is an operational database, the data model is not suited for analytical applications.

Having a well-defined task and a mineable table including the potentially relevant data, we have to choose a data mining technique to build a model. A model can be viewed as a set of patterns that summarize the data under some representational assumptions. A number of basic representation formalisms or its combinations can be used such as probabilities, rules, trees, etc. Similarly, a number of algorithms from machine learning or statistics are available. We are not going to get into the specific details of the different families of algorithms. Rather, we emphasize the distinction between two approaches related to the intended function of the data mining model. The most popular use for a model is for *prediction* purposes. The patterns found are used to make generalizations that enable to perform predictions about previously unobserved data. Models can also be used for *description* purposes, so that they can be explored in order to find patterns and relationships that explain the data. Note that this is not a disjoint division, a predictive model can be descriptive as well.

Finally, deployment depends on the particular problem. The most relevant aspect in both approaches is that results must initiate action, i.e. they must provide knowledge that can lead to action. Sometimes it is enough with providing non-technical users with appropriate interfaces and indicators that are expressed in a comprehensible manner. In general, descriptive models tend to be deployed in this way, as text-based or graphic reports and require some user intervention before they can be put in use. Predictive models can also exploit this approach, but usually are also well suited to be integrated into the operational systems.

3 Defining data mining tasks for supporting tutoring

In the early days of e-learning and, in general, of any web-based application, everything was based around contents. At that time, just putting some HTML contents on the web was enough to attract attention. The main addition on delivering courses through the web over traditional means that the student more control over navigation. Nowadays, and especially with the proliferation of LMS platforms, the situation is different. Content delivery is still important, but there is also a concern in communication and collaboration issues. A virtual course is not only a set of contents anymore but may also include a collaboration spaces and tools such as forums, chats or shared document areas.

The content oriented setting is basically a web version of the traditional intelligent tutoring approach and the problems more commonly solved using data mining are related to student guidance tasks [4]. The task of providing this kind of, possibly personalized, guidance is referred to as *adaptive navigation support* [5]. Usually, it provides the student with information such as the most appropriate links to follow in each stage of the learning process, building personalized pages or hiding some contents among others.

Virtual learning communities can also provide content and, therefore, take advantage of the mentioned adaptive tasks. But in this scenario, a student must work in collaborative activities carried out in a shared workspace. Actually, we can think of course settings in which relatively little content is provided and most of the work is developed through collaborative activities. This shift is important in determining useful data mining tasks because in the content based course layout the main problems are related to supporting students. Of course, tutors can be fed with some information or analysis about student performance, but their ability to influence in the course development is limited once the contents are designed. Now there are two actors equally involved, a student who has to perform the proposed activities and communicate and collaborate with other students, and the tutor who has to manage the group and organize the work.

Obviously, collaborative workspaces again pose some problems for students, who may feel overwhelmed because of the diversity of interactions available or have difficulties in finding someone to work with, for example. But since collaborative activities require a regular work by the student, tutors need to follow more closely the activities carried out in the course and the usage of the collaborative services available in the community.

Supporting students and tutors in their interaction with the group is an important factor to make virtual learning communities effective. This task is usually known as *adaptive collaboration support* (ACS), which is intended to provide support in groups that involve communication between multiple persons, and, potentially, collaboration towards common objectives [6]. Clearly, ACS can be the source for defining problems that can be solved with data mining techniques, especially since LMSs provide very diverse data about user interactions.

We have pointed out the need of formulating data mining tasks in a manner that states clearly the expected benefits in a particular domain, the intended users and, in general, the application context. ACS provides a convenient framework to achieve this goal. The notion of adaptive systems may appear to suggest that ACS tasks are mainly related to support students during a course. While this is true, we propose a wider view of ACS that also includes tutors, who in fact are part of the group albeit having a very particular role. Supporting tutors has largely been neglected in the literature, perhaps because sometimes it appears that simple reporting tools are enough to do the job. However, we think that this area is one in which data mining can have a significant impact.

3.1 A working problem

The course from which we collected the data was aimed to teach the use of the Internet in education. We set up a workgroup for the students and instructors providing forums, news, chats, file storage areas and personal web pages areas. At the beginning of the course we presented the students with a survey in order to evaluate how familiar they were with educational software, the Internet and several computer applications. Additionally, they could fill another survey indicating their interests (distance education, psychology, pedagogy, web design, etc.). In most cases the students were in turn lecturers interested in the use of the Internet in education, and, on the whole, they had little experience in the use of computers and Internet services.

Tutors closely monitored the students solving, on demand, the difficulties that arose. They proposed several collaborative activities to the students, mainly forum discussions and promoted using the platform services to help their peers. These activities were part of a larger course project used to assess students, but collaboration was not mandatory. Although there was also the possibility of contacting the instructors by other means, the main channels of communication were the course forums and electronic mail. The instructors also visited the chat room established for the course to detect if the students had difficulties in the course.

Given this scenario, our goal is to address the following ACS tasks for supporting tutors:

- Support for the assessment of the course by characterizing patterns of student performance that help to determine profiles of weak students and how to detect and improve this type of behaviors in future courses.
- Support in determining future activity levels during the course that might be indicators of student performance and in correcting undesirable behaviors.
- Support for detecting and characterizing behavioral patterns that may help to determine different student roles and manage groups in collaborative activities.

The formulation of these problems is what should drive the modeling effort more than choosing any particular state of the art technique. We will refer to the particular implications of each of these tasks in pre-processing the data, choosing a modeling data mining technique or evaluating the results in later sections. However, note that tutor support tasks are not only defined in terms of dynamic, continuous adaptation during a course, as are more student support tasks. Supporting tutors lends also naturally to assessment tasks at the end of a course that can be approached with a more traditional one-shot model building strategy.

4 Data pre-processing

The first step in any data mining application consists of gathering the relevant data. Under our assumptions, LMSs manage all their services through a relational database. This setting provides an integrated source of data that saves some pre-processing effort compared to other data mining applications. Note that we are presenting here a basic scenario. More sophisticated schemes that integrate additional information about students, which might be available in an educational organization, would require additional work.

As is the case in other environments, the data collected by LMSs are organized to optimize transactional performance, i.e. updation of records in the database. This is achieved by designing highly normalized database schemes that break down the data into multiple tables in order to avoid duplications. Accordingly, student and interaction data is spread over several tables, which becomes a problem for mining algorithms that require data to be assembled into a single, integrated and, in short, mineable table. We will refer to this table as the *analysis table*.

The contents of the analysis table are to some extend domain dependent and even, inside a particular domain, task dependent. An important initial decision is concerned with the granularity of the information contained in this table, or what we could refer to as the *unit of analysis*. For example, predicting student performance in a course may require a unit of analysis at the student level. That is, each row of the analysis table would represent the relevant information available for each single student. On the other hand, suppose we are analyzing student performance in a working session, i.e. the period of time between logging in and out of the platform. If we try to predict whether the student is going to complete a given task at the end of a session, we could think of the session as the unit of analysis instead of the student.

The schemes used in relational databases require an extensive pre-processing of data before obtaining a single analysis table, but they offer an advantage over data stored in plain text files, such as web logs. Processing the latter demands ad hoc implementations and a deep understanding of the log structure while relational databases provide powerful and widely known means of manipulating data through SQL clauses. Furthermore, the structure of a relational scheme is much easier to understand than custom logs.

Basic data preparation with SQL is performed by filtering sets of rows, selecting relevant columns, grouping rows to obtain aggregated columns and joining the tables resulting from several of these processes into a single analysis table. Frequently, the original data may contain errors and inconsistencies, so that a data cleaning process is also needed. Finally, we can enrich or transform the original data by adding new information or deriving new columns. It is interesting to remark here that the data gathered by an LMS may require less cleaning than data collected in other situations. Integrating data collection into a single source reduces the chance of inconsistencies and, assuming that the implementation has no flaws, the data should not contain many errors.

We will illustrate the process using our running example. As our first source of information we considered interaction data. Our goals required the unit of analysis to be the student, so we designed and executed a set of SQL queries in order to obtain aggregated data for each student in the course and each collaborative service. We ended up with a first set of columns reflecting the number of times that each student had used a given service or performed certain actions on the platform, as shown in Table 1.

Since the main collaborative activities in the course were carried out in the forums, we considered this service a good source of information to extract

Table 1: Columns reflecting data about user interaction with the system.

Number of sessions started
Number of entrances to the course chat
Number of messages sent to the course chat
Number of messages sent to the course forum
Number of files in the file storage area of the course
Activated alerts in the forum of the course
Created forum
Published a web presentation
Added bookmarks
Sent a email to the whole course
Registered in other courses
Number of messages sent to other forums
Number of entrances to other chats
Number of messages sent to other chats
Number of files in other file storage areas
Activated alerts in other forums
Number of static course pages visited
Number of threads started in the course forum
Number of threads replied by other students in the course forum
Number of threads finished in the course forum

additional columns. Particularly, we extracted the last three columns in Table 1 that included not only number of accesses, but more detailed use of the forum such as threads started, threads replied by other students and threads finished. Note than in a different setting additional information could be extracted if there is some intuition that it is relevant for the problem at hand.

Although most of the columns might be considered as generic for many data mining goals, some pre-processing is always task dependent. In our case, we differentiated between two different problems, namely, performing analysis aimed to give tutors an insight of what happened on a full course and developing more dynamic analysis models that can be used to make predictions through the course. In this latter case, time frames play an important role because evaluating a data mining model that makes use of the data gathered at the end of the course makes no sense if we want to use the model to perform a prediction during the course, when only partial data is available. We take this fact into account by generating an alternative analysis table that included service usage columns by periods determined by course activities.

Another simple but important step is filter the data in order to exclude information that is not considered relevant in our particular task. For example, we removed responses from the student who started the thread and from the tutors, but these data could have been considered under a different point of view.

Most of the previously described processes generate numeric columns. Considering that in our tasks the goal is support tutors, we regard comprehensibility of the resulting data mining models as a very important factor. Numerical columns may pose some problems for the interpretation of the models if they refer to magnitudes that tutors are not familiar with. For example, consider the following hypothetical rule characterizing student performance:

```
IF NumMsgForum >= 15 AND ActivityGrade > 8
THEN FinalGrade = pass
```

A tutor can quickly realize that the grade for the activity is high, because the ranges of the measurement are well known. However, it can be much more difficult to perceive whether 15 messages is an important quantity.

A solution is to perform the discretization of numerical columns so that they are divided into a set of intervals that can be mapped to categorical values. We discretized our data manually by observing the histograms of each column, but there are several discretization algorithms available. Using automatic methods can simplify the process but, as in other pre-processing steps, specific knowledge of the mining task should be taken into account. For example, we could enforce a special category for the null value, because we consider it interesting to distinguish students who have not used a service at all, independently of the automatically obtained intervals. The number of categories is another important issue if comprehensibility of the models is a requirement.

After obtaining the information related to user interaction, we decided to enrich the data with two additional types of information. First, we included personal data about students such as having a portrait, a bio or an URL. Second, we included data about general user interests and computer-related skills obtained from surveys. The latter needed some additional pre-processing since it is a typical case where null values have a different meaning depending on whether other options have been checked (negative responses) or not (non-existent).

5 Building predictive models

As in traditional classrooms, tutors in virtual learning communities, need to monitor student interactions. They need to detect or anticipate problems in student performance and to analyze and evaluate what had happened in the course to make improvements in future editions. In this section we describe how we applied predictive modeling to support three of the previously mentioned ACS tasks aimed to help tutors.

First, course assessment can be supported through predictive techniques by constructing models that characterize behaviors regarding some variable of interest (e.g. students who had failed the course). Although this goal has a descriptive modeling flavor, we include it in this section because we accomplish it by means of predictive techniques. However, unlike purely predictive modeling tasks in this case, in addition to accuracy it is necessary to take into account the comprehensibility of the models.

Anticipating a particular situation during the course differs from the previous task in that models cannot be constructed using all the data available at the end of the course. Since they should be able to provide predictions about a given variable during all the course, modeling techniques need to be evaluated as regard their capacity of reaching reasonably predictive accuracies at early stages of the course, when only partial behavior data is available.

5.1 Supporting tutors in course assessment

There are many different possible ways of considering the problem of course assessment but in our case, we set the goal of characterizing students who had failed the course. The idea is to get insight into the behavior of these students and find patterns that may confirm or deny tutor intuitions about the course and, possibly, particular cases of interest.

Given these goals, we considered that simply measuring overall accuracy was not a good performance indicator. Instead, we were concerned with obtaining the best characterizations regarding a particular label value, namely, failing students. Therefore we aimed at maximizing the accuracy of predicting if a student will fail. We aimed to cover as many weak students as possible, even though this meant labeling as failing some students who had actually passed the course. Additionally, we wanted to minimize the number of failing students labeled as passing the course. These notions can be formalized by using a confusion matrix and focusing on the true positives (TP) of predicting students who fail and the false positives (FP) of predicting students who passed the course.

As we remarked above, since our aim is to gain insight into the student behavior, it is important to employ predictive techniques that build models which can be easily inspected by the tutors. Particularly we employed three types of modeling techniques included in the Weka library [7]: decision trees (J48, the C4.5 implementation in Weka [8]), rule generation (PART [9] and JRip, the Weka implementation of Ripper [10]) and naive Bayes [11]. Since naive Bayes models consist of the set of conditioned probabilities between each feature and the class, we employed a wrapper feature selection method to obtain the list of the most relevant features which are presented to the users in order to provide a more simple interpretation of the model.

In our first attempt we employed all the data available from the pre-processing step described in Section 4 including personal information, survey responses and usage data. We will refer to this data set as DS1. Table 2 shows the results obtained for each algorithm. Looking at the overall accuracy seems that J48 is the best algorithm. However, a closer look at the confusion matrix reveals that most of this accuracy is achieved by correctly predicting if students passed the course but the accuracy of predicting failure is mediocre. Actually, JRip and naive Bayes provide the best combined results following our particular criteria for this task.

Exploring the resulting models revealed that they are too simple in order to provide interesting explanations about student behavior. Figure 1(a) shows an example of the rules obtained with JRip. Although it suggests that students who provided

Table 2: Results of applying several prediction algorithms to different versions of the data.

Data set	Algorithm	Accuracy	Failed		Passed	
			TP	FP	TP	FP
DS1	J48	0.72	0.64	0.19	0.81	0.36
	PART	0.70	0.67	0.26	0.74	0.33
	JRip	0.69	0.78	0.41	0.59	0.22
	Naive Bayes	0.70	0.75	0.37	0.64	0.25
DS2	J48	0.71	0.67	0.26	0.74	0.33
	PART	0.68	0.72	0.36	0.64	0.28
	JRip	0.71	0.76	0.35	0.66	0.24
	Naive Bayes	0.70	0.78	0.40	0.60	0.22
DS3	J48	0.72	0.81	0.38	0.62	0.19
	PART	0.66	0.76	0.47	0.53	0.24
	JRip	0.72	0.82	0.40	0.60	0.18
	Naive Bayes	0.64	0.76	0.50	0.50	0.24

an URL as personal information tended to pass, and that this feature is probably an indicator of interest in the course, there is not much more insight provided. Note that no rule describing failing performances is obtained, since they are covered by default. Looking at the most relevant features detected by naive Bayes, we also observed the presence of several survey-related features and the previously noted feature related to the student URL that were difficult to interpret.

From these results, we created a second data set, DS2, in which we removed the personal information and the responses to the survey. In order not to discard completely all this information, we added two binary features indicating whether the preferences and skills surveys were answered or not. Results in Table 2. Again, JRip and naive Bayes were the best performers, although the other two algorithms provided improved results.

The obtained models were somewhat better at explaining student behavior, particularly those obtained with J48 and PART, but they still trade too much accuracy compared with the other two algorithms. Figure 1(b) shows the new set of rules obtained by JRip. While it provides some additional insight with respect to the results obtained with DS1, they are still limited. We observe that creating a presentation in the course and a high number of sessions are good indicators. This results match the relevant features obtained by the naive Bayes model.

A problem that appeared to be in both datasets is that the number of messages sent to the forum was a very strong predictor of performance, so that alternative features that could described failing students were discarded. Although this makes sense due to the type of activities proposed in the course, this is a more or less obvious information for tutors so that it does not provides information.

(a)
```
IF NumMsgForum = medium THEN pass
IF URL = yes THEN pass
default: fail
-----------------------
```
(b)
```
IF NumMsgForum = medium THEN pass
IF NumMsgForum = low and ThreadStarted = none THEN pass
IF NumSessions = high THEN pass
IF CreatePresentation = yes THEN pass
default: fail
-----------------
```
(c)
```
NumSessions = veryLow
| EntranceChat = veryFewOrNothing
| | ThreadStartedNotReplied = yes
| | | Spam = yes: pass
| | | Spam = no
| | | | EmailAlerts = veryFew: fail
| | | | EmailAlerts = medium
| | | | | EntranceOtherChats = yes: fail
| | | | | EntranceOtherChats = no: pass
| | | | EmailAlerts = many: pass
| | ThreadStartedNotReplied = no: fail
| EntranceChat = few
| | MsgForumOut = no: pass
| | MsgForumOut = yes: fail
NumSessions = low
| TicketSent = yes: pass
| TicketSent = no
| | MsgForumOut = no: fail
| | MsgForumOut = yes: pass
NumSessions = medium
| TicketSent = yes: pass
| TicketSent = no
| | ThreadsOutReplied = yes: fail
| | ThreadsOutReplied = no
| | | PreferenceSurvey = no: pass
| | | PreferenceSurvey = yes
| | | | EmailAlertsOut = yes: pass
| | | | EmailAlertsOut = no
| | | | | EntranceOtherChats = yes: pass
| | | | | EntranceOtherChats = no: fail
```

Figure 1: Examples of different models obtained: (a) JRip with DS1, (b) JRip with DS2 and (c) part of the decision tree of J48 with DS3.

Therefore, we generated a third data set from DS2 that we call DS3 in which the number of messages to the forum were removed.

Results are now much better under our criteria for J48 and JRip, even though overall accuracy is largely unaffected. Figure 1 shows part of the decision tree obtained from which several patterns can be observed. For example, a pattern suggests that students who fail are not only those who have a low number of sessions but also those who are relatively unaware of the development of the course, as indicated by not having activated alerts or notifications (spam and email alerts).

5.2 Supporting tutors in anticipating student activity levels

The shift from traditional content-based courses to virtual learning communities is not merely a technical change, but means a course design oriented toward group work with strong emphasis in communication issues. Monitoring students is not just a matter of gathering and evaluating qualifications. Tutors need to observe their activity to determine their implication and participation in the course. In our running example, collaborative activities were developed mainly through forums and chats and, therefore, the eagerness to interact with these services should be a good indicator of the student performance.

Although monitoring activity could simply be a matter of manually observing access statistics for these two collaboration services, predictive models could help to improve performance at least from two points of view. First, we could have students who can be labeled as active even though their use of these services is limited, because they make use of other communication tools. Second, some unexpected patterns may arise that can be captured by the predictive model and improve overall performance.

Refining the formulation of the goals for our particular case, we found some differences with the task presented before. In this case, we were interested in a good overall prediction rate because we require to detect both weak and very active students. In the first case, tutors can correct the situation encouraging students to interact more. On the other hand, potentially active students can be good candidates as leaders or moderators of collaborative activities.

In our example, tutors labeled each student at the end of the course regarding their subjective assessment on their level of activity. In this case, modeling cannot be performed over the final data set that includes the student data over all the course. The correct model assessment need to simulate different situations during the course in which only partial interaction data is available. As we described in the pre-processing section, we generate different data sets by periods with accumulated information corresponding to the time frame of activities of the course.

We conducted some preliminary experiments using a decision tree to predict at different stages of the course the level of activity of each student. Without many specific tuning of the data sets we were able to reach an accuracy around 65% from early stages of the course, which turns out to be difficult to improve beyond 70% by observing more student interactions.

6 Building descriptive models

Predictive models are powerful analysis tools, but they still require defining a particular target of interest in advance. Sometimes, though, there is no particular variable to predict and the goal is to discover structure in the data and gain some insight. Although we have reviewed the explanatory approach in the previous section, here we will focus on *unsupervised* methods that are descriptive in nature.

In our experiences, we built descriptive models to address two different goals. First, tutors needed some support in determining student profiles in order to exploit them when assigning roles in collaborative activities. We employed clustering techniques to discover groups of students who show common behavioral trends [12]. Second, we wanted again to provide support in assessing the course, but this time without focusing in any particular target variable as we described in Section 5.1. We achieved this goal by simply adding a different interpretation to the clusters that allowed to assess if behavioral patterns were correlated with known goals.

6.1 Supporting tutors in determining behavioral patterns

There exists a large number of clustering algorithms and the choice depends on the particular application. For our purposes, we require an algorithm capable of dealing with categorical data. Model-based clustering is an approach that has gained wide popularity in the literature for both continuous and discrete data [13].

To help instructors interpret the clustering results in terms of the input features, we provide two pieces of information. First, we list all the features ordered by the degree of discrimination they provide between the different clusters. Additionally, we show a measure indicating how different the probability of each feature value in a given cluster is from the average probability in the full data. This measure of *lift*, commonly used to determine the interestingness of rules in association rule mining, reflects subsets of data inside a cluster that represent a behavior departing from the general tendency. The first information serves for the purpose of a general and comparative characterization of the groups while the second detects more particular behaviors derived from the segmentation obtained.

An examination of discriminant features for our first results indicated that the main characteristics used to form the clusters were the responses to the interests and skills surveys. While this clustering could make sense for some particular purpose, in our case we found difficult to obtain some insight. This is the same problem observed in previous section, so we used the data set we referred to as DS2 in Section 5.1. With this modification we not only reduced the influence of this sort of features but also changed the perspective of the data. After some experiments, we obtained a final set of six clusters that seemed to be reasonably explanatory.

Table 3 shows examples of group profiles obtained from the most discriminant features. Additionally, it includes interesting properties found in each cluster (differing from the average) but not covering all the members and the external

Table 3: Student profiles including discriminant features, interesting features and an external profiling feature (pass/fail).

Cluster (%)	Discriminant	Interesting	External
1 (0.10)	High initiative, promote discussions, high participation in forum	Create forums, publish presentations, participate in external forums	Pass (0.77/0.23)
2 (0.07)	Medium/low initiative, do not promote discussions, high participation in forum high participation in chat	Participate in external chats, create bookmarks, high number of sessions	Mixed (0.49/0.51)
3 (0.41)	Low initiative, low participation in forum and chat		Mixed (0.57/0.43)
4 (0.32)	High initiative, promote discussions, low participation in forum, low participation in chat		Fail (0.25/0.75)
5 (0.03)	Average in all areas	High number of visits to static pages, activate external alerts, participate in external forums, activate spam	Pass (1.0/0.0)
6 (0.07)	Low initiative, average participation in forum, low/high participation in chat	Activate alerts, use file storage area	Pass (0.89/0.11)

profiling feature. They can be used by tutors, for example, to identify some effects derived from group behavior.

For example, students in cluster 1 are highly collaborative and appear to help their peers promoting discussion and, in some cases, creating new forums or publishing presentations. This cluster tends to represent our ideal collaboration profile. In cluster 2, students tend to participate but at the same time their contributions do not generate too much interest. Since students appear to be motivated, a instructor could encourage this group to work harder in the course contents to better exploit their interactions. Students in cluster 3 exhibit a passive behavior. They could be representative of free-riders, learners that do not know how to work in the group or simply lack of motivation for social work. Additional information on passive interactions (e.g. reading messages) would help to determine whether they are taking profit of their peer contributions or just worked alone. Depending on the interpretation, an instructor could encourage this group to work harder or provide clues about how to contribute, among other actions.

In intermediate steps of the course, we could have used these profiles to help the tutor in creating groups of students to perform collaborative activities. They can also be exploited to assign roles into groups. For instance, members of cluster 1 could be a choice for moderators. Similarly, it can be taken into account that if cluster 3 represent free-riders, it may be counterproductive to join several of their members with a member of cluster 1, since this can promote the sucker effect. Obviously, these decisions would depend on the particular pedagogical strategy to be applied.

6.2 Supporting tutors in course assessment

To assess the course we should help tutors in understanding the groups obtained in the previous section in terms of known measures of interest. A strategy sometimes employed in data mining applications consists in defining a set of external characterization features that are not used to build the model. In our experiments we follow this scheme using an external feature that indicates whether a student has pass or failed the course.

It is important to note the differences between this approach and using predictive modeling to develop explanatory models. The patterns obtained in the previous section were aimed to explain a particular target while using unsupervised techniques we obtain first general patterns and then verify if they correlate to domain knowledge. We have used grades in this example, but other course dependent measures could have been added as well.

Note that there is no need to change the data mining technique and it is just a matter of enriching the interpretation provided to the user. As a result (see the last column in Table 3), we obtain a profile for each cluster described both in terms of the input features as before and the value of the profiling feature.

Results do not allow to conclude that collaboration patterns are always correlated with performance. For example, cluster 4 contains students with high initiative and that promote discussions but were not engaged in the forum activities. This suggests that collaborative activities may have some impact in student performance. On the contrary, cluster 3 consists of a group of students exhibiting low participation but with mixed results. In this case, this seems to evidence that collaboration was not necessary to pass the course.

7 Challenges and lessons learned

LMSs provide a suitable infrastructure to build e-learning courses offering a range of communication, information sharing and content delivering and evaluation facilities. However, they tend not to provide much support to tutors except for simple activity reports. In this context, we think that there is an opportunity for developing specific applications of data mining technology that unveil and predict student behavioral patterns.

The ultimate target of our research is the development of embedded data mining applications that fulfill the previous goals and are integrated seamlessly into an LMS. This objective requires incorporating all the data mining process into these tools while hiding most of the particular technical details to users. In this chapter we have described several experiences of applying data mining aimed to different tutor problems and using different assumptions and techniques. Next we review the lessons learned from these experiences and the challenges ahead.

7.1 Definition of data mining tasks

A concise definition of the problem to be solved using data mining is recognized as an important issue, and it gains even more importance if the process is to be automated. In this regard, we think that research should advance towards defining generic ACS tasks that can be shared between courses of different disciplines and that can benefit from applying data mining techniques. The tasks we have proposed are along these lines, but their generality stems from the fact that they include few domain specific knowledge. The support that they provide to tutors can be adapted to virtually any e-learning course over the same LMS and using typical services such as forums or chats. Solving problems relying on more specific domain knowledge appears to be desirable to build fully vertical applications, but, on the other hand, excessive specialization may cut down flexibility. Some LMSs provide not only basic services, but specialized activities which have their own pedagogical structure but, at the same time, can be applied to different contents. We think that future research should follow this idea by defining general templates that include collaborative activities together with ACS tasks and goals that can be solved with data mining techniques.

7.2 Data preparation

Creating a mineable table requires significant data transformations from operational systems. Usually, in business applications, beyond the technical complexities of the process, preparation is challenging because it needs to integrate data from different areas, each with its own focus and orientation. Using modern database-backed LMSs for e-learning provides us with a single and uniform source of data that alleviates some of these problems. Several common data preparation stages are greatly simplified or unnecessary, because there are few inconsistencies and errors.

Working with a common data model for any e-learning course, independently of its contents, should lead to a better automation of the preparation process. For example, we could provide a standard set of features out-of-the-box from a given service such as a forum. We should be able to provide easily not only simple measures such as the number of messages sent by a student, but many other derived features such as ratios by session, deviations from averages, etc. We should point out here that in our experiences we made a very limited use of derived features and that this is an issue seldom explored in the literature of data mining in our particular domain. It is known that generating derived features that provide a different perspective of the data can improve mining models, so experimenting with different alternatives to decide a good set of predefined preparation steps is an important research direction.

As is the case in defining generic goals, data preparation is still too complex and diverse to guarantee a complete automation of the process. A particularly challenging problem is that data preparation is intimately intertwined with the model building process so that data mining is usually a refinement process that iterates between these stages. One course of action could be to provide intuitive model validation measures so that end users are only required to iterate between model building and feature selection from a wide set of predefined features. Following this approach, an important research issue would be the impact and utility of automatic feature selection techniques [14]. As we have described, selecting the proper feature set has proved to be an important part in obtaining good models. However, while most of the feature selection research is aimed to simply improve predictive accuracy, we have also seen that in this domain there are other important concerns such as comprehensibility.

7.3 Model building

The problem of shifting the responsibility of model building from a technical data analyst to a end user is that the latter has the domain knowledge needed for the task but lacks the technical expertise. Although we have not given details in parameter selection for the different algorithms, once a validation measure is defined, this is not difficult to automate. We have seen that depending on the problem, the choice of a particular model is not only made taking into account total predictive accuracy. In our experience distinctions among different type of errors turn out to be important. Using a confusion matrix is only one simple way of tackling the problem, but other approaches could be tested such as different measures or cost-based learning systems. Depending on the intended use of the model, the goal might not be to reach the higher possible score of a given quality measure. Adaptive applications that are supposed to be used and refined over time may ask for other desirable properties such as rapid learning [15], even sacrificing some global performance. In any case, defining good validation measures for this domain is an important research issue. Ideally, the definition of generic data mining tasks should help to define associated validation strategies to fulfill each particular goal.

We have found interesting that comprehensibility for end users may not always be correlated with the common technical interpretation of the term, i.e. simplicity. Sometimes, a somewhat larger set of rules can provide a better insight to characterize student behaviors. Moreover, some models with high predictive values can rely on a few good predictors that are obvious in a particular setting and provide little real value. In this sense, there are several type of models that are commonly considered as more comprehensible but that, in practice, show some drawbacks. For example, decision lists such as those generated by the PART algorithm are not so easy to interpret because they are ordered and each rule depends on not matching the previous ones. Additionally, typical strategies to generate rule sets or decision trees select a single feature at each step discarding others that might be similarly relevant but that are considered redundant for prediction. For characterization purposes, redundancy may be in fact useful because it provides different interpretations of the model. This suggests either studying modifications to existing algorithms or – a possibly more reasonable direction – developing post-processing procedures that generate different model views.

Finally, as pointed out in [1], while in many business applications one of the main concerns is dealing with a large number of observations, in virtual learning courses this may be the exception rather than the rule. The need for larger data sets is also a recognized problem in machine learning for user modeling [16].

8 Concluding remarks

In our experience, data mining has proved to be a potentially useful tool to provide a good support for tutors in virtual learning communities. Nevertheless, automating data mining functionalities into LMSs still requires solving some research problems. On one hand, an LMS provides a very desirable capability, integrated data collection and management. By developing general ACS task definitions and data preparation templates, we have hidden part of these processes to end users. However, we have also seen that in order to obtain the best results, a high degree of expertise and user interaction is still needed.

In any case, once we have a working mining model, we think that the final deployment to support tutors in an LMS could be a relatively easy task. For example, for a given cluster we could easily obtain from the database the corresponding list of students and perform some action such as role assignment. In general, the only requirement would be to develop some integrated interfaces linking model descriptions to the LMS database.

References

[1]   Lavrac, N., Motoda, H., Fawcett, T., Holte, R., Langley, P. & Adriaans, P., Lessons learned from data mining applications and collaborative problem solving. *Machine Learning*, **57(1–2)**, pp. 13–34, 2004.

[2]   Srivastava, J., Cooley, R., Deshpande, M. & Tan, P., Web usage mining: discovery and applications of usage patterns from web data. *SIGKDD Explorations*, **1(2)**, pp. 12–23, 2000.

[3]   Ansari, S., Kohavi, R., Mason, L. & Zheng, Z., Integrating e-commerce and data mining: architecture and challenges. *The 2001 IEEE International Conference on Data Mining, ICDM01*, pp. 27–34, 2001.

[4]   Weber, G. & Specht, M., User modeling and adaptive navigation support in www-based tutoring systems. *Proc. of the Sixth Int. Conf. on User Modeling*, pp. 289–300, 1997.

[5]   Brusilovsky, P., Adaptive hypermedia. *User Modelling and User Adapted Interaction*, **11(1)**, pp. 87–110, 2001.

[6]   Paramythis, A. & Loidl-Reisinger, S., Adaptive learning environments and e-learning standards. *Second European Conference on e-Learning*, pp. 369–379, 2003.

[7]   Witten, I.H. & Frank, E., *Data Mining: Practical Machine Learning Tools and Techniques with Java Implementations*. Morgan Kaufmann: San Francisco, CA, USA, 1999.

[8]   Quinlan, J.R., *C4.5: Programs for Machine Learning*, Morgan Kaufmann: San Francisco, CA, USA, 1993.

[9]   Frank, E. & Witten, I.H., Generating accurate rule sets without global optimization. *Proc. of the Fifteenth Int. Conf. on Machine Learning, ICML98*, pp. 144–151, 1998.

[10] Cohen, W.W., Fast effective rule induction. *Proc. of the 12th Int. Conf. on Machine Learning, ICML95*, pp. 115–123, 1995.

[11] Langley, P., Iba, W. & Thompson, K., An analysis of Bayesian classifiers. *Proc. of the Tenth National Conf. on Artificial Intelligence*, pp. 223–228, 1992.

[12] Talavera, L. & Gaudioso, E., Mining student data to characterize similar behavior groups in unstructured collaboration spaces. *Proc. of the Workshop on Artificial Intelligence in CSCL. 16th European Conf. on Artificial Intelligence, (ECAI 2004)*, Valencia, Spain, pp. 17–23, 2004.

[13] Meila, M. & Heckerman, D., An experimental comparison of model-based clustering methods. *Machine Learning*, **42(1/2)**, pp. 9–29, 2001.

[14] Kohavi, R. & John, G.H., Wrappers for feature selection. *AI Journal, Special Issue on Relevance*, **97(1–2)**, pp. 273–324, 1997.

[15] Langley, P., User modeling in adaptive interfaces. *Proc. of the Seventh Int. Conf. on User Modeling*, Banff, Canada, 1999.

[16] Webb, G.I., Pazzani, M.J. & Billsus, D., Machine learning for user modeling. *User Modelling and User Adapted Interaction*, **11(1)**, pp. 19–29, 2001.

CHAPTER 13

Analysis of user navigational behavior for e-learning personalization

E. Mor, J. Minguillón & J.M. Carbó
Computer Science and Multimedia Studies,
Universitat Oberta de Catalunya, Spain.

Abstract

Personalization is an important issue in e-learning as it might help to improve both student performance and experience of use. In this chapter we describe a framework for studying the navigational behavior of the users of an e-learning environment integrated in a virtual campus. The students navigate through the web based virtual campus interacting with learning resources which are structured following the SCORM e-learning standard. These learning resources are structured following the concept of itinerary which it is basically a temporal scheduling involving several activities and the use of several learning resources. Itineraries may be structured depending on several personalization issues, ranging from student preferences to instructional designer and teacher teams expertise, including also knowledge extracted from the usage in previous semesters. Our main goal is to analyze such user navigational behavior for extracting information that can be used to validate several aspects related to virtual campus design and usability but also to determine the optimal scheduling for each course depending on user profile. We intend to extend the sequencing capabilities of standard learning management systems to include the concept of recommended itinerary, by combining teachers expertise with learned experience acquired by virtual campus usage analysis.

1 Introduction

Web mining is becoming a useful and common tool for institutions, as more and more data is collected from the users browsing the increasing number of web pages with interesting content. The validity of web mining as a tool for extracting useful information in any web-based organization system is described in several papers [1–3]. Three types of data are to be managed in any corporation web site: content, structure and usage data, which is the goal of this study. There are several fields where web usage mining can be used for understanding user behavior and navigation [4]. This expertise about users' behavior can be reintegrated in the web-based system (offering user personalized services, for example) in order to improve both user experience and satisfaction, and hopefully, to strength the customer relationship model [5, 6].

On the other hand, e-learning is one of the most promising and growing issues in today's information society. The growth of the Internet is bringing online learning to people in corporations, institutes of higher education, the government and other sectors. The growing need of continuous education and the inclusion of new multimedia technologies become crucial factors for this expansion. The appearance of Learning Management Systems (LMSs) has been a remarkable event for the success of e-learning environments, because there is no longer the need to design specific software for both content delivery and user management.

Several interesting questions arise from the use of web mining techniques in e-learning virtual environments. The possibility of tracking user behavior in such environments creates new possibilities for both web-based system architects and designers, but also for the pedagogical and instructional designers, which create and organize the learning contents. One of the most interesting possibilities is the personalization of the e-learning process. Personalization, which is a term widely used in other environments [7] such as e-commerce, is one of the most well-known and desirable properties of any web-based system, as it pursues the improvement of user experience and satisfaction. Personalization arises from the knowledge extracted from the navigational behavior of the e-learning virtual environment users, mostly students in this particular scenario. In fact, such scenario is a 'closed' system in the sense that every action performed by the users are related to the learning process, and with a set of previously established goals. Therefore, interesting hypothesis about user behavior, navigational patterns and other issues related to the learning process can be formulated and validated by means of web mining tools.

Personalization is a set of technologies and functionalities used in the design of user experiences. The functionality that is part of the personalization can vary, from simply show the user name on a flat web page, to a complex cataloging of the user navigation and the adequacy of products and services based in complex user models [8]. In online learning, personalization is revealed of great utility and importance. The adequacy and adaptation of the learning process it is very interesting as much at educational level as a level from establishing a one to one relationship with the student, and in this sense, it allows to present and offer high quality services and advantages to an every time more satisfied student. It is interesting to note the difference between the personalization and the individualization of the learning process. It is not the invention of this work to individualize the learning process, but to bring a methodology that allows the system to adapt the formative itineraries to the student needs and behavior. The different aspects related to instructional design are not approached directly in this work but it is necessary to mention that instructional design issues are of special importance and they are not obviated, in the sense that those issues are regarded as fundamental for the personalization system proposed goals. In fact, personalization is not an exclusive issue for information systems, but also for a wide range of applications (see [7] for several examples in other fields).

This work is part of a project concerned with the design of a standards-based e-learning platform that permits the creation of personalize user training itineraries [9], using reusable learning objects as the basic building blocks of the system as well as arriving at a formal methodological and normative specification for automated and semi-automated processes normal for any virtual environment system in the area of e-learning. As regards personalize training itineraries, the basic idea is to convert any current teaching plan (which is usually a completely linear document, static and isolated), into the skeleton of a dynamic and variable process which involves aspects of instructional design for user centered personalization (i.e. the student) and it is related to all the learning objectives which appear throughout an academic period (materials, resources, activities, teaching calendar, etc.), giving rise to what is called a learning itinerary. In this way, learning objects, structured and labeled using standards (LOM for example), are combined according to pedagogical criteria, the know-how of the teaching team, and the recommendations derived from observational studies realized previously with the users of the virtual classrooms (students principally, but also tutors and teachers), creating different possible formative itineraries. The itineraries form a non-linear graph structure which permits the expression of the whole richness of the learning process (obligatory and optional activities, repetition of activities, etc.). Regarding the specification of processes, we will develop a methodology which permits us to define consistent, unambiguous behaviors in learning systems, as currently the concept of itinerary, which are valid for any educative environment based on e-learning. The utilization of the SCORM standard for the representation of these itineraries assures a correct presentation of those contents so that the student has the liberty to advance at his/her own rhythm, but within a framework which has been defined previously by the teaching team.

The system follows all the user actions with two objectives: first, to adapt the learning process according to the rhythm and the actions of each user, as well as the results obtained; secondly, to collect information which can be analyzed later in order to extract useful information for usability evaluation, designing itineraries and measuring the quality of the personalization system, to detect possible problems and unclear points. The adequate combination of learning objects can be automated or semi-automated due to the existence of basic processes formally defined using an ontology and a standard language of definition of learning objects, in such a way that the system can use the process descriptions in the specification of processes that might be automated (to acquire learning processes, or compose new ones based on the learning objectives defined and the needs of the user, to cite some examples). Finally, the usability criteria and interaction between the user and the personalization system is also an important aspect to take into account when designing the system, in order to obtain a balance between privacy, flexibility and supervision, and assure the quality and accessibility of the proposed system.

2 E-learning environments

The intensive use of Internet possibilities not only for content searching and delivery but also for interface design and implementation has completely changed the visions in the open distance education field. E-learning is one of the most promising and growing issues in the information society nowadays. The growth of the Internet is bringing online education to people in corporations, institutes of higher education, the government and other sectors [10]. The growing need of continuous education and the inclusion of new multimedia technologies become crucial factors for this expansion.

One of the most interesting possibilities in any virtual environment is tracking user navigational behavior for analysis purposes, as it may help to discover unusual facts about the system itself. For example, having a user navigational model [11] may be used to perform an automated usability evaluation, detecting whether the system web interface was properly designed or not, and where users find obstacles and difficulties to reach out their objectives. It can be also used to detect bottleneck problems or web areas not used by most users. In the case of a virtual e-learning environment, several analysis levels can be determined and different research questions can be answered with the aid of web mining tools. Instructional designers, teachers and web designers need powerful tools for visualizing all the information collected in a virtual e-learning environment in order to improve the learning process and, thus, user experience and satisfaction, by means of an adaptive [12] environment: monitoring and interpreting the activities of its users [13], inferring user requirements and preferences, and acting upon the available knowledge on its users.

One of the related problems with the design of an e-learning environment is to obtain information about the users' actions, behavior and navigation and about the system usage. As it is described in [1], it is difficult to monitor what the users really do and what is expected they do in the form of navigation and behavior patterns. E-learning environments are usually designed taking usability into account, but it is not easy to determine whether the users feel comfortable with the environment or not, and whether they are capable of carrying out the tasks and actions related with the learning process or not. The extraction of the real learning and training patterns can be of great utility, among other purposes, to determine the degree of quality of the e-learning environment design and to evaluate the concordance degree among the usability requirements and the navigation behavior of the users. For example, it could be very interesting to find correlation among behavior patterns and the instructional and pedagogic design issues. The extraction of behavior and learning patterns must not be used in anyway with the aim of inspecting users and obtaining data that can be used with other goals than just guaranteeing a satisfactory learning and training process. The privacy aspects related to mining user behavior data and system usage data are described in [14], and some real scenario cases can be found in [15]. In Internet and e-learning environments it is not clear yet which indicators, metrics and usability data are suitable and relevant when designing processes and making decisions to design the end-user experience. There are still many design decisions based on hypotheses that are not contrasted with any type of objective data or real facts. The approach described in this chapter faces these issues and suggests a methodology that can serve to obtain data and results that they provide knowledge about users, their behavior and the environment usage, beyond the usual and common metrics like the hits or the number of accesses to a page [16]. Analyzing the log files generated and stored by an e-learning environment or platform and taking the information about the user's interactions and activities that the system stores, certain navigation paths and patterns can be obtained [17, 18]. Many times, in order to construct accurate paths, the information in the log files should be complemented with other sources of data as embedded marks placed in several points of the virtual environment.

2.1 The UOC virtual campus

The Universitat Oberta de Catalunya [19] (UOC [20], known as Open University of Catalonia in English) is a completely virtual campus which offers 19 official degrees, several graduate programs and post-graduate studies, and a doctoral degree, with more than 35,000 students and more than 1500 people including instructional designers, teachers, tutors, academic and technical staff. The UOC virtual campus is an integrated e-learning environment which allows users to communicate with other users using a mail system and includes an agenda, a news system, virtual classrooms, a digital library and other related e-learning tools. Although the use of classical text printed books is still massive, there is also a growing use of web based e-books and other online learning resources, so the introduction of new e-learning standards such as SCORM [21] is becoming a necessity for maintaining the constant evolution of the virtual campus.

Figure 1 shows the typical initial page that is loaded once an user logs into the virtual campus. Basically, this page includes a left vertical frame with a dynamic menu for accessing all the parts of the virtual campus, a top horizontal frame with recursive navigational buttons for the general and most common actions and, depending on user profile, a set links with all the information of the subjects he or she is enrolled to, and all the latest news in the virtual campus.

Basically, a student taking part in a course has an environment for communicating with the teachers and the other students, a learning plan and a calendar which includes a basic schedule for the activities needed to follow the course. This calendar is a default learning itinerary which is created by the instructional designers and the teachers of the course. The student has access to several learning resources (documents, exercises, etc.) accordingly to such itinerary. Because of the typology of the institution and the courses, which usually are taken in one academic semester (actually, around 15 weeks), the time unit used for designing itineraries is one week. Therefore, when we talk about navigational patterns we need to combine all the different user sessions along the academic semester in a single long-term session, rather than using the information contained in a single login session. It is remarkable that, although it is not possible to predict user behavior for a single session, the set of possible actions and activities is known, as the student navigates through a closed e-learning environment with a specific goal, i.e. to successfully achieve the learning

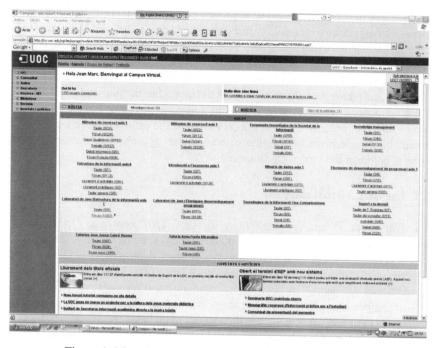

Figure 1: Virtual campus start page once user has logged in.

goals and fulfill the course requirements in order to pass the course exams. This fact can be also used to determine the variables used in the experimental setup. Each course involves a team of instructional designers, a team of teachers, the students which will take part of such course, and a set of learning resources. These learning resources are structured following the concept of itinerary which it is basically a temporal scheduling involving several activities and the use of several learning resources.

The UOC virtual campus is undergoing a structural revision in order to incorporate the use of new e-learning standards for improving user experience by means of personalization [9]. The inclusion of e-learning standards will allow a better tracking of students behavior (using the SCORM 2004 standard [21] capabilities) when accessing the learning resources, shifting also from a blended offline and online learning style towards a more online oriented learning.

2.2 Virtual campus architecture and services

The UOC virtual campus is built upon a complex database server system which uses a hierarchical structure of servers which deal with different kinds of user requests. There are up to 24 front-end servers (depending on the server load at each moment), and an automated load-balance system moves each user login to the front-end with lower load at that moment, switching on and off the total number of front-ends depending on system load. Other database servers for the digital library, the corporate intranet services, and other management requirements are also connected to the main database server system.

Briefly, the virtual campus uses client-server web technology and common interface to integrate a series of services and functionalities. These functionalities include: access to online educational materials, library resources, and general academic and cultural information; student enquiries management service; and interaction with professors and other students through predefined communication channels (e.g. forums, virtual laboratories, activity spaces). Among others, the following services are offered to students: an email account; a collection of virtual classrooms, where each one has several communication spaces where students and teachers can interact and share learning resources; a digital library which integrates all the digital and non-digital contents into the virtual campus. When users navigate through these services, they leave a track which can be posteriorly analyzed for user modeling purposes. Most of this information is collected by the web servers in the form of server log files, according to the Apache common log format.

3 Navigational behavior analysis

Navigation behavior analysis and user studies may cover a very wide range of potential research and methods, varying from the study of user navigation and choices in a virtual library or in a online store, to the qualitative discovery of user needs and expectations when navigating through a web site. There are many approaches to study and obtain information about user behavior in a computer system or in a web environment. Some of them are quantitative, taking into account the data and events generated and collected by the system [22] these quantitative methods usually focus on statistical analysis using, in some cases, visualization techniques to better understand what users do [23]. Gathering data related with usability parameters and measures may be useful for automating usability evaluation [24] and quality assessment. Other approaches are more qualitative, using methods to handle the complexity of human behavior. In all those different approaches similar issues are addressed and a set of common goals related with usability and with usability data are pursued. Moreover, the combination and fusion of such approaches and methods has been shown its great potential for carrying out user behavior studies [25].

This work focuses the users' knowledge and modeling on the information of their navigation paths and once obtained, the construction of navigation behavior patterns, with the aims of better re-designing the system not only to remove obstacles to the users activities, but also to tailor such design to user characteristics [22]. Following this approach, three different user navigation and behavior patterns levels are distinguished: session level, academic course level and lifelong learning level. Each of these levels of navigation, use and behavior will provide relevant information for constructing the user model and will allow achieving different kind of goals. These three levels arise in a natural way from the use that the students make of the virtual campus and the distinctive dynamics of their learning and training when carrying out online distance studies.

3.1 Navigational levels

Within the virtual campus framework, student behavior may be different depending on the level of analysis that is to be performed. One of the hypothesis that are interesting from a pedagogical point of view is to establish the connection pattern of each student, and to prove that different students follow different connection patterns but that these patterns are limited to a few, mostly because of course structure and temporal restrictions, but also depending on user particularities. In the context of a university, where each subject (several subjects within a course) is taken during an academic semester (i.e. around 15 weeks), two semesters each year, three different navigational levels can be identified: the session level, the course level, and the lifelong level.

The first level, namely the session level, captures the way users navigate with particular goals in mind. For example, how users use the e-mail service or how they access the proposed exercises. At this level, the short-term navigation behavior is studied, i.e. what each individual user does every time that he or she connects to the virtual campus. In this case, a web mining analysis could be helpful to detect problems with the web interface, for automatic usability evaluation purposes [24]. The information obtained at this level will allow validating these and other work hypotheses used for designing formative actions and learning plans. Many times, when designing learning plans, the starting points are hypothesis such as that students connect to the virtual campus in sessions of 20 min, and then they check their personal mailbox first and afterwards they access the courses they have registered for. The usability issues addressed at this level are related to evaluate task flows, detect navigation obstacles, analyze information flows and detect user's most preferred actions and spaces. For example, in the UOC virtual campus, the information provided at this level analysis would display whether students have difficulties when borrowing a book from the digital library, whether they read the academic news and whether the community and social services fit their needs or not.

The second level, namely the course level, tries to join all the single user sessions in a continuous flow during a longer period of time, with a limit of an academic semester. All the aggregated session information will provide a sort of user general course behavior. At this level it is also required to make a follow-up of the different navigation sessions of each user, to observe if each user has similar navigation patterns during a period of time, for example. This medium-term navigation behavior will be useful to validate hypothesis about the relationships of user actions and his or her results, which are related to the way learning resources are organized. The main goals of this level are to determine the navigational patterns followed by users but at a higher scale than in the previous level. For example, it can be interesting to study whether students connect every day or not, or whether they make extensive use of the virtual classroom forums during the weekends or not. All the information collected at this level could be used to feed an intelligent tutoring or adaptive hypermedia system [26]; with personalization purposes.

The third level, namely the lifelong learning level, can be considered a long-term navigational behavior analysis. In this case, the main interest is to analyze how students evolve from the beginning of a degree until they successfully finish it (or less successfully, they give up). This includes the study of several stages in the student life-cycle: approach and university access, first and following registrations, and so. Performing a data mining analysis at this level could help tutors and mentors to choose more carefully the subjects each student is enrolled to each semester [27]. At this level it may be interesting to discover inappropriate combinations of subjects that might lead to an excessive teaching burden.

In fact, the virtual campus is a rich scenario for experiment design, as different research questions involving different analysis levels can be imagined. Depending on the available information (collected usage data, surveys, academic results, etc.) and the desired goals, different experiments can be designed.

4 Experimental results

In order to test the validity of the assumptions about the navigational behavior of the students in a virtual campus and the connections with their academic performance, an experiment in the course level has been planned. This experiment implies, at it will be shown, to measure several user actions more related to the session level, such as accessing the virtual classroom or the time between consecutive sessions. Two different subsets of 569 and 111 students taking a degree in Computer Science, who enrolled in the subjects 'Foundations of Programming' (an introductory course to programming for new students in their first semester) and 'Compilers I' (a course for advanced students), respectively, have been selected as the matter of study. These students may also be enrolled in other subjects, but we will focus in the navigational actions related to the subject matter of study. Nevertheless, for a real personalization scenario all user actions should be taken into account for the profile analysis, but with an attempt to find a trade-off between model accuracy and complexity.

Basically, students connect to the virtual campus and access the virtual classroom to follow the learning activities designed for each subject, according to a previously established scheduling. In the case of the subjects studied in this chapter, students are asked to solve an optional exercise which is published during the first week (once the course has started) and that it must be solved and returned back to the teacher within 12 days (including one or two weekends, depending on each course). Students have specific places for both accessing the exercise description and rendering their solution. These spaces can be identified in the log file, so the exact moment when students perform the action of exercise download or upload is known. It is worth mentioning that this exercise is not mandatory, but it is strongly recommended as the final subject evaluation can be broken apart in several continuous evaluation activities such as the proposed exercise. Therefore, all students are supposed to follow the proposed activities, because those who do not follow them must take a final exam at the end of the semester, which usually has a higher degree of difficulty. We are interested in studying which students decide not to do the first exercise (or if they do it, but with poor results) in order to see whether such failure is somehow related to the way they navigate through the virtual campus and to their socio-demographic background. As mentioned before, this information can be collected

Table 1: Marks obtained by the students in the first exercise.

Mark	A	B	C+	C−	D	N	Total
Foundations of Programming	216	26	63	0	49	215	569
Compilers I	22	65	12	1	0	11	111

online by an intelligent tutoring system and helps each student fulfill his or her learning path much better, under a improved and personalized learning process.

Table 1 shows the results obtained by the students in the first exercise (it is worth mentioning that it is a simple exercise to introduce them to the subject of study, with a medium degree of difficulty, so it is not expected that many students will get poor marks, i.e. 'C−' or 'D', but on the contrary more students are not doing it, i.e. 'N'). Notice that, as expected, figures are different depending on the subject. For 'Foundations of Programming', 216 out of 569 students (37.8%) do not make the proposed exercise, and 49 more present a very poor exercise (8.6%). This is a well known fact for this course, so any information about the profile of users failing in this exercise would be very helpful. On the other hand, for 'Compilers I', only 11 students decided not to do the proposed exercise, and only one did it poorly and fails.

4.1 Server log files

For each action a user performs in the virtual campus, one or more lines representing such actions are logged in several servers. Furthermore, depending on the type of action, several servers might log the same action but using different information. In this work we have used mainly the log files from the Apache servers which act as front-ends, once they have been joined in a single file, generated every day. This file is firstly pre-processed in order to remove all those log lines which are surely not hits produced by the user, such as the load of icons, style sheets, banners, and so. This pre-processing reduces the amount of lines in a 90%. Nevertheless, during a typical week, the total number of lines that needs to be processed is still about 24 million, approximately 12 GB, which is a very large figure. Therefore, a second pre-processing, more oriented towards narrowing the experiment, is required, as described in [28].

Users can be uniquely identified because there is a unique session number generated each time a user logs into the virtual campus using his or her username and password. IP addresses are discarded because there is the possibility of many user accessing through the same proxy server which might mask the real IP address. Therefore, it is possible not only to identify individual users but also each individual session, which is useful to establish the different navigational levels described in the following section. When the user browses areas of the virtual campus where the session number is not required (public areas, for example), it cannot be successfully tracked, so those lines without session number are also removed.

All user interactions with the virtual campus are logged by one or more servers (web servers, database servers, etc). As we have stated before, the UOC's virtual campus has 24 Apache front-end web servers. Our work is currently focused in analyzing the standard Apache server log files generated by these 24 front-end servers. The variables recorded in the log files are: originating request IP number, local date and time, request URL and referrer URL. To facilitate tracking user and session information all the virtual campus features that require user authentication use an encrypted string embedded into the request or referrer URLs. These are the only interactions we take into account in our analysis because the remaining requests can not be traced down to a user or session context.

To deal with privacy issues, the encrypted string carrying user and session information is removed from the original requested and referrer URLs and substituted with a new user and session identifiers that cannot be traced back to the original user. These new user and session identifiers have a one-to-one map with the original users and sessions. This mangling process enhances privacy while retaining the ability to cross join user interaction data with other user demographic and academic data obtained from UOC administrative databases. Although this study may raise several concerns about privacy issues [14], all collected information is used only for academic purposes. All students are aware of the fact that all their interactions within the virtual campus are being logged and that all private record data is used only within the institution.

The analysis process has several steps, as outlined in Fig. 2. This process is only partially automated. Each day, all the log files that come out of the 24 front-end servers are joined into a single log file. Next, the request lines that have no useful information from the user interaction point of view – image, cascading style sheets, etc. – are removed from the original log file. All lines that lack user and session information (as we have pointed out above) are also removed. This step reduces the total size of the log file by a 90%. After this initial reduction, the average size of the log file is still 12 GB or 24 million lines per week.

Depending on the kind of analysis we want to undertake, this stripped down log file is further reduced by selecting the interaction lines on a user basis. In order to perform the experiments described in this chapter, we have used two different student sets. The first set stores all the interactions of a group of 569 students enrolled in a course named 'Foundations of Programming', with dates ranging from

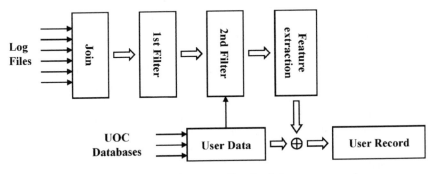

Figure 2: Preprocessing steps for obtaining user records.

23 February 2005 to 11 March 2005. The filtered log file for this set is 1,300,000 lines long. The second set stores the same information a group of 111 students enrolled in a course named 'Compilers I', with dates ranging from the same initial date to 17 March 2005. In this case, the filtered log file for this second set has around 220000 lines. The intersection between the two sets is void, as they are students from different degrees.

The rationale for selecting these sets of students and the related timeframes is the following. First, the datasets are small enough to allow us to experiment with different analysis methodologies. Second, the time frame starts at the very beginning of the course (23 February) and goes on till the students are requested to deliver their first practical exercise (deadline 12 or 17 March, depending on the course). The practical exercise (named PAC in UOC terminology) is of moderate difficulty, as it server as an introductory exercise according to the UOC pedagogical model [19]. As mentioned before, the submission of the PAC is optional but scoring a high mark helps the students in their final course performance evaluation, whilst not doing or failing the PAC has no negative consequences in the final course mark. Finally, this data comes from a closed e-learning environment where all user actions relate to the e-learning goals. Other user data like number of subjects enrolled during the term, number of book loans requested, total number of terms attending UOC is also readily available.

4.2 Data pre-processing and feature extraction

The experiments are performed using a reduced log file which removes all the useless information present in the Apache common log file, filtering out also those students not enrolled in each course matter of the study. The final log files have 13,000,000 and 220,000 lines approximately, which are reasonable data set sizes for studying user navigational behavior in a focused environment. Figure 2 shows all the pre-processing steps, starting from the original log files and databases, until the final data set is generated.

The main advantage of being in such a closed environment (the virtual campus) is that there are other available user data which may be relevant for analysis purposes. For example, from the transcript of each student we can extract the total number of subjects he or she is enrolled in, the number of semesters he or she has been studying in the UOC, and so on. Other information, such as the number of book loans requested or user satisfaction surveys are also available. Although this study may give rise to several questions about privacy issues [14], all the information collected about students is used only for academic purposes. Furthermore, all the students are aware of the fact that all actions in the virtual campus are logged, and that all private record data is used only within the institution. After the initial pre-processing, two filters are applied one for each of the session and course levels of analysis.

The first filter applied to the raw log file is the session filter. The aim of this first filter is to aggregate all user requests within a session into a single set of variables. The initial problem we face when we try to perform a session level analysis is clearly identifying the start and the end of a particular session. We have identified three kinds of sessions according to their start-end pattern: regular, aborted and fuzzy. Regular sessions are those sessions where the user starts interacting with the virtual campus and he or she is assigned a new session identifier. When the user decides to end the session he or she presses the virtual campus exit link. Aborted sessions are like regular sessions but do not end with the virtual campus exit link, the user ends just by closing the web browser. Aborted sessions need to be summarized at the end of the log file sequential analysis. Fuzzy sessions are, in fact, artifacts from the current virtual campus setup. Due to the load balancing nature of the web server layer, and its multi-threaded behavior, some users are not assigned a new session number each time they login; instead, they retain their previous session identifier. Thus, the only way to track session start and session end in this context is to account for inactivity intervals. When the lap between two consecutive session lines is greater than 20 min, a new session is accounted for regardless of the session identifier.

The first filter algorithm sequentially walks through the log file recording the following primary and derived session variables: user identifier, session identifier, session start local date and time, session end local date and time, user's hit count, session duration in minutes, day of week at the start of the session and hour at the start of the session. These are what we call generic variables. We also take into account some extra variables that are only relevant to a particular experiment at hand. The analysis that we present in this chapter takes into account several additional variables: the number of messages posted to the course forum and virtual laboratory during the session, local date and time of exercise proposal download if any, and local date and time of exercise resolution submission if any. In the next section we will explain why these extra variables are relevant in the context we are presenting. Identifying these extra variables usually implies writing specialized code modules to undercover the events to be taken into account. We use the extensive regular expression facilities of the Perl language to help extracting this kind of information out of the raw URLs. The asymptotic time cost of this first stage algorithm is linear to the amount of log lines and the asymptotic space cost depends almost exclusively of the amount of aborted sessions because they need to be processed at the end of the sequential walk.

The user level analysis follows the session level analysis (see Fig. 2). The aim of this second filter stage is to collapse all session tuples into one single course tuple for each user. Therefore, we will use the following variables as the input for the classification and clustering algorithms:

- GENDER: Although it is usual to have much more men studying engineering degrees than women, it is interesting to include it in this study to confirm the intuitive idea that gender is unimportant.
- AGE: This variable might provide important information about the socio-demographic background of students. For example, older students usually have greater family obligations than younger ones.
- NEW: Whether the student is new to the UOC virtual campus or not. New students may experience difficulties using the virtual campus, so it is interesting to validate such hypothesis.

- FIRST: Whether the student takes the course for first time or not. The students that failed to pass the course in the past semester are more likely to behave differently because they have information about their own experience.
- TOTALCREDS/ADAPTEDCREDS: The total number of course credits which the student is enrolled to / adapts from previous studies. The TOTALCREDS variable is directly related to the amount of time that the student needs to dedicate in order to follow all the proposed activities, so students with a large amount of credits are more likely to drop out from one or more courses, thus not doing the proposed exercises.

This information will be combined with the navigational behavior extracted from a very basic analysis of their navigational patterns during the period of time determined by the course starting and the day after the first proposed exercise must be rendered:

- *A set of information related to the session level*: the number of total sessions in the virtual campus (TOTALSESS), the mean delay between two consecutive sessions (MEANINTDUR), the mean length of each session (MEANDUR), and the mean number of hits (user-driven actions) in each session (MEANHITS). Although the exact intention of user actions in each session is unknown, these variables describe a basic navigational pattern in the period of time which is being analyzed. In order to study student habits, the number of total of sessions is also computed for each day of the week, creating seven new variables WD_i ($i = 1$ for Monday and $i = 7$ for Sunday). Then, a simple index measuring whether the student connects preferably on weekends or not is computed as $(WD_6 + WD_7)/\sum_{i=1}^{i=7} WD_i$ (namely WEEKENDPCT).
- *A set of information related to the course level*: the number of messages posted in the appropriate virtual classroom forum (FORUM), the number of messages posted in the associated laboratory forum (LAB), and the delay between the moment that the proposed exercise is published and the moment student accesses to its content (DELAY).

Therefore, a total of 21 variables are used for clustering and classification purposes. We are interested in somehow predicting which mark will have a given student, or at least, whether he or she will pass or fail the proposed exercise. For the course 'Compilers I', as only one student presents a poor exercise (marked with a 'C−'), this is almost equivalent to study whether a student renders or not the proposed exercise. On the other hand, for the course 'Foundations of Programming' there is an important set of students which are marked with a 'D', showing a very different behavior with respect the other set. It is worth mentioning that the global aim of this study is to understand user navigational behavior and to explain some well-known facts beyond intuition, but no building an accurate system for predicting a particular scenario such the described experiment. Therefore, any personalization effort must take into account not only students behavior but also the whole learning context.

It is worth to mention that there is navigational data for all the students in the 'Compilers I' course, but this is not the case for 'Foundations of Programming', as 25 students (4.4%) never connect to the virtual campus, and obviously they do not do the proposed activities. Therefore, the experiments described in the following section are performed using only the data of the other 544 students. During the pre-processing stage, it was detected that one of this 25 students had a 'A' mark for the proposed exercise, showing that the teacher made a mistake during the process of introducing the qualifications into the system. This illustrates the necessity of a higher degree of control by the system itself in order to avoid human mistakes, i.e. if a student has not uploaded the proposed exercise, automatically mark him or her with an 'N' without any teacher intervention. This case is a good example of how usability, utility and personalization may be improved by analyzing the data obtained from the virtual campus users activity.

4.3 Web mining

Once the data described in the previous section has been tabulated, and a single record describes the collected data for every student, several data mining techniques can be applied. Among others, unsupervised clustering by means of the TwoStep algorithm [29] and supervised classification by means of classification and regression trees [30] are the most useful because of the interpretability of the obtained results, despite the fact that both techniques might not achieve the optimal classification accuracy.

4.3.1 Variable relevance

Decision trees can also be used to measure variable importance, as suggested by [30]. Although several methods have been proposed in the literature [31], we will use one developed by the authors which tries to exploit decision tree diversity when trees are built from similar sets created using a bagging approach [32]. Basically, this method builds a large number of similar decision trees, one for each possible bagging training set, and then variable relevance is computed by weighting the number of times each possible classification feature is selected and its position in the decision tree, giving more importance to variables near the root of the tree.

For the 'Foundations of Programming' course, the most important variables are DELAY, TOTALSESS, and surprisingly, WD_5 (the exercise must be delivered on this day, though) and WD_2. The variable MEANDUR also deserves a special mention. Regarding the 'Compilers I' course, the most important variables are MEANINTDUR, TOTALCREDS, TOTALSESS, MEANDUR and DELAY. In this case, as most students do the proposed exercise, DELAY does not become so relevant as in the other course. It is also surprising that interaction variables (FORUM and LAB) are not considered important for classification purposes. On the other hand, GENDER and ADAPTEDCREDS are the least relevant variables, as expected. Both WD_6 and WD_7 are also considered irrelevant, which is also surprising, as most students are supposed to have little time for studying during the working week. Therefore, the hypotheses about user interaction during the weekends must be revised.

This simple experiment shows that the same classification features are not relevant for different data sets, although some variables (TOTALSESS, MEANDUR, DELAY) seem to be more robust for describing user behavior even for different learning contexts. DELAY is obviously a variable which contains relevant information which may be used for personalizing the course level: if a student waits too long to download the proposed exercise, he or she will be probably not able to finish it or to obtain a good mark. Therefore, an automatic system response could be designed to warn students (or their teacher) that they are approaching a deadline (a threshold, for example). This threshold could be estimated by combining teacher expertise and previous results. For example, a personalized banner or a tailored mail could be helpful to make the student aware of the proposed exercise and, optionally, downloading it or discarding it.

4.3.2 Unsupervised clustering

The second experiment tries to group students according to their navigational behavior, without taking into account student's socio-demographic background or the mark that they obtain. The TwoStep algorithm is used to discover patterns in the set of input fields. Records are grouped so that records within a group or cluster tend to be similar to each other, but records in different groups are dissimilar. The number of clusters is automatically selected. This study tries to identify which variables are relevant for classification purposes but from a different approach. A posterior supervised classification analysis could be then devised to design a recommendation system or an adaptive system for tutoring purposes combining both approaches.

For the 'Compilers I' students, two clusters are generated, with 27 and 84 records, respectively. The most relevant variables for clustering purposes are TOTALSESS, MEANINTDUR (which are obviously correlated), FORUM and LAB, which are significant at $p < 0.001$, and DELAY, which is significant at $p < 0.05$. MEANHITS, MEANDUR (both are strongly correlated) and WEEKENDPCT are not significant at all. These two clusters capture very well students' interactions: the students who connect more irregularly to the virtual campus do not post messages in the classroom spaces, and DELAY is also higher for these students than for the rest. On the other hand, the 'Foundations of Programming' students are grouped in three clusters, with 91, 318 and 135 records, respectively. In this case, user behavior is so different that all variables become significant at $p < 0.001$ except WEEKENDPCT, which is not relevant at all. Once again, though, students with a higher interaction pattern obtain better results than the rest (cluster 1 in Table 2), while the other two clusters show different values for DELAY, for example.

Table 2 shows the marks obtained by the students in each cluster. Notice that for 'Compilers I', the students who render a simple solution (a 'C+' mark) have a navigational behavior more similar to those who decide not to do it than to those who successfully solve the exercise. For 'Foundations of Programming', this separation is not so clear and needs to be analyzed more deeply.

Table 2: Marks distribution according to the obtained clustering.

Cluster	Foundations of Programming						Compilers I					
	A	B	C+	C–	D	N	A	B	C+	C–	D	N
1	69	4	9	0	4	5	11	13	2	0	0	0
2	127	16	44	0	38	93	11	52	10	1	0	11
3	19	6	10	0	7	93	–					

4.4 Data fusion

At present, UOC is introducing the use of the SCORM 2004 standard [21] for both course development and tracking purposes, as described in [9]. Nevertheless, other LMSs also incorporate the tracking capability, widening the options for obtaining data about the students, such as WebCT [33, 34]. Furthermore, when students browse other virtual campus services such as the digital library, for example, they also leave a track that can be used for personalization purposes [35]. Therefore, a reasonable data standardization process is needed to ensure that all these data can be properly described [36]. This process, which is called 'data fusion' based on the nomenclature used in other fields (e.g. remote sensing), might be very useful for overcoming all the classical log files problems: user identification, huge size, lack of user goals, etc.

In fact, the combination of different navigational strategies for the same goal (distance learning using a virtual campus with blended online and offline activities) will change the way students interact with the virtual campus and, therefore, the learning context. Moreover, having SCORM compliant courses will generate enough usage and academic data, which accurately analyzed will serve to adapt and personalize the learning process. These new personalized courses may lead to new ways of interaction and learning contexts and, hence, the system usage data collected could be different and consequently new processing and analyzing methods will be required. Simultaneously, an adaptive system for processing, analyzing and personalization purposes will be necessary.

5 Conclusions

In this chapter we have described an analysis performed in the UOC virtual campus with the aim of studying the relationship between user navigational patterns and the academic results achieved by the students enrolled to several subjects in computer science, namely 'Foundations of Programming' and 'Compilers I'. Three possible levels of analysis are described, and an experiment designed for the course level is outlined to show the possibilities that arise from the use of web mining tools in an e-learning environment for personalization purposes. Although the results shown in this chapter are preliminary and they are part of an ongoing project, it is worth to mention that some intuitive ideas that the teachers and instructional designers have about users navigational behavior can be validated with a simple clustering analysis. Obviously, a deeper analysis is required to better understand the complexity of the actions taken by the students. Results show that even a simple analysis may be useful to determine which variables are relevant for both clustering and classification purposes (for example, all the variables related to the interaction patterns), while other variables are not relevant at all (the percentage of sessions during the weekend, for example).

Further research in this area should include the use of other clustering and classification techniques for extracting information relevant to the learning process. The inclusion of other variables which may be also relevant to study user behavior may also improve both prediction accuracy and results interpretation. The extension of this study to other subjects with larger subsets of students or with different background (taking a degree in Social Sciences, for example) is also under consideration, specially for subjects with a known poor academic performance, as such criterion is directly related to user satisfaction. Finally, data fusion from different sources (web logs, internal marks, external databases, e-learning standards tracking tools) is also an interesting possibility.

Acknowledgments

This work is partially supported by the Spanish MCYT and the FEDER funds under grant TIC2003-08604-C04-04 MULTIMARK.

References

[1] Srivastava, J., Cooley, R., Deshpande, M. & Tan, P.N., Web usage mining: discovery and applications of usage patterns from web data. *SIGKDD Explorations*, **1(2)**, pp. 12–23, 2000.

[2] Kosala, R. & Blockeel, H., Web mining research: a survey. *SIGKDD Explorations*, **2**, pp. 1–15, 2000.

[3] Zhang, F. & Chang, H.Y., Research and development in web usage mining system-key issues and proposed solutions: a survey. *Proc. of the 2002 Int. Conf. on Machine Learning and Cybernetics*, Vol. 2, pp. 986–990, 2002.

[4] Chi, E.H., Pirolli, P. & Pitkow, J., The scent of a site: a system for analyzing and predicting information scent, usage, and usability of a web site. *Proc. of the SIGCHI Conf. on Human Factors in Computing Systems*, ACM Press: New York, NY, pp. 161–168, 2000.

[5] Spiliopoulou, M., Web usage mining for web site evaluation. *Communications of the ACM*, **43(8)**, pp. 127–134, 2000.

[6] Marsico, M.D. & Levialdi, S., Evaluating web sites: exploiting user's expectations. *International Journal of Human-Computer Studies*, **60(3)**, pp. 381–416, 2004.

[7]   Riecken, D., Personalized views of personalization. *Communications of the ACM*, **43(8)**, pp. 27–28, 2000.

[8]   Kramer, J., Noronha, S. & Vergo, J., A user-centered design approach to personalization. *Communications of the ACM*, **43(8)**, pp. 44–48, 2000.

[9]   Mor, E. & Minguillón, J., E-learning personalization based on itineraries and long-term navigational behavior. *Proc. of the Thirteenth World Wide Web Conference*, New York City, NY, Vol. 2, pp. 264–265, 2004.

[10]   Rosenberg, M.J., *E-Learning: Strategies for Delivering Knowledge in the Digital Age*, McGraw-Hill, Inc.: New York, NY, 2002.

[11]   Kay, J. & Lum, A., Creating user models from web logs. *Proc. of the Intelligent User Interfaces Workshop: Behavior-Based User Interface Customization*, 2004.

[12]   Paramythis, A. & Loidl-Reisinger, S., Adaptive learning environments and e-learning standards. *Electronic Journal of e-Learning*, **2(2)**, pp. 181–194, 2004.

[13]   Thomas, R., Kennedy, G., Draper, S., Mancy, R., Crease, M., Evans, H. & Gray, P., Generic usage monitoring of programming students. *Proc. of the ASCILITE 2003 Conference*, Adelaide, Australia, pp. 715–719, 2003.

[14]   Clifton, C. & Estivill-Castro, V., (eds.), *Proc. of the ICDM 2002, Workshop on Privacy, Security and Data Mining*, Vol. 14, ACS, Maebashi City, Japan, 2002.

[15]   Spinello, R.A., *Case Studies in Information Technology Ethics*, Prentice Hall: Upper Saddle River, NJ, 1996.

[16]   Spiliopoulou, M., Pohle, C. & Faulstich, L., Improving the effectiveness of a web site with web usage mining. *Proc. of the Int. Workshop on Web Usage Analysis and User Profiling*, Springer-Verlag: London, Vol. 1836, pp. 142–162, 1999.

[17]   Bucklin, R.E. & Sismeiro, C., A model of web site browsing behavior estimated on clickstream data. *Marketing Research*, **XL**, pp. 249–267, 2003.

[18]   Cadez, I.V., Heckerman, D., Meek, C., Smyth, P. & White, S., Visualization of navigation patterns on a web site using model-based clustering. *Proc. of the 6th ACM SIGKDD Int. Conf. on Knowledge Discovery and Data Mining*, Boston, MA, pp. 280–284, 2000.

[19]   Sangrà, A., A new learning model for the information and knowledge society: The case of the UOC. *International Review of Research in Open and Distance Learning*, **2(2)**, pp. 1–19, 2002.

[20]   UOC, http://www.uoc.edu

[21]   ADL, Sharable Content Object Reference Model (SCORM) 2004, 2nd edn, overview, 2004.

[22]   Hilbert, D.M. & Redmiles, D.F., Extracting usability information from user interface events. *ACM Computing Surveys*, **32(4)**, pp. 384–421, 2000.

[23]   Chi, E.H., Improving web usability through visualization. *IEEE Internet Computing*, **6(2)**, pp. 64–71, 2002.

[24]   Ivory, M. & Hearst, M., The state of the art in automated usability evaluation of user interfaces. *ACM Computing Surveys*, **33(4)**, pp. 173–197, 2001.

[25]   Juvina, I., Trausan-Matu, S., Iosif, G., Veer, G.v.d., Marhan, A. & Chisalita, C., Analysis of web browsing behavior – a great potential for psychological research. *Proc. of 1st Int. Workshop on Task models and Diagrams for user interface design*, Bucharest, Romania, 2002.

[26]   Brusilovsky, P., Adaptive hypermedia. *User Modeling and User-Adapted Interaction*, **11(1–2)**, pp. 87–110, 2001.

[27]   Tattersall, C., van den Berg, B., van Es, R., Janssen, J., Manderveld, J. & Koper, R., Swarm-based adaptation: Wayfinding support for lifelong learners. *Proc. of the Third Int. Conf. on Adaptive Hypermedia and Adaptive Web-Based Systems*, Eindhoven, The Netherlands, Lecture Notes in Computer Science, Vol. 3137, pp. 336–339, 2004.

[28]   Cooley, R., Mobasher, B. & Srivastava, J., Data preparation for mining world wide web browsing patterns. *Knowledge and Information Systems*, **1(1)**, pp. 5–32, 1999.

[29]   Zhang, T., Ramakrishnan, R. & Livny, M., BIRCH: an efficient data clustering method for very large databases. *Proc. of ACM SIGMOD Conf. on Management of Data*, Montreal, Canada, pp. 103–114, 1996.

[30]   Breiman, L., Friedman, J.H., Olshen, R.A. & Stone, C.J., *Classification and Regression Trees*. Wadsworth International Group, 1984.

[31]   Duda, R.O., Hart, P.E. & Stork, D.G., *Pattern Classification*, 2nd edn, John Wiley & Sons: New York, 2000.

[32]   Breiman, L., Bagging predictors. *Machine Learning*, **24(2)**, pp. 123–140, 1996.

[33]   Marquardt, C., Becker, K. & Ruiz, D., A pre-processing tool for web usage mining in the distance education domain. *Proc. of the Int. Database Engineering and Applications Symposium*, pp. 78–87, 2004.

[34]   Mazza, R. & Dimitrova, V., Visualising student tracking data to support instructors in web-based distance education. *Proc. of the 13th Int. World Wide Web Conf.* (alternate track papers & posters), ACM Press: New York, NY, USA, pp. 154–161, 2004.

[35]   Ferran, N., Mor, E. & Minguillón, J., Towards personalization in digital libraries through ontologies. *Library Management Journal*, **26(4/5)**, pp. 206–217, 2005.

[36]   Avgeriou, P., Papasalouros, A., Retalis, S. & Skordalakis, M., Towards a pattern language for learning management systems. *Educational Technology and Society*, **6(2)**, pp. 11–24, 2003.

CHAPTER 14

Automatically constructing an e-textbook via web mining

J. Chen & Q. Li
Department of Computer Engineering and Information Technology,
City University of Hong Kong, Hong Kong.

Abstract

A good e-textbook can greatly assist a learner in accomplishing his/her learning goals. How to automatically generate an e-textbook for a user-specified topic hierarchy is a novel yet important task in e-learning research. In this chapter, an approach to use web mining technologies as an aid in constructing an e-textbook will be introduced, in which several tasks are combined to fulfill the goal. First, building concept hierarchies over a web document collection is examined. Next, a pre-processing step commonly employed before mining is taken: web pages are segmented according to their layout and noisy content is detected and filtered. A ranking strategy is introduced to evaluate the web page's suitability to be included in the e-textbook. Then in order to analyze the 'suitability', concept features are extracted from the unstructured text with an automatically mined pattern set. An example system is used to depict how web mining techniques are applied throughout the process of e-book construction.

1 Introduction

With the development of web-based technologies, applications in distance learning have become common practice. Typical web-based learning environments such as Virtual-U [1] and Web-CT [2] achieve increasing popularity in universities and companies. As the people are getting more familiar with online learning systems and the number of e-learning users increases, researchers have been trying to enhance the learning experience. One of the popular means is through web mining.

Web mining [3] is the application of data mining technologies to the content, structure and usage of web resources, corresponding to the three different areas of web mining: web content mining, web structure mining and web usage mining. Web content mining refers to analyzing the content of web pages. Web structure mining focuses on the structure of the Web, exploiting the implicit information in the structure of the connected web pages. Web usage mining mainly involves mining records of the requests by users to a web site, most often collected by a web server log.

Among the three areas, web usage mining has been most excessively applied to distance learning [4, 5]. Researchers have long noticed that the experience of distance learning is similar to that of electronic commerce and, for both applications, understanding user behavior is a crucial goal. The standard routines to apply mining approaches to learn user behavior are dividing students into learning groups with clustering or classification approaches, making use of their student profiles or log files, or mining their navigational behavior and academic results for patterns through sequential mining. Most popularly, a combination of the approaches is used to achieve an adaptive environment for students.

While web usage mining has been most enthusiastically adopted by e-learning applications, the two other web mining categories have been long neglected, and we will focus on web content mining in the rest of this chapter. Web content mining involves several close research areas, such as information retrieval, information extraction and natural language processing, especially information retrieval. With the prosperity of a large information retrieval application, the web search engine, it is now feasible to employ web content mining techniques to aid applications in e-learning.

In this chapter, we will discuss several tasks in web content mining and information retrieval, and examine how they can be applied to generate an e-textbook on the Web. All tasks are more or less related to the web search engine. First, building concept hierarchies over a web document collection is examined. Next is fundamental in web content mining, segmenting web pages and detecting noise, which is usually a pre-processing step for many web mining applications. A ranking strategy, which is commonly employed in information retrieval systems, is introduced to evaluate the suitability of the web page to be included in an e-textbook. Then in order to analyze the 'suitability', concept features are extracted from the unstructured text with an automatically mined pattern set. An example system is used to depict how web content mining techniques are applied throughout the process of e-book construction.

2 System architecture

Our system (Fig. 1) starts from a user-specified *concept hierarchy*. It is similar to the table of content found in a traditional book. Each entry in the hierarchy is a concept. The root concept is the topic that the user is interested in and the sub-concepts extend the root further.

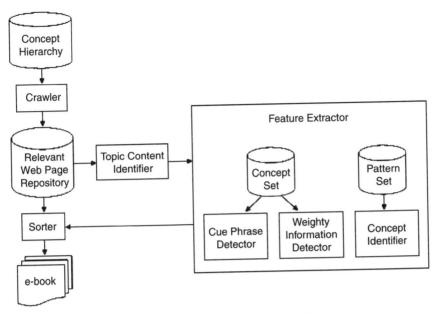

Figure 1: Architecture of the e-book construction process.

The concepts in the hierarchy are used to generate queries for a search engine. The queries can be generated by concept-based query expansion techniques [6], making use of the relationship of concepts in the hierarchy. The *crawler* then gathers the according URLs returned in the result list of the search engine. The collected documents constitute a *relevant web page repository* in the view of the search engine. However, the search engine is not designed to retrieve web pages that fulfill the requirements of learning. Pages that are highly ranked do not necessarily describe a concept, or provide an overview of related topics. Thus, further mining is required.

Several steps are taken to re-evaluate the importance of a web page. First, through the *topic content identifier*, the topic content of a page is obtained, excluding noisy blocks in the original page. Then the topic content along with the title and the URL are sent to the *feature extractor* to calculate characteristic features, including weight of cue phrases, information in weighty tags and concept features. To discover the concepts in web pages, a set of syntactic patterns are automatically obtained by performing a typical data mining technique, frequent sequential pattern mining. The mined patterns are then used to find new concepts in the given web pages. At last, the features extracted are sent to the *sorter*, which integrates their influence to determine the final weight of each web page.

In the final e-textbook, the concept hierarchy plays a similar role as the table of content for a traditional book. The tree structure on the left in Fig. 2 is a concept hierarchy for 'data structures and algorithms', which serves as an index for browsing the compiled e-book. When a concept node in the hierarchy is extended, its sub-concepts are displayed, and by selecting a particular concept in the tree, the

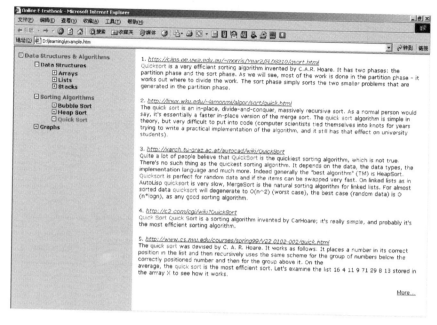

Figure 2: The final e-textbook.

abstract of the highly ranked web pages are presented. For each concept, 5–10 pages are reserved and organized as a list similar to the ranking list of the search engine. The difference of the e-book from the search engine ranking list is that the pages in the e-book all contain some descriptive paragraphs about the selected concept, one of which used as the abstract for the web page. A detailed description of the e-textbook construction process can be found in [7].

3 Building concept hierarchies

The concept hierarchy is frequently used in the e-textbook construction process. Its role in the final representation of the e-textbook as a table of content is quite natural, yet its necessity as being user-specified makes the approach less useful. To make the e-book construction process more attractive to users, building an understandable concept hierarchy for a given topic seems much more reasonable. Unfortunately, such a goal has not been successfully achieved by now. The closest success for hierarchy construction for a learning purpose should be the interactive approach proposed by Liu [8]. For a given topic, it exploits the existing hierarchical structures contained in web pages, extracts important concepts and presents them to the user. Then the user decides which concept to exploit further. Other attempts in hierarchy construction mainly involve clustering web documents or their snippets (e.g. their abstract provided by the search engine) and naming the clusters [9, 10]. Further efforts are required on the attempt to build a reasonable concept hierarchy over a specified topic and complete the e-textbook construction task.

4 Topic content identification

The topic content identification process is equivalent to a web page cleaning operation. A web page typically contains many information blocks. Apart from the main content blocks, it usually has such noisy blocks as navigation panels, copyright and privacy notices, and advertisements. Web page cleaning is a pre-processing step which 'cleans' the web page by analyzing their HTML source codes and identifying and eliminating noisy blocks. It has been widely noticed that to obtain satisfactory web mining results, a web page cleaning stage is necessary.

Many proposed web page cleaning algorithms [11, 12] involve two stages: web page segmenting and block analyzing. In the first stage, a web page is segmented according to its HTML tags into a tree structure. Then the visual blocks (nodes) in the tree are analyzed and noisy blocks are filtered.

To have a better understanding of the different roles of web pages, we classify them into two categories: topic page and hub page (Fig. 3). For many web mining applications, only topic pages are desired. This is especially the case for e-book construction.

- *Topic page*: A topic page has a main theme and the theme is described concretely through paragraphs of text. A news page, for example, is a typical topic page. We call the main content blocks for topic pages the topic content.
- *Hub page*: Compared to a topic page, a hub page does not describe a theme in detail, but it provides links to some valuable pages related. For example, the homepage of web directories such as Yahoo, is a typical hub page.

4.1 Segmenting web pages

The nested nature of HTML tags allows us to convert an HTML page into a tree representation. The most popular tree representation of an HTML file is the

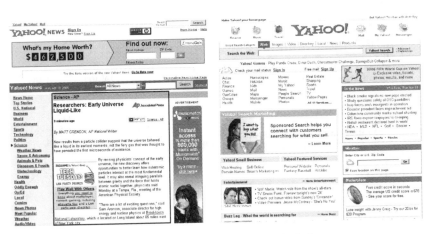

Figure 3: Example of a topic page and a hub page.

Document Object Model (DOM) proposed by W3C. In the DOM tree, each HTML tag is a node, and display properties of the tag are attached.

However, the DOM representation is often regarded as insufficient for the web page cleaning task. It stresses on every tag within each individual web page. For this reason, researchers have proposed several similar representation models that concentrate on either the commonalities of documents within a web site or heuristically pruning an individual tree. Mining documents in a single web site for commonalities is more accurate yet limited in power; while the heuristic approach is effective and can be more widely used sacrificing some accuracy.

Our method belongs to the second category, focusing on two specified kinds of HTML tags, namely, *container tags* and *weighty tags*. Container tags add structure to documents and partition a page into visual chunks, the 'content blocks'. Typical container tags include <HR>, <TABLE>, <TR>, <TD>, <P> and <DIV>. Weighty tags are those that specify display properties in terms of color, font and size, and highlight the tag content, such as <B>, <I> and <STRONG>. Unlike the DOM tree, only the <BODY> tag and container tags are picked by our approach to construct the HTML tag tree. Weighty tags are added as attributes to the content blocks they belong to. Figure 4 depicts how an HTML tag tree is derived from a web page; each block in Fig. 4(b) represents a 'content block'; weighty tag <I> is recorded as attributes of the first and third <TD> block.

4.2 Identifying the topic content for topic pages

Only topic pages are suitable for constructing the e-textbook. They are naturally descriptive, and those relevant to the concept have a high probability to contain a

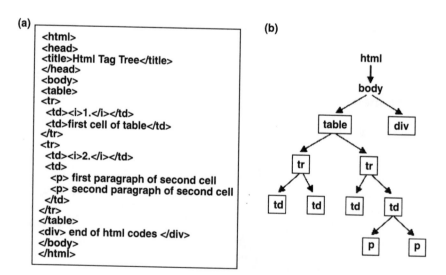

Figure 4: A derived HTML tag tree.

concept definition. The difference in designing purposes determines that hub pages will not provide adequate information about a concept.

To distinguish between topic and hub pages, two simple heuristic rules are introduced:

- If a content block is mainly constituted by hyperlinks, it is regarded as a hub block, otherwise a topic block;
- If the main content blocks of a web page are mostly hub blocks, the web page is a hub page; otherwise a topic page.

The type of a content block is decided by the proportion of terms embedded in the hyperlinks in the block to the total number of terms within the content block. The main content blocks are those that lie in the central area of the web page, which can be recognized by inspecting the properties of the container tags [12]. These simple heuristics have been proven to be efficient and effective.

5 Ranking algorithm

Given a query, calculating the similarity from web pages in a data collection to the query is the most common task in information retrieval. In the case of building the e-textbook, the criteria for a good web page can be interpreted as 'suitability' for belonging to the e-textbook. A web page is regarded as 'suitable' for the e-textbook if it contains intuitive descriptions or definitions of interested concepts. For example, a page describing a concept should provide an explicit explanation of the concept, and a general description of its sub-topics would also be helpful. The *relevant web page repository* contains web pages in the retrieved list of the search engine, and reflects the notion of the search engine in judging them as relevant. However, relevancy does not guarantee that a web page is suitable for generating the e-book. In order to find documents that are suitable for the e-book, further mining is necessary.

To pick out the web pages that fit the e-book, we extract several features for a web page to evaluate whether it is appropriate for the e-book. As seen in Fig. 2, the features include the weight of cue phrases, the weight of the information in weighty tags and the weight of concepts in the topic content. The original ranking provided by the search engine is another feature that can be measured. Most of the features can be extracted quite easily, except for the weight of concepts in the topic content. This is much more complicated in that only concepts appearing in a descriptive sentence or a concept definition are beneficial for learning. To address this, a pattern-based concept discovery algorithm is utilized, and the pattern set can be obtained automatically with a frequent sequence mining approach. The extracted features are used to calculate a weight for the web page, which decides its 'suitability' for the e-book. Web pages with a high 'suitability' form a ranking list similar to that of the search engine, except that the web pages contained are much more readable for users.

5.1 Original rank

The original rank of pages, given by an existing search engine like Google, is a fundamental feature used in the ranking algorithm and mainly includes two factors:

1. PageRank: the importance of a web page on the Web;
2. Textual match: the topic coverage of the query in the page.

PageRank is independent of the query or textual content. It suggests that surfing on the Web is a random walk and defines a measure of prestige over it. The PageRank value of a web page corresponds to its popularity in the whole Web. Textual match is decided at query time. The exact algorithm used to match query terms and retrieved documents is not available, but it is widely known that it takes into account many factors, such as keywords, phrase matches, match proximity and anti-spamming [13]. The combination of PageRank and textual match tries to meet the most general needs of searching on the Web, showing great flexibility and quality in many cases.

5.2 Cue phrases

Some URLs contain terms that imply the content of a page. For instance, the URL 'http://www.cs.bu.edu/teaching/cs113/spring-2000/sort/' contains terms like 'edu', 'teaching' and 'sort', from which we may 'guess' that it is a web page generated for educational purposes and its main subject is about sorting algorithms. The example indicates two kinds of beneficial terms. The first kind includes terms that suggest the writing objective of the author, such as 'teaching' and 'course', which we call implicit key items (IKIs). The other kind has terms that include salient concepts in the concept hierarchy, like 'sort'. We can call these terms explicit key items (EKIs).

Similarly, cue phrases can also be detected in the title of web pages. Title is an author-given summarization of the web page. It is available in the returned ranking list of a search engine. If IKIs and EKIs can be found in the URL and/or title, a page should be weighted.

5.3 Weighty tags

Weighty HTML tags specify the display properties of the text embedded, demonstrating the author's notion of importance. Thus text in weighty tags can give clue of what a web page is centered upon. In many web pages, the detailed descriptions of concepts and sub-concepts are led by a highlighted heading of the discussed concept.

Different weighty tags show different levels of importance, and thus are associated with a tag credit to measure this importance. The credit is determined by the HTML features of the tag, as shown in Table 1.

Previously, weighty HTML tags were attached as attributes to a content block. For the content blocks in the topic content, text embedded in the weighty tags are matched with a concept set, consisting of the concepts in the hierarchy. The matching of the embedded text with the selected concept and the other

Table 1: Tag credit of weighty tags.

Weighty tags	Tag credit
H1	4
H2	3
H3,B,STRONG	2
Others	1

concepts are counted separately, and extra weight is given to the appearance of the selected concept.

5.4 Concept descriptions and definitions

Concept definitions and descriptions are naturally beneficial to the e-textbook, because people usually prefer pages that give definitions and examples of a concept when they learn knowledge about a topic. Yet discovering concept definitions and concept descriptions is a non-trivial text extraction problem. It can be viewed as an information extraction task based on several techniques in natural language processing and data mining, mostly requiring a set of manually labeled examples to train the extractor [14, 15]. Another feasible method is to identify concept descriptions and definitions by patterns. Liu et al.'s approach [8] gives an efficient pattern-based routine to identify definitions of concepts with a set of predefined patterns. For example, '<CD:Concept> is defined as', where <CD:Concept> represents a concept in the user-specified hierarchy.

Although the predefined pattern set method has been proven to be effective, the pattern set is rarely complete and often limited to a single web site or a particular application. Matching the predefined pattern set to an arbitrarily chosen web page often results in only a few concepts discovered, if any. In the e-book construction process, concept descriptions and definitions play a vital role and we cannot afford such a low recall. Thus an automatic approach for mining an adequate pattern set is needed, as introduced in the following.

5.4.1 Pattern set mining

The input of the pattern mining process (Fig. 5) is also a set of concept hierarchies. The concept hierarchies should belong to several different broad topics. For example, in our experiment, 12 concept hierarchies in 12 different areas were used, including 'data structures and algorithms', 'data mining', 'series', 'computer architecture', 'algebraic structures', 'botanical science', etc. The wide range of topics reduces the influence of a specific topic over the result patterns. It is not required that a concept hierarchy should enumerate all concepts about a topic, as long as the parent–son relationships of concepts are correctly depicted in the hierarchy.

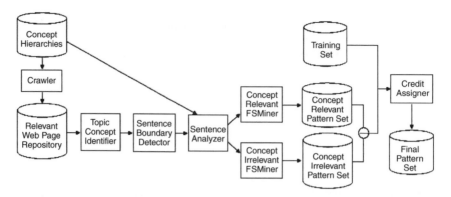

Figure 5: Pattern mining architecture.

- *Crawler:* The *crawler* works similarly as the crawler in Fig. 1, except that it takes in a set of concept hierarchies, and uses them to generate queries.

- *Topic content identifier:* The *topic content identifier* is identical to the module in Fig. 1.

- *Sentence boundary detector:* The *sentence boundary detector* breaks down a web page into sentences. Detecting sentence boundaries is not as simple as it appears to be. Most sentences use a period at the end. However, a period can be associated with an abbreviation, such as 'Mr.' or represent a decimal point in a number like $12.58. Also in HTML pages, the period is an essential component of a URL. There are generally two classes of sentence boundary detectors. The first, also employed in our system, uses manually defined rules to identify abbreviations, numbers, etc. The second belongs to the machine learning family, treating the sentence boundary disambiguation task as a classification problem.

- *Sentence analyzer:* The *sentence analyzer* has several functions. A sentence first goes through a part-of-speech parser commonly used in natural language tasks, which assigns each word with a part-of-speech tag (e.g. he/pronoun). And a stemming algorithm is applied to the words in sentences. In many application of information retrieval, morphological variants of words have similar semantic interpretations and can be considered as equivalent (e.g. 'book' and 'books'). A stemming algorithm aims to reduce a word to its stem or root form. The *sentence analyzer* then inspects each sentence and matches the phrases in the sentence with the concepts appearing in the concept hierarchy. If a match is found, the concept in the sentence is substituted with a label '<CD:Concept>'. If more than two concepts appear in one sentence, the sentence is filtered. An example of a processed sentence is as follows:

Original: *Data mining* can be defined as
Result: *<CD:Concept>* can be defined as

At last, those sentences with only one concept substitution are sent to the concept relevant frequent sequence miner; and those without any concepts are sent to the concept irrelevant frequent sequence miner.

- *Concept relevant frequent sequence miner and concept irrelevant frequent sequence miner:* Both the concept relevant and concept irrelevant FSminers apply a frequent sequence mining algorithm to their input. Sequential pattern mining [16] is a data mining task that discovers frequent subsequences as patterns in a sequence database. The target of the concept relevant FSminer is to find syntactic patterns that describe or define a concept; while the concept irrelevant FSminer aims for common syntactic patterns that may appear in any natural language sentence.

  Given a set of sequences and a user-specified min_support threshold, the problem of sequential pattern mining is to find all the frequent subsequences, i.e., the subsequences whose occurrence frequency in the set of sequences is no less than min_support. Let $I = \{i_1, i_2, \ldots, i_n\}$ be a set of all items. An itemset is a subset of items. A sequence is an ordered list of itemsets. A sequence s is denoted by $<s_1 s_2 \ldots s_j \ldots s_l>$, where s_j is an itemset, also called an element. The number of items in a sequence is called the length of the sequence. For mining natural language patterns, the sequential pattern mining problem is simplified so that each sentence is a sequence for mining, words are the corresponding elements, and the length of a sequence is the number of words in the sentence.

  In sequential pattern mining, besides the min_support, min_length is widely used in many applications to constrain the minimum length of result sequences. To mine the natural language patterns, another parameter, min_coverage, is introduced to minimize the influence of a single knowledge domain (corresponding to a concept hierarchy) on the resulting patterns. Every knowledge domain has its own frequent vocabulary, hence tends to produce its own high frequency sequences. A constraint on min_coverage ensures that only patterns that occur in no less than min_coverage domains can be recorded as resulting patterns. In the end, corresponding to the separate input, the sequential patterns that are longer than min_length and occur no less than min_support times in at least min_coverage domains are recorded into two pattern sets: the concept relevant pattern set and the concept irrelevant pattern set. The common part of the two pattern sets is the patterns that are common in natural language, and should be filtered from the concept relevant pattern set. So the difference set of the two pattern sets is obtained as the final pattern set, as depicted in Fig. 5.
- *Credit Assigner:* The credit assigner gives a credit to each pattern in the *Final Pattern Set*. The credit measures how accurate a pattern identifies a concept. An annotated training set is used to determine the credit of a pattern. In [17], an automatic annotation process was introduced. Each pattern in the final pattern set was matched with a sentence in the training set. If all words other than the concept label <CD:Concept> can be found in the sentence and the order of the words in the sentence are identical to that of the pattern, the pattern is regarded

as a 'matching' pattern of the sentence. The words in the sentence corresponding to the concept label in the pattern are the concept in the view of the matching pattern. If the concept identified is actually a concept according to the annotation in the training set, it is regarded that the pattern made a right decision; otherwise a wrong decision is made. Because of the complexity in human language, almost all patterns make both right and wrong decisions. The proportion of times it makes a right decision to a wrong one indicates the accuracy rate of the pattern. For example, if the credit of a pattern is 0.8, we get a conclusion that the pattern has made a decision that has an 80% probability to be right. In our context, this is equivalent to say a candidate concept is a real concept with an 80% probability. Also, if the credit of a pattern is 0, we can get a conclusion that the candidate concept discovered by the pattern is generally not a real concept. If the credit of a pattern is 0.5, it means that the pattern makes decisions quite randomly, so its decision does not give us any useful information.

5.4.2 Concept discovery

Provided with a set of patterns with an associated credit each, the next questions is if two or more patterns all identify a candidate concept from a given sentence, which candidate should be regarded as the final identified concept. For example, assume the pattern set is comprised of three patterns, $\{p_a, p_b, p_c\}$, with the corresponding credits $\{0.9, 0.3, 0.6\}$. Given a sentence $\{word_1\ word_2\ word_3\}$, after matching the pattern set with the sentence, $word_1$ is identified by p_a and p_b, and $word_2$ is identified by p_c. Should $word_1$ or $word_2$ be the identified concept? Here a voting algorithm is introduced to settle this problem.

Given a credit set $\{C_1, C_2, ..., C_i, ...\}$ corresponding to the final pattern set FPS $= \{p_1, p_2, ..., p_i, ...\}$. Consider a sentence S $= \{word_1, word_2, ..., word_j, ..., word_n\}$. Through matching each pattern with the sentence, some phrases are identified as candidate concepts. For each candidate concept, we can compute the probability that the candidate concept is really a concept according to the credits of the patterns that identify the candidate concept. If a phrase, PH, is identified as a candidate concept by a set of patterns P' (which is a sub-set of FPS), then the probability that it is a real concept is:

$$Pr(PH) = \frac{\prod_{p_i \in P'} C_i}{\prod_{p_i \in P'} C_i + \prod_{p_i \in P'} (1 - C_i)}, \tag{1}$$

where PH is the candidate concept discovered by pattern set P', $Pr(PH)$ is the probability that PH is really a concept, C_i is the corresponding credit of pattern p_i that belongs to P'. If PH is really a concept, it also means that all the patterns in P' have made a right decision. And all the patterns make decisions independently, so the probability of it is $\prod_{p_i \in P'} C_i$. Also, if PH is not a real concept, it means that all the patterns in P' have made a wrong decision, so the probability of it is $\prod_{p_i \in P'} (1 - C_i)$. If $Pr(PH)$ is larger than 0.5, it means that the probability that PH is a concept is larger than the probability that it is not a concept. Following the above example, $Pr(word_1)$ and $Pr(word_2)$ can be computed as follows: $Pr(word_1) = (0.9 * 0.3)/(0.9 * 0.3 + (1 - 0.9) * (1 - 0.3)) = 0.27/(0.27 + 0.07) = 0.8$, and $Pr(word_2) = 0.6$. In this example, $Pr(word_1)$ and $Pr(word_2)$ are all larger than 0.5, so both of them can be regarded as concepts. But compared with $word_2$, $word_1$ has a larger possibility and is chosen as the final detected concept.

5.5 Integrating extracted features

The four features discussed above, viz., the original rank, cue phases, weighty information and concept definitions and descriptions all can affect the new rank of pages. The following formula integrates the features, and calculates a weight as the 'suitability' of the web page:

$$W_i = \lambda_1 \cdot \frac{f_{R_i}}{\sum_{j=1}^{N} f_{R_j}} + \lambda_2 \cdot \frac{f_{U_i}}{\sum_{j=1}^{N} f_{U_j}} + \lambda_3 \cdot \frac{f_{D_i}}{\sum_{j=1}^{N} f_{D_j}} + \lambda_4 \cdot \frac{f_{T_i}}{\sum_{j=1}^{N} f_{T_j}}, \qquad (2)$$

where N is the number of the pages retrieved for each concept in the concept hierarchy; λ_1, λ_2, λ_3 and λ_4 ($\lambda_1 + \lambda_2 + \lambda_3 + \lambda_4 = 1$) are the parameters to tune the relative importance of the four features.

6 Conclusions

Building an e-textbook via web mining is a relatively novel topic for distance learning. In this chapter, we use a prototype e-book construction system to examine how web content mining can be applied to aid e-learning experiences. As web content mining roots in several other areas, such as information retrieval, information extraction and natural language processing, existing methods in these related research areas can contribute a lot to fulfill the task of e-book construction.

Although the advances in web content mining and related areas have made the process of building an e-textbook feasible, the challenge is that this area still needs to be explored to make the e-textbook construction system more attractive to users.

References

[1]   Harasim, L., Calvert, T. & Groeneboer, C., Virtual-U: a web based system to support collaborative learning. *Web-Based Instruction*, ed. B. Khan, Educational Technology Publications: Englewood Cliffs, NJ, 1997.
[2]   WebCT, http://www.webct.com/
[3]   Kosala, R. & Blockeel, H., Web mining research: A survey. *SIGKDD Explorations*, **2(1)**, 2000.
[4]   Zaiane, O.R., Web usage mining for a better web-based learning environment. *Conference on Advanced Technology for Education*, Banff, Alberta, Canada, pp. 60–64, 2001.

[5]   Guo, L., Xiang, X. & Shi, Y., Use web usage mining to assist online e-learning assessment. *IEEE International Conference on Advanced Learning Technologies (ICALT'04)*, pp. 912–913, 2004.

[6]   Qiu, Y. & Frei, H.P., Concept-based query expansion. *Proc. of SIGIR-93, 16th ACM Int. Conf. on Research and Development in Information Retrieval*, Pittsburgh, pp. 160–169, 1993.

[7]   Chen, J., Li, Q., Wang, L. & Jia, W., Automatically generating an e-textbook on the web. *Int. Conf. on Web-Based Learning*, Beijing, China, pp. 35–42, 2004.

[8]   Liu, B., Chin, C.W. & Ng, H.T., Mining topic-specific concepts and definitions on the web. *The Twelfth Int. Conf. on World Wide Web*, Budapest, Hungary, pp. 251–260, 2003.

[9]   Zamir, O. & Etzioni, O., Grouper: a dynamic clustering interface to web search results. *Computer Networks (Amsterdam, Netherlands: 1999)*, **31(11–16)**, pp. 1361–1374, 1999.

[10] Lawrie, D.J. & Croft, W.B., Generating hierarchical summaries for web searches. *The 26th Int. ACM SIGIR Conf. on Research and Development in Information Retrieval*, Toronto, Canada, pp. 457–458, 2003.

[11] Yi, L., Liu, B. & Li, X., Eliminating noisy information in web pages for data mining. *The Ninth ACM SIGKDD Int. Conf. on Knowledge Discovery and Data Mining*, Washington, DC, USA, pp. 296–305, 2003.

[12] Zhang, Z., Chen, J. & Li, X., A preprocessing framework and approach for web applications. *Journal of Web Engineering*, **2(3)**, pp. 175–191, 2004.

[13] Chakrabarti, S., *Mining the Web: Discovering Knowledge from Hypertext Data*, Morgan Kaufmann: San Francisco, CA, 2002.

[14] Cohen, W.W. & Sarawagi, S., Exploiting dictionaries in named entity extraction: Combining semi-Markov extraction processes and data integration methods. *The 2004 ACM SIGKDD Int. Conf. on Knowledge Discovery and Data Mining*, Seattle, USA, pp. 89–98, 2004.

[15] Hu, M. & Liu, B., Mining and summarizing customer reviews. *The 2004 ACM SIGKDD Int. Conf. on Knowledge Discovery and Data Mining*, Seattle, USA, pp. 168–177, 2004.

[16] Pei, J., Han, J., Mortazavi-Asl, B. & Pinto, H., Prefixspan: mining sequential patterns efficiently by prefix projected pattern growth. *The 17th Int. Conf. on Data Engineering*, Washington, DC, pp. 215–226, 2001.

[17] Chen, J., Zhang, Z., Li, Q. & Li, X., A pattern-based voting approach for concept discovery on the web. *The Seventh Asia Pacific Web Conf.*, Shanghai, China, pp. 109–120, 2005.

CHAPTER 15

Online outlier detection of learners' irregular learning processes

M. Ueno
Faculty of Engineering, Nagaoka University of Technology, Japan.

Abstract

Distance education using e-learning has become popular in educational situations. One problem is that the instruction strategy tends to be one way, so sometimes learners find it more boring than conventional instruction methods. This chapter proposes a method of online outlier detection of learners' irregular learning processes using the learners' response time to e-learning content. The unique features of this method are as follows: (1) It uses the Bayesian predictive distribution, (2) It can be used for small samples, (3) It unifies the methods of various statistical tests using a hyper-parameter and provides more accurate test results than one of the traditional methods alone. (4) It assists two-way instruction using data mining results of learners learning processes. (5) Outlier statistics are estimated by considering both students' abilities and the difficulty of content. In addition, this chapter proposes an animated agent which provides adaptive messages to the learners using the data mining. Moreover, the system was evaluated and the results showed the effectiveness of the system.

1 Introduction

Motivation is essential to learning and performance, particularly in e-learning environments where learners must take an active role and be self-directed in their learning [1]. Despite the importance of motivation to learning, between 1988 and 2000, less than one percent of papers at the international conferences concerned with distance education focused on motivational issues. Keller (1999) argues that although motivation is idiosyncratic, learner motivation can also be affected by external aspects [2]. Visser reported that motivational messages can reduce dropout rates [3] and later attempted to improve motivation in e-learning situations using such messages [4]. Gabrielle applied technology-mediated instructional strategies to Gagnes events of instruction and showed the effects of these strategies on motivation [5]. These studies emphasize the effects of the teacher's motivational messages adapted to a learner's status. However, when the number of learners is large, it becomes difficult for a teacher to individualize and personalize messages to students.

On the other hand, acquiring huge amounts of learning history data using e-learning is easy because it is automatically saved as log-data in learning history data-base. In this situation, it is important how we save or use this data. In this sense, the data mining technologies has become one of notable techniques to discover useful knowledge from the huge amounts of data [6, 7].

The main idea of this work in this chapter is to develop a method of detecting students who requires the previous mentioned motivational messages using the data mining technologies. The main the proposal in this chapter is an online outlier detection of learners' irregular learning processes using response times to e-learning content. Although many outlier detection techniques have been proposed, the techniques can be classified into the following two. One is a detection technique using statistical test methods [8, 9] and another is one using neural network techniques [10–13]. However, applying the conventional outlier techniques to the problem of detecting irregular learning processes in e-learning has the following problems.

- If a learner starts learning using irregular learning processes, then regular learning processes will be regarded as irregular.
- The conventional techniques assume that all data in a time series are for the same task. However, in educational situations, tasks(= content) in a time series differ in the sense of difficulty.
- In the conventional techniques, the criteria that specify outliers are not statistically well defined.

Considering these problems, this chapter proposes a new outlier detection technique to detect learners' irregular e-learning processes. The unique advantages of this method are as follows:

- It can use prior knowledge reflecting the response time characteristics of each content using Bayesian approach. This prior knowledge can avoid regarding regular processes as irregular at the beginning of the learning processes.
- The proposed method uses a model that incorporates task difficulties parameters and learner's ability parameters. Outlier statistics are estimated considering both students' abilities and the difficulty of the content, so the method efficiently detects irregular learning.
- The proposed method uses a unified statistical test derived from Bayesian approach. By changing the value of the hyper-parameter in the model, the proposed method can express various statistical test methods. This test has a clear mean and criterion in the sense of a statistical predictive distribution.

The author also developed a learning management system (LMS) called 'Samurai' that uses the online outlier detection method. This system supports online outlier detection of learners' irregular learning processes and enables two-way instruction by mining data on learners' learning processes. The system was used for actual classes and shown to be efficient.

2 Learning management system 'Samurai'

In this section, an outline of an LMS I previously developed [13, 14] is introduced. The author has developed a LMS called 'Samurai' (See Ueno 2003), and has provided many e-learning courses (now the LMS provides 78 e-learning courses from my university). The LMS consists of a Contents Presentation System (CPS), a Contents Database (CD), a Learning Histories Database (LHD), and a Data Mining System (DMS). The CPS integrates various kinds of content and presents the integrated information on a web page.

Figure 1 shows a typical e-learning content presentation by Samurai. The contents are presented the contents by clicking on the menu button. A sound track of the teacher's narration is also presented according to [15], and the red pointer automatically moves as the narration proceeds.

This lesson corresponds to a 90-minute lecture at university and includes 42 topics. Although the content in Fig. 1 is text, the system also provides illustrations, animation or computer graphics, and video clips. In this lesson, there are 11 text contents, eleven illustrations, ten animations, and ten video clips. The system also

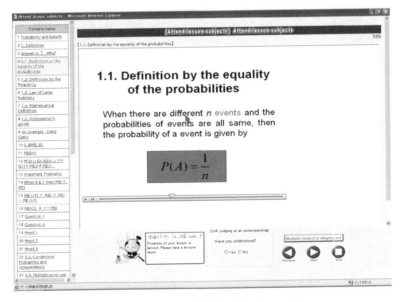

Figure 1: Example of e-learning instruction.

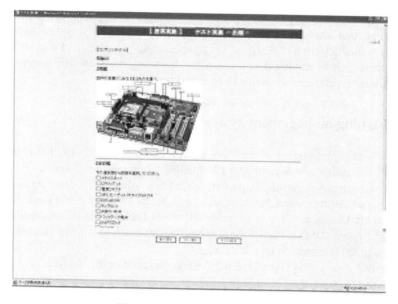

Figure 2: Example of test frame.

presents some test items to assess the learners' degree of comprehension as soon as lessons have been completed (Fig. 2).

The CD consists of various kinds of media, text, jpeg, mpeg, and so on. The proposed platform monitors learners' learning processes and saves them as log data in the LHD. The teacher makes prepares a lecture, and saves its contents in the CD. Then, the CPS automatically integrates the contents, and presents them to the learners.

The learners can learn them through the Internet. Learning history log data are saved in the LHD and analyzed in the DMS. The DMS provides feedback to the learners and teacher.

The LMS monitors learners' learning processes and stores them as log data in the LHD. The stored data consists a Contents ID, a Learner ID, the number of topics which the learner has completed, a Test Item ID, an Operation Order ID (which indicates what operation was done), a Date and Time ID (which indicates the time and date of an operation started), and a Time ID (which indicates the time it took to complete operation). This data enables the system to recount the learner's behaviors in e-learning.

3 Online outlier detection

3.1 Data

Response time data is used to detect learner's irregular learning processes, as shown in Fig. 3. The horizontal axis indicates the number of content items a learner has accessed, and the vertical axis indicates the response time for the content.

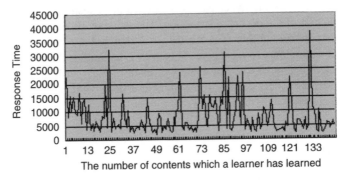

Figure 3: Learning time data for content items.

The horizontal axis indicates the number of contents which a learner has learned, and the vertical axis indicates the response time for the content. Using this data, we can discover irregular learning processes. To do this, this chapter proposes a new method to detect learner's irregular learning processes. The main idea is to derive a Bayesian predictive distribution of a new data item, x_{n+1}, given a learner's learning processes data, $x_1, \ldots, x_n$, and provides a test for outlier detection of the new data item.

3.2 Model

This section derives a Bayesian predictive distribution of a new data item, x_{n+1}, given a learner's learning processes data, $x_1, \ldots, x_n$. Let w_{ij} be a learner j's response time for the ith content item, and consider the following linear equation

$$x_{ij} = \frac{w_{ij} - \overline{w}_i}{s_i} = \mu_j + e_j, \tag{1}$$

where $\overline{w}_i$ indicates the average response time and s_i indicates the variance of response time of ith content item.

A Bayesian predictive distribution of a new data x_{n+1} given the learner's learning processes data item, $x_1, \ldots, x_n$, can be derived as follows:

$$p(x_{n+1}|X) = \int\int p(x_{n+1}|\mu, \sigma^2)p(\mu, \sigma^2|x_1, \ldots, x_n)d\mu d\sigma^2$$

$$\left(1 + \left[\frac{(x_{n+1} - \mu_*)}{\sqrt{\frac{n_0+n+1}{(n_0+n)v}}\lambda_*^2}\right]^2 \middle/ v\right)^{-\frac{v+1}{2}}, \tag{2}$$

where

$$t = \frac{(x_{n+1} - \mu_*)}{\sqrt{\frac{(n_0+n+1)}{(n_0+n)v}}\lambda_*^2}. \tag{3}$$

Then, t has a t distribution with degrees of freedom $v = n_0 + n - 1$.

Here, μ_* indicates the hyper parameter of the prior distribution, which is the mean parameter of the normal distribution. The value of μ_* is determined by the mean of data item x. In this case, the data x is standardized with mean zero and standard deviation one, so μ_* is zero. This prior can combine the prior knowledge with objective data analysis. For examples, even if a learner begins by using an irregular learning processes, the proposed method does not regard the processes as regular processes.

3.3 Model

Using eqn (3), we can detect outliers of learning processes. The procedure is as follows:

1. Get a new data item x_{ij} during a learner is learning
2. Calculate the value of t using eqn (3)
3. If the value of t is greater than the value of t in a t distribution with α or the value of t is less than the value of negative t in the t distribution with α, then the new data item is detected as an outlier.

One unique feature of this method is that it unifies various statistical test methods. Changing the value of the hyper-parameter, n_0, has the following effect:

- When n_0 is large enough, the method is equivalent to the Z test.
- When n_0 is equivalent to zero (called a non-information prior distribution), the method is equivalent to the traditional t test.

Thus, the proposed method unifies two major traditional test methods. In addition, the proposed method expresses various statistical methods which have different characteristics from the traditional test methods.

3.4 Outlier detection curves and examples

To detect irregular learning processes, this study proposes a method called outlier detection curve. The curve corresponds to a learner's learning processes to a lecture. For example, Fig. 4 shows learner 4's (outlier) detection curve, corresponding to Fig. 3. The four parallel lines in Fig. 4 indicate the outlier detection line. For example, if the t value corresponding to a learning process exceeds the top detection curve, it means that the learning process was too long. If the t value exceeds the bottom detection curve, it means that the learning process was too short.

In Fig. 4, outlier processes were used to learn content items 129–145. We should note that the response times, which may seem comparatively very long or short in Fig. 3, are not always judged as outlier processes. The reason is that the statistical value of t for the outlier detection is estimated by considering both the student's ability to learn and the difficulty of content items. For example, even if we find

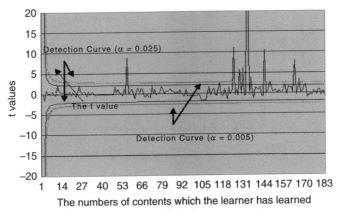

Figure 4: Outlier detection curve corresponding to Fig. 3.

responses that took longer than others, we cannot say that they are outlier processes because the content may require more time than other content.

These features are quite different from the traditional data mining methods using the outlier system; for example, discovering robberies using depositing processes in banks and discovering invasions into computer networks do not require such complex methods because they need not consider respectively different tasks in a series.

An example of raw learning time data and detection curve when outlier processes are rare is shown in Fig. 5. From the raw data, it seems that learning times for content items 72–92 are irregularly long, but only the learning processes for items 77 and 78 are detected as outliers. An example of raw learning time data and detection curve when outlier processes are common is shown in Fig. 6. Note that the shape of the curve that shows the raw learning time data in Fig. 6 is very similar to one in Fig. 5. However, the outlier detection curve in Fig. 6 shows many outliers in the learning processes. This learner may not have studied hard. Thus, the proposed method can detect outlier learning processes that we cannot notice by only analyzing raw learning time data. In practical use for distance education, a teacher cannot track all students' learning processes. The teacher can detect learners who should be taken care of and send them e-mails with messages like 'Did you have trouble understanding some of the content?', 'Are you studying hard enough?', and 'Are you bored?'. These messages will show students who have some learning problems that the teacher notices them, and I expect that it will motivate their learning.

4 Simulation experiments

Although the proposed method represents various statistical test methods using a hyper-parameter, n_0, the way to determine the value of n_0 is unknown. In this

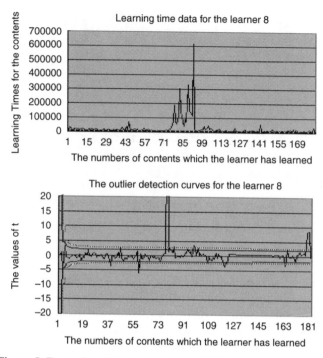

Figure 5: Example of detection curve with few outlier processes.

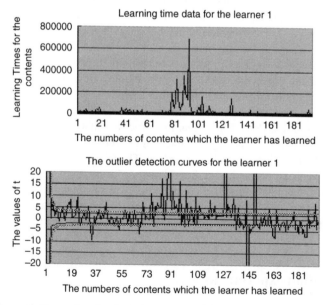

Figure 6: Example of a detection curve with many outlier processes.

section, I describe some simulation experiments to determine the optimum value of the hyper-parameter. The flow of the simulation experiments is as follows:

Fix a learner, j, and generate random data using

$$x_{ij} = \frac{t_{ij} - \bar{t}_i}{s_i} = \mu_j + e_j.$$

- Apply my method to the generated data.
- Repeat these procedures 1000 times.
- Calculate the probabilities that the method correctly detects irregular processes and incorrectly detects regular processes by changing the value of the hyper-parameter.

The results are shown in Table 1. Column n indicates which random data sequences were used for the outlier detection. For example, 1–10 indicates that the outlier detection procedure used the first through tenth items in the random data sequence. The calculated probabilities are the averages of the probabilities that the method incorrectly detects regular processes and the probabilities that the method correctly detects irregular processes using different values of the hyper-parameter. The results show that the probability that the method correctly detects irregular processes in each range of n increases as the hyper-parameter increases. As the hyper-parameter increases, the probabilities get closer to the probabilities of the Z test. The results also show that the probability that the method incorrectly detects regular processes in each range of n increases as the value of the hyper-parameter decreases. The probabilities when $n_0 = 0$ are equivalent to the probabilities of the t test. Thus, we have to consider the balance between the two probabilities when choose the value of the hyper-parameter. Here, this considers that minimizing the probability that the method incorrectly detects regular processes is important, so this study used $n_0 = 1$.

5 System

The author developed a LMS including the outlier detection system. The outlier detection system is shown in Fig. 7. The system presents a graph called 'Outlier detection curve' as shown in Fig. 7. Figure 7 corresponds to a learner's learning processes to a lecture.

The horizontal axis of the graph indicates the number of content items a learner has accessed, and the vertical axis indicates the value of t in eqn (3). Furthermore, there are two lines which indicate the value of t in a t distribution with α in the graph. If the value of t is greater than the value of t in a t distribution with α or the value of t is less than the value of negative t in the t distribution with α, then the new data item is detected as an outlier. For example, Fig. 4 shows that the number of irregular processes increases as the learner proceeds to learn the contents items. Thus, the learners' irregular learning processes are detected using an online system. If an irregular process is detected, the teacher investigates the learner's learning processes and sends an e-mail with some comments later.

Table 1: The outlier detection results changing the value of the hyper-parameter.

n	$\frac{Z}{\text{test}}$	$n_0 = 0$	$n_0 = 1$	$n_0 = 5$	$n_0 = 10$	$n_0 = 15$	$n_0 = 20$
Probabilities that method incorrectly detects regular processes							
1–10	0.37	0.07	0.057	0.10	0.15	0.21	0.25
11–20	0.47	0.12	0.11	0.19	0.28	0.36	0.42
21–30	0.44	0.11	0.10	0.16	0.24	0.31	0.37
31–40	0.47	0.14	0.12	0.20	0.28	0.37	0.43
41–50	0.46	0.15	0.14	0.20	0.29	0.37	0.43
51–60	0.46	0.15	0.14	0.21	0.29	0.37	0.43
61–70	0.46	0.15	0.14	0.21	0.29	0.37	0.43
71–80	0.45	0.15	0.14	0.21	0.28	0.37	0.43
81–90	0.44	0.16	0.15	0.21	0.29	0.37	0.43
91–100	0.45	0.16	0.15	0.22	0.29	0.37	0.43
Probabilities that method correctly detects irregular processes							
1–10	0.89	0.72	0.74	0.82	0.86	0.87	0.88
11–20	0.98	0.88	0.90	0.97	0.99	0.99	1.00
21–30	0.95	0.84	0.85	0.92	0.95	0.95	0.96
31–40	0.98	0.91	0.92	0.97	0.99	0.99	0.99
41–50	0.99	0.97	0.97	0.99	0.99	0.99	1.00
51–60	0.99	0.97	0.98	0.95	1.00	1.00	1.00
61–70	0.99	0.98	0.98	0.99	1.00	1.00	1.00
71–80	0.99	0.98	0.99	0.99	1.00	1.00	1.00
81–90	0.99	0.99	0.99	0.99	1.00	1.00	1.00
91–100	0.99	0.99	0.99	0.99	1.00	1.00	1.00

6 Evaluation

In this section, some experiments to evaluate the effects of this system are described. The author gave the learners the following instructions during their learning.

'If you feel that the learning process you used in this section had some problems, please click the 'No' button. If you understand the content, please click the 'Yes' button.'

The learners' responses are divided into three categories: yes, no, and no response. We can consider that students who answer 'Yes' have no problems, but those who answer 'No' or give no response might have some problems. We can consider that a 'No' response indicates that the learner did not understand the content and that no response indicates that the learner might not have completed the content.

Table 2 shows the conditional probabilities of the responses to the above question given the learners' learning processes are or are not detected as irregular.

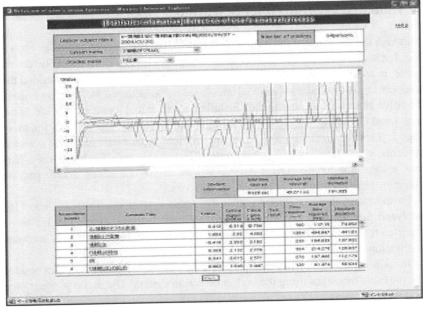

Figure 7: Online outlier detection system.

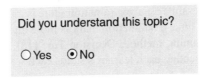

Figure 8: Yes–No button used in experiment.

Table 2: Comparisons of detected irregular processes and learners' statements.

	Learning process detected as irregular	Learning process not detected as irregular
1. 'Yes'	0.24	0.95
2. 'No'	0.31	0.02
3. No response	0.45	0.03

Table 2 indicates that the detection system efficiently detected learners' irregular processes. The probability of a 'Yes' response when a learning process is detected as an irregular process is comparatively large; this indicates that the detection criterion is somewhat strict.

7 Animated agent to enhance learning

Although the feedback of the outlier detection to the teacher is presented as shown Fig. 7, it is very difficult for a teacher to understand and interpret the outlier detection curve. In addition, even if the teacher can understand the curve, it will overload the teachers much to send motivational messages to the detected students by e-mail. To solve this problem, the author installed an animated agent to provide some motivated messages generated from the data mining results into the LMS shown in Figs 1, 9 and 10. In this system, the agent provides some messages to the detected students, e.g. 'Didn't you skip the content 21, 22, 23, and 29? Try again', 'You took a long time for the content 41, 42, and 51. If you are having trouble with the contents, please consult your teacher.', and so on.

Furthermore, there is evidence that the agent system is effective. Ueno [16] analyzed that learners begin to be bored of their learning every 18 min, so he reported that the animated agent system is very effective in attracting the learners' motivation.

In addition, the LMS 'Samurai' provides various motivational messages besides the previous messages using the outlier detection system. The message generation system is as follows [17].

The method is to apply a data mining method to the huge amount of stored data and construct a learner model to predict each learner's final status: (1) Failed (Final examination score below 60); (2) Abandon (The learner withdraws before the final examination); (3) Successful (Final examination score is more than 60 but less than 80); and (4) Excellent (Final examination mark is more than 80). For this purpose, the well-known data mining method, Decision Tree [18], is employed using the following variables reflecting each learner's status each week:

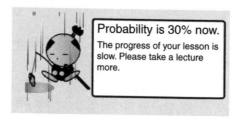

Figure 9: An intelligent agent system.

Figure 10: Various actions of the agent.

1. The number of topics which the learner has learned.
2. The number of times the learner accessed the e-learning system.
3. The average number of times the learner has completed each topic. (This implies the time the learner repeated each topic.)
4. The average learning time for each lecture, which consists of several types of contents and runs 90 min.
5. The average of the degree of understanding of each topic. (This is measured by the response to the question which is corresponding to each topic.)
6. The average learning time for each course which consists of fifteen lectures.
7. The average number of times the learner has changed the answer to the questions in the e-Learning.
8. The number of times which the learner has posted opinions or comments to the discussion board.
9. The average learning time for each topic.

Because all courses run for 15 weeks, fifteen decision trees are estimated corresponding to learners' learning histories data for the fifteen weeks. We use the ID3 algorithm [18] as a learning algorithm for the decision trees. The program was developed using Java and installed in Samurai. The decision trees are always estimated using updated learning histories. Therefore, the decision trees structures for predicting the learner's final status always change. In this algorithm, all variables are always used. A decision tree learned from 1,344 learners' data is shown in Fig. 11. This tree was estimated using 14 weeks of learning history data. The two values in parentheses indicate the number of cases in which the inference is correct and incorrect. For example, (408/18) indicates that the probability of the correct inference is 408/426. In this system, decision trees corresponding to the weekly learner's status are always being constructed.

The agent provides adaptive messages to the learner using the learner model. And the agent system also performs various actions based on the learner's current status as shown in Fig. 10. The instructional messages to a learner are generated as follows:

1. The system predicts the target learner's future status and it's probability using the constructed decision tree.
2. If the predicted status is 'Excellent', then the agent provides messages like 'Looking great!', 'Continually do your best.', and 'Probability of success is xx%'. If the predicted status is not 'Excellent', the system then searches for the closest 'Excellent' node from the current predicted status node. For example, let us consider a part of the decision tree in Fig. 11 (see Fig. 12). If the predicted status is 'Failed', the nearest node 'Excellent' is the gray node in the figure. The system finds the nearest node 'Excellent' and determines the operations that will change the learner's predicted status to 'Excellent'. In this case, 'the average learning time for each topic' is detected. The system provides the messages with the predicted future status, the probability of success estimated by the decision tree, and the instructional messages according to Table 3.

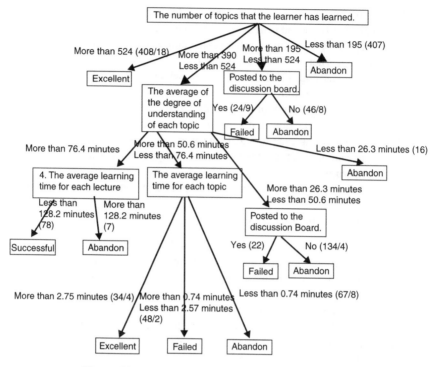

Figure 11: An example of constructed decision trees.

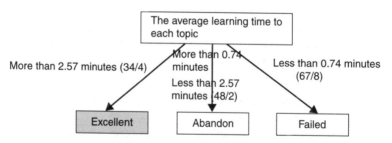

Figure 12: A part of the decision tree in Fig. 11.

Ueno [17] reported that this agent system reduced the dropout rate of e-learning to about one-third. This is a remarkable effect of the agent system.

8 Conclusions

This chapter proposed a method of online outlier detection of learners' irregular learning processes using learner response times to e-learning content. The unique

Table 3: Instructional messages corresponding to the detected variables.

Variables	Instructional messages
1. The number of topics which the learner has learned.	1. Progress in your lesson is behind. Please take more lectures.
	2. Progress in the lesson is liable to be slow. Let's take more lectures.
2. The number of times the learner accessed the e-learning system.	3. You have not engaged the lesson well. Let's access the system more.
3. The average number of times the learner has completed each topic.	4. Don't forget the previous contents! Let's confirm the previous contents again.
4. The average learning time for each lecture, which consists of several types of contents and runs 90 minutes.	5. It seems that you are working through the lecture too quickly. Please spend more time on each lecture.
5. The average of the degree of understanding of each topic (This is measured by the response to the question which is corresponding to each topic).	6. Were the contents of the lesson difficult? Let's take the lecture from the beginning once again.
	7. When there is something you don't understand, let's ask a question on a discussion board.
6. The average learning time for each course which consists of fifteen lectures.	8. You have not engaged in the lesson well. Let's access the system and study more slowly and carefully.
7. The average number of times the learner has changed the answer to the questions in the e-Learning.	9. It looks as if your knowledge is not so robust. Let's take a lecture from the beginning once again.
8. The number of times which the learner has posted opinions or comments to the discussion board.	10. Learning is better done between learners. Let's participate in and contribute to the discussion board.
9. The average learning time for each topic.	11. Did you do the lecture correctly? Ordinarily, a lesson should take more time.

features of this method are as follows: (1) It uses an outlier detection method using a Bayesian predictive distribution. (2) It can be used for small samples. (3) It can conveniently calculate predictive distributions. (4) It assists two-way instruction using data mining results on learners' learning processes. (5) The outlier statistics are estimated by considering both students' abilities and the difficulty of content.

The system was used for actual classes, and the results show the efficiency of the system.

The advantages of this outlier detection method are that it represents various statistical test methods by using a changing hyper-parameter and that the model, which depends on learners' learning ability and the difficulty of items, provides results that cannot be seen by only looking at raw learning time data.

In addition, the author proposed an animated agent which provides motivational messages to the learners using the data mining methods. The evaluation results show that these methods are effective enough.

References

[1]   Lee, C.Y., Student motivation in the online learning environment, *Journal of Educational Media & Library Sciences*, **37(4)**, pp. 365–375, 2000.

[2]   Keller, J.M., Motivation in cyber learning environments, *International Journal of Instructional of Educational Technology*, **1(1)**, pp. 7–30, 1999.

[3]   Visser, L. & Keller, J.M., The clinical use of motivational messages: An inquiry into the validity of the ARCS model to motivational design, *Instructional Science*, **19**, pp. 467–500, 1990.

[4]   Visser, L., Plomp, T. & Kuiper, W., Development research applied to improve motivation in distance education, Association for Educational Communications and Technology, Houston, TX, 1999.

[5]   Gabrielle, D.M., The effects of technology – mediated instructional strategies on motivation, performance, and self directed learning, *Proc. of ED-Media*, pp. 2569–2575, 2000.

[6]   Ueno, M., Learning log database and data mining system for e-Learning, *Proc. of IEEE Int. Conf. on Advanced Learning Technologies 2002*, IEEE Computer Society: Kazan, pp. 436–438, 2002.

[7]   Ueno, M., Data mining and text mining technologies for collaborative learning in LMS SAMURAI, in special invited lecture 'Collaborative Technology and New e-Pedagogy', *Proc. of IEEE Int. Conf. on Advanced Learning Technologies Conference*, Published by IEEE Computer Society, Joensuu, pp. 1052–1053, 2004.

[8]   Barnett, V. & Lewis, T., *Outliers in Statistical Data*, John Wiley & Sons: New York, 1994.

[9]   Burge, P. & Shaw-Taylor, J., Detecting cellular fraud using adaptive prototypes, *Proc. of AAAI Workshop, Approaches to Fraud Detection and Risk Management*, Providence, pp. 9–13, 1997.

[10] Bonchi, F., Giannotti, F., Mainetto, G. & Pedeschi, D., A classification-based methodology for planning audit strategies in fraud detection, *Proc. of KDD-99*, San Diego, pp. 175–184, 1999.

[11] Fawsett, T. & Provost, F., Combining data mining and machine learning for effective fraud detection, *Proc. of AAAI Workshop, Approaches to Fraud Detection and Risk Management*, Providence, pp. 14–19, 1997.

[12] Lee, W., Stolfo, S.J. & Mok, K.W., Mining in data-flow environment: experience in network intrusion detection, *Proc. of KDD-99*, San Diego, pp. 114–124, 1999.

[13] Ueno, M., E-learning platform with learning historical data and data mining, *Proc. of ICALT 2002*, Kazan, 2002.

[14] Ueno, M., LMS with irregular learning processes detection system, *World Conference on E-Learning in Corp., Govt., Health., & Higher Ed.*, pp. 2486–2493, 2003.

[15] Mayer, R.E. & Anderson, R.B., Animation need narrations. *Journal of Educational Psychology*, **83(4)**, pp. 484–490, 1991.

[16] Ueno, M., Animated agent to maintain learner's attention in e-learning. *World Conference on E-Learning in Corp., Govt., Health., & Higher Ed.*, pp. 194–201, 2004.

[17] Ueno, M., Intelligent agent based on decision tree for e-learning histories data, *Proc. of IEEE Int. Conf. on Advanced Learning Technologies Conference*, IEEE Computer Society: Kaoshin, 2005.

[18] Quinlan, J.R., Induction of decision trees. *Machine Learning*, **1**, pp. 81–106, 1986.

CHAPTER 16

Use of data mining to examine an outreach call center's effectiveness and build a predictive model for classifying future marketing targets

J. Luan, C. Summa & M. Wieland
Cabrillo College, USA.

Abstract

Data mining is demonstrated through the evaluation of an enrollment management call center at a community college in the US with predictive modeling of data mining being the dominant tool for the key research questions. In responding to the three research questions, the study found a statistically significant 5% higher registration rate in a four way post facto control and experimental analysis. Through examining the applicants by the manner in which they were reached by the call center, the study found that those who spoke directly with the call center staff had at least a 10% increase in registering for classes compared to those who had no contact with the call center. After removing the applicants who interacted with the call center directly, data mining analysis identified six rules for applicants who would register for classes and another six for those who would not. Further, the data mining analysis built a predictive model with an 85% accuracy to predict those who would be less likely to register in a future semester. In conclusion, there is enough evidence to suggest that data mining has a place in enrollment management.

1 Background

A call center is a medium through which organizations communicate with their members and with which service providers keep in touch with their customers, mostly through the use of telephones staffed by trained personnel. In higher education in America, call centers have been used to perform similar functions, with actual tasks varying from fund raising, to enrollment follow-up, to survey research, such as those at Piedmont and Sinclair Community Colleges. Sometimes call centers are named 'phone banks'. If done well, call centers may provide a positive impact on college enrollment.

Personal touch in an era of a fast-paced, impersonal lifestyle can leave a person reached by the call center with a lasting impression, not the least of which is the power of persuasion inherently present in a call from a college representative compared to receiving a piece of mail. To reinforce this concept, in the March 2005 issue of *Campus Technologies* [1], an article entitled 'Getting Personal' discussed strategies being implemented at various institutions to boost their enrollment. Ferris State, for example, attributed the increase of 2327 students up from 9495 a couple of years ago to customized recruiting. After providing many examples, the article stated that 'Campuses ... to interact with potential students have reported success in meeting their enrollment goals'. In the *University Business* [2] magazine published in the same month, the article 'A New Definition of Marketing' discussed the concept of engaging students through organizational as well as departmental marketing efforts.

Students enroll and leave college without graduation for many reasons [3]. Hossler in 1984 [4] systematically identified several factors influencing students' enrollment. College reputation, cost, financial aid, all played certain roles. Active outreach, or customer relationship management concepts borrowing a modern term, did not receive significant mention in Hossler's work. Neither was information driven analytical approaches, such as data mining. Rounds [5] in 1984 discussed several promising practices in attrition and retention of community college students, which helped shed light on establishing a focal point on interpreting some of the behaviors of students, such as peer influence and inertia. Luan and several scholars [6, 7] in 2004 and 2005 presented case studies to demonstrate the use of data mining in managing applicants' yield, outreach, and predictive modeling for both registration and attrition. Their work helped with designing the data mining approach.

Spring 2005 marked another round of California community college fee increases enacted by the California legislature. Past fee increases had proven to negatively impact enrollment. For example, one study conducted by Borden [8] showed that for every fee increase, there had been a corresponding drop in enrollment. A S13 increase would effect a 6% drop in headcounts, which translates into hundreds of students not enrolling. In confirmation of this, in 2004 the Chancellor's Office for the 109 California's community colleges estimated that system-wide annually a total of 142,500 students would be 'lost' due to such an increase [9].

In anticipation of a potential enrollment dip, Cabrillo College's Marketing & Communications department, with assistance from several areas of the college, helped form the enrollment fee task force with the goal to maintain, if not increase, the spring 2005 enrollment. Among many areas identified as worthy of improvement, the issue of low registration rate from a large pool of applicants rose to the top. Although a majority of the applicants would register, thousands may never proceed beyond turning in their applications. Back in spring 2004, a total of 1836 applicants out of 7137 did not register for classes. Therefore, one of the strategies identified by the taskforce was to direct call center outreach activities to those who have applied, but have not registered in spring 2005. As of January 18, 2005, roughly a month before the spring census day, a total of 2649 applicants were identified. Between January 10 and January 30, 2005, Cabrillo College, with the generous donation of time from 50 volunteers, made calls to a list of applicants at the beginning of the spring 2005 semester.

The purpose of the call center was to maintain or increase enrollment for spring 2005. The specific objectives of the call center effort were the following:

- Primary: to remind and encourage students to register.
- Secondary: to help students resolve problems stopping them from registering.
- Tertiary: to gather data about registration problems and identify any trends.

2 Three key questions addressed

This study addresses three key questions in evaluating the spring 2005 call center effectiveness. The general term of effectiveness used here means to include yield rate and productivity. Yield refers to the number of applicants who have become registrants as a result of the call center's efforts. Productivity refers to the average units taken by these registrants. An additional question for designing a predictive model by pre-classifying future applicants into groups scaled according to their likelihood to register is also explored by the study. A predictive model would reduce the cost of call center by identifying those who are less or least likely to register, so that calls are more focused and targeted.

Specifically, this study addresses three questions:

- Question one (yield): How many of the applied-but-not-registered applicants became registrants as a result of being reached by the call center?
- Question two (productivity): What are the average units taken by the registrants as compared to other registrants who were not directly reached by the call center?
- Question three (predictive modeling): How many applicants can be predicted to be less likely to register so that the call center can concentrate on these applicants?
- For the sake of saving space, answers to the productivity question are not stated in this chapter.

3 Data sources

Cabrillo College's Computing Resources (CR) department provided lists of applicants who applied, but had not registered, for select dates based on request from the call center volunteers. CR also provided summary counts of applicants for both the current semester and the historical spring 2004 semester. The call center provided feedback data in the form of notes taken by the call center volunteers. The Planning and Research Office (PRO) conducted data matching where possible prior to conducting statistical analyses.

4 Design and method

In order to answer all three questions, this study employed a variety of methods and tools. The study adopted a post facto control and experimental design for seeking answers to question one. Chi-square statistics was used for question one. Regression equations, neural networks, and classification and regression tree (C&RT) were used for algorithm bias analysis for question three. Also, data were split into training and test sets for empirical accuracy validation. Data warehousing and SQL (structured query language) technologies directly supported the datasets merging and querying tasks.

The results of the call center were hand coded into an Excel worksheet that was imported into Brio Query, a business intelligence (BI) tool for the purpose of querying and pivoting variables (building various reports). Most of the answers to question one and question two are provided by Brio Query, assisted by Excel and SPSS (another statistical analysis tool). For question three of predicative modeling, the study utilized data mining and a tool called Clementine, a leading industrial strength business analytics (BA) application.

The study chose Clementine as the data mining tool because of its ability to directly interface with static or live relational databases, to calculate new fields using GUI (graphical user interface) guided nodes, to convert transactional data files into analytical data files, and to allow infinite number of scenarios to be built and examined using its 16 modeling algorithms. All analyses are conducted inside one data stream, which makes it much easier for cross-validation, interpretation, replication and documentation. The screenshot in Fig. 1 illustrates the 'data stream' built within Clementine for the entire study, including the nodes used for calculating new fields (variables).

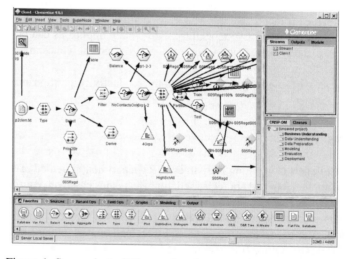

Figure 1: Screenshot of Clementine data stream on design canvas.

Since Brio Query queried the datasets and produced a data cube containing most of the needed data elements that lent themselves readily as input variables for the data mining tasks, Clementine directly imported a tab delimited text files from Brio Query as its data source.

5 Findings

5.1 Yield

The answer to question one was obtained through two separate steps. The first step examined the differences in registration rates between a control group and an experimental group. The experimental group would be the group that had the presence of a call center and the control group had not. To compute specific yield rates, which was the second step, required those in the experimental group who were identified to be those who applied but had not yet registered for classes for the call center to contact. Not all applicants could be contacted by the call center.

5.1.1 Step one for answering question one: overall effect of the presence of call center

As the first step in addressing question one, the study made refinement to the original pair of a control group and an experimental group by splitting them further. The rationale is as follows. As mentioned earlier, all those who turned in their applications as of spring 2004 semester census date (February 23, 2004) became a pseudo-control group because no call center activities took place in that semester. All those who had their applications on file as of spring 2005 semester census date (February 22, 2005) were the experimental group. The call center only functioned for a brief period of time, a month before the start of the spring 2005 semester and the college continued to receive applicants since the lists of applicants were extracted for the calls. This has provided a good opportunity to examine the registration rates with and without the call center in the same semester. Therefore, applicants in both groups were then split by a specific date. For spring 2005, the date of January 19 was chosen because none of the applicants who turned in their applications after 19 January were contacted. This group is called 'Pool A'. January 19, 2005, was 31 days before the census day of spring 2005. For spring 2004, the date of January 20, 2004, was chosen (31 days before spring 2004 census date). This group is called 'Pool B'. Hypothetically speaking, if call center had no effect, then the rates for Pools A and Pools B in their respective semesters should be very similar.

The following table presents the rates of registration for the control (Pools A & B) and experimental groups (Pools A & B).

Table 1 shows that those spring 2005 students in Pool A had a higher registration rate than Pool B. The difference is 5%. Both the equivalent pools of students in spring 2004 showed no change in their registration rate.

Is the observed 5% difference statistically significant? The study turned to chi-square analysis for answers. The following output from chi-square analysis showed a high level of significance.

Table 1: Registration rates by treatment and control groups.

		Spring 2005		Spring 2004
Pool A	Call Center Available	71%	No Call Center	74%
Pool B	No Call Center	66% Difference = 5%	No Call Center	74% Difference = 0%

Note:

1. Pool A contain all applicants who turned in their applications as of spring census date. For Pool A from spring 2005, a sub-group of the applicants, namely those who applied but had not registered as of the date of January 19, 2005, was the group contacted by the call center and consequently discussed in detail in the study.
2. Online application was made available for the first time in spring 2005. A great number of students utilized it to apply online. This is a key difference other than a call center available to both Pool A and Pool B in spring 2005.

$$\chi^2 = \Sigma\,(O\text{-}E)^2/E = \quad 24.52$$
$$\text{degrees of freedom} = 1$$
$$p = 0.000001$$

Figure 2: Chi-square output.

The chi-square analysis indicates that the observed 5% difference was statistically a significant event for the registration rate for those who applied but had not registered in spring 2005. The occurrence of a difference of 5% purely by chance is deemed to be one in 100,000, or very unlikely.

Although the 5% difference is considered statistically significant, in order to completely answer the question on the yield rate the next step is to look at the actual number of yields.

5.1.2 Step two for answering question one: computing specific yield rates

The applicants under study have been categorized into several distinct groups. Those who spoke with the call center staff directly and said they were going to register were in the Promised group. Those who received a voice mail message from the call center volunteers were in the Left Msg. group. Those whose phones never answered were in the Not Accessible group. Those who spoke Spanish only were in the Spanish Spk group. Those who provided a wrong number on their applications were in the Wrong No. group. Those whose phone numbers had an area code other than 831 were in the Out of Area group. Table 2 contains detailed information on these groups.

In Table 2, of the applicants who had not registered by January 19, 2005, 370 of them spoke with the call center staff directly and said they would register. Eventually, 194 of them were found to have registered as of spring 2005 semester census day, thus producing a yield rate of 52% for the Promised group. Across all

Table 2: Yield rates by all applicant types.

	Applicants*	Yield	Rate**
Promised	370	194	52%
Left Msg.	842	400	48%
Not Accessible	259	120	46%
Spanish Spk	12	5	42%
Wrong No.	288	115	40%
Out of Area	86	26	30%

*Applicants column has been revised by removing those who had already registered by January 19, 2005.
**Rate refers to the number of actual registrants (yields) from within each category of the applicants. This way the rate can be clearly computed to indicate the yield.

categories of applicants in Table 2, this is by far the highest yield rate. The next group that had the highest yield rate (48%) was those who received a voice mail message from the callers.

The study removed all cases from all categories if they were found to have a registration date prior to January 19, 2005. This will help with making sure that the subjects under study have not been included in error. Secondly, the researchers went through the actual survey forms filled out by the call center volunteers and paid particular attention to those in the Promised group. The purpose of examining the actual feedback from the applicants was to get a sense of the reasons behind those 194 direct yields. Many of them stated reasons such as 'not clear on what to do next', 'have not gotten the time', or 'procrastinating'. Many were thankful that they got the call. It was clear that they indeed may not have registered if they had not receive the calls.

Apart from those who received a voice mail message from the callers, those who registered without speaking directly with the call center volunteers (or without being reached by the callers) can be regarded as those who enrolled in classes of their own volition; therefore, subjects with no contact from call center (without receiving any treatment). They were the groups of Not Accessible, Wrong No. and Out of Area. After collapsing the above six application types (Table 3) into only three, the yield rate of the applicants for the Promised group is ranked 11% higher than the All Other group and is still 3% higher than all others after it is combined with the Left Msg. group (Promised & Msg) (Fig. 3).

5.2 Predictive modeling

Question three: How would predictive modeling help with identifying among the future applicants those who are less likely to register to help better focus on calls made by the call center?.

Table 3: Yield rates by collapsed applicants types.

	Applicants*	Yield	Rate
Promised	370	194	52%
Promised & Msg	1212	594	49%
All Other	633	261	41%

Promised denotes those who spoke to the callers directly and promised to register. Promised & Msg denotes those of the Promised group as well as those who received a voice mail message. All Other denotes those who were not reachable, wrong number, and out of the area (who are likely distant or non-residents).

*Applicants column has been revised by removing those who had already registered by January 19, 2005.

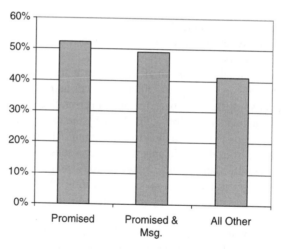

Figure 3: Yield rates by collapsed applicant types.

To answer this question, the study first used a Venn diagram to group the 2949 applicants based on their presence in the college's MIS data warehouse and the spring 2005 census database. A Venn diagram, developed by John Venn, a logician, is an effective way to visually identify subgroups (also called sets in algebra) of any populations, particularly when there is a large amount of overlapping. Venn diagrams have found use in many fields, such as database design, combinatorics [10], and assessment of learning [11].

The following Venn diagram (Fig. 4) indicates the overlapping of the population of 2949 applicants with the colleges' MIS historical data warehouse and the spring 2005 census database. Four distinct groups are therefore clearly visible. They are:

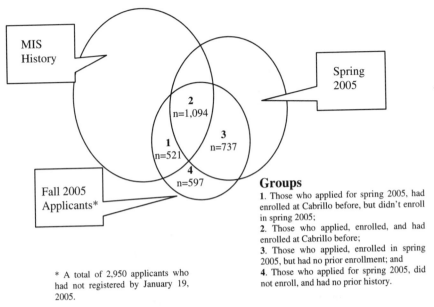

MIS
History

Spring
2005

2
n=1,094

3
n=737

1
n=521

4
n=597

Fall 2005
Applicants*

Groups
1. Those who applied for spring 2005, had enrolled at Cabrillo before, but didn't enroll in spring 2005;
2. Those who applied, enrolled, and had enrolled at Cabrillo before;
3. Those who applied, enrolled in spring 2005, but had no prior enrollment; and
4. Those who applied for spring 2005, did not enroll, and had no prior history.

* A total of 2,950 applicants who had not registered by January 19, 2005.

Figure 4: Venn diagram of four groups of the 2949 applicants.

Group 1: Those who applied for spring 2005, had enrolled at Cabrillo before, but did not enroll in spring 2005 ($n = 521$);

Group 2: Those who applied, enrolled, and had enrolled at Cabrillo before ($n = 1094$);

Group 3: Those who applied, enrolled in spring 2005, but had no prior enrollment ($n = 737$); and

Group 4: Those who applied for spring 2005, did not enroll, and had no prior history ($n = 597$).

These groups helped the rest of the analysis by making it possible to focus on each of them while drilling down to its population details. They guided the rest of the study and are frequently referenced.

Since Venn diagrams do not display data in proportion to their distributions in a dataset, a pie chart below will correct that by making the distributions adjusted to their appropriate scale. First, for those who eventually registered, the majority (62%, Groups 2 and 3) of the 2949 applicants eventually registered as of spring 2005 census time. At least a quarter (25%) of the applicants was new to Cabrillo College because no prior academic records existed for them in the college MIS historical data warehouse going back 15 years.

For those who never registered, regardless of being reached by the call center or not, over a third (38%, Groups 1 and 4) of the 2,949 applicants on the call list did not eventually register, but half of them (Group 1) had attended Cabrillo College before. The other half, or 20% of the 2949 applicants, had never been to Cabrillo College.

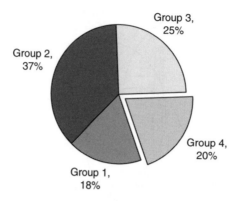

Figure 5: Registration percent distribution of applicants to be called ($n = 2949$).

Overall, 45% (Groups 3 and 4, $n = 1334$) of the 2949 applicants had never been to Cabrillo College before. It is unique to have so many of the potential 'new' students among the 2949 applicants to be called by the call center. Was there a reason for a disproportionate number of applicants who had never been to Cabrillo College to be slow in registering for classes? Spring 2005 enrollment statistics showed that a total of 2741 students enrolled were new students. Hypothetically, the number of new students could have been 3338 (2741 + 597 of Group 4). In other words, 17.8% (597/3338) were missing from the new students pool.

The pie chart (Fig. 5) also seems to indicate that the 2949 applicants almost had an equal 25% chance in falling into any of the four groups. Overall, having been to Cabrillo College seemed to increase the chance of registering for classes (37%, Group 2). For those who had never been to Cabrillo, their chances of registration were about 50/50. This means that the outcomes of the applicants are really a set of four: those who had been to Cabrillo but did not register and those who did register; those who were new to Cabrillo and registered; and those who did not register and their prior background information is unknown.

The following five charts (figures) and tables display background characteristics of the groups identified in the Venn diagram. However, Group 4 is not in any of the analysis due to lack of data.

Figure 6 above shows the distribution of age ranges across the three Venn diagram groups.

Overall, the age of students in Group 1 (those applicants who had been at Cabrillo before but did not eventually register) was higher than the other two groups. Compared to Groups 2 and 3, Group 1 had fewer students younger than 20. The reverse is true for Groups 2 and 3.

Students ages 17 and below or 19 and below as shown in Fig. 5 are likely concurrently enrolled students. For Group 2 (the group of applicants who had taken classes at Cabrillo College and registered), there were fewer students in the age range of a recent high school graduate (18–19) compared to Group 3 (new applicants who had never been to Cabrillo). Comparing Group 2 to Group 3, fewer

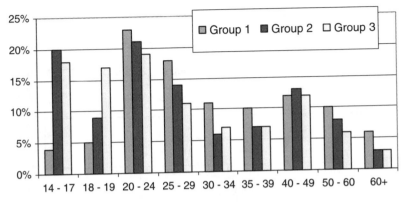

Figure 6: Age distribution by Venn diagram groups.

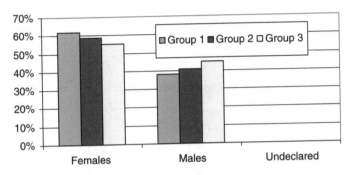

Figure 7: Gender distribution by Venn diagram groups.

students in Group 2 were from the age range of 18 to 19. The missing ones may have been recent high school graduates who had decided to move on following their study at Cabrillo College.

Figure 7 above shows the distribution of gender across the three Venn diagram groups. Across the three groups, gender seemed to have an opposing trend. More females were in Group 1, less in Group 2 and much less in Group 3, but the reverse is true for males. New applicants (Group 3) tended to be male. Applicants who had been to Cabrillo College and had not registered tended to be female.

Figure 8 above shows the distribution of ethnicities across the three Venn diagram groups. There is no major difference across major ethnic minorities among all three groups of applicants. There appeared to be fewer white students in Group 3 (new applicants without Cabrillo College experience) while there is an increase in the Unknown category in Group 3. Research has shown that most of the students in 'unknown' or 'unreported' categories tend to be White students.

Figure 9 above shows the distribution of education background across the three Venn diagram groups. There were fewer concurrently enrolled students in Group 1 (those applicants who had been to Cabrillo College, but never registered) compared

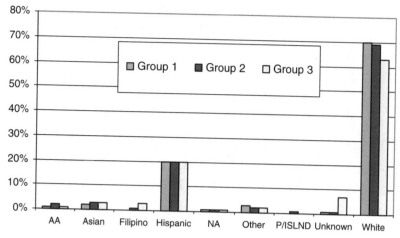

Figure 8: Ethnicity distribution by Venn diagram groups.

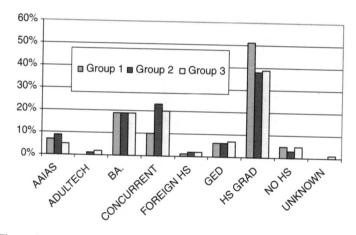

Figure 9: Education background distribution by Venn diagram groups.

to other groups. This is a validation of the observations made about their age. More of them in Group 1, on the other hand, were high school graduates, but not necessarily recent high school graduates.

Figure 10 above shows the distribution of enrollment status across the three Venn diagram groups.

The largest portion of Group 1 was those who were continuing students when they applied. The largest portion of applicants in Group 2 was those who were new. The largest portion of applicants for Group 3 was those who were new, too.

Distributions of enrollment status for the three groups of applicants were generally very diverse. Very few in Group 1 were concurrently enrolled students. Very few in Group 2 were continuing students when they applied.

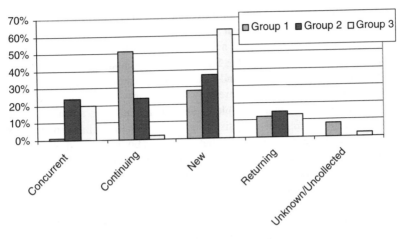

Figure 10: Enrollment status by venn diagram groups.

5.2.1 Data mining rationale and discoveries

The above visual analysis by five select background variables of demographics and academic status help develop an impression of the different characteristics of the applicants in Groups 1, 2 and 3. However, the impression is at best a fuzzy one, not accurate or evidential to help classify individual future applicants into respective groups. Plus, should one decide to cross tabulate the groups by two or more variables, the examination of these background variables using the method above can go on forever and there can be infinite number of tables and charts.

A 3-dimensional environment with multiple variables intermingled in a myriad of ways is impossible for the human eyes to quickly spot trends or monitor changes. It is precisely such a spatial sphere in which hidden patterns exist that can lead to new information on how the applicants become a registrant. Conventional tools may start to show inadequacies in handling the infinite number of coordinates in such a spatial sphere. Even the traditional regression analysis, which computes the residual statistics of multiple variables around a mean to determine their contribution to explain the variance of a phenomenon, is not entire adequate.

For example, there may be a dozen variables going into a regression analysis to identify the key ones that would determine whether or not an applicant would register. The regression analysis may find that among these variables gender, ethnicity, age, location, and GPA would be significant. It then provides a specific value (odds ratio) associated with each variable to determine the likelihood of an applicant's registration status. The equation typically functions as a polynomial model: if the value of a variable changes by one unit, such as one year of age increase for an applicant, the likelihood of registration would change by an X amount. Plugging in an applicant whose age is 18, gender is male, and ethnicity is Asian, out comes the likelihood of his registering for classes.

This likelihood is essentially a quadratic equation following a Sigmoid curve (regression line) with its values ranging from 0 to 1. Every new case is fit into this regression equation. The sizes of the confidence intervals drawn for individual cases are much greater or wider than those drawn for the averages predicted by the regression lines [12]. For example, not necessarily every 18 year old, male, Asian applicant would be likely to register. Some 18-year-old male Asian applicants may register because of variables A, B, and C, and others because of variables C, D and F.

Another regression test, the linear regression has long been considered inadequate to address most social science problems and has remained as an introduction to modern regression statistical analysis [13]. Approaches to nonlinear data do exist, such as Nonlinear Regression (NLR), but it requires both input and output data to be quantitative. Many data mining algorithms do not have such requirement. In addition, the Neural Net algorithm, for example, does not make assumptions about the data, nor does it require data to be coded any particular way [14].

Jesus Mena in 1998 [15] observed the differences between statistics and data mining by classifying traditional statistics as a top down approach and data mining bottom up. Mena stated that traditional statistics require the researcher to first formulize a theory in the form of a hypothesis and then query the data to prove or disprove the theory. Data mining on the other hand relies on data to self-organize and may not ever rise up to the level of formulating a theory [16]. Mena also discussed scaling both the analytical prowess and data file to speed and size that is particularly important in a fast moving business environment. For example, according to Mena, a typical database may contain 100 attributes about customers, which would mean, for any customer, there would be 100×99 combinations of attributes to consider. A small task such as classifying customers into high, medium or low groups, would mean 970,200 ($100 \times 99 \times 98$) possible combinations.

The rest of the study moved beyond data visualization and employed predictive modeling data mining technique. Specifically, the study used Neural Net and C&RT nodes. Both of them are predictive modeling nodes based on artificial intelligence and machine learning. The predicative modeling nodes, to state simply, has the ability to study known cases in order to make predictions onto unknown cases. The unknown cases would be incoming applicants for a future semester. Along the way, data mining also provides a number of sophisticated ways of examining and describing the data.

Not all cases have been used for the predictive modeling. First, hundreds of applicants spoke directly with the call center staff, which could have contaminated the subjects because of the extra intervention they received. The direct interaction with the call center staff would artificially make the likelihood of registering for classes higher, particularly such an interaction has been proven to be effective in generating enrollments. Therefore, the study removed these 370 applicants. Secondly, the study removed the entire Group 4, because there was no background data for this group of applicants who never registered. Thirdly, Group 3 (those who had no prior records at Cabrillo but eventually registered) presented another dilemma. The most significant marker for this group is that they had no prior records, which would trick the algorithm to put too much weight on this fact that could overwhelm all other variables. Therefore, the entire group was removed as well. The remaining 1413 applicants came from Group 1 ($n = 463$) and Group 2 ($n = 950$).

Between applicants registering for classes and not registering for classes, of interest to the study is those who did not register. The reason is simple. If data mining algorithms can predictively identify those who are less likely to register, then the call center staff can concentrate on these applicants, which is a far effective use of time and resources. Defined as between group accuracy, all the applicants who did not register (Actual) should be 'predicated' as not having registered (Predicted). The idea is for the data mining algorithms to first examine all the variables associated with each applicant's registration outcome to learn the rules and then apply the rules to similar cases to predict their registration outcome. Since the focus of the predictive modeling is on those who would not register, the level of Between Group Accuracy should be higher than 85%, which means out of all the applicants predicted to be less likely to register, it would get 9 out of 10 of them correct. The outcome variable, S05Regd, is binary: registered 'S05' and not registered 'NoS05'.

The Neural Net node was run first with the sensitivity statistics shown in Table 4.

The sensitivity statistics from the Neural Net node helps the analysts understand the level of importance of input variables that determine an outcome. In this case, the outcome is registered or not registered. The node indicates (Table 4) that the enrollment status is the most important variable and gender is the least important variable.

Yet, the predication accuracy by the Neural Net node is not impressive. The between group predictive accuracy of Neural Net node for those who did not register is low (55.9%), evidenced by the following matrix (Table 5). This represents a slightly better chance than a coin toss. Neural Net node was not used after this discovery.

The C&RT node was used next without any adjustments inside the node to accommodate for misclassification. Misclassification is the equivalent of false positives. It is often used when the analysts choose to err on the side of predicting more cases favoring one outcome over the other, such as not registering for classes, so as to increase the chances of getting more cases of one side (type) correctly predicted at the expense of the other.

Table 4: Relative importance of inputs of Neural Net node.

Variable name	System variable names	Sensitivity
Enrollment Status	Group of EnrlStatAll	0.40344
High School Origin	HighSchAll	0.33039
Age (in ranges)	AgeRange2005	0.307335
Ethnicity	Group of EthnicityAll	0.30281
Education Background	Group of EdStatusAll	0.249625
Number of Terms Previously Enrolled	CntDTL	0.176079
Gender	GenderAll	0.115245

Note: Neural Net node: 71.2% accuracy; 59 neurons, 1 hidden layer; Quick, seed = true.

Table 5: Between group accuracy matrix by Neural Net node.

Actual		Predicted Not Reg'd	Registered
Not Reg'd	Count	259	204
	Row %	55.9	44.1
Registered	Count	160	790
	Row %	16.8	83.2

Table 6: Between group accuracy matrix by C&RT node.

Actual		Predicted Not Reg'd	Registered
Not Reg'd	Count	393	70
	Row %	84.9	15.1
Registered	Count	344	606
	Row %	36.2	63.8

In Table 6, the between group predictive accuracy produced by the C&RT node for those who did not register is much better (85.7%) than those who eventually registered (70.4%).

The rest of the analysis utilized a decision tree graph and rule sets from the C&RT node.

Figure 11 is a partial screenshot of a binary decision tree produced by the C&RT algorithm. The tree is six branches deep from the first node of registration status ($R-S05Regd), but only the first four top branches can fit on a landscape page in this report. The top branches typically contain variables more influential to the outcome than the rest toward the bottom.

In the decision tree graph (Fig. 11), applicants' latest Enrollment Status seemed to be most important, therefore, it became the first split. Those who were Concurrently Enrolled, New or Returning applicants ($n = 905$) were split from those who were Continuing or with unknown status ($n = 508$). Of those 905 applicants, 21.3% ($n = 193$) did not register and 78.7% of them did. For the sake of understanding the tree graph, let us focus on these 193 applicants who did not register. In the next split that occurred on the variable of Education Background, 183 were left. They were those who had already obtained a Baceelaureate degree, or a Foreign High School Diploma, or a General Education Degree, and those who either graduated or did not graduate from high school. The next split took place on the variable of number of terms enrolled at Cabrillo College prior to applying for college (CntDTL), 109 applicants who had less than 1.5 total terms enrolled were left. They reside in the terminal node, which means no further split occurred. Therefore, tracing the above splits, it can be reasonably stated that the 109 applicants who did not register were those who had a very short or no prior attendance at the college, who had a Bachelaureate degree, or a high school diploma, regardless of their high school

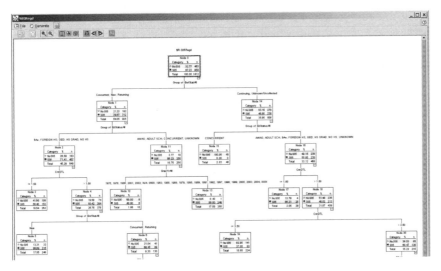

Figure 11: Decision tree (partial) from C&RT.

graduation status, and were either concurrently enrolled, or a new or returning to college after a brief stop out.

To identify these patterns by studying the decision tree diagram can be cumbersome. Fortunately the data mining algorithm has already combed through the tree diagram and produced a list of the patterns, called rules. There are a total of six rules for those who did not register and another set of 6 rules for those who did. If more variables were introduced to the algorithm, the number of rules would likely increase. The first rule reads as follows:

Rules for No Registration - contains 6 rule(s)
        Rule 1 for No Registration (262, 0.584)
            if Group of Enrollment Status in ["Concurrent" "New" "Returning"]
                and Group of Education Background in
["BA+" "FOREIGN HS" "GED" "HS GRAD" "NO HS"]
                and Number of Terms Ever Enrolled <= 1.500
                then No Registration
        Rule 2 for No Registration (36, 0.528)
            if Group of Enrollment Status in ["Concurrent" "New" "Returning"]
                and Group of Education Background in
["BA+" "FOREIGN HS" "GED" "HS GRAD" "NO HS"]
                and Number of Terms Ever Enrolled CntDTL > 1.500
                and Group of Enrollment Status in ["Concurrent" "Returning"]
                and City Locations in
["Aptos" "Campbell" "Capitola" "Moss Landing" "Mount Hermon" "Santa Cruz" "Soquel" "Watsonville"]
                and Age Range in ["25 - 29" "35 - 39"]
                then No Registration

The first rule corresponds to the observations made early for the 109 applicants. Because 153 of those who actually registered were also classified into the terminal node with the 109 applicants, therefore, the rule states at the beginning that there were a total of 262 cases and the confidence is only 58%. It is not unusual that the accuracy for individual rules may not be always high. The fourth rule had 40 cases in it and it had a confidence level of 100%. The rules are listed without a hierarchical order. The first rule is as important as the last rule. Let us take a look at the first rule for those who would register.

Rules for Registration- contains 6 rule(s)
        Rule 1 for Registration (248, 0.867)
           if Group of Enrollment Status in ["Concurrent" "New" "Returning"]
               and Group of Education Background in
["BA+" "FOREIGN HS" "GED" "HS GRAD" "NO HS"]
               and Number of Terms Ever Enrolled > 1.500
               and Group of Enrollment Status in ["New"]
               then Registered.

There were a total of 248 cases belonging to this rule and its confidence level was 87%.

It is clear through just viewing a few of the rules that there are many different profiles that could determine the final outcome of registering for classes. This proves that there is no one equation that can adequately illustrate the highly various nature behind the registration status of all the applicants. Case in point, only about 40 students fit the fourth rule for those who did not register. Another 248 of the applicants fit the first rule for those who registered.

The 2949 applicants, a subset of all the applicants for spring 2005, were those who for some reason had not registered just days before the semester was to start, the analysis of their behaviors and background information should bear in mind that real reasons and the motivation factor were unknown. Some of them may be straddlers or stragglers, others may have a legitimate reason to be slow. As the notes taken by the call center staff showed, some applicants were confused by the registration process, some were waiting for their appointment dates, some took a backseat when they realized they had to go through assessment. Quite a few applicants reached by the call center said they were moving out of the area, had financial aid issues, or downright unmotivated and 'lazy' quoting their own words.

At the time of this study, academic history data is only available for Groups 1 and 2. When background data becomes available for Group 4, the predictive modeling may be further enhanced.

6 Discussion

In responding to the three research questions, the study uncovered the following findings. In terms of call center effectiveness as defined by yields and significance of the yields (question one), the study found a statistically significant 5% higher registration rate in a four way post facto control and experimental analysis. But this significance should also take into consideration a few college initiated changes, although no specific impact to any of the four way analyses was immediately perceivable. For example, the college implemented online application in spring 2005, which increased the total applicants by 12% as compared to the spring a year earlier.

The study found a noticeable difference in registration rate large enough to attribute the increase in registration to the call center after examining the different categories of applicants coded for callers. Those who spoke directly with the call center staff had at least a 10% increase in registering for classes compared to those who had no contact with the call center. Yet in answers to question three on productivity (not discussed in this chapter), the increase was found at best to have helped maintain the level of FTES, a productivity measure. However, it can be viewed that without the call center, there could have been a perceivable drop in both headcounts and FTES in spring 2005. From a summative evaluation perspective, the call center receives a B+.

After removing the applicants who interacted with the call center directly, data mining analysis identified six rules for applicants who would register for classes and another six for those who would not. Further, the data mining analysis built a predictive model with an 85% accuracy to predict those who would be less likely to register in a future semester.

References

[1] Tansey, F., Getting Personal – eRecruiting technologies now enable schools to match their strengths to prospective students' individual expectations. *Campus Technologies*, 2005.

[2] Sevier, R.A., New Definition of Marketing – The AMA's update can mean enormous opportunities for higher education. *University Business*, 2005.

[3] Digby, K.E., A study of the factors which influence adult enrollment in a technical institute. *ERIC* (ED273319), 1986.

[4] Hossler, D., *Enrollment Management – An Integrated Approach*, The College Board: New York, 1986.

[5] Rounds, J.C., Attrition and Retention of Community College Students: Problem and Promising Practices. ERIC (ED242377), 1984.

[6] Luan, J., Zhai, M., Chen, J., Chow, T., Chang, L. & Zhao, C., Concepts, Myths, and Case Studies of Data Mining in Higher Education, Presentation at 44th AIR Forum. Boston, MA, 2004.

[7] Luan, J., Kumar, T., Chang, L., Eykamp, P., Sujitparapitaya, S., Williams, M. & Stamoulis, L., Concepts, Myths, and Case Studies of Data Mining in Higher Education, Presentation at 45th AIR Forum. San Diego, CA, 2005.

[8] Borden, R., Projected impact of fee hike on Cabrillo fall enrollment 2003 to 2007, Cabrillo College Publication, 2003.

[9]   Fluentes-Michel, D. & Perry, P., Student fees, Presentation at the Study Session of the Board of Governors Meeting of California Community Colleges, 2003.

[10]   Ruskey, F.A., Survey of Venn diagrams. *The Electronic Journal of Combinatorics*, 1997.

[11]   Dixon, J., http://www.valdosta.edu/~jharris/assessment.html, 2005.

[12]   Chang, L., A Case Study Applying Data Mining Technology in Modeling and Predicting Admissions Yield in Higher Education, AIR Forum, San Diego, 2005.

[13]   Fetterer, F. & Knowles, K., *Sea Ice Index*, National Snow and Ice Data Center: Boulder, CO, Digital media, 2002.

[14]   Shachmurove, Y., Applying Artificial Neural Networks to Business, Economics and Finance (online: http://qudata.com/lib/neuronet/), 2004.

[15]   Mena, J., Data Mining FAQs, DM Review, 1998.

[16]   Zhao, C.M. & Luan, J., Chapter One (draft): Introduction to Data Mining Applications for Enrollment Management. Data Mining Concepts, Myths & Its Applications in Enrollment Management. Proposed issue for *New Directions for Institutional Research*, 2005.

Index

Computational Finance and its Applications II

Edited by: M. COSTANTINO, Royal Bank of Scotland Financial Markets, UK, C. A. BREBBIA, Wessex Institute of Technology, UK

Computational systems have become increasingly important in many financial applications, such as trading strategy, risk management, derivatives pricing, and many others. At the same time, traditional financial techniques have been constantly improved and developed as a result of the increased power of modern computer systems. Featuring papers from the Second International Conference on Computational Finance and its Applications, the text includes papers that encompass a wide range of topics such as: Risk Management; Derivatives Pricing; Credit Risk; Trading Strategies; Portfolio Management and Asset Allocation; Market Analysis, Dynamics and Simulation; Computational Economics and Agent-based Markets; Forecasting; Data Mining and Knowledge Discovery; Pattern Recognition; Intelligent Trading Agents; Time Series Analysis and Forecasting; High Frequency Financial Data; Export Systems and Decision Support; Advanced Computing and Simulation.
WIT Transactions on Modelling and Simulation Volume 43

ISBN: 1-84564-174-4   2006   apx 450pp apx £165.00/US$295.00/€247.50

All prices correct at time of going to press but subject to change.
WIT Press books are available through your bookseller or direct from the publisher.

Risk Analysis V

Computer Simulation in Risk Analysis and Hazard Mitigation V

Edited by: V. POPOV, Wessex Institute of Technology, UK, C. A. BREBBIA, Wessex Institute of Technology, UK

Covering a series of important topics, which are of current research interest and have practical applications, this book examines all aspects of risk analysis and hazard mitigation, ranging from specific assessment of risk to mitigation associated with both natural and anthropogenic hazards. Originally presented at the Fifth International Conference on Computer Simulation in Risk Analysis and Hazard Mitigation, the papers cover topics such as: Risk Mitigation; Estimation of Risk; Hazard Prevention; Management and Control; Data Collection and Analysis; Information Society Technologies in Risk; Man-made Risk; Seismic Hazard; Marine and Maritime Risk; Landslides and Slope Movements; Floods and Droughts; Soil, Water and Air Contamination; Health Issues; Policy and Decision Making; Risk and Sustainability and Operational Issues such as Energy Response; Risk Communication; Risk Perception.
WIT Transactions on Ecology and the Environment Volume 91

ISBN: 1-84564-172-8   2006   apx 400pp apx £145.00/US$265.00/€217.50

We are now able to supply you with details of new WIT Press titles via E-Mail. To subscribe to this free service, or for information on any of our titles, please contact the Marketing Department, WIT Press, Ashurst Lodge, Ashurst, Southampton, SO40 7AA, UK
Tel: +44 (0) 238 029 3223
Fax: +44 (0) 238 029 2853
E-mail: marketing@witpress.com

Risk Analysis IV

Editor: C.A. BREBBIA, Wessex Institute of Technology, UK

This book contains over 70 papers from the fourth in this popular international conference series. Topics covered include: Seismic Risk; Floods and Droughts; Man-Made Risk; Estimation of Risk; Risk Assessment and Management; and Risk Mitigation.
Contributions from three special sessions highlighting the work of renowned international experts are also featured. These deal with Geomorphic Hazard and Risk, Seismic Risk Analysis in Mediterranean Cities, and Landslides from Hazard to Risk Prevention.
Series: Management Information Systems, Vol 9

ISBN: 1-85312-736-1 2004 832pp
£291.00/US$465.00/€436.50

Data Mining VI

Data Mining, Text Mining and their Business Applications

Edited by: A. ZANASI, TEMIS Text Mining Solutions SA, Italy,
C. A. BREBBIA, Wessex Institute of Technology, UK, N. F. F. EBECKEN, COPPE/UFRJ, Brazil

This book contains most of the papers presented at the Sixth International Conference on Data Mining held in Skiathos, Greece. Twenty-five countries from all the continents are represented in the papers published in the book, offering a real multinational and multicultural range of experiences and ideas.
There has been an explosion of interest in data mining applications to unstructured data and this is reflected in a large increase in text mining. Consequently it is not difficult to forecast that in the next months several applications will appear dedicated to analysis of content coming from the billions of available web pages, newsgroups, emails, chat lines and message boards, and that the interest in unstructured data mining and text mining will grow amongst researchers, OEM and system integrators working in sectors as information retrieval, semantic web, linguistics, and knowledge management. In business applications, the most promising areas are those regarding National Security, Competitive Intelligence and Customer Relationship Management. They can all be incorporated into the area of Intelligence Analysis, of especial interest for textual data mining and text mining applications.
Contents include: Data mining; Text mining; Neural networks and decision trees; Link analysis; Clustering and categorization; Consumer and strategic intelligence; Applications in science, engineering and life sciences, and Applications in business, industry and government.
WIT Transactions on Information and Communication Technologies Volume 35

ISBN: 1-84564-017-9 2005 568pp
£199.00/US$318.00/€298.50

WIT eLibrary

Home of the Transactions of the Wessex Institute, the WIT electronic-library provides the international scientific community with immediate and permanent access to individual papers presented at WIT conferences. Visitors to the WIT eLibrary can freely browse and search abstracts of all papers in the collection before progressing to download their full text.

Visit the WIT eLibrary at
http://library.witpress.com

Methods and Technologies for Learning

Edited by: G. CHIAZZESE, Istituto per le Tecnologie Didattiche, Italy,
M. ALLEGRA, Istituto per le Tecnologie Didattiche, Italy, A. CHIFARI, Istituto per le Tecnologie Didattiche, Italy,
S. OTTAVIANO, Istituto per le Tecnologie Didattiche, Italy

For more then a decade the rapid growth of ICT and its use in education have generated a lot of changes in traditional educational structures as well as interest in defining new models for designing advanced learning solutions.

This book provides an overview of international perspectives regarding the latest innovations and results in different fields of education. In particular, it is addressed to all those who are interested in exploring methodologies and extending their knowledge of current research in education and training technologies.

The wide variety of contributions provides an interesting and useful account of some of the major issues and controversies facing researchers, academicians, professors, educational scientists and technologists in most of the educational contexts in which ICT is applied.

Over 90 papers are featured and these are divided under headings including: Online Education and Training; Innovative Teaching and Learning Technologies; Collaborative Learning Environments; Navigation Strategies and Comprehension; Mobile Learning; Quality Issues of Distance Learning Processes; Knowledge Management and E-learning; Learning Technologies for Primary and Secondary Schools; Educational System for People with Special Needs.

ISBN: 1-84564-155-8   2005   648pp
£227.00/US$363.00/€340.50

Modelling of High Complexity Systems with Applications

F. STANCIULESCU, Research Institute for Informatics, Romania

This book is a research monograph, of an interdisciplinary scope, that brings together complexity system analysis, hybrid modelling and simulation, knowledge-based and fuzzy control engineering. The author takes PC-based numerical insights into solving natural systems problems, and man-developed systems problems, and exemplifies all his assertions.

The book sets out to provide new methods and techniques for computer modelling of high complexity systems. Development of simulation and control techniques, and of problem-solving applications, is the aim.

Modelling of High Complexity Systems addresses a large readership: computer scientists, system analysts, modellers, simulationists, control engineers, naturalists, ecologists, environment experts and managers, teachers, students/masters of science, doctoral students and others. The CD-ROM provides the application software for modelling, simulation and control of high complexity natural systems, e.g. ecological systems (big lakes, rivers, river deltas, soil systems, forests, agro-ecosystems) and for environmental protection (diffusion of industrial chemical pollutants in urban atmosphere, air quality control).

ISBN: 1-85312-778-7   2005
376pp+CD-ROM
£149.00/US$238.00/€223.50

WITPress
Ashurst Lodge, Ashurst, Southampton, SO40 7AA, UK.
Tel: 44 (0) 238 029 3223
Fax: 44 (0) 238 029 2853
E-Mail: marketing@witpress.com